SELF-HANDICAPPING
LEADERSHIP

SELF-HANDICAPPING LEADERSHIP

The Nine Behaviors Holding Back Employees, Managers, and Companies, and How to Overcome Them

Phillip Decker

Jordan Mitchell

Publisher: Paul Boger
Editor-in-Chief: Amy Neidlinger
Executive Editor: Charlotte Maiorana
Cover Designer: Chuti Prasertsith
Managing Editor: Kristy Hart
Project Editor: Andy Beaster
Copy Editor: Cenveo® Publisher Services
Proofreader: Cenveo Publisher Services
Indexer: Cenveo Publisher Services
Compositor: Cenveo Publisher Services
Manufacturing Buyer: Dan Uhrig

Published by Pearson Education, Inc.
Old Tappan, New Jersey 07675

For information about buying this title in bulk quantities, or for special sales opportunities (which may include electronic versions; custom cover designs; and content particular to your business, training goals, marketing focus, or branding interests), please contact our corporate sales department at corpsales@pearsoned.com or (800) 382-3419.

For government sales inquiries, please contact governmentsales@pearsoned.com.

For questions about sales outside the U.S., please contact international@pearsoned.com.

Company and product names mentioned herein are the trademarks or registered trademarks of their respective owners.

Printed in the United States of America

First Printing November 2015

ISBN-10: 0-13-411972-X
ISBN-13: 978-0-13-411972-4

Pearson Education LTD.
Pearson Education Australia PTY, Limited
Pearson Education Singapore, Pte. Ltd.
Pearson Education Asia, Ltd.
Pearson Education Canada, Ltd.
Pearson Educación de Mexico, S.A. de C.V.
Pearson Education—Japan
Pearson Education Malaysia, Pte. Ltd.

Library of Congress Control Number: 2015949481

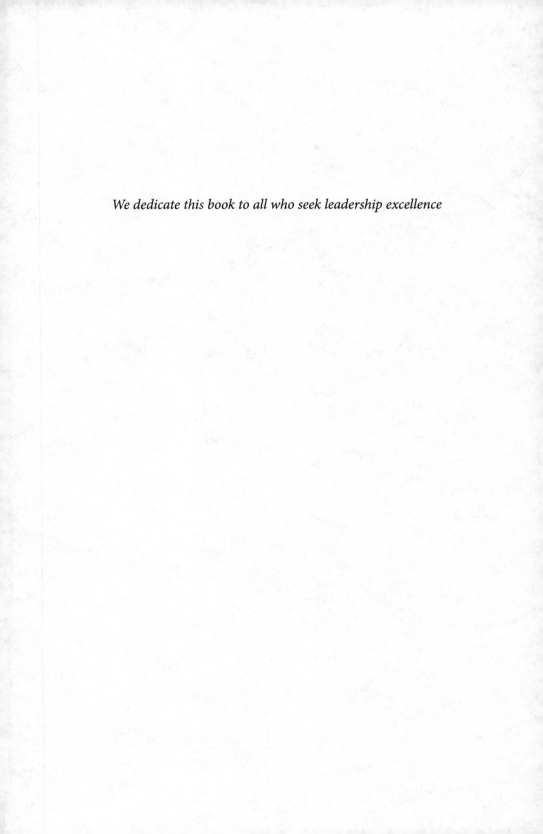

We dedicate this book to all who seek leadership excellence

Contents

Authors' Notes

Most of us would like to believe our problems stem from too much to do in a workday or our poor bosses and ignore what we do to ourselves. *But, the greatest limits on leadership are those that leaders place on themselves.* Our focus is this self-handicapping because there is no current conversation about it in business—especially about overcoming it. When this conversation is started, leaders will see significant improvement in their organizations. This is why we wrote this book. It is the story of what we do to self-sabotage ourselves at work and what to do about it.

This is not a self-help book or the "10 Things You Do to Be a Better Leader" book you read on the airplane. It is a handbook to refer to when things are not going well. Whether individual contributor, middle manager, or senior executive, chances are you are shooting yourself in the foot somehow. Overcoming this self-handicapping will open doors to exceptional leadership. We want to start the conversation. The rest will come along. This book is your reference book for the journey.

Several years ago, we began studying the idea of self-handicapping in leadership. A lot of people have supported us in this journey. First, we both would like to thank our wives, Kay and Bethany. Beyond their support and patience, they spent many nights reading "in progress" chapters and added insight that shaped the book. Second, we truly appreciate the countless hours of proofing, researching, and editing from Neha Singh; we could not have written this book without her efforts. We are pleased to recognize all the major contributions from the many executives and managers we have encountered in over 30 years of consulting and management/leadership training.

This book would not exist without the confidence and support of the team at Pearson/Financial Times. We wish to sincerely thank those at Pearson who made this happen:

Paul Boger, Amy Neidlinger, Charlotte Maiorana, Alan Clements, Kristy Hart, Andy Beaster, Cenveo® Publisher Services, and Dan Uhrig.

The idea of self-handicapping and leadership would not have taken off without the help of the first two semesters of our new leadership course and we thank those enrolled Fall 2013 and Spring 2014 for their help developing these ideas. Most of all, we thank them for putting up with the fact that self-handicapping was the only thing in their professors' brains throughout. The students attending our first pilot workshops at the University of Houston Clear Lake TMC campus offered invaluable advice.

We also had significant help along the way from many executives. In the formulation stage, we received valuable guidance about self-handicapping topics and training from Todd Caliva and Nancy Edgar. Craig Cordola believed in us from the beginning and allowed one of his organizations (Memorial Hermann Hospital) to be used as our laboratory. Ellen Bubak organized, recruited, and participated in the focus groups and beginning training programs where we ran our ideas in front of executives and directors. They are responsible for much of what you will see here. Finally, throughout this project, Julie Rabit-Torkie provided practical insight, organized people to help, and believed in this project even when it was just an idea on paper.

We received invaluable comments and suggestions from a number of leaders as the book chapters took form. Christy McCormack served as our guiding angel and put up with a thousand questions and ideas. Others included James Maynard, Craig Cordola, Dr. Timothy Doyle, Jason Decker, David Bernard, Suzzette Bagalman, Santosh Patel, Niki Decker, David Skinner, Raymond Khoury, W. Kenyon Chichowski, Jayne Johnston, Shannon Wright, Judy Hodges, Laurie Christensen, Chris Denman, Ben Benitez, Pam Potter, and Greta Cardenas. Finally, we would like to thank our colleagues and the administration at UHCL for their continued support and their many contributions to this project.

We use the term, "leader," throughout because the book is offered to all who aspire to be better leaders. We tried to make it relevant for business students, early careerists, managers, and executives. Our aim was to hit in the middle but you might find we drift from student to executive at times. We believe each population will find wisdom in it and continue to come back to its pages as leadership situations arise.

Before we get started on this journey, let us apologize for using the pronoun "he" throughout as a convenience, but we men self-handicap slightly more than women. While the research is not clear, it also suggests that men set up more roadblocks while women use more excuses to self-handicap themselves. Women evaluate the use of handicaps by others more negatively than men. So, we thought the use of "he" was appropriate.

About the Authors

Phillip J. Decker, PhD, is a Professor in the Business School at the University of Houston, Clear Lake, Texas Medical Center. Following his discharge from the US Navy, where he was a nuclear non-destructive test specialist working on submarines, Dr. Decker received his PhD in Industrial/Organizational Psychology from The Ohio State University. He has consulted in numerous Fortune 100 companies and hundreds of hospitals, been an expert witness in EEO cases, testified before Congressional committees, and consulted internationally. Dr. Decker has published over 90 articles and written 13 books in management, human resources management, and leadership. And, he is still working to overcome all of his self-handicapping.

Jordan Mitchell, PhD, is an Assistant Professor in the Business School at the University of Houston, Clear Lake, Texas Medical Center. Dr. Mitchell received his PhD in Health Services Policy and Management from the University of South Carolina. He has authored and co-authored peer-reviewed journal articles, federally funded technical reports, and conference proceedings in the fields of finance, information management, and rural health. Finally, he believes that if leaders can recognize their self-handicapping, they can overcome it.

1

Introduction to Self-Handicapping

Chapter Takeaways

- ► Understand the self-handicapping process
- ► Learn the relationship between excuses, self-defeating behavior, and poor leadership
- ► Define the different types of self-handicaps
- ► Understand how self-handicapping is triggered by situations
- ► Understand the ERO Spiral
- ► Understand the Box of Blame
- ► Learn about WHAT and HOW questions
- ► Understand the three steps to reversing the self-handicapping process

Employees witness self-sabotage daily from their leaders—not confronting errant employees, inconsistent leadership, hiring the wrong people, blaming everyone, acting like a control freak, self-centered decision making, or not keeping their word. These can cause employees to be apathetic, unmotivated, and lack ownership; so why do leaders do these things? Given the Internet, the hundreds of books, and the training programs available, it is probably not lack of education. Most leaders know *what* to do—make effective decisions, engage and motivate employees with a compelling mission and vision, build trust with full transparency and accountability, drive outcomes, and overcome resistance. Yet, Gallup research reveals that only about one in ten leaders consistently do all of those things. There is something else that gets in the way.[1]

In reality, the problem stems from leaders being uncertain and relying on the success of their impression management actions.

Leaders let the excuses used in managing how others view them lead to reduced effort and learning. Because the excuses are successful, they do it again and again instead of finding a better way. This lack of effort and learning will ultimately lead to those poor leadership behaviors that cause all that bad employee reaction. Here is an example of how it starts and is reinforced. When a leader walks into a presentation and says, "Please be patient with me, I haven't been trained on PowerPoint," the audience immediately gives him a break and expects less. If he does present a poor slide deck, they don't blame him, they blame the company for not training him. Conversely, if he presents a great slide deck, they think he is a hero for doing so well with no training. *Either way, the excuse covered his actions—"great" impression management.*

So he does it again and again. Some leaders will have a tendency to keep giving the same excuse presentation after presentation rather than get the training or read a book on PowerPoint. It is easy and seems to keep everyone happy. It becomes a habit and is repeated without a conscious decision. Two things will eventually happen: (1) The audience (or his boss) will get tired of the excuses and finally attribute his lack of PowerPoint skills to laziness—"poor" impression management; they think he had ample time to get educated on PowerPoint. (2) Further down the road, the day will also come where the PowerPoint presentation was so bad he lost a client, angered his employees, or lost favor with his boss—then he has created a real obstacle to success. These actions go well beyond just poor impression management, they represent ineffective leadership and poor outcomes. *This process is a slippery slope and it is called self-handicapping.*

Self-handicapping is the process where "people withdraw effort, create obstacles to success, or make excuses so they can maintain a public or self-image of competence."[2] *It provides an explanation for potential failure or sets the stage for an individual to receive more personal credit for success than might otherwise* accrue (enhancement).[3] Self-handicapping is a before-the-event strategy with two varieties: (1) Claimed; and (2) Behavioral self-handicapping. *Claimed* self-handicapping is coming up with an excuse for potential failure and *behavioral* self-handicapping is when a person creates an obstacle for themselves. Both can be internal or external to the person (Table 1.1) and excuses commonly lead to behavioral handicaps. Self-handicapping allows individuals to externalize failure and avoid the personal accountability for learning from it. It can be a very attractive strategy for any leader unsure of himself—a common occurrence in business.

Self-handicapping influences observers' impressions of a leader through two processes: (1) Before the task (lowering expectations); and (2) After it (changing attributions about the individual).[4] Following performance, it may discount the blame ordinarily associated with failure.[5] People tend to use self-handicapping when others are watching them (and presumably would have knowledge of their behavior/excuse).[6]

Table 1.1 Types of Handicaps

	Behavior	Internal Handicap	External Handicap
Claimed	*Excuse*	"I don't know how to use PowerPoint very well."	"My boss made me hire that employee."
Behavioral	*Reduced Effort*	Not learning how to use PowerPoint more effectively	Lack of mentoring/ training the unwanted employee
	Create obstacle	Produce a poor PPT slide deck	Assign new, unwanted employee to a failing project

Claimed self-handicapping is common; leaders claim anxiety, lack of time, task difficulty, lack of authority, and lack of resources (whether or not these are actually true). Behavioral self-handicapping is used slightly less often (setting unrealistic goals, avoiding accountability, drug and alcohol use, and reducing effort).[7] Internal handicaps (being unprepared, claiming an injury) are less likely to be used than external ones (the boss, workload, the organization) because leaders must appear competent and some internal handicaps like drug and alcohol use violate norms of organizational conduct. Yet, behavioral self-handicaps are more effective because they are less disputable and more tied to actual performance.[8] Self-handicapping does not always undermine immediate performance because it reduces the stress of self-evaluation and that allows the person to focus on the immediate task and perform better. So there are positive short-term effects from self-handicapping;[9] but it does inhibit long-term performance by creating obstacles to success. Frequent self-handicapping lowers observer impressions over time.[10]

Let's look at a more complex example—a team meeting with a dozen managers seated around a conference table and the senior leader at the head of table. The leader is worried about poor customer satisfaction scores and his ability to influence them in his department. He says to the group, "I'm tired of all of the customer complaints. Stop second-guessing your employees' decisions with customers and let them do their work." By this point, everyone in that meeting is thinking the same thing. "Well, why do you think we're doing that? If any employee makes the slightest mistake and it gets back to you, you will be down here yelling at us and making us look like fools." Of course, no one says that aloud. The leader hasn't really offered any meaningful solution or created any individual accountabilities to solve the poor customer satisfaction; he just dumps his demand on the group. None of the team offers up a meaningful solution that would really solve the customer satisfaction issues. Nor does anyone explicitly say, "Yes, I'll do that, boss!" and take accountability. The discussion likely goes in circles with everyone nodding or saying, "We should do this" a lot ("We" meaning the boss), while no real action happens.

Even though the leader's apprehensions may be the hottest topic of conversation when the leader is back in his office, why don't these managers speak up in the meeting and try to get the real problem on the table? Why doesn't the leader magically change his ways and assign accountabilities? Where is that brave employee who will speak up and lead the team out of the mess? Why doesn't the entire group stop and brainstorm meaningful solutions together? We know the answers—they don't want to get on the leader's bad side or feel any other repercussions from speaking up, they don't think anything they can do will really change the situation, and, ultimately, no one wants to look stupid or be embarrassed in front of their peers. Everyone is managing impressions rather than solving real problems. But the impression management becomes self-defeating behavior—something that once was useful but now causes problems. This process can't be discussed openly; nor can the embarrassment and fear around it be discussed directly (an *undiscussable*). The result is a huge cover up for the boss's poor leadership skills and for the group's lack of action. This situation is self-handicapping for everyone involved and happens every day. Eventually, this poor leadership trickles down to even lower customer satisfaction.

These things that managers do to sabotage their own leadership is our focus. This self-handicapping is the explanation why many leaders and organizations stay good and never reach exceptional. Excuses used in impression management often lead to self-defeating behavior that causes significant obstacles to leading effectively. Here is how it works— the excuse, "I am not good at PowerPoint," leads to reduced effort to learn PowerPoint (self-defeating behavior) which then leads to a poor presentation in a key meeting (obstacle) and that creates dissatisfied or lost customers (poor outcomes). *Because of the focus on what leaders do to self-sabotage themselves, this book will profoundly alter how you think about leadership.* These leadership missteps rarely lead to failure; the work still gets done. Self-handicapping simply inhibits—keeps leaders and their teams from growing, innovating, and working at their fullest; they get bogged down with excuses and self-sabotaging behavior. The group went back to work and achieved something; they probably didn't improve customer satisfaction, but work got done and the enterprise went on. As the customer satisfaction gets worse, the leader may be replaced. But as we all know, that will bring a host of new leadership problems to be managed. This is why the process is called self-handicapping—not suicidal behavior. *Eliminating self-handicapping is the key to exceptional leadership.*

The Self-Handicaps

Here are the most common behavioral handicaps leaders do to themselves. Each leads to many obstacles for leading employees or creating change in organizations.

1. *Avoiding Accountability*—Avoiding conflict and confrontation; making excuses or blaming others; playing "devil's advocate" constantly; poor presentation of self in public, or social media; and not holding others accountable.

2. *Tunnel Vision*—Focusing on the small picture (ie, continuously developing "tools" to solve problems in order to avoid big picture thinking); attending to people only until you get your way; being linear (tackling only one problem at a time); and not effectively prioritizing or juggling projects.

3. *Lack of Awareness*—Little or no self-assessment of one's traits, strengths, or leader behaviors; little or no consistent direction or vision for oneself or others; not understanding one's personal impact—what is left in your wake, and not burning bridges.

4. *Poor Analysis and Decision Making*—Not asking the right questions; frame blindness in decision making; not knowing what you don't know; not questioning yourself or your organization; and making decisions for instant gratification, impulse, selfishness, or to please others.

5. *Poor Communication Culture*—An inability to create transparency and trust; not being consistent and open; lacking listening

skills; being defensive or unable to take constructive feedback; not allowing vulnerability or expression of doubt in meetings; and ignoring the wisdom of the crowd.

6. *Poor Engagement*—Viewing everything as a transaction, rather than as a partnership; not adding value to relationships; poor networking; talking about others behind their back; and aligning with only a few individuals (pack mentality).

7. *Poor Talent Development*—Hiring the wrong people; not being on the lookout for talent that can be grown in your organization; avoiding coaching, mentoring, and sponsoring deserving employees; not paying attention to the fit of people in the team; and allowing coaching and mentoring from bad leaders.

8. *Micromanaging*—Leading through fear, coercion, and intimidation; constantly looking for fault and who to punish; being unable to cope with uncertainty or the unexpected; choosing situations where no unexpected challenge or event will take place; and not understanding interpersonal boundaries.

9. *Not Driving for Results*—Anything that keeps one from focusing on outcomes (confusing effort with results or confusing internal results for customer outcomes); avoiding challenge and risk; spending time thinking about how things should be instead of taking action; and not using baby steps.

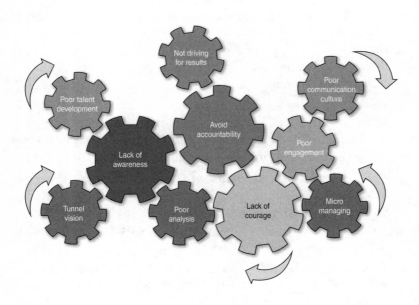

These categories are not completely distinct or a simple list of handicaps. One category can easily blend into one or more of the others. They are not in any particular order, but there does seem to be certain progressions from one to another. Like all things in life, a little self-handicapping is manageable, and can be coped with; but habitual use keeps leaders from performing well and learning. *There are simple reasons leaders do this things; we will analyze each and find solutions.*

The Slippery Slope

Most business leaders feel uncertainty with new or complex tasks; this is common in business. Self-handicapping comes from this uncertainty and can help create a comfort zone in those situations. The early excuses can quickly become habitual because *self-handicapping is extremely effective.* It helps peers or bosses think the self-handicapper's problems are caused by some external agent, keeps them from blaming him personally, reduces any sanctions for failure they may impose for failure, and may enhance their attributions of him. It is much easier to self-handicap than expend all the energy needed to determine competencies and then attain them; or to put up the determined fight to solve problems and overcome challenges. In other words, *self-handicapping in impression management is easier than learning, growing, and overcoming challenges. We all do it.*

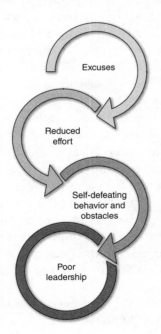

But *those excuses are the start of a vicious cycle leading to failure of leadership.* A leader who routinely self-handicaps does not typically improve the impressions of his boss or peers over time. Even more devastating is that *self-handicapping directly leads to poor leadership.* First comes the excuse, "I can't spend all this time to engage my employees; I am too busy." This may save time, but the reduced effort that follows means the leader is avoiding learning better ways to interact with his employees or fighting through the feelings keeping him from relating to employees on a one-on-one level. His behavior leads to a huge obstacle—disengaged employees. His employees neither own their own work nor the goals of the organization. Customers suffer.

Here is an example of a behavioral handicap. When faced with motivating an employee with the rationale behind a request versus with a demand, leaders often use the demand. It is quick, it works, *and it maintains the image of the leader as a tough guy*; the problem gets solved, the work gets done, and the leader moves on. The success of his demanding can make those actions habitual over time. But this choice to save effort and reduce interpersonal engagement on the short-term creates an obstacle to effective leadership because the employee is resentful, becomes disengaged, and the issue shows up later in poor work or even sabotage. You can see the pattern—uncertainty, excuses and expedient choices of leadership behavior, positive short-term outcomes from self-handicapping, reduced effort to learn and gain greater competence, obstacles to effective leadership with employees and customers, and ultimately, a bogged down career. We call this the Excuses-Reduced Effort-Obstacles Spiral (ERO Spiral). The ERO Spiral is the hidden slippery slope to poor leadership for many of us. *Great leaders stay off this slope. We will tell you how.*

For the leader, it is more difficult to face up to and eliminate behavioral than claimed self-handicaps. We have found that leaders immediately see their excuses and confess to them when they understand the self-handicapping process. But admitting to the impact of the self-defeating behavior that results from using the excuses is much more difficult. There are three reasons for this: (1) It is embarrassing to admit to one's own self-defeating behaviors affecting employees; (2) It is a habit, and we don't know we are doing it; or (3) It is suppressed and we deny doing it even if confronted with the evidence. When it is pure habit or suppressed, many leaders fail to recognize or admit to its impact on them and others.

We have found that the key for leaders to reverse self-handicapping is to *recognize* what they do, *admit* to its impact on others, and then *adjust*—find and practice alternative behaviors to break these ingrained habitual tendencies. This requires self-reflection and practice. When leaders see the ERO Spiral and how "innocent" excuses lead down a road to disengaged employees and dissatisfied customers, they are often ready to find better ways. The way out is to find what is triggering this behavior; every habit has a trigger. Training and coaching, of course, can have a significant effect, but we think a conversation in the workforce about the process of self-handicapping will accelerate this effect greatly. *Our aim is to start this conversation.*

Now for the truly hard part—if self-handicapping is done over years to the point where a leader's style only creates obstacles, it can cause the leader to withdraw into a shell and blame everyone else for his problems and the bad outcomes. If not short-circuited at the excuse or self-defeating behavior level, this "Box of Blame," as we call it, will be the end result. *This is the worst place to try to intervene.* By that stage, the leader is using blame consistently as his self-handicap of choice and will resist self-reflection or learning new behaviors. In their book *Leadership and Self-Deception: Getting Out of the Box*, the Arbinger Institute explores how managers can treat others as objects to help accomplish goals (termed being "in the Box") as opposed to viewing others as people, with their own hopes and dreams (being "out of the Box").[11] We have extended this concept into the self-handicapping process. When excuses are exhausted and what the leader does is mostly self-defeating, it becomes overwhelming to take total personal accountability and find a way out. There comes a point when it is easiest to throw all blame outward—to the employees, the boss, peers, the company—to avoid the devastating thoughts that you may have failed in your profession. This is when a leader is in the Box of Blame. Great leaders never go there and will not let their employees go there either.

Every leader can choose to honor what is right or betray it—act contrary to what they feel they should do.[12] As an example, take us—we are teachers. We get up every day knowing that our job is to help students learn. When we face a difficult situation where a given student or group of students is not learning, we can choose between thinking "What am I doing wrong here?" (honoring our commitment) or, "These students must be stupid" (dishonoring our commitment). When we choose the "stupid" route, we become the *victim* because the administration gave us students who are stupid and don't want to learn, we have to *work extra hard* because we have stupid students, *it is unfair* because we have to put up with their uncaring behavior, we become *smarter* because we contrast ourselves with these "stupid" individuals, and more *honorable* because we keep at it despite these hardships. We think of ourselves as pretty heroic and blame the students and administration for *our failure to teach*. We blame our colleagues for not thinking as we do. Once this cycle begins, it grows because the students' and administration's response to our blame is to create their own Box of Blame and blame us back. Constructive feedback ceases on both sides. But if you step back and look, we put ourselves into the Box of Blame. We chose this route— to inflate others' faults, our virtue, and blame others because of continued self-handicapping. This is the ultimate self-handicap—*the Box of Blame—and even it can be stopped* although it is very difficult to do so.

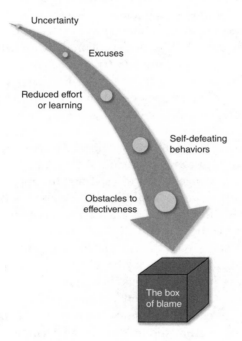

Gerald Piaget tells a story about a man sitting on his roof tearing up newspaper and throwing it off.[13] When his neighbor asked him why he was doing such a messy (useless) task, the man on the roof replied that he was keeping the wolves away. Exasperated with the mess, the neighbor exclaimed, "But, there aren't any wolves around here!" The man on the roof said, "See!" implying that "tearing up the newspaper is working!" The neighbor just walked away shaking his head in disbelief. As far as the man on the roof is concerned, he is doing what he knows brings success—no wolves—and he is keeping all of his neighbors safe. The message in his head is that things are working and there is no need for change. He does not know that the wolf problem was solved a century ago and he could now be doing more productive things with his time. As far as he is concerned tearing up newspaper is not a waste. It is a necessary task. His neighbor thinks he is causing a mess and wasting time but takes the issue no further. He feels sorry for him, walks away, says no more, and avoids him in the future. Employees witness self-handicapping like this daily from their leaders—and often think it is this crazy—not confronting bad employees or playing the blame game. They wish for the day their leader would be "rational."

One reason a leader may not appear rational in the employees' eyes, is that his perception follows the same logic as the guy on the roof, and the self-handicapping is facilitated by the fact that the employees or peers watching are unlikely to deliver anything but ambiguous, mildly negative feedback at worst. Employees rarely confront their boss with his self-defeating behavior or the obstacles this causes. Employees don't see the ERO Spiral that got the manager to that stage; they just see the poor leadership today. The self-handicapping leader, therefore, is likely to perceive that the costs of his behavior are much less than they actually are. Employees know they cannot solve his problems and peers don't want to be seen as the bad guy confronting him and suffer the repercussions. So, the leader is comfortable, as he goes nowhere. Meanwhile, the employees and the team are *not* comfortable. The obstacles emanating from a stifled, disengaged workforce have far more impact and importance than a leader saving face or avoiding accountability.

There are solutions. We believe that leaders can stop the excuses (when the self-handicapping conversation is started) and change their behavior to alternatives that are successful—not obstacles—with some self-reflection and effort. When leaders stop placing handicaps on themselves and reduce the negative consequences of that on employees and customers, they have time to move forward, to be humble, and to think about mastering the job of leadership. *Exceptional leadership comes from eliminating self-handicapping.* That is the focus of the following chapters. Self-handicapping does not have to inevitably lead down the road to failure. We want you to see this book as a reference for when you are uncomfortable—when things aren't working. It is not the short read on the plane about the ten things that will make you exceptional. *This book is about how to do things differently to be an exceptional leader.*

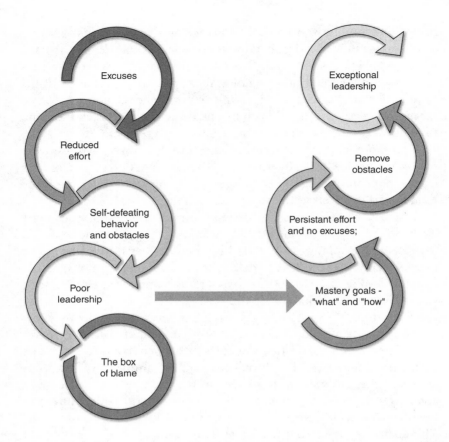

John Miller, in his book *QBQ: The Question behind the Question,* proposes a very easy formula that we use to think about reversing self-handicapping and moving to a quest for mastery of leadership skill.[14] Instead of asking "Why me?" or "Why don't other people do their jobs right?" and using the answers for excuses, one should only ask "What can I do?" and "How can I solve that?" These questions cannot be used as excuses and are the keys to a mastery goal-orientation in leadership. Notice that these questions do not include "Why," "When," or "Who." "Why" questions are about being the victim and avoiding accountability. "Who" questions are about finding a scapegoat. "When" questions are about waiting and procrastination. "What" and "How" questions lead to solutions, add value for the customer, and produce action. *They are the questions of a person seeking to reverse self-handicapping and be an exceptional leader.* Of course, those words must be coupled with "I," not "you," or "we."

Eliminating self-handicapping is not about changing others; it is about changing you and these questions are where to start. "What?"

and "How?" questions are the effective solution to starting to reverse self-handicapping. Even so, leaders must find new ways of operating, practice them, and keep from falling back into old habits. This requires understanding what triggers one's self-handicapping, acknowledging and admitting to what you do, and asking "What?" and "How?" It may sound elementary, but try it for a day or two and see how hard it is to get out of your habitual impression management behaviors.

Picture trying to get the paper-tearing guy down off his roof. He must first *recognize* the things he does are self-handicapping and have become self-defeating. Then, he will need to *admit* the impact of his behavior. It is wasted effort and creates a mess for others. This won't be easy as he has been in a state self-deception about it for some time. He will then have to *adjust*—find the things that trigger his habits and learn new behaviors to replace the newspaper tearing. Of course, he will want to make sure that they work before he gives up what he knows. Leaders can't just stop being pessimistic, they have to learn how to be optimistic, and then be reinforced for optimism (and yes, optimism can be learned).[15] Paying attention to the triggers for self-handicapping and the *impact* of one's leadership style are a big part of jolting individuals out of their comfort zone and reversing the negative effects of self-handicapping.

Here is an example—many leaders are late to meetings because somewhere along the line, they learned that 12 minutes late is not really late—just like the airlines. If someone says to the leader, "You are always late (even jokingly)," the leader *can honor his position and choose to* say, "Yes, I am," and ask himself "What am I *really* doing?" and "How can I change it?" If these steps occur, he has *recognized* and *acknowledged* his self-handicapping. Part of the "what" question here is what is triggering this behavior. He can ask himself "Why did it become habit?" Is it because he is disorganized in arranging his schedule or is it disrespect for the team? If he says, "No, I'm not." we likely have a case of self-denial (the "Box") with no acknowledgment, recognition, or admission. It may take lots of people very directly saying, "You are always late" (instead of giving the usual ambiguous, indirect feedback) to get this leader to move toward acknowledging or admitting his behavior.

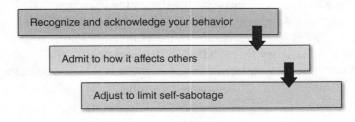

Recognize and acknowledge your behavior

Admit to how it affects others

Adjust to limit self-sabotage

When the leader *admits* to the impact his lateness has on himself and others (the disrespect team members feel for their time and retaliation of coming late next time—or not coming), he has started to reverse the self-handicapping. He can then *adjust* by changing the context that is triggering the habit (morning meetings, meetings directly after lunch, crammed schedule) or finding better ways of operating (plan more time to get to the meeting, schedule them at different times, or let others know that he is running late). He then needs to practice these new ways until they are the new habits. He could even apologize for his past lateness.

Mentally look at your interactions with people. Do you know someone who does not admit to themselves or others that they understand the implications of their actions? Do they neglect to say, "I am sorry?" (or even better, "I am sorry and I won't do it again.") Are they in complete self-deception about it all? Or are they trying to find new ways of behaving? As you read this book, you may be like a reformed smoker and not be able to tolerate "the smokers" as you work on self-handicapping. The more you rid yourself of the tendency to shoot yourself in the foot, acknowledge the self-sabotage, and adjust to better ways of dealing with situations, the more you will be able to identify and acknowledge these behaviors in others and see the negative impacts. *But remember, if you want to change the world, you have to change yourself first. Telling others what to do rarely is effective.* They may not appreciate your advice to stop their "bad" behavior and need to discover this themselves. Forget labeling others, talking behind their backs, or telling them how to change. Become a role model and change them by showing them your exceptional leadership and offering stories about self-handicapping and how you reversed yours. *Help us start the conversation.*

Why Leaders Are Not Talking About Self-Handicapping?

Self-handicapping is almost always hidden, subtle, and hard to nail down—often denied by the individual and undiscussable by the crowd (an undiscussable is something no one can discuss in front of the boss but is the main topic of discussion without the boss present). There is virtually no research about self-handicapping in business. Think about your situation at work. Deep down, the employees know something is not going right. They know what exceptional leadership is supposed to look like, but they never see or feel it. With a little exposure to what self-handicapping is all about, managers and employees can start to see the layer of excuses and the impression management going on. Saying something like, "I didn't get a good night's sleep last night," just seems to roll off the tongue in an unconscious effort when you are uncertain about your ability to get something done or do it well. Leaders doing this may not "see" themselves doing it or be able to admit to the impact they have. That is because the behaviors have become "natural tendencies" over time—habits. It leads down the ERO Spiral quickly.

Simply put, there is no conversation about self-handicapping in business—especially about overcoming it. When this conversation is started, leaders can begin to reverse their self-handicapping behaviors, find more time to master their job, remove the obstacles they place on the workers and themselves, and see significant improvement in their area of responsibility. Their confidence will improve; they will be more humble. They will reverse the ERO Spiral. That is the road to exceptional leadership.

In emergencies, people have a way of cutting through all the bureaucracy and red tape. They just get the work done and the objectives met. They organize; they have two-way conversations; and they divide work without complaint. They express their fears and needs. They work harder. So, why in everyday organizational life do we evolve into this mess of avoidance, impression management, and self-handicapping? Part of it is that we avoid talking about it. Picture someone in a meeting keeping some project out of his budgetary responsibility because he thinks it may fail. He is avoiding accountability because he knows 70-90 percent of all projects fail, so having nothing to do with it is best. And then no one brings that up as an issue! That is *avoiding talking about self-handicapping*. Self-handicapping is bad enough; making it undiscussable is worse. This is why we want to give you a vocabulary and start a conversation about self-handicapping. Picture it—we are all in a big swamp bogged down and no one wants to say anything about it. When we can see self-handicapping clearly, laugh at ourselves for doing it, and role model so others reverse it, we free ourselves to solve real problems and add true value for customers. We may then find those actually "fun" times when we were free to try anything to solve the emergency and were heroes when we did.

Another reason for no discussion is that leaders are often uncomfortable dealing with or talking about human issues. This has always been a problem in team building, crucial conversations, performance management, and coaching. They don't like to judge people or deal with "psychological" issues. So, leaders often avoid the very things that are likely their core problems in not achieving the mission—people problems—specifically self-imposed people problems. But ignoring self-handicapping will not make it magically go away. We want it out in the open. The principle of developing a common language among members of any community to facilitate effective change is well-established.[16] Right now, there is no common vocabulary for talking about self-handicapping in business. We find it fascinating how many leaders identify these issues in their employees but have no tools to deal with them. They often see it as trait-based—a personality defect—and too difficult to tackle head-on. It is also interesting how many of those very leaders do not see their own self-handicapping.

Furthermore, there is currently no cute, nonthreatening way of pointing out these problems at work such as the monkey being on your shoulder when you delegate accountability poorly. None of us yet have a picture in our heads of the "self-handicapping rabbit" running down the rabbit hole of poor leadership because of his tunnel vision, avoidance of accountability, or poor talent management. Managers often talk about leaders falling down the proverbial "rabbit hole" when they are "burned out" and leading poorly. We think self-handicapping is a severe case of "running down the rabbit hole" so we offer up the rabbit who self-handicaps by hiding in the hole. The rabbit hole is his "comfort zone" where he goes to find the easy way out. We encourage our readers to use the "self-handicapping rabbit" as part of the new conversation about self-handicapping at work.

A leader who self-handicaps also reinforces a workforce to self-handicap such as the team not speaking up. That is why every leader needs to make an effort to overcome all claimed handicaps and then take the high road to eliminating the behavioral handicaps he may be using. We believe self-handicapping also contributes to organizational change initiative failure. Employees overvalue their old habits and what they currently gain from them—status and comfort zone—while leadership overvalues the new strategy and potential long-term results without helping the employees navigate the road to the new. Great leaders overcome their self-handicapping and find ways to protect the employees' status and provide new rewards/status to replace those lost in the transition. There is a focus on "overcoming resistance to change" in business but those very words are self-handicapping. They imply that the leader must do something to employees, but this creates an obstacle—more resistance. A leader who says, "What rewards can I offer employees to make the change willingly?" and "How can I help my employees retain their status in this change?" (WHAT and HOW) removes obstacles and allows the employees to want to move toward the change.

Let's look at another example. One leader that comes to mind was very bright, but young in the role. This leader overpowered in meetings, spoke loudly, and was somewhat a bully (creating an obstacle). He felt and acted like he knew everything. This was a coping mechanism for his insecurity in his new role and resulted in him always trying to be the "expert." While his insecurity was covered up in the short term by this self-handicapping behavior, the long-term obstacle to success was a stifled work group, with little engagement and motivation to speak up or contribute. In situations like this, the leader's bosses eventually see the impact of this behavior on employees, customers, and his "numbers." Many of his employees assume he is a "know-it-all," "control freak" and stay out of the way. Some see right through his behavior to the real problem—insecurity—but say nothing.

The trouble is that management will react eventually. If the young leader is lucky, he will have a boss who recognizes the real problem and coaches him about his behavior and impact—overcome the insecurity, tone down the "need to be an expert" mentality, and he eliminates the self-handicapping obstacles to his leadership. His negative impact on employees can be reversed and he is ultimately successful and moves up in his career. The downside is that his superiors are only attending to the numbers and make the conclusion that he "just does not have what it takes." and is replaced. What are the odds of either occurrence? Well, the knowledgeable, caring boss is rare. It is more likely that this would be a ruined career and a stifled employee. Without help to overcome self-handicapping, these situations can destroy any chances for advancement at work. And no one will tell him the "real" reason why. *We want the conversation about self-handicapping and the ERO Spiral out in the open so bosses and managers in these situations can talk and grow rather than create further obstacles for employees and ruin careers.*

Most business fads offer lots of prescription and little description. They say things like, "motivate your employees" or "drive for results" but unless managers know precisely *what to do* and why they don't (in a way they understand clearly), they may not be successful. For example, if a leader tries motivating employees with the rewards that he values—more challenge or solving work problems—we can almost guarantee he will not be successful in increasing the effort level of his employees. They don't value those rewards. The leader sets out to do the "right" thing, but handicapped himself with poor techniques. *It is one thing to understand self-handicapping, it is another to be able to remove the things causing it and to develop and master new effective techniques. We offer details on "What" and "How" in every chapter.*

Why We Self-Handicap?

Self-handicapping is often a habitual, knee-jerk reaction to uncertainty and apprehension. We know it is done to avoid accountability and externalize blame. It can be very effective as an impression management tool, and therefore, continued use is reinforced, but in using it, the leader also avoids consideration of any long-term consequences and often slides down the ERO Spiral. You might think one of the major keys to reversing self-handicapping is the motivation behind the action. Yet we all know changing minds is not easy and does not necessarily mean changing behavior. Look at all the public health campaigns to get us to stop doing something bad—they don't work very well. Think about the last time you tried to lose weight. Unless we find new ways of doing things, the old eating habits have a magical way of coming back. The reason for this is that habits are not guided by goals, but by situations *and are triggered.* Failure to change habits does not necessarily indicate poor willpower or weak goals, but instead, the power of situations to trigger responses—we all choose the expedient response under pressure, avoid irritating situations and things we fear, etc. Time is always an issue in business and creates many situations that trigger self-handicapping. Habitual triggers often keep us doing what we have always done, despite our best intentions to act otherwise. *Reversing self-handicapping is a search for triggers, not a search of one's personality for bad motivation or lack of clear goals.*

Self-handicapping is usually triggered by three things—expediency (saving time/effort), avoidance, or apprehension. It also emanates from self-deception but that is easier thought of as a result of long-term self-handicapping than a trigger. When in the Box, one is in a cycle—*blame begets more blame*. These triggers can drive us to use habitual excuse and behavioral handicaps—learned anywhere from childhood on—and are difficult to change without understanding and removing the triggers. When the doing is easier than the thinking, people do. We all work on automatic sometimes and that is a significant driver for self-handicapping. Under time pressure, leaders do what is quick and works without thinking about it (the guy on the roof). Recognizing your self-handicapping triggers and finding different responses to them is an important key to success in eliminating self-handicapping. It is a major part of *recognizing* and *acknowledging* your self-handicapping. These triggers are expanded as follows to show the situations that may cause them to appear. As you progress down this scale, the issues become more painful and are more difficult to unlearn to break the binds to self-handicapping.

Expediency

The leader is on automatic and doesn't see or acknowledge the behavior or the impact. He:

- Doesn't have the time so he chooses what is easy
- Isn't interested so he delegates inappropriately or does what requires less time
- Is on automatic and his mind is elsewhere
- Is truly doing the only thing he knows but it isn't the best way

Avoidance

The leader sees and acknowledges the behavior, but is avoiding the impact. He:

- Is doing habitual behavior and doesn't see a need to change
- Is avoiding admitting his lack of competence—low self-efficacy
- Is using ineffective trait-based (eg, introverted or pessimistic) behaviors
- Doesn't know what to do, so he is consciously faking to avoid embarrassment
- Is consciously trying to not look bad—managing up
- Is consciously doing things to protect his self-esteem—bragging, exaggerating

Apprehension

The leader sees it, may or may not acknowledge the behavior, but fears the impact. He:

- Has a legitimate fear of his dysfunctional leaders
- Is driven by the culture of his team or organization
- Is doing things that work satisfactorily and fears risking trying something different
- Is driven by fear of failure—making mistakes
- Believes he lacks competence—shame

Self-Deception

The leader does not see or acknowledge the behavior or the impact—He has suppressed it. He:

- Is unconsciously doing things to protect his self-esteem
- Fears losing control
- Is in a cycle of blame
- Is doing things because of some unknown fear—possibly from childhood

What is critical in looking through this list is that, in attempting to influence how others view us or how we view ourselves, we can do bad things to ourselves. These situations have very little to do with solving problems, helping others, or furthering the mission of the team or organization. *Self-handicapping—whether excuses or self-defeating behavior—is not solution building; it is to protect the individual by managing impressions.* Each of these examples is about a leader solving an immediate personal problem—not providing leadership. As we explore each self-handicap category in the following chapters, we examine each of these triggers so that you can reflect on what situations may drive your self-handicapping.

What Is It Costing You?

Robert Sutton suggested organizations would be convinced to take his advice if they estimated the total cost of the actions of the type of employees he discusses.[17] So, from his example, we provide an informal estimate of one's Total Cost of Self-Handicapping (TCSH). Calculating exactly how many hours are lost, nerves shattered, dollars spent, heath problems started, employees disengaged, or customers/friends forced away

Table 1.2 Total Cost of Self-Handicapping Calculation

	Cost of the hours you spend in coaching/discipline	Costs associated with what you take home	Cost of disengaged, dissatisfied employees	Cost of blame, conflict, and retaliation	Cost of lost sales, productivity or innovation	Health problems and emotional costs to you	Time spent with your boss	Sub-total cost per SH area
Lack of awareness								
Tunnel vision								
Avoiding accountability								
Poor talent development								
Poor communication								
Micromanaging and lack of boundaries								
Poor analysis and decision making								
Not driving for results								
Poor engagement								
Sub-total cost per function								GRAND TOTAL COST:

by self-handicapping is probably impossible; however, even with crude measurement, going through this quick exercise to calculate your TCSH Score is illustrative of what this problem is costing you. Try it. Consider all of the self-handicap categories to begin to calculate (see Table 1.2).

You don't have to spend an inordinate amount of time on this exercise to realize self-handicapping costs individuals far more than they realize. Self-handicapping is learned; and therefore, can be unlearned, reduced and overcome. It may not be easy—those behaviors have served since childhood and early career.

Where to Go from Here?

Today, most companies spend extensive effort addressing employee motivation, engagement, and performance. The results are generally underwhelming. New approaches come along weekly that are designed to open up dialogue, increase trust, engage people, and put customer outcomes first. Of course, most leaders understand this; they just can't get there. We think they have neither calculated the costs of folks shooting themselves in the foot nor tried to open a conversation to reverse self-handicapping in their organizations.

Final Personal Takeaways

Baby Steps

In every chapter, we provide a list of baby steps—the things *to do tomorrow* or this week that can be a foundation for everything else to come. Sometimes we don't even take the first step because it seems too overwhelming and intimidating. Don't give up before you even start—*success in baby steps reinforces success in subsequent larger steps and builds confidence.*

The baby steps for this chapter are as follows:

- Take one situation that is not working well for you at work. Use Table 1.3 and think through the ERO Spiral for this situation.

- Reveal one self-handicapping excuse and one self-defeating behavior and analyze its triggers and what to do to reverse each. Here is the action plan (Table 1.4) for analyzing the triggers for your self-handicapping and finding solutions.

- Keep a log and track where you used blame to avoid accountability for an entire day. Ask yourself how much blame you heap out each day and its impact on you and your employees/peers.

Table 1.3 Examining the ERO Spiral

The situation	The excuses you are using for it	How it has or will build to self-defeating behavior	The obstacles you are creating for employees	The obstacles you have created for yourself	The outcomes

Table 1.4 Analyzing Self-Handicap Triggers

Excuse or self-defeating behaviors	What is the situation?	Trigger	Impact on others	What to do/ when
Excuse		__Expedient __Avoiding __Apprehension __Self-deception		
Self-defeating behavior		__Expedient __Avoiding __Apprehension __Self-deception		

Follow-Up Questions

1. Which chapter on self-defeating behavior will I learn the most? Need the most? Why?

2. What do you think your employees and peers are thinking and saying about you regarding self-handicapping?

3. Can you see your excuses used in self-handicapping? Can you see your self-defeating behaviors creating obstacles for your employees? If not, what is your plan of action?

4. Are you humble? Do you always strive for mastery of what you are doing—to know more and be better? How do these affect your self-handicapping?

Endnotes

1. Why Good Managers Are So Rare. See https://hbr.org/2014/03/why-good-managers-are-so-rare. Accessed February 6, 2015.

2. Hugh Kearns, Angus Forbes, Maria Gardiner, et al, "When a High Distinction Isn't Good Enough: A Review of Perfectionism and Self-Handicapping," *AER,* 35(3), December 2008, 21–36.

3. JM Crant and TS Bateman, "Assignment of Credit and Blame for Performance Outcomes," *Acad Manag J*, 36(1), 1993, 7–27.

4. PA Siegel and J Brockner, "Individual and Organizational Consequences of CEO Claimed Handicapping: What Is Good for the CEO May Not be Good for the Firm," *Organ Behav Hum Decis Process,* 96, 2005, 1–22.

5. CR Snyder, "Self-Handicapping Processes and Sequelae: On the Taking of a Psychological Dive," In RL Higgins, CR Snyder, and S. Berglas (eds.), *Self-Handicapping: The Paradox That Isn't,* New York: Plenum Press, 1990, 107–150.

6. A Kolditz Thomas and Robert M Arkin, "An Impression Management Interpretation of the Self-Handicapping Strategy," *Pers Soc Psychol,* 43, 1982, 492, 495.

7. DA Hoffman, "Self-Handicapping and Manager's Duty of Care," Legal Studies Research Paper Series No. 2007-09, Beasley School of Law, Temple University, 42 Wake Forest Law Review, 2007, 803.

8. Miron Zuckerman and Fen-Fang Tsai, "Costs of Self-Handicapping," *J Personality,* 73, 2005, 411.

9. Seligman, EP Martin, Susan Nolen-Hoeksema, et al. "Explanatory Style as a Mechanism of Disappointing Athletic Performance," *Psychol Sci,* 1(2), 1990, 143–146; MS McCrea, ER Hirt, "The Role of Ability Judgments in Self-Handicapping," *Pers Soc Psychol B,* 27(10), 2001, 1378-1389; Lis P Drexler, Anthony H. Ahrens, and David A. Haaga, "The Affective Consequences of Self-Handicapping," *J Soc Behav Pers,* 10, 1995, 861-870; and T Garcia, "The Role of Motivational Strategies in Self-Regulated Learning," *New Directions for Teaching and Learning,* 63, 1995, 29–42.

10. RA Giacalone and SB Knouse, "Justifying Wrongful Employee Behavior: The Role of Personality in Organizational Sabotage," *J Bus Ethics,* 9, 1990, 55–61.

11. The Arbinger Institute, "Leadership and Self-Deception: Getting Out of the Box," Berrett-Koehler Publishers, San Francisco, 2010.

12. For a detailed description, see The Arbinger Institute, *Leadership and Self-Deception,* San Francisco, CA: Berrett-Koehler Publishers, 2010.

13. See Gerald Piaget, *Control Freaks.* Doubleday, The Knopf Doubleday Group 1745 Broadway, New York, 1991.

14. John Miller, *QBQ: The Question behind the Question,* see http://qbq.com/qbq-the-question-behind-the-question/ (accessed February 6, 2015).

15. See Martin E.P Seligman, *Learned Optimism,* New York, NY: Vintage Books/Random House, 2006; and Martin Seligman, "Learned Optimism Test". http://web.stanford.edu/class/msande271/onlinetools/LearnedOpt.html (accessed May 3, 2015).

16. Summary of Balanced Insight, "The Power of a Common Business Language". http://www.balancedinsight.com/wp-content/files/BIWhitepaper_ThePowerOf-CommonBusinessLanguage.pdf (accessed February 6, 2015).

17. RI Sutton, *The No Asshole Rule,* Business Plus, an imprint of the Hachette Group, New York, NY: Grand Central Publishing, 2007, pp 44–51.

2

Overcoming Self-Handicapping

Chapter Takeaways

- ▶ Learn more about the causes and consequences of self-handicapping
- ▶ See the entire self-handicapping process in one diagram
- ▶ Learn the triggers of self-handicapping and how to deal with them
- ▶ Learn how to reverse and eliminate self-handicapping

A long time ago, an Italian economist, Vilfredo Pareto, found that 20 percent of the pea pods in his garden held 80 percent of the peas and that 20 percent of the Italians at the time owned 80 percent of the land. Thus was born Pareto's 80/20 principle. We have since found that 20 percent of the workers cause 80 percent of everything—accidents, sales, profit, and so forth. At work, you have 20 percent engaged self-starters and 80 percent that come to work and function as required. The 80 percent wait for orders, keep their heads down, do what is required, and stay out of trouble – in other words, they do their job. All leaders hope to find more of the engaged 20 percent using some magic *talent management,* but usually don't. We suggest want is needed is a company-wide conversation about self-handicapping. Then, if leaders walk the talk and get out of the way of the 80 percent, they should see some of them become part of the 20 percent. All employees want to have fun, do a good job, and work toward something useful—at least, in the beginning. By not dealing with the effects of self-handicapping, we have taught ourselves and impose on our employees a huge burden of self-defeating behaviors. Just think about moving half of those 80 percent folks over to the 20 percent column. How would that affect your work day?

This can be done by eliminating self-handicapping. It frees up enormous time that can be redirected to excellence. Individuals in the top 20 percent are more focused and more efficient because they have not started self-handicapping. Focusing on the right issues and being effective and efficient largely comes from being 100 percent focused on the mission and staying away from self-defeating behaviors and obstacles. Extensive effort is wasted on self-handicapping that truly gets in the way of being happy at work, building careers, and being part of productive work teams. It bogs organizations down. To facilitate the conversation about overcoming self-handicapping, we will first review the causes of self-handicapping, how it works, and what effects it has on people. Then we can use that information to discuss known methods to reverse and eliminate it. Since most of the causes of self-handicapping are habitual and can be changed, the ERO Spiral can be stopped in its tracks.

What Causes Self-Handicapping?

Let us look at self-handicapping in business. Siegel and Brockner examined *external* and *internal self-handicaps* presented in the annual letters sent by CEOs to shareholders.[1] External handicaps were obstacles outside the firm and internal handicaps included issues such as restructuring and loss of personnel. External handicaps influenced valuations of the firm and CEO compensation. When prior CEO performance was negative, external handicaps negatively affected the valuation of the firm, while not affecting CEO compensation. The self-handicapping from CEOs by writing a letter explaining external handicaps seems to serve the classic short-term goal of deflecting blame for failure. Crant and Bateman sampled 120 accountants on the assignment of credit and blame in self-handicapping.[2] They found that the use of external self-handicaps diminished blame for failure but did not affect assignment of credit for success. McElrroy and Crant examined the effects of source and frequency of handicapping on observer impressions of managers and the perceived credibility of handicap.[3] They showed that repeated use of handicapping creates considerable risk for the leader. Finally, Ishida showed mathematically that incorporating uncertainty and self-handicapping into a business contracting situation yields implications that run counter to conventional economic wisdom—that is, the standard tradeoff between risk and incentives may break down in the presence of self-esteem uncertainty and the use of self-handicapping.[4]

This research is the sum total of all information about self-handicapping in the business research literature. Self-handicapping may mitigate blame for failure in business operations and affects some economic decision making. We actually know much more about self-handicapping—its antecedents, process, and consequences—but from other areas such as education and sports. It makes sense that educators need to be aware of students' self-handicapping in test taking and major assignments. It also follows that athletes will self-handicap in the competitive world of sports and that these sports-researchers would study the concept. Business is just as competitive, the stakes are just as high, and the participants just as unsure of their ability to perform; yet the research is sparse. Self-handicapping occurs in business situations—you see it in yourself by now. There is virtually no conversation about self-handicapping in the business world, even though *it may be the missing link that can tip good organizations to excellence.*

What do we know about self-handicapping from these other areas? We know that students and athletes self-handicap in numerous situations because of both situational and personal causes. Self-handicapping is greatest when individuals are uncertain about themselves (or their specific competence) or feel vulnerable.[5] This can occur in situations that are evaluative or competitive (testing, sporting events, and many business environments). Other factors that drive an individual to use self-handicapping include how important the task is to the person, his goal orientation, and how public it may be. The more competitive the atmosphere in a classroom, the more students tend to self-handicap. A classroom in which the emphasis is on cooperation and collaboration and where students do not anticipate public comparison of their results, there is less self-handicapping. We also know some factors that explain why self-handicapping is used over other impression management strategies—task importance, competitive situation, emotional exhaustion, stress, and uncertainty. Clearly the research done on self-handicapping depicts it as a dynamic, contextually driven strategy, rather than a static personality trait. *In other words, self-handicapping is very strongly influenced by variables that might be easily altered.*

Personal causes for self-handicapping include fear of failure, perfectionism, self-doubt, low self-esteem, and low self-efficacy (one's belief in his/her ability to complete tasks or reach goals).[6] *Neither individuals with low self-esteem/self-efficacy nor with strong self-esteem/self-efficacy have much incentive to self-handicap. They are either certain they will lose or they can handle anything, respectively.* Because of this, self-handicapping is greatest when individuals are uncertain about their abilities to succeed—a common situation is business where leaders are often not clear on how they stand in the eyes of their bosses, tasks are unclear, and accountability is fuzzy. These can be altered in the workplace so that the tendency for self-handicapping will be reduced. One's belief in one's ability can be bolstered by successive small victories on small parts of the task. Self-doubt can be eliminated by praise and supportive environments.

There is an aspect of psychological maturity that is important in self-handicapping. It pertains to people's attitude toward the unknown. To children, the world around them is an immense unknown and there are things they are not yet able to understand. Independent adults recognize that there are things that they do not yet know and *need to learn*. They do not entertain the child's conclusion that there are things unknowable in principle to them. Nor do they accept the notion that intelligence is fixed. An important aspect of cutting off the triggers to self-handicapping is changing one's attitude toward learning and intelligence. Accepting that there is much to be uncertain about, and that the best response is *to always be open to learning defeats self-handicapping*.

Some people believe that intelligence is a fixed trait—that they have been given a certain amount of intelligence—and that it is it, forever. This is called an *entity theory of intelligence*. Others believe that intelligence is a quality they can continually develop through their effort

Causes of Self-Handicapping

Personal

- Uncertainty about one's performance
- Sense of vulnerability
- Low self-esteem
- Low self-efficacy
- Theory of intelligence and goal orientation (performance goals)

Situational

- Evaluative or competitive situations
- Unsupportive environment
- Public

and education. This is called an *incremental theory of intelligence.* These individuals are focused on learning and becoming smarter. On the other hand, those with entity theories are more likely to self-handicap because it allows failure to be attributed to something other than one's intelligence.[7] If they fail to perform it indicates a lack of intelligence, which they perceive to be unchangeable. Even when entity theorists are successful, they attribute this success to external factors, such as luck, and not to internal factors, such as practice.

Theory of intelligence is important because individuals can strive to achieve for different purposes—mastery, performance-approach, and performance-avoidance.[8] Incremental theorists strive for mastery goals—a desire to *develop* competence and continually learn. Entity theorists have performance-approach goals—a concern to *demonstrate* competence by outperforming others, or performance-avoidance goals—the desire to avoid appearing incompetent or less competent than others. People with performance goals are more worried about external judgments of their work and have a poor sense of their own capacity to perform the work. Therefore, they are often uncertain and self-handicap more. Those with mastery goals do not self-handicap— they don't need to because they see the task as a challenge to be mastered and to be learned. They know they can find a way. Those with performance goals (especially performance-avoidance goals) spend time avoiding errors and trying to win.

This may sound complicated but it should give us all a great deal of hope for the future. Everything shown to cause self-handicapping can be changed in the management process. Business will always be a competitive environment, but the outcomes and prizes can be shifted to lessen self-handicapping. For example, classroom structure that includes involvement, teacher support, student cohesiveness, cooperation, and equity reduces self-handicapping.[9] In business, read this as engagement, accountability, and team building. Leaders can build work environments that emphasize understanding and improvement of customer outcomes (rather than being best or avoiding error at all costs). Success should be defined by improvement, with value placed on the process of learning and being more competent. Work should involve a climate that helps employees feel they can take risks, make mistakes, and reveal their lack of understanding in order to learn and grow. This environment fosters mastery goals rather than performance goals. Plainly put, *an environment emphasizing only performance goals will never produce excellence because it fosters self-handicapping.* Furthermore, there are many ways to help employees with low self-efficacy (and even self-esteem)—build their confidence. How individuals are introduced to new tasks is important; success in baby steps builds self-efficacy. Let us review the consequences of self-handicapping; then we can dive into a full discussion of how it works and how to reverse and eliminate self-handicapping.

Consequences of Self-Handicapping

Consequences of habitual self-handicapping can be negative for several reasons—some behavioral self-handicaps (eg, alcohol consumption) are hazardous to health, all eventually impede performance, have wide ranging effects on self-esteem, and lead to self-deception.[10] Self-handicaps can eventually lead to denial of their use. Over time, self-handicapping and the problems it produces reinforce each other. Self-handicappers report a loss in perceived competence and intrinsic motivation for their jobs. They also have lower performance, poorer study habits, and lower self-esteem than those who don't self-handicap. They also have low levels of intrinsic goals, poor rehearsal strategies, and poor time management practices. Finally, and most important, *self-handicappers*

Consequences of Self-Handicapping

Positive

- Discounting blame
- Positive attributions from others
- Enhanced attributions
- Better short-term performance and less perceived stress
- Less punitive sanctions for failure

Negative

- Poor attributions long-term
- Self-defeating behaviors leading to serious employee issues
- Low job satisfaction
- Poor job performance
- Reduced learning and mastery
- More self-handicapping
- Little focus on adding value to customers

---

fail in their jobs and education more often than those who do not self-handicap. This all sounds pretty horrible—and it can be—if the ERO Spiral is allowed to progress into self-deception. But remember, the cycle can be stopped. Reducing or eliminating self-handicapping will be very advantageous for any leader. Early careerists must be aware of where their excuses can lead them.

Although self-handicapping can bolster self-esteem and (perhaps) performance in the short-term, it eventually undermines both. The two-way relationship of self-handicapping with self-esteem suggests a vicious circle of reciprocal reinforcement downward—the ERO Spiral.[11] Self-handicappers report higher use of avoidance coping (eg, denial, disengagement) and turning against the self (self-blame and shame). Self-handicappers may not always be aware of the true nature of their excuse making and, over time, become wedded to these handicaps.

Most researchers suggest that self-handicapping is rarely if ever *just* a public impression management tool, and typically, *self-handicappers are likely trying to deceive themselves and others at the same time. So, self-reflection about the impacts of self-handicapping is important.* Let us review a complete model of the self-handicapping process before we move on.

Process

We know that handicaps include excuses, reduced effort, and obstacles created as a reason for potential poor performance. To summarize:

- Self-handicapping is an impression management technique designed to change peers' attributions about us (provide a reason for failure or enhancement with success) and lessen blame for failure.

- Reduced effort means less learning, studying, or preparing.

- Self-handicapping is increased in environments that emphasize performance goals—to win, show competence, or not make mistakes.

- Self-handicapping is reinforced for several reasons. It relieves some of the stress of evaluation that causes us to concentrate on the task and creates positive attributions.

- Self-handicapping also causes several very negative consequences. It can result in poor attributions from others with long-term use, and excuses can lead to self-defeating behaviors which can cause serious employee obstacles.

- Continued self-handicapping leads to reduced effort which translates eventually into reduced competence.

- Reducing the effort spent learning and gaining mastery of one's competence negatively impacts customers and employees.

- *The focus in self-handicapping is on protecting the self, not on adding value to customers and solving their problems. Therefore, self-handicapping is a major drag on the mission and vision of any organization.*

We provide the model in Figure 2.1 to bring all of this together in one picture for you. After studying self-handicapping across several sciences, we have concluded that self-handicapping is a slippery slope to poor leadership. Excuses used for impression management are the start of a vicious cycle leading to self-defeating behavior that seriously hinders attempts to positively influence employees and customers. A leader who continually self-handicaps does not typically improve the impressions of

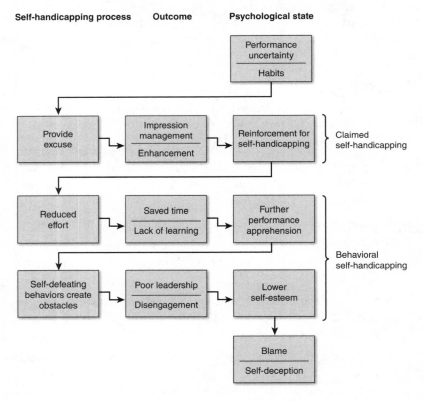

Figure 2.1   A Model of Self-Handicapping in Business

his boss or peers over time, make himself happier, engage his employees, or move forward the mission of the organization.

As shown in Figure 2.1, uncertainty in competitive, evaluative situations leads to habitual use of excuses as a self-handicapping strategy. The excuses prevent peers and bosses thinking failure is due to incompetence, lessens blame for failure, or enhances their attributions if one succeeds. This is reinforcing, so a leader will use the strategy again. And, then reduce effort—spending less time in preparation or getting the necessary education for future attempts. He doesn't grow; and performance goals further enhance this problem. Continued, it will cause obstacles either because employees, peers, or bosses get tired of the self-handicapping or more likely his skills erode due to lack of learning and growth. Reduced effort causes poor leadership; poor leadership causes unmotivated, disengaged, poorly trained and equipped, nonaccountable employees. They will spend more time attending to the leader and his problems than customers or organizational goals. This further increases the leader's performance apprehension and may lead to the Box of Blame—at minimum, it starts the cycle over again.

The most important boxes in this model for *any leader* to think about are "Reduced Effort" and "Saved Time/Lack of Learning." No one can avoid the fact that reducing effort to learn or grow will lead to poor performance in a world that is moving quickly forward. Think about *not* learning to operate a smart phone or the Internet due to your "reduced effort." You would miss out on many great things most of us have learned and take for granted. When you said "I don't have enough time," you didn't learn to operate the devices and you created obstacles for yourself (having no handy mapping tool or weather forecasting program). But that doesn't bother you because you did not know the possibilities of picture taking, map reading, instant weather reports, or product code scanning even existed. Only you are affected by this slide down the ERO Spiral. *Yet, when you progress to management*, the stakes become much higher and your reduced effort/ learning directly impacts employees, customers, and organizational outcomes. Not using a smart phone becomes a major obstacle—no one can text you, you have to wait until you get back to the office before you can check your email (if you have an office), and you can't access dashboard information for your unit. Customers are annoyed; they move on to places where they get faster communication, employees disengage and slow up, and bosses are irritated. You fail in achieving your goals and the goals of the organization and customers. Leaders cannot let the reduced effort that follows excuses lead them down the ERO Spiral or into the Box of Blame. Exceptional leaders are those that overcome this cycle.

How to Handle Self-Handicapping Triggers

In trying to recognize and acknowledge self-handicapping, it is important to analyze the triggers for it. When we are uncertain, self-handicapping starts with habitual behavior—the "innocent" excuse or the small obstacle created to preempt possible embarrassment. No one wants to look bad at work and we all self-handicap to some extent—it is the easiest way to look competent. It is almost automatically triggered by the situation. Even exceptional leaders self-handicap; the difference between them and us (the 80 percent who feel more uncertainty) is they catch themselves and eliminate the triggers that cause the self-handicapping. Their mastery goals help them remain humble, focused on learning what success really is, and how to build competence—rather than the need to look good. We (with our performance goals) are trying to prove our competence or not make mistakes and stay out of trouble. So, we habitually self-handicap more. This means that we limit our effort toward building competence. *Self-handicapping always starts with habitual behavior*—that is why the exceptional leaders can also be seen to do it once in a while.

Understanding and acknowledging the excuses one offers in self-handicapping is fairly easy. We have found that managers quickly say something like, "Wow, I do that all the time!" What they are talking about, of course, are the habitual excuses that come whenever they are unsure; such as, "I'm not good with PowerPoint." before a presentation, "I didn't get a good night's sleep." before one attempts a task, or "I'm not sure that will work." before taking accountability for something. A little self-reflection, identifying triggers, or deliberate action to break the old habits can reverse excuse self-handicapping. A work team can agree to call each other out on these excuses—make a joke of it—and they disappear quickly. When these excuses lead to reduced effort to be competent they start the downward spiral.

To help find the trigger behind the self-handicap being used, we suggest the "5 Whys Method" used by Toyota in their quality program.[12] By repeating "Why?" five times, the nature of the problem as well as the solution becomes clear. Let's try dieting:

- Why eat so much?
  + Because it tastes good and I have great food in the house.
- Why is it there?
  + Because I stock my shelves well with food that tastes good.

- Why is taste so important?
  - Because I don't want to fill my stomach with food I dislike.
- Why do you want to fill your stomach?
  - So I don't feel hungry all day.
- Why is feeling hungry bad?
  - Because it hurts and I want to avoid that feeling.

Now, we are down to the real issues—lots of good food available and a need to avoid the feeling of being hungry. One can take deliberate action to change the situation in the grocery store—don't go shopping while hungry and think about buying more sensible foods that still taste good. One would deal with the feelings of fullness in baby steps—gradually eat less and less—to avoid the feeling of being hungry. The first step to changing a habit is finding the triggers. Stop and acknowledge why you do something before you do it.

Habits are highly dependent on the context—where you perform it, how you feel—your fears and stressors, who is there, and what needs to be done. One can change the context or plan a different response. Action plans help one reflect on the triggers and context. If there is enough trust, doing this in a team helps—public declarations of a team commitment to reduce self-handicapping increases the likelihood it will be achieved. Here are some apps you can download to help change your personal habits—*HabitBull* (Android), *Balanced* (iOS), *Lift* (Android and iOS), *Way of Life* (iOS), and *Good Habits* (iOS).

Self-Handicapping Triggers with Solutions

- **Expediency**—Practice deliberate action and repetition of new behaviors to overcome the habit

- **Avoidance**—Increase self-efficacy (the belief you can do something) through baby steps

- **Facing Apprehension and Fear**—Face your fear and practice the task; change your need to impress

- **Self-deception**—Look and listen very carefully for feedback from anyone and everyone

---

Let's revisit the list of triggers for self-handicapping. What is interesting about this list is that we can look at the array of triggers for self-handicapping and immediately start to contemplate the behavioral solutions. And there are solutions! *Expediency* can be dealt with by practicing deliberate action and repetition of new behaviors to overcome the habitual nature of them. *Avoidance* can be handled by increasing self-efficacy (the belief you can do something) through baby steps. *Apprehension* can be faced. Facing fear and practicing the task takes some courage but it can be done. The need to impress causes much of the uncertainty underlying self-handicapping so facing that is a key. *Self-deception* is the toughest. It requires a leader to look and listen very carefully for feedback from anyone and everyone. When in the box, it is near impossible to receive and reflect on feedback about one's behavior. Let's explore each:

Deliberate Action

David Marquet, in his book *Turn the Ship Around,* uses the term *taking deliberate action.*[13] On his submarine, this means before taking an action, you pause and vocalize what you will do while gesturing toward what you are about to do. The intent of this is to eliminate "automatic mistakes" by causing you to pause and deliberate on what you are doing. It gives time for others to correct you if wrong. We want you to take deliberate action so you can discover triggers and reflect on the impact of the self-handicapping you are about to do—especially the long-term impacts on employees, the team, and organization. Then, you can determine if you are self-handicapping on automatic rather than thinking about the longer-term mission of the organization.

Self-Efficacy

Self-efficacy is the strength of one's belief in one's own ability to complete tasks and reach goals.[14] It is the calculation you have in your head concerning the likelihood that if you put in effort you could achieve a performance. Self-efficacy is the key to effort; without self-efficacy, people don't try. Most of us did not sign up for the 90-meter ski jump in the last Olympics because we thought that no matter how hard we tried, we would surely fail—low self-efficacy. When there is no self-efficacy, there is no effort. Low self-efficacy at work drives many to feel the same way and to avoid trying. Employees also avoid challenging tasks and believe that difficult tasks and situations are beyond their capabilities. People with high self-efficacy are more likely to make an effort and persist longer than those with low self-efficacy.[15] The keys to increasing self-efficacy are starting small and gaining successes at each step.

When workers evaluate themselves in terms of whether they perform well or poorly there are two common explanations—ability (I got it done because I'm smart.) and effort (I did it because I worked really hard.).[16] When performance is good, it may seem that there is little difference between explaining performance in terms of ability or effort. But when performance is not good and the employee is in the habit of explaining performance in terms of ability, he will not only feel bad about the results, but will also have little desire to try harder in the future. Leaders must create environments that help employees avoid feeling hopeless about improving their performance in the future. In contrast, after a failure, an employee should be helped to see his excuses and think instead, "Wow, I probably would have done better if I had prepared better." This explanation might help him focus on his competencies/skills and how to improve his performance the next time.

Self-efficacy is not an enduring trait; it can be changed relatively easily. Self-efficacy is increased, in part, through success—small achievements over time. Even reminiscing on past successes and visualization of success can create a greater sense of self-efficacy. Use "baby steps" to practice. Start small and gain success; then build on that foundation. Self-efficacy can also be increased by witnessing other people successfully completing the task and through persuasion to believe that you have the skills and capabilities to succeed. So, a team commitment to eliminate self-handicapping should help self-efficacy.

Apprehension

We all fear uncertainty—we want to be in control—to make things predictable. Apprehension and fear drives us to self-sabotaging actions. Fear of embarrassment, not being seen to do a good job, not following the rules, and making mistakes all come from performance goal environments. Fear can stem from childhood upbringing, from one or two very negative work-based episodes, or from a dysfunctional environment created by a boss. Regardless of the source, we all have a choice to move forward or not. If a leader fears giving a speech, he can face it, prepare well, and maybe do a good job; or he can procrastinate, self-handicap, and in the end, *do* a bad job. He can give in to fear or try his best to master the speech and learn—these are the tough choices we all make daily. The simple choice to master the skill of presentation will reduce self-handicapping and keep you out of the ERO Spiral. Even in the worst of circumstances one can face the fear of leaving the organization for a new position.

Surprisingly, recognition of fear starts when we begin listing what you want to be.[17] Write that down in the form of goals. After making sure each one of these goals is internally motivated, realistic, and specific, create a list of payoffs for each. Leaving a bad work situation may be one of them. Now for each goal, list all the worries, problems, and fears you have about trying to make this goal come true. You will see that you are clearly articulating what causes your fears. The last step is to list the emotional obstacles, excuses, and barriers (self-handicaps) you are erecting to protect yourself from these fears. Also, start talking in the third person, finding the positive, and looking at the problem as it was someone else you are advising—this has been found to be very helpful. Say, "Phil, you need to practice your presentation;" not, "I need to give better presentations." It really works.

Self-Deception

If you are thinking any of the following—"I can't fail," "It's impossible to take me by surprise," "It's not my fault," "Jordan is the bad guy," you have a tendency to blame things on others, or you have an excuse for everything, you may be deceiving yourself about self-handicapping. There are five basic types of self-deception that you may put into practice. These are as follows:[18]

- The existence of a problem
- The significance of the problem
- The options available
- The time urgency of a problem
- Your personal ability to change

Our prescription is to *look and listen carefully for feedback from any source on each of these.* This means paying attention to the feedback coming at you from others. Remember, it may not be in words, it will be subtle, and there may be none at all. No feedback or very quiet feedback is probably a clear sign you are doing something wrong. So listen carefully and watch for the signs. Picture the guy on the roof—he was left to his mess by his neighbor who did not want to intervene. The neighbor walked off after a few words, shaking his head slightly, not looking back. He didn't even pick up any of the torn paper. Your peers will do the same. *Look and listen to these kinds of signs carefully!* Lack of feedback or expression of concerns and quickly backing off by employees or peers in such situations is almost a sure sign of "the Box."

So increase your awareness, stay plugged in to all feedback sources, and be willing to ask for suggestions. If people don't show concern for your behavior (or heaping blame back your way), it means you are in the "Box" and doing something wrong. Remember that self-deception is a coping mechanism which helps postpone the need to deal with the truth of a situation. *In doing so, you also deny help.* So if you see yourself blaming or blame is directed at you, look and listen for feedback about self-handicapping like never before, get an executive coach, start a conversation about it in your workgroup, and invite feedback on self-handicapping behavior from all sources.

Reversing and Eliminating Self-Handicapping

There are several points of intervention with the self-handicapping process—*the person, the situation, his excuses, his behavior, and dealing with his self-deception.* Researchers have looked for ways to reduce the tendency to self-handicap by changing how individuals think about themselves and how individuals react to others' impressions of them.[19] Simply reinforcing a series of baby steps to build a greater sense of accomplishment can change how an individual sees his own self-efficacy. A leader can recognize uncertainty, know that it can trigger self-handicapping, and defer his reactions to the uncertainty to avoid using the self-handicap. He has the power to know that he is in this state and can defer acting until his mind has cleared.

What Reverses Self-Handicapping

- Eliminate triggers
- Enhance self-confidence
- "Talk back" and challenge your under-confidence
- Change to a mastery goal orientation—ask "What?" and "How?"
- Use self-reflection to catch the excuses
- Identify self-defeating/self-sabotaging behaviors and replace them with better methods
- Examine the possibility that you may be in the Box and think about how to get out
- Find an executive coach that understands self-handicapping

Person

Working on self-esteem helps. Those with higher self-esteem do not tend to self-handicap. Self-esteem is a subjective value judgment that people make about their personal worth. The less concerned a leader is with the evaluation or attributions of others, the less self-handicapping occurs; so removing evaluation or helping one ignore it helps. Training or coaching time could be spent on making leaders less susceptible to other's opinions; as will bolstering self-esteem in other ways. When a leader reaches the point where he knows he can do it or will find a way to do it regardless of what others think is when the ERO Spiral is arrested. This is also one avenue into mastery goals.

Since self-confidence is expected of business leaders, it might be hard to generate concern about managers with uncertain self-confidence. Furthermore, senior leaders may have little patience for self-affirmation sessions to bolster their managers' self-esteem—that is admitting to the failure of the leader selection systems. Yet, this lack of empathy for those more susceptible to self-handicapping is all the more reason to focus on eliminating excuses and shortcutting the self-handicapping behavioral process before it leads to obstacles. By the time an individual is in management, he should be able to see and arrest his habitual excuses with some exposure to the concepts of self-handicapping. In training and coaching, it may be best to focus on what is harder to change—his self-sabotaging behavior. *We believe that if we can change the behavior, the mindset will follow.* Even so, there is ample room for executive coaches to explore the underlying issues leading to self-handicapping as the workgroup and bosses focus on changing behavior. Working on mindfulness would also help. If the leader can create a cooperative culture where there is less competition and evaluation and more focus on mastery and the mission, this should lower the likelihood individuals would need to self-handicap.

Situation

Research has shown that students exposed to mastery-oriented teaching practices will develop a preference for strategies that enhance their learning. We have a pretty good picture of what it takes to create a mastery-oriented classroom. Students are taught to be concerned with ability versus effort, emphasize quality of thinking over memorization, find the meaning of tasks, have autonomy to explore, understand the meaning behind making mistakes, and view assessment as having relevance to their mastery of content and competence rather than being scored and compared.[20] Students who are taught to be mastery oriented focus on effort, use appropriate learning strategies, make choices that are challenging and engaging, and develop a positive orientation toward learning.

When managers emphasize performance goals, employees can have a tendency to worry about lack of ability. This triggers self-handicapping. In the long term, it is better to discourage this anxiety, foster long-term learning, and instill a belief that effort is tied to success. Managers should emphasize goals of understanding and improvement (rather than being best or avoiding error). They should convey an activity's meaning and real-world significance—tying it to adding value for customers, rather than the department or the boss. Employees should be involved in decision-making to develop responsibility, independence, and self-directed learning strategies. This is how they take over the accountability for their own competence (mastery). Self-regulated learners tend to develop a high sense of self-efficacy and attribute poor performance to controllable areas like insufficient practice. Success should be defined by improvement, with value placed on learning. Praise should be informational rather than directive of future performance. Finally, work should involve a climate that helps employees feel they can take risks, make mistakes, and talk about their apprehensions. They should feel comfortable asking questions.[21] Much of the focus of this book is to teach managers to create this type of climate in order to reduce self-handicapping.

Excuses

According to Burns, one thing a leader can do right away is to talk back to himself and as we said, it is best to talk back to yourself in the third person.[22] Any sense of uncertainty is created by you within yourself, so start talking back to yourself. One way is to train yourself to recognize self-critical thoughts as they go through your mind and practice talking back to them. This way you create a more realistic and positive self-evaluation system and thereby reduce uncertainty. Of course, you will have to understand why these thoughts are distorted in order to talk back. For example, these are all distorted thinking:

- *All or Nothing Thinking*—Seeing things in black or white. You are either perfect or a failure.

- *Overgeneralization*—You see a single negative event as a never ending pattern of defeat.

- *Mental Filter*—You pick out a single negative detail and focus on it exclusively.

- *Disqualifying The Positive*—You reject positive information.

- *Jumping to Conclusions*—You make a negative interpretation even though there are no facts to back it up.

- *Magnification or Minimization*—You exaggerate the importance of things if they are bad and shrink things when they are good.

- *Emotional Reasoning*—You think that since you feel it, therefore, it must be true.

- *Should Statements*—You try to motivate yourself with "should" and "ought."

- *Labeling*—Instead of describing an error or mistake you attach a negative label to yourself, such as I'm a loser.

- *Personalization*—You see yourself as the cause of some negative external event when in fact you were not primarily responsible for it.

After figuring out what mental distortion you are using, the next step is to substitute a thought of certainty (or mastery) over the situation. Instead of, "I am such a failure at this," talk back with "Come on Phil, find out how to get this done well." Burns also suggests that you keep track of the number of negative thoughts that you have. By facing these self-criticisms and distortions, you will begin to cope rather than feel like a victim.

Very recent research adds significantly to Burn's positive, short-circuiting of one's distorted thinking. Kross and his colleagues[23] suggest that *how* you talk to yourself makes a great difference. They demonstrated that third person language use (compared with first-person) leads people to appraise stressors as a fixable challenge rather than unfixable, and therefore, in less threatening terms. In other words, saying, "Phil, what are [you] nervous about? It's not the end of the world. You can do this, Phil." is a much more powerful way to approach challenges than saying, "I am scared. I don't know what to do. I can't do this." The first-person approach does not remove the uncertainty driving self-handicapping. The third person back talk is positive and distanced—which is much like what is required in practice on mindfulness. Simply saying, "Jordan, you can do this; try again" may change your entire leadership style. Using your own name in private talk minimizes social anxiety, the fear of being evaluated in a social context, and reduces post event processing—what we do after the fact to "chew over" our performance. Using *I* or *me* in self-talk means you have to work much harder to talk yourself into a positive view. Kross contends that the psychological distance gained by using one's name "gives you wisdom." It shifts the focus away from the self (where we are all more critical) to reasoning about the social problems of another (where we are all much wiser). As you can see, this concept may seriously help you reverse the mechanisms triggering self-handicapping. Try it. Sometimes the most simple of things can have profound effects. It seems that more positive self-talk using your own name may be one of those things. "Phil, what you just said was a self-handicapping excuse." "Stop it!" "Try that again."

Behavior

The fourth intervention is to change self-defeating behaviors that come behind the excuses. For example, lack of learning, and unwillingness to expend effort on employees or processes creates obstacles—disengaged employees, indecisive decision making, lack of accountability, or not driving for results. These behaviors become habitual methods of operating for the leader and this cycle becomes truly self-defeating. Since much of our day is characterized by repetition, we form habits so we can do things with minimal conscious control.[24] This reduces the thinking needed to take the next behavioral action. An example is driving home instead of where you really wanted to go (because you were thinking about something else). The context of the streets leading to your house triggers habitual behavior, which can even overpower your specific goals such as getting to the cleaners. Another is walking to meetings without engaging or acknowledging employees by name. You are in a hurry and the natural tendency is to look down and just get there. Peter Drucker said "effectiveness is a habit—a series of practices that can be learned."[25] Self-handicapping is a bad habit that gets in the way of exceptional leadership and it can be *unlearned*. This is a handbook for that purpose.

Self-Deception

The last intervention is the worst—when someone is in complete self-deception about their self-handicapping. They are probably in the Box of Blame. To be honest, we do not have a solution for those totally in the Box. Our aim is to start the conversation about self-handicapping so it would be presumptuous on our part to say that we have all the solutions—we don't. There is much left to business researchers and executive coaches to sort out. For example, we know there is self-handicapping going on in business, but we don't know how much. We are not exactly sure how the ERO Spiral works in business settings though we clearly see it all the time. We do not know how to get managers out of the Box of Blame. Simply put, business researchers have a lot of work ahead of them to explain self-handicapping and how to reverse it in business. They are well behind their colleagues in education and sports psychology.

We highly suggest the Arbinger Institute, *Leadership and Self-Deception: Getting Out of the Box*, as a start to exploring self-deception in self-handicapping.[26] It explores how managers can treat others as objects and get "in the Box," however, they do not have all the answers for getting out of the Box either. When in the Box, a leader starts to blame others and begins to feel justified in blaming them. Lots of things then build up to keep the leader in the Box and force his employees into their own boxes. He feels their blame is unjust and blames them more. He inflates their faults, inflates his own virtue, and the value of things that justify his self-betrayal. Once this cycle begins, it grows. Both parties response to the other's blame is to stay inside their own Box; provoking each other to commit more of the negative actions that they so resist from the other.

Executive coaches or patient bosses can help leaders explore the reason behind the blame and the effects it is having. This would be a very healthy intervention, but the coach must understand the self-handicapping process. However, we know that the most common intervention for those in the Box is termination. It is easier to start over again with another candidate than it is to invest in coaching and counseling someone who is resisting reality. That is why our focus is on arresting the cycle at excuses, or at self-defeating

---

What Is Easy and What Is Hard

- **Excuses**—Easy to see and with reflection, easy to overcome; better with a team commitment.

- **Reduced effort**—Hard to face but with a mastery goal orientation it becomes easier; start with refection; can be changed through performance management.

- **Self-defeating behaviors**—Hard to admit to and change; start with reflection; performance management and team commitment help; usually requires behavioral practice.

- **Obstacles**—What is built up from self-defeating behavior; use the wisdom of the crowd; performance management and behavioral practice are required.

- **Self-Denial**—Hard to see and hard to change; termination is usual; beyond team commitment; coaching and counseling required.

---

behavior, before the ERO Spiral gets down to the point of major obstacles affecting employees. When the obstacles build up too heavily, and the manager deceives himself about why the obstacles are there—or even IF they are there—he can easily fall into the Box and not get out. Yet sometimes, a leader can be jolted hard enough to step back and see the Box and the path out of it. A leader would have to look and listen very, very carefully for feedback in executive coaching or from a very patient boss. That coach or boss would have to be very resilient, and fully expect that the in-the-Box leader, when pushed too hard, will simply find another position in another organization.

Relapse

Whenever someone is trying to replace a behavior that causes problems with a more positive response, relapse to the old behaviors can occur. If you are trying to lose weight and you come home to find that your significant other cooked a tray of brownies, your initial response may be to take one small piece to taste. This is your first relapse. You immediately start to think, "What the heck, I might as well have a bigger piece. It tastes really good!" Second relapse. Very quickly you've eaten half the pan of brownies. Then you are guilty and your commitment to losing weight is in jeopardy. You have relapsed because you hit a high-risk situation with no plan, no coping response, or alternative behavior. It works the same with self-handicapping. We help you plan for these situations—have your "action plan." We want you to identify these high-risk situations, their impact, and develop better ways to handle them. We provide alternative behavioral approaches. Relapse prevention involves identifying high-risk situations, developing alternate skills for those situations, and practicing them until they become the new habit.

What Is Next?

This book is heavily focused on the concepts of relapse prevention—Chapters 3–11 each discuss high risk situations where self-handicapping behaviors lead to self-defeating behavior and obstacles. We want you to identify these situations, their impacts and triggers, and develop better ways to handle them. In each chapter we do these things:

- *Define The Self-Handicap*—Excuses and self-defeating behavior.
- *Discuss The Impact of The Handicap*—Obstacles and what we see as the real issues to explore.
- *Short Self-Test*—Provide a short self-test.
- *Discuss What to Do*—In each category for exceptional leadership.

- *Talk About Why You May Not*—Within each of the four triggers—expediency, avoidance, apprehension, and self-deception.

- *Provide Five-Six Alternate Behaviors*—By discussing recognition, acknowledgment, and adjusting. We provide key behaviors for adjustment.

- *Personal Takeaways*—Finally, we provide "personal takeaways"—an action plan, baby steps, and follow-up questions.

Self-handicapping is nothing more than a set *bad habits learned long ago to cope with uncertainty in evaluative situations. The problem, of course, is that when one becomes a leader, these habits spawn obstacles that hurt other people—that are very self-sabotaging.* Self-handicapping is a slippery slope to self-defeating behaviors and obstacles that affect employees and customers in very negative ways. The result is poor leadership and lack of organizational outcomes. All of this can be changed. These "better ways" are often nothing more than good management and good leadership—things you know. If you take deliberate action—slow up—and avoid the allure self-handicapping and impression management, you will find the road to exceptional leadership.

Final Personal Takeaways

Baby Steps

Remember: Don't give up before you even start—*success in baby steps reinforces success in subsequent larger steps and builds self-efficacy.*

The baby steps for this chapter are as follows:

- Identify the situations where you are the most uncertain. Determine what self-handicaps you use in those situations.

- Write down how you might change your area of responsibility so that it is supportive of increasing employee mastery goals.

Follow-Up Questions

1. Where will you start? What will you do tomorrow?
2. Do I have self-efficacy issues? Where could I safely start to practice baby steps to build confidence?
3. Have my excuses made me reduce effort, not learn, or set up deliberate obstacles to better performance?
4. What is my theory of intelligence? How does it affect me?

Endnotes

1. PA Siegel and J Brockner, "Individual and Organizational Consequences of CEO Claimed Handicapping: What Is Good for the CEO May Not be Good for the Firm," *Organ Behav Hum Decis Process*, 2005, 96, 1–22.

2. JM Crant and TS Bateman, "Assignment of Credit and Blame for Performance Outcomes," *Acad Manage J*, 1993, 36(1), 7–27.

3. JC McElrroy and JM Crant, (2008). "Handicapping: The Effects of Its Source and Frequency," *J App Psychol*, 2008, 93(4), 893–900.

4. J Ishida, "Contracting with Self-Esteem Concerns," *J Econ Behav Organ*, Feb. 2012, 81(2), 329–340.

5. For the research findings cited in this paragraph, see Wikipedia—Self-Handicapping http://en.wikipedia.org/wiki/Self-handicapping, (accessed June 23, 2015); CR Snyder, "Self-Handicapping Processes and Sequelae: On the Taking of a Psychological Dive," RL Higgins, CR Snyder, and S. Berglas (eds.), *Self-Handicapping: The Paradox That Isn't*. Springer US. 1990. (pp. 107–150); RF Baumeister, JC Hamilton, and DM Tice, "Public VersusPrivate Expectancy of Success: Confidence Booster or Performance Pressure?,"*J Pers Soc Psychol*, 1985, 48, 1447-1457; D Simek and DK Grum, "The Role of Different Aspects of Academic Motivation and Competitiveness in Explaining Self-Handicapping," *Horizons of Psychology*, 2010, 19(1), 25–41; JP Dorman, JE Adams, and JM Ferguson, "Psychosocial Environment and Student Self-Handicapping in Secondary School Mathematics Classes: A Cross-National Study," *J Educ Psychol*, 2002, 22, 499–511.

6. For the research findings cited in this paragraph, see RF Baumeister, JC Hamilton, and DM Tice, "Public Versus Private Expectancy of Success: Confidence Booster or Performance Pressure?," *J Pers Soc Psychol*, 1985, 48, 1447–1457; DL Feick and F Rhodewalt, "The Double-Edged Sword of Self-Handicapping: Discounting, Augmentation, and the Protection and Enhancement of Self-Esteem," *Motiv Emotion*, 1997, 21, 147-163; and DM Tice, "Esteem Protection or Enhancement? Self-Handicapping Motives and Attributions Differ by Trait Self-Esteem," *J Pers Soc Psychol*, 1991, 60, 711–725.

7. For the research findings cited in this paragraph, see Nicolette P. Rickert, Inez L. Meras, Melissa R. Witkow, "Theories of Intelligence and Students' Daily Self-Handicapping Behaviors," *Learn Individ Differs*, December 2014, 36, 1–8.

8. For the research findings cited in this paragraph, see TB Urdan, "Predictors of Academic Self-Handicapping and Achievement: Examining Achievement Goals, Classroom Goal Structures, and Culture," *J Educ Psychol*, 2004, 96(2), 251–264; Joseph M. Furner and Alyssa Gonzalez-DeHass, "How do Students' Mastery and Performance Goals Relate to Math Anxiety?," *Eurasia J Math, Sci & Tech Educ*, 2011, 7(4), 227-242; EA Gardner, "Instruction in Mastery Goal Orientation: Developing Problem Solving and Persistence for Clinical Settings, J Nursing Education, September 2006, 45(9):343-347; and V Mesa, "Achievement Goal Orientation of Community College Mathematics Students and the Misalignment of Instructors' Perceptions," Paper presented at the Annual Meeting of the American Educational Research Association, New Orleans, LA, April 8, 2011.

9. C. Garcia Teresa, "Predictors of Self-Handicapping: An Examination of Personal and Contextual Factors," Paper presented at the Annual Meeting of the American Educational Research Association, New York, NY, April 8–12, 1996.

10. For the research findings cited in this paragraph, see Ibid; DA Hoffman, "Self-Handicapping and Manager's Duty of Care," Legal Studies Research Paper Series No. 2007-09, Beasley School of Law, Temple University, 42 Wake Forest Law Review, 2007, 803; CR Snyder, "Self-Handicapping Processes and Sequelae: On the Taking of a Psychological Dive," In RL Higgins, CR Snyder, and S Berglas (eds.), *Self-Handicapping: The Paradox That Isn't,* New York, NY: Plenum Press, 1990, 107–150; and Miron Zuckerman and Fen-Fang Tsai, "Costs of Self-Handicapping," *Journal of Personality,* 2005, 73, 411.

11. See Miron Zuckerman and Fen-Fang Tsai, "Costs of Self-Handicapping," *Journal of Personality,* 2005, 73, 411; and Steven Berglas and Edward E. Jones, "Drug Choice as a Self-Handicapping Strategy in Response to Non-Contingent Success," *J Pers Soc Psychol,* 1978, 36, 405.

12. From N Eyal, *Hooked: How to Build Habit Forming Products,* New York, NY: Portfolio/Penguin, 2014.

13. D Marquet, *Turning the Ship Around: A True Story of Turning Followers into Leaders,* New York, NY: Penguin Group, 2012.

14. Adapted from http://psychology.about.com/od/theoriesofpersonality/a/self_efficacy.htm (accessed February 6, 2015).

15. See Wikipedia, "Self-Efficacy", http://en.wikipedia.org/wiki/Self-efficacy (accessed February 6, 2015).

16. From Amanda Durik, "Helping Your Adolescent Think Constructively About Academic Performance". http://www.niu.edu/cea/publications/newsletters/HowToThinkAboutCompetence.pdf (accessed June 23, 2015).

17. For a fuller description, see J Alpert and A Bowman, *Be Fearless: Change Your Life in 28 Days,* New York, NY: Hachette Book Group, 2012.

18. Summarized from Spiritual River, "Breaking Through Self-Deception". http://www.spiritualriver.com/breaking-through-Self-deception/; Boxing Scene, "How to Deal with Denial". http://www.boxingscene.com/motivation/2657.php and Caring.com, "How to Deal with Self-Deception". http://www.caring.com/articles/deal-with-Self-deception?page=3 (accessed February 6, 2015).

19. Ibid. See also notes 1 and 21.

20. Summarized from M Joseph, Furner and Alyssa Gonzalez-DeHass, "How do Students' Mastery and Performance Goals Relate to Math Anxiety?" *Eurasia J Math, Sci & Tech Educ,* 2011, 7(4), 227-242 and EA Gardner, "Instruction in Mastery Goal Orientation: Developing Problem Solving and Persistence for Clinical Settings," *J Nurs Educ,* September 2006, 45(9):343–347.

21. Ibid.

22. E Burns, *Feeling Good: The New Mood Therapy,* New York, NY: Harper Collins, 2008.

23. E Kross, "Self-Talk as a Regulatory Mechanism: How You Do It Matters," *J Pers Soc Psychol,* 2014, 106(2), 304-324, and Elizabeth Bernstein, "'Self Talk': When Talking

to Yourself, the Way You Do It Makes a Difference". http://selfcontrol.psych.lsa.umich.edu/wp-content/uploads/2014/05/Kross-SelfTalk-WSJ.pdf (accessed May 3, 2015). See also, P Weintraub, "The Voice of Reason," *Psychol Today*, June 2015.

24. Summarized from David T. Neal, Wendy Wood, and Jeffrey M. Quinn, "Habits—A Repeat Performance," *Curr Dir Psychol Sci*, 2006, 15(4), 198–202.

25. P Drucker, *The Effective Executive*. New York, NY: Harper Business, 2006, 23.

26. For a detailed description, see The Arbinger Institute, *Leadership and Self-Deception*. San Francisco, CA: Berrett-Koehler Publishers, 2010.

3

Accountability

O f all the things we expect of leaders, such as taking charge and setting strategy, being accountable and holding employees accountable are often problem areas.[1] *Accountability* is a personal choice to rise above one's circumstances and demonstrate the ownership necessary for achieving desired results—to "see it, own it, solve it, and do it."[2] This means continually asking, "*What else can I do* to be better able to help customers and *how to achieve the results* that they and the organization desire?" Being accountable requires a level of ownership that includes making, keeping, and answering for personal commitments. It incorporates liability for one's actions.

In business, accountability is needed on multiple levels. A leader can be *personally* accountable, responsible for making *employees, peers, and bosses* accountable, and/or responsible for the *organization's* accountability. When accountability lives in an organization on all levels, the organizational culture has:

- Trust within teams and across departments
- People who know that they can depend on one another
- Leaders and workers who know each will keep their word
- People who speak up and hold others accountable

■

Many workers do their best to avoid accountability because it can be used as ammunition for blame or punishment. Picture yourself in a team meeting with a dozen people and the senior leader at the head of the table.[3] The leader says to the group, "I'm holding all of you accountable for the goals we have established in this meeting." Now look around at your peers and see the pressure on their faces. It is there because the minute the leader said he was going to hold all of you accountable, the tone of the meeting became much more negative than the constructive strategy meeting that was taking place prior to this statement. There are real reasons for the worry initiated by the leader's comment—team members do not have enough time to meet the goals, they don't know what they are individually responsible for, they don't have all the tools, skills, and authority needed to accomplish the tasks, or they are just plain worried about the "across the board" accountability. Without prior work laying the foundation for accountability, "holding people accountable" will always cause stress. The accountability is back-loaded into the business process; it only shows up when things go wrong and people start to lay blame. And in doing this, the leader is creating an obstacle for himself— self-handicapping—in order to protect his image in case things do not work out.

When leaders delegate tasks, they must delegate responsibility, authority, and *accountability*.

- *Responsibility*—An obligation to perform assigned duties to the best of one's ability.

- *Authority*—The power assigned to a leader in order to achieve certain organizational objectives.

- *Accountability*—The answerability for performance of the assigned duties—living with the outcomes.

Most leaders do not do a good job of passing accountability on to the subordinate when delegating. This could come from a controlling attitude, not knowing how, or expediency in the delegation. This is what makes accountability such an issue in most organizations.

The Real Issues

Watching the news can make one believe that nobody is at fault for anything anymore; rather, it is the result of disease, addiction, chemical imbalance, the other political party, the boss, or the company—nothing but excuses. But leaders always have a choice to accept accountability or to avoid it—to honor their commitments or not.[4] *Avoiding accountability is a self-handicap that quickly leads down the ERO Spiral and right into the "Box of Blame."* Not making a choice is also a choice—*a choice to allow other people or events to make choices for you.* When self-assured leaders make the choice for accountability, you typically don't see them on the news giving excuses. Picture Volkswagen's diesel engines. They know they have some degree of control and that avoidance is self-handicapping. They choose positive action over words and excuses. They apologize. Survivors of extreme difficulties have shown that instead of fighting and arguing against the new reality, and trying to stop the change, they face what is happening.[5] Great leaders take ownership and get to work on positive solutions. They ask "What?" and "How?"

Use of "I" for successes and "you" or "we" for failures, overpowering at meetings, pretending to know everything when one doesn't, blaming others for one's failures, and reverting to activities and behaviors of one's old job when things get tough are all self-handicaps that fall under "avoiding personal accountability." When leaders don't learn from mistakes, they are avoiding accountability. Leaders avoiding situations where they anticipate there may be conflict and confrontation, not holding peers accountable, holding staff accountable reactively rather than proactively, or a leader surrounding himself with a loyal group of direct-report staff that don't call him on his bad actions are all avoidance of accountability. They are self-imposed behavioral handicaps.

Avoiding accountability can be subtle or obvious. For instance, the age of social media has allowed wide access to colleagues, possible mentors, or just sharing pictures of the weekend barbeque with friends. It has also created a subtle form of avoiding accountability, "ghosting." *Ghosting* is cutting off all communication with a person. It isn't something you announce; it just happens, and the person being ghosted is often left with uncertainty and wondering what happened. It's been around since people have had telephones, but it's now much more common, thanks to texting, Twitter, and other social media where you don't have to face someone. The problem is that it is a subtle, but a very strong avoidance of accountability and lack of common courtesy. It is a form of avoidance of confrontation that can lead down the ERO Spiral. First ghosting, then avoiding a crucial confrontation dearly needed for workplace efficiency, and so on into the box of blame. It is happening in business because so many of us are sending text messages and emails instead of direct interaction. There are peers or employees out there in hopes of getting a response and never knowing what happened. Another example is hitting the "Reply to All" button and blasting someone to the entire workforce.

Because of this level of subtlety, holding peers and bosses accountable is usually very difficult for most managers. Furthermore, there are many reasons you may have to approach your boss about accountability—he does not care about the employees, he doesn't understand the realities of the marketplace or work, his skills are outdated, or he focuses only on himself. In business today, it's the manager's job to take charge of his boss. Don't wait; ask yourself, *"What can I do to help him be more effective?"* and *"How can I approach him?"* You may have a very open boss or one who needs to think that your conversation is all his idea. Either way, always have your house in order before you approach your boss about his house. But approaching a boss about accountability is a real issue for most leaders. It is especially difficult in places such as health care where the physician controls patient care but is not an employee.

Impact

Avoiding accountability can be detrimental to employees and organizations. Many of the new tools developed in organizations require a collaborative culture, but turf protection dies hard. For example, while the leadership of an organization may promote quality improvement, middle leaders can sabotage this intent by continuing to make contrary decisions within their department or division. Power comes with departmental budget authority, not from cross-functional programs designed to increase collective accountability for quality improvement.

In the spring of 2010, at a British Petroleum (BP) oil lease in the Gulf of Mexico, several subcontractors were drilling for oil in over a mile of water and 2½ miles below the seabed. Deep water drilling was relatively new and extremely complex. At the Macondo drilling rig, various problems had put the job behind schedule and over budget.[6] Contractors cut corners to maintain schedule and budget. When the well started to blow out, the managers realized they had a problem, but confusion over authority delayed assessment of its severity and caused hesitation in initiating attempts to activate the blowout preventer and disconnect the rig from the mile-long pipe to the seafloor. The subsequent explosion killed 11 people and destroyed the rig. The broken pipe at the seafloor continued spilling oil for several months. Billions of dollars of damage was caused around the Gulf. A lot of what went wrong involved matters of judgment and technology, but perhaps the main lesson in this incident is that even with literally billions of dollars and many lives at stake, accountability at one level to hurry and make budget can seem more important in the moment, at the site, than the long-term accountabilities of the company—to work safely, stay out of the news media, produce oil and gas, and to make money for stockholders. The on-site managers forgot they were playing on a much larger team with much bigger accountabilities than their own. The managers' concern about what was good for them at the site hurt BP and its stockholders dearly.

Even at the personal level, a leader can have significant impact by avoiding accountability. Have you ever been on a team where you could have positively contributed to a project, but there was something in your head that told you not to do it because of a high likelihood of failure? You chose to drag your feet or keep a low profile because you feared being part of that "group that failed." Doing nothing may be safe but it is avoiding accountability. There can also be a reluctance to disclose data because data is often used to blame and punish rather than to learn new ways of doing things. For example, we know that many physicians and hospitals object to sharing internal data that can put them in a bad light, hurt their marketing efforts, or expose them to liability problems. Hotel chains resisted consumer reviews for years until overwhelmed by social media (and consumers have became savvy about sorting through the many reviews). There are also leaders that find pointing fingers and creating crises can be a strategy for avoiding accountability. But accountability is about transparency—anything less is self-handicapping.

What to Do?

Personal Accountability

Exceptional leaders take ownership of situations for which they are responsible or involved in. When things begin to go wrong, they see them through, try new ways of solving problems, and do not blame others. They accept responsibility for what happens whether it is good or bad and strive to master the situation. One executive told us that when he was an intern, significant crises happened about once a year. When he took his first management job that went up to once a quarter. As a vice president, it was once a week; and as a chief executive officer, once a day. His point was that, as a leader, you have to learn to be calm, accept accountability, look for solutions, and not panic. It is your job. *A leader is at his best when people barely know he exists—when there is no self-handicapping.*

It can be difficult to take personal accountability. It requires a leader to be secure within himself, have courage, and have healthy, respectful relationships with coworkers. It takes time and planning to face things one doesn't like such as confrontation. Our formula for overcoming the ERO Spiral—What and How questions—is the same formula to keep oneself accountable. Instead of asking "Why me?" or "Why don't other people do their jobs right?" one should only ask "What can I do?" or "How can I solve that?" These questions are the keys to a mastery goal-orientation. Remember that "Why" questions are about being the victim and passing accountability, "Who" questions are about finding a scapegoat, and "When" questions are about procrastination. "What" and "How" questions are the questions of a person accepting accountability. Personal accountability is one of the foundations of great leadership.

Here are our hints for accepting personal accountability:

- Step up and confess as soon as you realize what went wrong or take charge if you are not.
- Ask only "What" and "How" questions.
- Don't skate around the issue or beat around the bush; don't try to shift even a part of the blame. Persistently drive for solutions.
- Don't play the "if only" game—justifying failures by saying you could turn things around if only x, y, or z would happen.
- Accept the consequences. Take your punishment as courageously as possible, and when it's done, it's over. If it was extra work to solve a problem, focus on the good things the customer is feeling.
- Learn your lesson; either don't do it again or change the process to avoid it again.
- Recover gracefully. Hold your head up and move on.

Holding Others Accountable

Patrick Lencioni, in his book, *The Five Dysfunctions of a Team*, says that *failing to hold someone accountable is ultimately an act of selfishness.* For most leaders, it is safer to concentrate on work than it is to call a peer or boss on his or her avoidance of accountability. When a leader confronts a peer on lack of accountability, he becomes subject to being called out on his behavior (glass houses). Additionally, most leaders don't like to talk about behavior—or anything nontechnical. It's much easier to ignore situations than to talk about the psychology of any situation.

DailyFeats has created a model in which an individual can list the positive actions they make on a daily basis that aggregates to a daily life score. This score is supposed to be a reflection of the good that we do every day. The notion of what's good in this website is defined by you, so you can define it as not avoiding accountability every day and keep track on your cell phone.[7]

Brian Cole has provided the following hints for holding employees accountable:[8]

- **Set Expectations**—Employees do not automatically know what is expected. Understanding expectations, timelines, and goals up-front will eliminate any chance for arguing and blaming later.

- **Invite Commitment**—Discuss with your employees how these goals will benefit them personally and the organization. Ask them to be committed to a project once they know this information.

- **Measure Progress**—Measure ongoing performance and gauge whether or not the employee is meeting the goals and expectations to which they had committed.

- **Provide Feedback**—Employees need continuous feedback about where performance is falling short of expectations. Most of the time, giving objective behavioral feedback is all it takes.

- **Link to Consequences**—Administer appropriate consequences to help guide and focus behavior and encourage employees to take their commitments seriously.

- **Evaluate Effectiveness**—Look at the expectations and goals that were set at the beginning of the project, evaluate how effective they were in creating accountability in the employees.

Great leaders trust employees and allow them to take ownership of their jobs. They believe that employees are capable and will do the right thing for the organization. On the other hand, employees who do not trust their leaders will not choose to be accountable.

How You Avoid Accountability?

Survey: Do I Avoid Accountability or Not?
(Y = Yes, N= No, DK = Don't Know)

_____ I shy away from confrontation.

_____ Coaching or dealing with poor performance of employees can be a problem for me.

_____ I sometimes make excuses or blame others.

_____ I often play devil's advocate.

_____ I can sometimes present myself poorly—in dress, presentations, or in public, social media.

_____ I cover up my weaknesses sometimes.

_____ When problems occur I ask "Why" and "Who" right off the bat.

_____ It is common for me to use "I" for successes rather than "we."

_____ My employees might say I overpower at meetings.

_____ I have been known to try to know everything and be the "expert."

_____ My direct reports are all pretty loyal to me.

_____ I sometimes have poor time management with subordinates.

_____ I have been known to revert to activities and behaviors of my old job.

_____ I have inconsistently held people accountable across units or shifts.

_____ I don't like learning all the time; it hurts.

_____ I don't think I always do a good job separating responsibility, authority, and accountability for my staff.

_____ My employees don't think I'm very consistent and treat everyone by the same rules.

Scores

12–16 Y's—You are avoiding accountability.

6–11—You are inconsistent on accountability (which is the same as not very accountable).

1–5—You are very accountable.

What was your degree of fudging on these questions? When not sure, did you round up to yes? This assessment is only as good as your honesty to yourself.

So Why Don't We Do These Things?

Expediency

Sometimes we aren't accountable because no one has told us how to be, we may need certain tools, or we simply are unaware of our lack of accountability. Being constantly late to meetings, starting meetings late, letting things slip through the cracks, telling people what they want to hear instead of, "I can't get that done on your timeframe," and not preparing for tough situations are all forms of expedient avoidance of accountability. The excuses for avoiding accountability come easily due to poor time management or passive communication techniques. Often the person giving excuses because he gets little feedback. Not doing what you promised (lack of integrity) is the tip of the iceberg and can be seen by everyone—bosses, employees, and customers. There are a number of great apps out there for people to keep track of work assignments and commitments (we prefer *Asana*).[9] Regardless, do not let time be your excuse for lack of accountability.

Here are some tips for dealing with the time issue in avoiding accountability:[10]

- Be clear about what you are responsible for—Know your role, responsibilities and the expectations for your role and the same with your employees.

- Plan your time and do not procrastinate or overcommit—When something falls through cracks, you let someone down. Acknowledge it, apologize, and fix it.

- Use accountability as a learning tool—When something has not gone according to plan, ask for feedback, and try to do things differently in the future.

- Watch your self-talk—It is easy to let excuses roll off your tongue a priori to a task to set up a reason you are truly not accountable. It is even easier to tell people what they want to hear and then do what you want to do. This is the start down the ERO Spiral.

- If you use "If only" in your conversations, remind yourself that "If only" is an excuse to blame time for your problems.

- If leaders who avoid being accountable get ahead in your organization, and those who take responsibility are rejected, maybe it is time to find an organization that values accountability.

How do you fail to be accountable for because of expediency?

_____

_____

Avoidance

Planning ahead or learning more about an issue are the easiest ways to begin to be accountable, but we often put this off (reduced effort); we avoid the impact of the extra work. If an individual does this enough, he creates obstacles to leadership. Improve your skills through practice, be prepared and you will be more accountable and productive. It is common to avoid accountability in confronting others. Find the time, get mentored, and practice the skill. Remember that it takes ball players thousands and thousands of at-bat practices to get to the "Show." Don't think that management skills are any easier to learn.

Healthy/respectful relationships make being accountable much easier; however, this can be a chicken and egg situation—which comes first? Is accountability required to have a healthy relationship or do healthy/respectful relationships cause accountability? We think you most likely have to start with accountability to build the trust required in healthy relationships. On the other hand, if you find yourself in a group of dysfunctional coworkers, you can probably be accountable every day and still not have healthy relationships. In these situations, you can only do what is in your power—that is, be honest, open, brave and accountable. Over time, individuals who are drawn to that type of relationship will gather around you and thus start to form a healthy relationship network. You can choose to avoid the dysfunctional types in most cases. The negative, unproductive, and time-consuming folks are not drawn to the assertive, humble, accountable type.

Many of the things that drive us to avoid accountability are *motivational*,[11] that is, we wish to avoid failure, making mistakes, and ultimately embarrassment—performance goals. Fear of making errors is an especially large problem in very technical industries. Avoiding stress and confrontation are common drivers for avoiding accountability. The nonuse of technology by employees may also be viewed as an avoidance of accountability. When employees shut off or ignore their communication devices, it can be to finish an important project or to avoid confrontation or stress. Another factor that has to be acknowledged is that most managers love stimulation and challenge. Since many responsibilities and accountabilities are not stimulating, managers gravitate away and avoid them.

What issues are you avoiding that are self-handicapping?

Fear

To talk about individual accountability, we have to talk about self-esteem. *Self-esteem* is confidence in one's own worth or abilities; it is self-respect. Humans are unique because we have the capacity to define who we are and then decide if we like ourselves or not. The problem is in the judgment. When one doesn't like himself, it is more difficult to meet people, interview for a job, push hard for something he believes in, be assertive, hear criticism, be certain of his abilities, and be *accountable*. To avoid too much judgment and particularly self-rejection, we erect defense barriers—blame others, bury ourselves in our work, and make excuses leading down the ERO Spiral. This is all self-handicapping; those with higher self-esteem spend less time avoiding accountability.

A habit of avoiding accountability can develop as a slow, relentless accumulation of thoughts about your faults and a message that those faults are permanent; in short, "I am not good." and "I'll never be good enough." Then it does not matter how well you perform; you discount it, and may even view yourself as a fraud when things go well. This is knee-jerk, automatic self-handicapping to avoid accountability. If you often believe you are responsible when you are not, practice perfectionism, or are highly critical of yourself, *start challenging those thoughts.*

Also, get over the idea that making mistakes is a bad thing. Aren't we all supposed to be building learning organizations? Even if bosses want to hold you accountable after the fact and the organization is on the dysfunctional side, you can be accountable to yourself and your employees. Being accountable to your word, acknowledging mistakes, and then working to make things right will cause people to respect you.

Steps for *being secure within yourself* are as follows:

- Stop telling yourself avoiding accountability doesn't matter—*It does!*

- Take a positive approach—Instead of feeling guilty about avoiding accountability, reward yourself for planning ahead and being more accountable—*Baby Steps.*

- Plan things out—*Action planning.*

- Announce ownership publicly of things to be done and then do them—*Mastery orientation.*

Self-efficacy is believing that you have the power to do something, and it comes from successive successes. Plan, learn, slow up, and take accountability in small doses; you will get better at it and have more confidence in yourself. It will grow on you and you might magically become very humble. Self-efficacy and self-esteem reduce self-handicapping and show up as humility. When you are confident, your peers, subordinates, and bosses will come to believe that you can do what you say you will do. You will also. Lots of good things come to those who are accountable for their own actions.

Now let's talk about *courage*.[12] It takes courage to be accountable because you have to claim your part in whatever was said or done. When confronted, it is a natural tendency to want to duck the truth. The moral courage to stand up and accept what happened can be difficult because sometimes you own something when those around you may be hiding. But, courage is the essence of leadership; you must find it in yourself and demand it from your employees. Being courageous means doing something despite fear.[13]Exposing yourself to things that you fear (in small doses just like inoculation) can help you overcome self-handicapping and make it easier for you to face issues. First responders all practice and train for the experiences they have to face. You can do the same. Gaining knowledge (think not reducing effort) also helps build your confidence. Don't hesitate. The longer your brain comes up with excuses, the harder facing the fear becomes. Learn from the results of that first attempt and do not become discouraged. Feel free to talk to someone—that is why we emphasize networking and having a mentor/coach. Talking can help you to articulate where your fear is originating and plan your response. Start small and pay attention to your limits. Don't let failures dictate who you are. It means that you are trying and have more to learn. We suggest Osho's, *Courage: The Joy of Living Dangerously*.[14]

How is fear driving you to self-handicap your accountability?

Self-Deception

How many times have you heard someone who said something mean or hurtful, rather than accept accountability?[15] Or they justify bad behavior by saying you had "made" him mad? Those are examples of using blame to excuse one's own bad behavior. It is denial of one's own responsibility to be accountable and is a sign one is far down the ERO Spiral of self-handicapping. Instead of taking responsibility for his action, the blamer begins to find reasons why he should be excused from the repercussions of it—repercussions that he doesn't believe he "deserved." Blaming others for one's actions is a slippery slope and makes avoidance of accountability difficult to self-recognize.

Knowing a little about why you are thinking the way you are can help you avoid knee-jerk reactions when confronted with failure. This is especially true when your thoughts are based on dire predictions, doubt in your coping skills, continual focus on negative events, negative explanations of others' behavior, or rigid rules about how people should behave. Take deliberate action. Step back and think about how your thinking may be driving your reactions. Talk back to this in your head. Ask for feedback from others and listen. We know this isn't easy, but instead of accepting blame and viewing these thoughts as absolute truths, see them as mental events to observe and evaluate.[16] Your thinking drives your actions. Be willing to challenge knee-jerk thoughts and replace them.

Can you pinpoint any self-deception about your accountability?

Behaviors To Change
Avoiding Conflict and Confrontation

Recognize

Almost all managers have avoided confronting employees/peers who are doing bad things—sometimes because they do not have the time to deal with the repercussions of confronting. Some employees say the inevitable, "It wasn't me!" which means a long, hard conversation ahead. Some employees may accuse others of being the problem. Peers will do the same. These individuals require even more time and effort to confront because of their denial. Some might say, "Okay, I will not do it again," and then next week do it again. Even those who say, "I'm sorry; please show me how to do it better," require more work on the manager's part. Sometimes it is just easier to let it slide. But, what happens? The manager gets mad when it is not fixed and angrier over time. Then he blows up and the situation gets worse. It would have been ideal to address and correct the problem when first seen—even if it took a few extra minutes. Many of us have a healthy fear of confrontation. For some it is a cultural thing. Regardless of why, *avoiding employee/peer accountability is very self-handicapping if you are a leader.*

Admit

Confrontation is part of management. You will have to accept the avoidance or fear in these situations and take action. Examine your expectations of bad outcomes—what you fear out of an encounter—and ask what you can do to avoid them. Develop coping responses (this is a high-risk situation). The answer is to spend a few minutes and plan for the encounter. How should it be approached? What will motivate the person to be confronted? What does he want out of the situation?

Adjust

The Center for Conflict Dynamics has built what it calls active constructive responses to help stop avoiding conflict and confrontation. They are:[17]

- **Reaching Out**—Restarting communications and asking if the other party would be willing to work through an issue.
- **Perspective Taking**—Putting yourself in the shoes of the other person and trying to understand where that other person is coming from.
- **Expressing Emotions and Creating Solutions**—Where you collaborate with the other party to try and find a solution. This final step helps turn an adversarial relationship into one of mutual problem-solving.

We also suggest you read Patterson and Grenny, *Crucial Conversations/Confrontations* books, McGraw-Hill, New York, 2002.

Healthy responses to conflict are characterized by the following:[18]

- The capacity to recognize and respond to important matters
- The ability to seek compromise and avoid punishing
- A belief that resolution can support the interests and needs of both parties
- A readiness to forgive and forget

Key Behaviors

Here are the key behaviors for conflict resolution:[19]

1. Diagnose the issue and person and choose your battles.
2. Reach out and ask the person to sit down and talk.
3. Have the discussion in a private area, if possible. Take some time to cool down if needed.
4. Give the other person time to vent. Watch your body language.
5. If someone starts getting upset, figure out why. Then try to stay calm and remain professional. Reschedule the meeting if needed.
6. Verify that you are accurately hearing each other. Use active listening if needed.
7. Acknowledge where you disagree and where you agree.
8. Discuss the matter on which you disagree, not the nature of the other person. Look for the "win-win" scenario.

9. Thank the person for working with you.

10. Keep the conflict between you and the other person.

11. Don't hold a grudge when it's all over.

External Locus of Control

Recognize

Blaming others and playing the victim is avoiding accountability. *Locus of control* refers to the extent to which individuals believe they can control events affecting them. People with an internal locus of control believe that they have control of their lives; those with an external locus of control believe that events and circumstances control them.[20] When a student says, "I earned an A," it is internal; when one says, "Dr. Mitchell gave me an A," it is an external locus of control. Those with an external locus of control self-handicap more than internals.

Admit

In situations where you are having a hard time and feel like a victim, it is likely that you have an external locus of control. No one wants to own up to this state of affairs; so remember, one can develop or learn a sense of internal locus of control. You always have a choice to allow other people or events to run your life or not. You choose to be accountable by not offering excuses and putting the effort in to do it.

Adjust

These behaviors are typically learned over a long period of time in relation to certain circumstances. Determine the circumstances and what you naturally do. Then plan deliberate action. Tools to develop an internal locus of control are:[21]

- Develop and work toward a personal vision (Chapter 4, Self-Awareness).

- Set goals for yourself (both personal and professional).

- Determine what pieces you might be able to influence today.

- When you feel trapped, make a list of all possible courses of action. Just brainstorm and write things down without evaluating them first.

- Stay positive in your self-talk; avoid "I have no choice," or "There's nothing I can do."

- Ask only "What" and "How" questions.

- Assess your decision-making and problem-solving skills (Chapter 7, Analysis and Decision Making). Then strengthen your problem-solving skills. As you do so, you will gain the confidence and the belief that you can tackle whatever challenges come your way.

Key Behaviors

Here are the key behaviors to follow when faced with a problem and you feel like a victim:

1. Say to yourself, "Phil, solve this on your own," over and over.

2. Get an accurate understanding of the problem. Get as much information about what's happening as you can.

3. Make a list of all possible courses of action.

4. Ask yourself, "What do I want?" or "What is my desired outcome?"

5. Ask yourself, "How can I do that?" or "How can I get that done?"

6. Take action. Pick a solution.

7. Develop a list of baby steps and carry it out.

8. List the effects of your action. What worked?

9. Modify your efforts with what you learned.

10. Write down your feelings about having succeeded.

Personal Accountability and Boundaries

Recognize

There is more discussion on boundaries later in Chapter 10, Micromanaging, but let's start the discussion here. A boundary is where you end and where another person begins. When we talk about needing space, setting limits, or determining acceptable behavior, we are talking about boundaries. Exploitation of a customer by a professional, or an employee by a leader, and expecting another person to be an extension of yourself are clear violations of boundaries. Often, those who have a poor sense of boundaries do not know that they do.

Interpersonal boundaries are where many violations occur. Interpersonal boundary parameters include the following:

- The tone people use with each other.

- The attitude and approach coworkers use with each other.

- How personal conflict is managed—with discussion or yelling.

- The ability to effectively set limits with others who have poor boundaries.
- Clearly defining the consequences when a boundary is violated and sticking to them.

Professional boundaries[22] include who reports to whom, who gives you assignments and feedback, who sets priorities, how information is used, and how people are treated. An effective leader understands that failing to define these boundaries or having no boundaries can have an unfavorable impact on their team. Often leaders revert to activities and behaviors of their old job or some equivalent comfort zone. They tend to jump into technical topics and minutiae to escape the uncomfortable responsibilities of leadership. This is self-handicapping in professional boundaries.

For instance, John, who is a senior leader of IT, was having a very hard time reconciling his yearly budget without resorting to laying off one or two employees. In order to avoid having to make the tough decision, John starts getting involved in projects to see where improvements can be made to speed up schedules and improve project budgets. He's comfortable doing this because he used to be a project leader; however, it is not his job to meddle at the project level. It is his job to develop a budget for the overall division and he must face all the decisions—even layoffs—that go with that. John is avoiding his leadership accountability by reverting to his project manager role.

Admit

Avoiding accountability in an organization inevitably leads to violation of someone else's boundaries. What you avoid, someone else has to do. There are two sides of this coin: (1) Do not violate others boundaries by avoiding accountability; and (2) Do not allow others to violate your boundaries. It is the job of the leader to make sure that he is consistent and helps establish boundaries for workers and customers. It is also the job of the leader to hold employees and peers accountable for their boundaries in work.

Regardless of the urges of the moment, it is also important to not avoid accountability for customer relations. Customers are like anyone else; once trust is violated it comes back very slowly (if at all). Violating customer trust is avoiding your accountability to the organization that pays you. The rules here are as follows:[23]

- Do not seek out a personal relationship with your clients.
- Do not have a sexual relationship with clients.
- Do not introduce clients to your own family. Work and home should be kept separate.

- Do not supply or use alcohol or smoke in front of clients.
- Don't arrive late and leave early. Clients notice.
- Do not ask for money, gifts, or special favors from your clients and vice versa.
- Do not give advice outside your skills and expertise.
- Do not discuss information about your clients or with clients.
- Do not criticize, complain about or discuss issues relating to your staff, or employer, with clients.

Adjust

It is the inability or unwillingness to call others on their violations of professional and interpersonal boundaries at work that allows avoidance of accountability on both sides of the coin. Remember, good leaders face their fears, respect boundaries, are accountable themselves, and hold peers and subordinates accountable. They watch what they do and try not to inappropriately cross others' boundaries. They ask rather than demand.

Key Behaviors

The key behaviors for confronting others on boundary violations are as follows:[24]

1. Think about and consciously set your boundaries. Write this down if necessary.

2. Once a boundary has been set, let others know what it is. If a coworker says he will call you in the evening, you can simply say, "Please don't call me after 8 pm."

3. When boundaries have been violated, address the issues as soon as possible in a controlled and positive manner.

4. Respectfully and tactfully tell people what the boundary was and what they did.

5. Do not defend the boundary. Do not beat around the bush or expect things to happen without your request.

6. Say what effect their behavior had on you, and request they do not do it again.

7. Clearly ask for what you need or want—over and over if needed.

8. Involve your supervisor when boundary violations continue to occur.

Holding Peers or Bosses Accountable

Recognize

Have you ever been part of a team that you knew had an accountability problem? What characteristics of the team set off the alarm? Were some members of the group just there to check off the box, collect a paycheck, and go home? In an effort to not be confrontational, did some avoid asking difficult questions? Did any of the team members exhibit poor behavior, and the other members not call his attention to it? Avoidance of accountability is often one of the major dysfunctions in teams.

While it may be hard to confront your direct reports about accountability, it is even more difficult to confront your peers and bosses especially in a team. Patrick Lencioni[25] suggests several things to improve your ability to hold a team or a boss accountable. These are as follows:

1. Publish commitments, goals, and expectations. Clearly document performance expectations, roles, and responsibilities in meeting minutes.

2. Hold simple and regular progress reviews. The published commitments, goals, and expectations will be effective if team members refer back to them to check on individual commitments. Use this peer pressure to ensure accountable behavior.

3. Improve your ability to effectively, yet respectively, work at the individual level and "call people out" especially on self-handicapping.

Always remember that relationships with bosses and peers can be improved and your avoidance of trying to do so helps no one. It is a self-handicap. Building effective relationships always demands a considerable investment on your part. Acknowledge that total success is not possible, but incremental success is. Dealing with a boss's problems is a process, not an occasion.

Admit

When team members become willing to tolerate avoidance of accountability, it is the leader's responsibility to call this out as well as train the team to stop it. If the leader is avoiding accountability, it is the team members who must step up and approach the boss about it. The more a team is prepared to tolerate the interpersonal discomfort that accompanies calling someone out on his or her behavior, the fewer accountability problems the team will have. Lencioni says that members of great teams overcome the natural inclination to hold back on this. *Remember, one of the most powerful self-handicapping emotions in business is the unwillingness to be embarrassed.* If this one area can be improved in a department or organization, you will see massive strides in efficiency, productivity, and the satisfaction of everyone involved.

Adjust

We have all been in situations where the behavior of a peer or boss has disrupted or delayed the progress of the group.[26] Problem behavior can be caused by transient or sporadic issues such as bad news, lack of sleep, stress at home, or other circumstances. The more serious type of problem behavior comes from people who are difficult all the time—those overpowering at meetings, knowing everything or being the "expert," blaming others, never owning anything, etc. *But, unless you confront it, you enable it.* We highly recommend Patrick Lencioni's, *The Five Dysfunctions of a Team: A Leadership Fable*[27] or *Overcoming the Five Dysfunctions of a Team: A Field Guide for Leaders, Leaders, and Facilitators* for more in-depth reading about accountability in teams.

Sometimes, team members have learned that being difficult handicaps others, who then accept their negative behavior as "typical." Robert Bramson, in *Coping with Difficult People*,[28] suggests there are seven types of difficult people and describes in detail how to cope with each. These types are described in Table 3.1 and ways to cope with their disruptions are discussed in the following paragraph. This table has columns for you to match the names of coworkers to the problem types and design a strategy for dealing with them. Make sure to place your name where appropriate.

Table 3.1 How to Plan for the Inappropriate Behavior of Others

Names of Your Coworkers	Inappropriate Meeting Behavior and Coping Style	What Will You do to Counter This Behavior
	Hostile/Aggressives are abusive, abrupt, and intimidating. They are bullies. They believe their "victims" are weak. There are three subtypes in this group:	
	Sherman Tanks need to be right and will plow over people to prove a point. Victims are overwhelmed—they aren't able to get a word in. They will attack your idea and you personally.	
	Snipers maintain cover and take cheap shots at their victims—innuendos, digs, and nonplayful teasing. They do this in public, where the victim is less likely to confront.	

Names of Your Coworkers	Inappropriate Meeting Behavior and Coping Style	What Will You do to Counter This Behavior
	Exploders throw temper tantrums. When met with any degree of resistance, the normal conversation will escalate into fury.	
	Complainers find fault with everything. They have a disguised message behind all their complaints that YOU should do something about them.	
	Clams become unresponsive at times where you need an answer. When faced with a difficult situation, they clam up.	
	Super-Agreeables are always pleasant and supportive of your ideas and projects. They leave you thinking that they are in agreement with you, only to let you down later.	
	Negativists are usually capable but feel very strongly that unless a project is in their hands, it will fail. They will say things like, "It's no use in trying," or "That won't work." When confronted, they reply with, "Nothing will work."	
	Know-It-Alls believe they are superior to others. The ideas of others are inferior to their wisdom. There are two types of Know-It-Alls: **Bulldozers** are very productive people, but are very forceful with their opinions to the resentment of coworkers. If things go wrong, they blame others. **Balloons** are phonies. They seek approval and respect of others by acting like experts. Often, they speak beyond their knowledge-base without realizing it.	
	Indecisives postpone decisions that may hurt others. As time progresses, the decision becomes obsolete—thus reinforcing indecisive behavior.	
	Ramblers talk too much. They are sometimes either misinformed or don't understand the topic and sometimes they tell stories from the "glory days."	

When dealing with:

- **Sherman Tanks**—Stand up for yourself. Give them time to run down, but you may have to interrupt to get into the conversation. Sitting down will take some aggression out of them. Speak from your own point of view, "I disagree with you...." They will not strike out at you as readily if you sit next to them.

- **Snipers**—Force them out into the open. Ask questions like, "What did you mean by that?" Give them an alternative with a direct question. Usually the sniper will deny the attack, but will then realize that you identified it, thus making a repeat snipe less likely.

- **Exploders**—Give the exploder time to run down. If there are no signs of a slowdown, loudly say, "Stop!" and follow-up with "I want to discuss this important matter with you, but not like this."

- **Complainers**—Acknowledge but don't agree with the complainer. Be prepared to interrupt with limiting responses, avoiding "always" and "never." Finally state facts without apology and invite the complainer to solve the real problem, (if there is one).

- **Clams**—Get them to talk. Ask open-ended questions; use a friendly, silent stare. Don't fill the empty space—give the clam time to come out. If needed, narrate what is going on to prompt a response.

- **Super-Agreeables**—Make them feel safe enough to disagree with you. Confront them if they make an unrealistic commitment.

- **Negativists**—Avoid getting drawn into their negative thinking. Don't argue with them, but do state your realistic optimism. Create a "worst case scenario," this may take some wind out of the negativist's sails.

- **Bulldozers**—Try to get bulldozers to consider alternatives without directly challenging their expertise. Prepare for the conversation. Understand all the facts. Listen carefully and acknowledge that you understand what the "expert" is saying. Question without confrontation.

- **Balloons**—State the correct facts as explicitly as possible and provide an escape route for the balloon. Give them a way out—without embarrassment.

- **Indecisives**—Make it easy for them to tell you the issue why they are stalling. Once the problems have surfaced, help them solve it; if the problem is you, acknowledge it and move on.

- **Ramblers**—Ramblers have to be gently brought back on track. Wait for a good pause in their ramble, and assertively interrupt to come back to the main issue.

Remember, this behavior comes from insecurity (the uncertainty which leads to self-handicapping behavior) and they will usually back down when confronted assertively by a peer or superior on their behavior. You have to have the courage to do it and ask the team to make a commitment to do it.

Key Behaviors

The key behaviors for confronting difficult peers for their avoidance of accountability are as follows:

1. Prepare before the encounter. Do not deny or ignore the problem. Develop a plan on how to deal with the situation.

2. If you have support persons, warn them that you may confront the individual.

3. Stand or sit directly in front of the person and give him or her direct eye contact.

4. Express genuine concern for the person. You are educating them, not punishing. Assume that the other person's intentions are good even if his or her actions are problematic.

5. Identify the specific conduct that is objectionable. Be very specific; express yourself clearly and directly. Express what emotions you feel or sense that others feel.

6. Ask that they cease the objectionable behavior. Speak tactfully, in a way you would like to be spoken to and be constructive. *Confront gently*.

7. State that this behavior is counterproductive to the mission. You can conclude with what would be a good next step for the person you're confronting.

8. Own your own message; don't apologize for your feelings or the organizational needs.

9. Avoid evaluating and interpreting the person (eg, identifying him as "controlling" or "a complainer"). (Do not use any labels from the table.)

10. Thank the person for never doing the objectionable behavior again.

11. Repeat as necessary.

12. Think about the benefits of speaking up versus being a "clam" on others' lack of accountability.

Leaders at successive levels have different but important skills that play key roles in any organization. Carefully examine your thoughts and feelings about this with respect to your boss. Understand how your boss is thinking before you approach him about accountability. Always have data and let the data speak for itself. Do not explain the data in a defensive manner, but rather use it as a tool. Understand that your boss deals with an array of matters and may need to vent too. Assertiveness, a firm and positive respect, and an ability to empathize with your boss will most often lead to successful relationships and getting him to look at his accountability. Honesty is the best policy; be open, transparent, and always close the loop. Be sure to follow up in order to assure the boss that you have not disregarded the situation.

Key Behaviors

The key behaviors for confronting bosses for their avoidance of accountability are as follows:

1. Consider yourself and the boss *equal* partners of a team working toward a mission.

2. Do not deny or ignore the problem. Develop a plan on how to approach your boss—understand his personality and how he will react.

3. Collect and provide data from a reliable source concerning the issue.

4. Identify the specific conduct that is objectionable. Be very specific; express yourself clearly and directly.

5. State that this behavior is counterproductive to the mission using the hints for each personality type shown earlier.

6. Listen and be considerate of his needs and/or desires. Reflect confidence and be assertive.

7. Ask what you can do to help the boss be accountable in this situation. Be honest and transparent without disclosing unnecessary information.

8. Ask what he will do to resolve the situation.

9. Be responsive and follow up.

Front-Loading Accountability

Recognize

Let's start with how to delegate. Remember that to be effective in delegating tasks, you must delegate responsibility, authority, and *accountability*—especially proactive accountability. Accountability is difficult for many of us; we never let the individual get to the point where they alone must live with the outcome of their actions. If we see them moving toward a mistake, we jump in and take over to avoid a failure that may be tagged to us. We also do this to our children, and then wonder why they grow up unaccountable and unable to make decisions for themselves. Let us be clear—*the fastest way to a nonaccountable workforce is to never let them have accountability.* We often fail to make employees own their outcomes and we don't use the language of accountability correctly. Finally, we don't "front-load" the accountability (proactive accountability) that we give to employees, rather we "back-load" it and use it as a tool to assign blame.

Admit

It is important to establish in your organization a precise language of accountability.[29] Henry Evans, the author of *Winning with Accountability*, says that some of the biggest offenders in language are—"soon," "ASAP," "right away," "I'll get right on it.," "try," "should," "best," "we," and "by the next time we meet." Do not tolerate terms like this in team meetings; instead, create clear expectations with precise language. One of the main reasons people do not live up to others' expectations is because they don't know precisely what they are expected to accomplish. They mentally see a different result than the person making the request. Evans says "there is no 'I' in teams and there is no 'team' in ownership."

We believe that accountability should be made public. Evans says that, "Accountability is born when two or more people know about a commitment." This is the approach used in Alcoholics Anonymous and other self-help groups. When you make commitments public, you are more likely to accomplish them. Increasing accountability this way may be at the heart of employee empowerment and engagement.

Research shows how leadership in times of heightened accountability affects the outcomes for employees.[30] With increased accountability, environments with abusive leaders experienced significantly more negative impacts on job satisfaction, tension, and burnout. In work environments where supervisors were not abusive, increased accountability actually led to better outcomes. So, whether supervisors jump in and take over or ridicule their subordinates, the bottom line is that leadership has to be supportive in an environment with increasing accountability. Therefore, there is a need for proactive accountability.

Adjust

Provide clear expectations about what is expected and measurement tools to determine outcome accomplishment. Employees must trust and believe that there is a fair and accurate process for keeping track of their actions and tying their personal outcomes to real consequences in the organization.

In order to engage employees in accepting accountability, leaders need to start by setting *SMART goals—specific, measurable, achievable, results-oriented, and time-bound* in delegation. As we all know, it is hard to remember to capture all these elements when delegating in busy leadership positions. But, it is important that both parties know all the specifics up-front so they know where responsibility and accountability lie. Due to competing projects and a lack of prioritization, employees often struggle to know which is more important and where to focus their time and efforts effectively. It's up to leaders to help employees figure this out. Leaders also should monitor progress toward these goals and use coaching to correct the trajectory if needed.

Key Behaviors

The key behaviors for front-loading accountability are as follows:

1. Develop SMART goals and write them down (Baby Steps are mentioned later).
2. Define your performance expectations behaviorally and tell the employee.
3. Identify possible barriers for success and write those down.
4. Develop solutions to these barriers to be done by either or both of you. Specify responsibilities.
5. Set a follow-up plan.
6. Recognize individuals performing to expectations.
7. Adjust performance of individuals failing to meet expectations (coaching).

These last two items must be done on a daily basis to ensure accountability of employees—recognizing accountable individuals and adjusting when avoidance of accountability occurs. Here is some guidance on doing both of those activities. These specific key behaviors can get you through difficult one-on-one employee interactions.

Key Behaviors

When recognizing individuals who have been accountable in their work, follow these key behaviors:[31]

1. Give feedback directly, NOT through messengers or messages. Make it timely.
2. Stand or sit directly in front of the person and give him direct eye contact.

3. State clearly what the employee did that deserves recognition.

4. Express your personal satisfaction with the employee and his performance. Be direct and sincere. Get to the point—mean what you say and say what you mean.

5. Explain why it is important to continue in this manner.

6. (Optional) Ask what you can do to help him continue the good performance.

Key Behaviors

When employees have avoided accountability and adjustment is needed, we provide the following key behaviors:[32]

1. Diagnose the situation. Is accountability the issue?

2. State your concern that accountability is lacking. Say why.

3. Listen to their reasoning (and for any obstacles/barriers.)

4. Ask, "What can they do to accept or reaccept accountability?"

5. Ask, "What can I do to help?" (in removal of barriers)

6. Agree by developing a plan to remove any barriers.

7. Ask yourself who has the accountability at this point (you or the employee). If you, rebuild their ownership.

8. Monitor progress. Repeat if necessary.

Final Personal Takeaways

Action Plan—Accepting Personal Accountability

So what will you do about your personal accountability? Be honest and complete this action plan. Check the items needed.

Personal Accountability Self-Handicap	What Is the Situation	Trigger	Impact on Others	What to Do/When
Lack of what/ how question asking		__Expedient __Avoiding __Fear __Self-deception		__Deliberate action____ __Self-efficacy_____ __Face it _____ __Look and listen_____
Playing "devil's advocate." Constantly, saying things won't work		__Expedient __Avoiding __Fear __Self-deception		__Deliberate action____ __Self-efficacy_____ __Face it _____ __Look and listen_____

Personal Accountability Self-Handicap	What Is the Situation	Trigger	Impact on Others	What to Do/When
Don't want to accept the consequences— hurts too much		__Expedient __Avoiding __Fear __Self-deception		__Deliberate action____ __Self-efficacy_____ __Face it _____ __Look and listen_____
Making excuses, blaming others, being a victim		__Expedient __Avoiding __Fear __Self-deception		__Deliberate action____ __Self-efficacy_____ __Face it _____ __Look and listen_____
Avoiding conflict and confrontation		__Expedient __Avoiding __Fear __Self-deception		__Deliberate action____ __Self-efficacy_____ __Face it _____ __Look and listen_____
My locus of control		__Expedient __Avoiding __Fear __Self-deception		__Deliberate action____ __Self-efficacy_____ __Face it _____ __Look and listen_____
Poor presentation of self—dress and speech in presentations, social media.		__Expedient __Avoiding __Fear __Self-deception		__Deliberate action____ __Self-efficacy_____ __Face it _____ __Look and listen_____
Ashamed to admit mistakes		__Expedient __Avoiding __Fear __Self-deception		__Deliberate action____ __Self-efficacy_____ __Face it _____ __Look and listen_____
Rather just hide or do my old job		__Expedient __Avoiding __Fear __Self-deception		__Deliberate action____ __Self-efficacy_____ __Face it _____ __Look and listen_____

What will you do about holding others accountable? Be honest and complete the action plan below.

Action Plan—Holding Others Accountable

Holding Others Accountable Self-Handicap	What Is the Situation?	Trigger	Impact of It	What to Do/When
Delegating responsibility, authority, and accountability to employees		__Expedient __Avoiding __Fear __Self-deception		__Deliberate action____ __Self-efficacy_____ __Face it _____ __Look and listen_____
Using account-ability with staff reactively rather than proactively		__Expedient __Avoiding __Fear __Self-deception		__Deliberate action____ __Self-efficacy_____ __Face it _____ __Look and listen_____
Using the correct "language of accountability"		__Expedient __Avoiding __Fear __Self-deception		__Deliberate action____ __Self-efficacy __Face it _____ __Look and listen_____
Recognizing employees who have been accountable to the organization, clients/customers, coworkers, etc.		__Expedient __Avoiding __Fear __Self-deception		__Deliberate action____ __Self-efficacy_____ __Face it _____ __Look and listen_____
Coaching those employees who have avoided accountability		__Expedient __Avoiding __Fear __Self-deception		__Deliberate action____ __Self-efficacy_____ __Face it _____ __Look and listen_____
Not holding peers accountable		__Expedient __Avoiding __Fear __Self-deception		__Deliberate action____ __Self-efficacy __Face it_____ __Look and listen_____
Not holding boss accountable		__Expedient __Avoiding __Fear __Self-deception		__Deliberate action____ __Self-efficacy_____ __Face it _____ __Look and listen_____

Baby Steps

In every chapter, we provide a list of baby steps—the things to do tomorrow or this week that can be a foundation for everything else to come behind them. Sometimes we don't even take the first step because it all seems so overwhelming and intimidating. Don't give up before you even start. *Success in baby steps reinforces success in subsequent larger steps and builds self-efficacy.*

The baby steps for this chapter are as follows:

- Arrive to your next meeting early and start it precisely on time.

- Announce ownership of one thing publicly to employees or peers *and do it*—all in one day.

- Step up and confess as soon as you realize something you did went wrong. Say you are sorry out loud. And ask yourself only What/How to solve it.

- Develop and write down a smart goal—specifying each element for an employee before delegation occurs.

Here are the key behaviors for announcing ownership/accountability:

1. Choose an issue you are responsible for that you can define as a smart goal.

2. Choose a public forum (team meeting, etc.) to announce your ownership of the issue.

3. Define the goal specifically.

4. State that you will be accountable to get it down by date and time.

5. Specify the concrete criteria used to determine whether you have attained of the goal.

Here are the key behaviors for SMART goals.[33] SMART goals are specific, measurable, achievable, results-oriented, and time bound.

1. To set a specific goal you must answer who, what, where, when, why, and which tools or constraints are involved.

2. Establish concrete criteria for measuring progress and ultimately the attainment of the goal. Ask how much or how many and determine a measuring tool.

3. Determine that the goal is not too easy or not achievable. Neither is motivating. Ask the employee if they can get it down on time, in budget.

4. Discuss with the employee the outcome of the goal. Make sure it is a goal related to the mission or a customer. It must represent an objective toward which you are both *willing* and *able* to work.

5. Anchor the end result outcome within a timeframe, set a date and time for completion.

6. Ask the employee if he heeds any other information to own and accomplish what is delegated.

Follow-Up Questions

1. How does your personal avoidance of accountability affect your holding others accountable?

2. What more do you need to learn about boundaries and accountability?

3. How must you prepare to confront your boss on accountability issues?

4. Which peers have you avoided confronting on avoidance of accountability? Why? How will you prepare to do it?

Endnotes

1. Adapted from Darren Overfield and Rob Kaiser, "One out of Every Two Managers is Terrible at Accountability." https://hbr.org/2012/11/one-out-of-every-two-managers-is-terrible-at-accountability/downloaded (accessed February 9, 2015).

2. Adapted from Roger Connors and Tom Smith, "How to Create a 'Culture of Accountability.'" https://www.asme.org/career-education/articles/management-professional-practice/how-to-create-a-culture-of-accountability and Shawn Galloway, "Safety Measurement: Boring, Uninspiring, and Fear-Inducing." http://epubs.democratprinting.com/article/Sustainable_Safety_Excellence/1159273/124103/article.html (accessed December 20, 2013).

3. Adapted from Evans, HJ. "Winning with Accountability: The Secret Language of High-Performing Organizations." CornerStone Leadership Institute, 2008.

4. Adapted from Caroline Smith, "Locus of Control: Are You in Charge of Your Destiny?" http://www.mindtools.com/pages/article/newCDV_90.htm.

5. Adapted from Brett and Kate McKay, "Building Your Resiliency: Part III – Taking Control of Your Life." http://www.artofmanliness.com/2010/02/16/building-your-resiliency-part-iii-taking-control-of-your-life/ (accessed October 21, 2014).

6. Adapted from: Carl Safina, "The 2010 Gulf of Mexico Oil Well Blowout: A Little Hindsight." http://journals.plos.org/plosbiology/article?id=10.1371/journal.pbio.1001049 (accessed October 21, 2014).

7. Go to www.dailyfeats.com and start an account.

8. Summarized from Brian Miller, "Holding Others Accountable Is SIMPLE." http://www.communicoltd.com/pages/338_holding_others_accountable_is_simple.cfm (accessed October 21, 2014).

9. See ASANA https://asana.com/start

10. Adapted from Caroline Smith, "Developing Personal Accountability: Taking Responsibility to Get Ahead." http://www.mindtools.com/pages/article/developing-personal-accountability.htm (accessed December 20, 2013).

11. Adapted from Brett and Kate McKay, "Personal Responsibility 102: The Importance of Owning Up to Your Mistakes and How to Do It." http://www.artofmanliness.com/2013/02/19/how-to-own-up-to-mistakes/ (accessed December 21, 2013).

12. Adapted from Lt. Col. Robert MacKenzie, "Commentary: Success Through Accountability, Courage, and Teamwork." http://www.hilltoptimes.com/content/success-through-accountability-courage-and-teamwork (accessed December 20, 2013).

13. Summarized from WikiHow, "Have to Have Courage" www.wikihow.com/Have-Courage

14. Osho, *Courage: The Joy of Living Dangerously*, St. Martin's Griffin, 1999.

15. Adapted from Marc MacYoung, "Blaming Justifies Your Own Bad Behavior." http://www.nononsenseselfdefense.com/blameBadBehavior.htm) (accessed December 21, 2013).

16. Adapted from Hazelden Publishing, "Overcoming Shame-Based Thinking." http://www.bhevolution.org/public/overcoming_shame_based_thinking.page (accessed December 21, 2013).

17. Adapted from Craig Runde, "The Trouble with Avoiding Conflict." http://www.conflictdynamics.org/blog/2012/04/the-trouble-with-avoiding-conflict/0 (accessed December 20, 2013).

18. Adapted from Edmonds Community College, "Conflict Resolution Skills." http://www.edcc.edu/counseling/documents/Conflict.pdf (accessed December 20, 2013).

19. Adapted from Edmonds Community College, "Conflict Resolution Skills." http://www.edcc.edu/counseling/documents/Conflict.pdf and Carter McNamara, "How to Dearl with Conflict." http://managementhelp.org/interpersonal/conflict.htm and Yahoo, "How to Deal with Workplace Tension and Conflict." http://voices.yahoo.com/how-deal-workplace-tension-conflict-in-1730043.html (accessed December 20, 2013).

20. Adapted from Totally Responsible Person, "Why 'Locus of Control' Matters—and How TRP Can Help." http://www.trpnet.com/locus-of-control/ and Caroline Smith, "Locus of Control: Are You in Charge of Your Destiny?" http://www.mindtools.com/pages/article/newCDV_90.htm and Allison Foskett, "3 Ways to Control Your 'Locus of Control' to Meet Your Career Goals." http://www.goal-setting-motivation.com/tag/external-locus-of-control/ (accessed December 21, 2013).

21. Ibid. (see Note 19).

22. Adapted from University of California San Francisco, "Setting Healthy Workplace Boundaries." http://ucsfhr.ucsf.edu/index.php/assist/article/setting-healthy-workplace-boundaries/ (accessed December 21, 2013).

23. Adapted from Queensland Health, "How to Build Good Boundaries in Support Work." http://www.health.qld.gov.au/abios/behaviour/professional/boundaries_pro.pdf (accessed December 21, 2013) and https://professionalboundaries.com/faq.php (accessed January 29, 2015).

24. Adapted from Gloria Garceau-Glaser, "Professional Boundaries in the Workplace." http://vhsp.dphhs.mt.gov/sltc/services/communityservices/ProfessionalBoundariesInTheWorkplace.pdf (accessed December 21, 2013).

25. Patrick Lencioni (2002), *The Five Dysfunctions of a Team*, Jossey-Bass.

26. Adapted from Carol Stewart-Kirkby, "Coping with Problem Behavior," Ontario Ministry of Agriculture and Food, http://www.omafra.gov.on.ca/english/rural/facts/96-003.htm# (accessed December 21, 2013).

27. Ibid. (see Note 24).

28. Robert M. Bramson, *Coping with Difficult People*. Garden City, New York, NY: Anchor Press/Doubleday, 1981.

29. Adapted from Evans, H J. *Winning with Accountability: The Secret Language of High-Performing Organizations*. CornerStone Leadership Institute, 2008.

30. Craig Dowden, "Increasing Employee Accountability: The Critical Role of Leadership." http://www.hrvoice.org/increasing-employee-accountability-the-critical-role-of-leadership/ (accessed December 20, 2013).

31. Adapted from Decker. P, *Supervision*. 1982.

32. Adapted from Shawn Galloway, "Accountability: Positive and Proactive or Negative and Reactive." http://proactsafety.com/articles/accountability-positive-and-proactive-or-negative-and-reactive (accessed January 13, 2014).

33. Adapted from Top Achievement, "Creating SMART Goals." http://topachievement.com/smart.html (accessed October 21, 2014).

4

Self-Awareness

► Be aware of yourself and your impact

► Find the best ways to assess yourself

► Understand why it is difficult to be self-aware

► Learn how to read the room

► Learn to fix what you left in your wake

► Learn the importance of a personal vision

► Establish a network and a personal brand

Out of all the examples of self-handicapping behavior in this book, perhaps none is as fundamental as self-awareness. We all like to think that we are aware—both self-aware and aware of our surroundings, coworkers, organization, and industry. But many leaders do not spend enough time looking at themselves or their environment. When we are aware, we notice change. This can be scary. Leaders self-handicap because of uncertainty—they would rather feel good about what they already know than try something and risk being embarrassed or being something less than perfect. They often protect and preserve, rather than be aware and grow.[1] Growth usually hurts—we all know that. But in this chapter, you will learn that not growing because of being unaware can hurt a lot more and much longer.

Self-awareness is having a clear perception of one's personality, competencies—strengths and weaknesses, thoughts, beliefs, motivation, and emotions. It allows a leader to understand other people, their perception of him, and his responses to them. It is also awareness of one's environment and managing that environment by taking control of it or predicting its future effects on one's team. A leader's external environment includes his employees, customers, organization, industry, and location. Self-awareness allows a leader to see where his thoughts and emotions are taking him. It is the first step in creating what he wants and mastering his competencies to get there—being a great leader. Until a leader is aware of his natural tendencies, emotions, and behavior, as well as the environmental forces affecting him, he will have difficulty becoming an exceptional leader.

We all think we know ourselves fairly well, but in reality most of us don't. Many of our business students are absolutely sure they are extroverted, flexible, optimistic, and not controlling. We ask them to do a self-assessment and most of them quickly find out that their initial perceptions are false. On average, business students are less extroverted, more linear, pessimistic, and controlling than they imagined. Of course, some individuals break that mold, but until the students do some hard self-assessment with valid instruments they may only be deluding themselves as to who they are, where they are going, how to get there, and how they interact with others. That is why we force self-assessment on them.

Choosing to be aware can be a difficult decision, but the choice to be aware or not is a choice we all make—*every minute of every day*. Even our students, when forced to do self-assessment, can still deny the results. A lot of us have selective awareness—being aware of the things that we like and avoiding things that we would rather not be aware of. This is a normal reaction. For example, look at Tim Cook, the Chief Executive of Apple. Mr. Cook is aware of his strengths and weaknesses. He has presented Apple annual meetings somewhat differently from when Steve Jobs was at the helm. While Tim Cook is talented, he is aware that other Apple directors are more effective in presenting a project's capabilities, so he lets them. The lesson here is to use one's strengths and find someone else that can compensate for one's weaknesses. Of course, in order to do this, a leader has to be aware of his own strengths and competencies.

Think of learning to be self-aware as learning to dance.[2] When learning to dance we practice and have to pay attention to how and where our feet move, our hands' and body's motions, what our partner is doing, music, the beat, floor space, and other dancers. It takes time and focus. Just like dancing, self-awareness isn't learned from books. After much practice, one finally achieves some mastery of dancing.

With effort and practice, anyone can learn to be self-aware. By the time we leave school, we all seem to think we have it all figured out. Furthermore, self-reflection isn't something that most of us want to spend time doing. This is why the majority of us have a pretty low level of self-awareness. It's unfortunate because self-awareness is fundamental for anyone to realize full leadership potential. Humility comes from full awareness.

Yet, being aware in itself is not enough to overcome self-sabotage. Put simply, a leader can be aware and not act on that awareness. Remember our students rejecting the results of their own testing. Remember how easy the excuses come when uncertain—we can easily avoid seeing ourselves for who we are. There are lots of reasons for not taking action. The most common is that we don't like what we see. The ability to judge ourselves makes us uniquely human, but often that judgment is negative and we don't like to face it. Don't forget that lack of awareness and those excuses lead to reduced effort, which really means lack of learning or growth. Being unaware can produce some huge obstacles in leadership due to lack of learning. How many managers, when fired, really look to themselves rather than blame the company, coworkers, or circumstances? Just like the employee who spends more effort getting out of work than if he had just done the work, some of us spend more time staying unaware than if we had just opened up and grown. It really takes more effort to reject, suppress, or ignore information than just being aware.

Impact

There is a controversy about whether a leader should work on his weaknesses or just find his strengths and use that to guide his career. Peter Drucker says a person can perform only from strength.[3] Throughout history, he says, people had little need to know their strengths because they were born into a position, but now people have choices and need to know their strengths in order to know where they belong. We think that early careerists must attend to weaknesses to add to their competencies and to find their strengths. Senior leaders can work toward strengths, but this entire book is based on the premise that no matter how senior or experienced one is, there is still a very serious need to attend to what is hidden and denied—the weakness of self-handicapping. Self-assessment is the first step toward identifying what is done to self-sabotage oneself. There is strong logic to working on strengths; people rarely argue against that philosophy. The missing key ingredient is what we do that we don't realize—what we do to self-sabotage those strengths. Self-handicapping is a huge weakness usually overlooked at every level.

An executive told us a story about increasing awareness of self-handicapping—first, in herself and then in her organization.[4] In training, she asked what is really being sabotaged. Is it one's mobility or the cost and strain on the organization? She supervised a manager who got the work done and looked good on the dashboards but who subtlety abused her employees to get the results. The executive said that without understanding self-handicapping she would have eventually promoted the manager, because from her perspective the manager was effective and her team seemed okay with her. The manager and organization were getting results, but could better results have been achieved more efficiently without the abuse? And what would be the long-term effects? As the executive thought about her own leadership skills and what had happened with that manager, she concluded that the manager's behavior created unnecessary stress for people and that detracted from the productivity that could have been achieved over time. She said, "This is where defining the audience becomes important. Some people just need to know about self-handicapping and how [to] stop being a jerk, others need to understand how to identify and eliminate it because it's making a mess in their organization." She said the manager, "was a crafty one, but her demeanor should have given me some hints. The problem is that these people are smart and I think many of them know how to toe the line with just enough to get done what's needed." In this situation, self-awareness flowed into organizational awareness. Lack of awareness can impact both the self and the organization. Some examples of obstacles caused by lack of awareness are presented as follows.

Lack of Self-Awareness

- *Stunted Professional Growth*—If a leader is not aware of areas that need improvement, his effectiveness will be limited.

- *Low Emotional Intelligence*—If a leader is not aware of how his employees are feeling or their apprehensions, he may force a project forward and employee resistance destroys any chance of successful implementation.

- *Impact On Others*—When a leader is giving a presentation and the audience is losing attention and he doesn't recognize and know how to pull them back.

- *Self-Imposed Barriers*—A leader may not be approachable—limiting any constructive feedback from his coworkers. Regardless of talent, people-skills matter. No one wants to work with a jerk.

Lack of Awareness of The Impact On The Organization

- **A Mediocre Manager**—When a leader lacks awareness of a new manager's weaknesses, he may put him in less-effective roles.

- **Inappropriate Market Positioning**—When a leader is confused about the benefits his organization offers to the consumer in relation to his competition, he limits the organization's advantage.

- **Vision to Operations Alignment**—Without constant awareness of how the organization's operations align to the vision, the mindsets of employees will become muddled and may create false motivations.

Emotional intelligence has long been theorized to contribute to effectiveness in leadership; however, empirical work demonstrating this link is not conclusive.[5] Yet, it is hard to dispute that there is an emotional component to leadership. Overall, businesses have not had good fortune when basing selection, promotion, or reward decisions on measurement of emotional intelligence; there are too many inconsistencies in the measurement of this trait. The answer may lie in understanding self-awareness; it may be more effective to simply show leaders how lack of awareness of their own behaviors affects leadership outcomes.

Bratton, et al. suggest that the notion of modesty is an effective leadership trait that seems to be less embraced by business practitioners and may be as or more important than emotional intelligence.[6] In business, we tend to look for and reward dominance and self-assuredness in our leaders. Humility often takes a back seat, but in our work, we have found that great leaders are humble. These authors' research supports previous findings that modesty may be a key component for transformational leaders. Research also shows that leaders' self-awareness of their own humility increases employee satisfaction, self-leadership, and effectiveness.[7] We think that modesty is an emotion that promotes mastery goals, may reduce the need to self-handicap, and warrants greater research in business. It may also be the "opening move" in self-awareness.

The Real Issues

Many people have a rudimentary concept of self-awareness. Often, they will say, "Whoops, I am failing at this again!" and believe they have awareness. This is only seeing what one is doing; not its impact. Picture a child learning "right from wrong"; they know what they are doing is wrong—being caught may cause unpleasantness, but they may not acknowledge how that behavior affects others or themselves in the long term. Applying this line of thought to the professional world, it is not enough for a leader to simply acknowledge and become aware of what he is doing and how that differs from what he should be doing; he must see the effects of his actions and take control.

It is important to review what was said in the first chapter about the impact of self-handicaps. *Recognizing* is seeing what one does. *Acknowledgment* is the act of understanding why that behavior is used—what are the triggers that cause one to choose self-handicapping over other ways of operating? The habits of self-handicapping are fairly automatic and are used for impression management. The next step, *Admitting* is accepting that the behavior affects others. This helps a leader see the impact his behaviors to himself and others—how the excuse to skip talking to an employee will affect that employee's engagement. Admitting is a key to being humble and helps him elevate himself above impression management to exceptional leadership. Breaking through this barrier is a crucial part of the awareness process. Finally, *Adjusting* is finding better ways of operating and practicing them until they are the new habits.

Let's review the example in Chapter 1. Leaders being late to meetings because they learned that those 12 minutes are not really late (Or, they simply don't have respect for the others in the meeting—whether consciously or not). To become aware, the leader must see the behavior and acknowledge its consequences. Recognition requires being humble enough (or just reducing self-centeredness enough) to be open to someone's feedback. Acknowledgment requires a set of ideals and principals regarding "right versus wrong"—saying "My behavior was wrong." Looking at Kohlberg's work reminds us of why some people don't learn what is right or wrong in a conventional sense.[8] Some people only think it is wrong if it comes back to hurt them. Some think something is wrong if everyone else thinks it is wrong. Some think it is wrong if it is a violation of their code of rules or vision for themselves—the Kohlberg levels of development, put simply. Recognition is when a leader is humble enough to see he is late at 12 minutes, acknowledges that is wrong, and admits how his behavior affects others in the meeting. Then it is time to adjust and plan more time to get to the meeting.

True awareness comes from acknowledging one's behavior, and then admitting how that behavior affects others. When a leader becomes aware of how his behavior affects others, he has reached a level where he can truly be humble and appreciate where others are and what they need to engage or be exceptional in *their* work. This allows the leader to stop blaming others to avoid looking at himself. Of course, we all think we do this, but we often don't. Mentally look around yourself at work.

Who do you know that does not acknowledge to themselves or others that they understand the implications of their actions. How many are really humble? Do these folks neglect to say, "I am sorry?" or even better, "I am sorry and I won't do it again." Do they stop and listen to others? Left unchecked, this becomes an endless cycle of lack of true awareness, self-handicapping, and never improving.

A lack of awareness can be caused by fear. But fear takes courage to face. Leaders can fear the unknown, a hyper-competitive environment, or situations they dislike. A leader must have the courage to identify those situations and the effects of his actions in them before he falls victim to some self-created obstacle that sinks the ship. By implementing strategies such as a self-assessment or executive coaching, a leader can right the ship. Simply by shutting one's mouth and sitting back humbly to listen to others could be the start of righting the ship. Remember that the uncertainty and apprehension driving self-handicapping often comes from a competitive, performance goal environment. Fighting through this fear or working to change the culture is crucial leadership behavior that can open a group to self-awareness. Perhaps the most difficult to correct is when lack of awareness has led to self-deception—especially the Box of Blame. It is important to note that leaders often slip right through these levels. Lack of awareness leads to excuses which lead to avoidance goals and ultimately obstacles such as the irritated employees waiting for the boss late to the meeting. This is self-handicapping by lack of awareness.

Do You Lack Awareness?

Survey

Do I Lack Awareness or Not? (Y = Yes, N= No, DK = Don't Know)

____Know what your weaknesses are, and find employees to complement you?

____Have an accurate feel for your traits and preferences?

____Have a personal vision for yourself?

____Know what your strengths and competencies are?

____Maintain constant awareness for your environment?

____Maintain constant awareness for your industry and business in general?

____Know the extent of how your actions affect others?

____Have a healthy work/life balance?

____Read unspoken reactions of others for feedback?

____Understand what is left in your wake/don't burn bridges?

____Have emotional intelligence for staff (and customers too)?

____Able to read the room/audience to pick up the unspoken?

____Have created a vision for your area of responsibility?

Scores
10–13—You are aware.
5–9—You are inconsistent in your awareness.
1–4—You are greatly self-handicapping yourself through unawareness.

What to Do?

An important area for self-assessment is boundaries. Boundaries are a common theme in this book because so many areas of self-handicapping (such as micromanagement and lack of accountability) are violations of others' boundaries. Boundaries define the limits and responsibilities of the people with whom a leader interacts. Poorly defined boundaries can lead to significant denial of the negative consequences resulting from what a leader does.

Effective leaders know where they end and where another person begins. When we talk about needing space, setting limits or determining acceptable behavior, we are really talking about boundaries.[9] Boundary violations can be subtle. For example, in your next meeting with both males and females, watch carefully and see if you can catch one of the males starting a sentence one or two words before the female speaker is done speaking. This is very quick. It becomes even worse when the male starts his response with "Yes, but...." These actions can come from a deep-seated, often not acknowledged, disrespect for females or it may be cultural on the part of the male. But both are very subtle emotional boundary violations—"put downs." Ask any woman if this has happened, and the answer will likely be "Yes, all the time!" Many males will say they do not know what you are talking about. Boundary violations in today's workplace are usually subtle, not acknowledged, and in this case, fester in half the workforce. But it is learned behavior and can be corrected. Leaders have to be aware of this level of impact in themselves and their team. When we adopt a higher-level of awareness and recognize how our behavior affects others, we then conceptualize and pay attention to the boundaries between others and ourselves. This is the beginning of being humble and of exceptional leadership of others.

A great exercise to understand boundary violation is to find and watch the movie, "What About Bob?" Bob was a psychiatric patient who was emotionally attached to his psychiatrist. He tracked his psychiatrist down on vacation and would not leave him and his family alone, violating professional and personal boundaries by the minute. *The key element in the movie is that a boundary violation involves two people—the first steps over a boundary and the other allows it to happen.* We violate others boundaries by what we do to them that we should not do, and by what we fail to do that we should have done. This includes taking advantage of their goodness, how we say things to others (such as ridicule, sarcasm, and putdowns), by the things we say through gossip, by manipulation of others, and/or avoidance of our own accountability. We also violate the boundaries of others through things like triangular communication—where one person sends a message to another person through a third party. We can also violate others' boundaries because they let us. It often starts small and works up to bigger and bigger intrusions. We do it because both parties don't perceive a boundary between them or deny it. Sometimes we temporarily violate boundaries in emergencies, when highly emotional, or angry.

Here are some signs a leader is not self-aware.[10] The first few are obvious but going down the list they can become more subtle. A leader:

- **Is a Bully**—Open or behind the scenes anger and aggression are often signs that a leader feels threatened or scared.

- **Is Defensive**—When genuine and objective feedback makes a leader agitated or even angry, that's a sure sign.

- **Is Controlling**—When a leader micromanages, it means he is not paying attention to something really important. Another sure sign.

- **Is Passive Aggressive**—When a leader says, "Sure, no problem," then turns around and does the exact opposite, it's a deflection. This is another flavor of controlling.

- **His Behavior Changes and Doesn't See It**—A leader says he doesn't have some trait or criticizes others for having it and then turns right around and does that trait.

- **Is Grandiose**—When a leader's strategies/goals defy objective reasoning, that's a sign he is genuinely in over his head and are overcompensating to appear like everything is under control.

- *Makes Excuses*—These are ways of avoiding or deflecting negative attention and the start of the ERO Spiral.
- *Blames Others*—This is a sure sign of self-deception.

Forbes suggested the following as first steps in becoming more self-aware:[11]

1. *Take a Personality Test*—There are many and they share common building blocks.

2. *Participate in a 360-Degree Assessment*—Including boss, peers, and subordinates. Even include family and friends if possible.

3. *Ask For Informal Feedback*—Try this when you are discussing professional development with a mentor or a leader of a team.

4. *Reflect on a Regular Basis*—Set aside time for this kind of introspection.

5. *Write in a Journal*—And review the connection between behavior and results.

6. *Practice Being Humble*—Avoid taking credit, praise others often, admit your mistakes immediately, and always go last.

7. *Be Interviewed*—Management coaches can help interpret a leader's thoughts and actions.

8. *Exercise and Seek Out Recreation*—Deliberately tuning out with exercise heightens perception when you tune back in.

Self-Assessment

Asking others for an assessment (and being open to constructive criticism) of one's strengths and weaknesses can be very helpful. Even with a spotless record, a leader is still vulnerable to blind spots. Asking others for help in identifying these "blind spots"—which usually are self-handicapping—can illuminate issues that a leader had no idea existed. Once he becomes aware of these blind spots he can then work on addressing them.

Sometimes we just need downtime to self-reflect. Most of us are all caught up in the "I have no time" lifestyle—resulting in little opportunity for self-reflection. Downtime doesn't necessarily mean a vacation; it can be 10 minutes every evening before one leaves work to ask, "What was I successful at today?" and "What should I have done differently?" By getting on a daily schedule with these probing questions—a leader will be more aware. Self-reflection is an audit of what, when, and how a leader thinks about and does things. Whatever method of self-reflection a leader chooses, a "one-shot" action will not sustain greater awareness. In a *Harvard Business Review* article entitled, "Managing Oneself," Peter Drucker advocated journaling key decisions that a leader makes and then later comparing what happened with what one expected to happen.[12] By making a journal and seeing the reasons why one makes a decision and comparing to actual results, a leader develops awareness of his reasoning skills.

In general, people's self-assessments are rarely as accurate as other people's predictions of their behavior.[13] Typically, the views of other people about you—subordinates, peers, and superiors—agree with each other more than with one's own self-assessment. "People overestimate the likelihood that they engage in desirable behaviors or favorable outcomes, furnish overly optimistic estimates of when they will complete future projects, and reach judgments with too much confidence."[14] There are several reasons for this. These are as follows:

- People often do not have the knowledge and expertise necessary to assess their own competence. Put simply, if a leader is incompetent at work, he will be incompetent at assessing that work.
- Leaders receive incomplete or no feedback about their actions, which can lead to overestimation of skills and outcomes.
- Leaders fail to appreciate the power fear, anxiety, and embarrassment have on employee feedback.
- Leaders often have difficulty predicting how they will respond to situations that have significant emotional components.

Because many managers are not very good at assessing their own performance and are reluctant to solicit feedback on their own, organizations adopt systems such as regular performance reviews or other assessment to clue employees to their strengths and weaknesses. But these tend to be relatively ineffective because the feedback is infrequent, often sugarcoated, and usually too late. It is also often threatening— it is tied to losing something or not gaining something. Feedback will also not work if people experience it as commentary about their character. Organizations try many things to solve these issues such as separating feedback from evaluation, providing more frequent "coaching" and using 360 reviews. This makes the evaluation process more costly and intense and often not any better. One technique shown to enhance assessment and to reduce self-handicapping is to bolster a person's sense of self-worth before they encounter the feedback. They then become more willing to accept it and to change their behavior. Regardless, our message is clear—exceptional leaders take charge of awareness and self-assess in every way possible.

Flawed self-assessments happens all the way up the corporate ladder. CEOs display overconfidence in their judgments, particularly when stepping into new markets or novel projects. Given that executives live in an isolated world with little objective feedback on their personal behavior, the magnitude of the problem can be magnified at this level. One answer is adding outside perspectives from an independent board or executive coaching. Yet, the conclusion we hope a leader makes is that assessment of one's behavior without expert help is relatively inaccurate.[15]

There are numerous places where a leader can take a complete battery of tests for free to determine strengths, weaknesses, and preferences. If a leader has never done this kind of assessment, we highly recommend it and we show you where to do it. A leader may not like the feedback, he may disagree with what it says, but it will get him thinking about himself. Any self-examination is the start of choosing to think about oneself objectively and discovering who you are, comparing what one thinks to what others think, and how that impacts one's world, family, career, and life. Remember that what is a strength now may be a weaknesses later. Being fairly controlling as a manager is good; being controlling as an executive is usually bad. It leads to lack of awareness. Self-assessment is a life-long process for an exceptional leader.

One of the standard self-assessments many companies use is the Meyers Briggs. This "test" provides identification of one's basic preferences in each of 16 distinctive personality types specified or implicit in Jung's personality theory.[16]

The Myers-Briggs has been taken by millions of people, but remember, none of the free personality tests purporting to determine one's MBTI® or Myers Briggs Personality Type on the web are the "real thing." So, use the real thing—the MBTI® publisher, CPP, Inc. (formerly Consulting Psychologists Press), has developed an online system for administering and interpreting the MBTI® called "MBTI® Complete"[17] Other useful free tests of a leader's preferences can be found at http://www.mypersonality.info/Take/. We suggest completing all.

The Self-Assessment Library is a learning tool that allows a leader to assess their knowledge, beliefs, feelings, and actions in regard to a wide range of personal skills, abilities, and interests. We use this book of 69 research-based instruments so our students have one source from which to learn more about themselves. Find it at http://www.pearsonhighered.com/educator/product/Self-Assessment-Library-34/9780136083764.page#sthash.Uu0ID8uF.dpuf or http://www.pearsonhighered.com/sal/

or http://www.amazon.com/Self-Assessment-Library-Stephen-Robbins/dp/0136083757#.

Going back to strengths, Gallup provides a survey based on the belief that people should focus on making the most of their talents, rather than struggling to work on their weaknesses. A strengths-based approach can have rapid payoffs in confidence and productivity. Gallup's basic analysis identifies people's five top traits, along with advice about how to put them to work. Check out this approach and complete the assessment at https://www.gallupstrengthscenter.com/?utm_source=googadwords&utm_medium=web&utm_campaign=newhomepage&gclid=CP-0_66wk8ACFSMV7AodHCUAww.

Another way to self-assess is to compare oneself against books that tell a leader what should be done. We highly recommend Barbara Pachter's book, *When the Little Things Count*, which lists 601 things every manager and executive should know (http://www.amazon.com/When-Little-Things-Count-Always/dp/1569242909. It is the best we have seen; we require reading it and developing an action plan from it of all our students. This activity is definitely not a one-shot assessment but should be reviewed annually.[18]

Matching up our personality with a suitable role can be vital to successful career change. If this is your situation, or think it might be, check out the website http://www.careershifters.org/. We wish to over-emphasize this point—*Measuring oneself against some outside frame of reference to gauge your traits, preferences, weaknesses, strengths, and self-sabotaging tendencies must not be skipped over, overlooked, or ignored.* Awareness is the first step to not shooting yourself in the foot at work, to not sabotaging a leadership career, and to being an exceptional leader. A leader must be aware of who he is before he tries to change employees or an organization. You may think you are aware, but remember—those who are not could be in some state of self-deception that quickly plateaus a career.

Using Executive Coaching

When a leader is more senior, he may look into executive coaching to build awareness. This coaching is useful when a leader has few role models to call on as mentors. Executive coaching provides leaders with tailored guidance on how to manage people and processes to improve organizational results.[19] Coaching targets future behavior and prior influencing factors so it can be useful to build awareness and learn new skills. *Executive coaching should include goals set for understanding and managing self-handicapping behavior.* Like all approaches to leadership development, executive coaching is not a cure-all. The presence of any "teachable moment" in coaching depends on the knowledge that self-handicapping is occurring and a readiness to deal with it. This may come from organizational forces resulting in bad outcomes or from self-generated data such as employee surveys or discussion.

Executive coaching should *not* be considered "remedial" but instead something that enhances awareness of problems and what it takes to achieve high performance, similar to how an elite athlete uses a coach.[20] Coaching is neither irrelevant to leadership nor of minor importance. "The higher a leader's position, the more he is dealing with psychological and relational issues. Successful leadership requires astuteness about others—their emotional and strategic personal drivers; their self-interest, overt and covert. These competencies rest on a foundation of self-knowledge and self-awareness. And a leader can't know the truth about another without knowing it about himself."[21]

Executive coaching may be in order for an executive when pushing a strategic shift concerning self-handicapping behavior in an organization. This will entail introducing a new skill set to a group managers and executives and must be modelled to be effective. Coaching can help the leader be a great role model. However, finding coaches familiar with self-handicapping and what to do about it may be difficult.

Using the Wisdom of the Crowd

We have used an evaluation methodology to estimate the likelihood of failures in organizational programs and projects that relies on the wisdom of a group of people about certain "markers" of problems (Chapter 7).[22] Similar complexity exists in self-handicapping behavior and there are markers of self-handicapping. We believe eliminating self-handicapping behavior, personally or organizationally, is a project to be taken on just like any other large business project and can be predicted. Remember that self-handicapping is almost always hidden, subtle, and hard to nail down—denied by the individual and undiscussable by the crowd. Hence the search for "markers" makes some sense. We contend that the likelihood of identifying self-handicapping is quickly and readily predictable using these markers and asking employees the extent of such behavior in an organization.

Crowds like employees and managers are better than experts at diagnosing and solving problems (if they are wise crowds). To be wise, crowds have to meet four necessary conditions: (1) Diversity of opinion—each person should have private information; (2) Independence—people's opinions are not determined by the opinions of those around them; (3) Decentralization—people specialize and draw on local knowledge; and (4) Aggregation—some type of mechanism exists to arrive at collective judgments. Employees can be very wise—especially about self-handicapping since they likely see it every day and it directly impacts them. It could be good to give them a positive outlet to identify, discuss, or deal with it, but most executives fear this level of exposure. Nevertheless, we have found considerable value in using the wisdom of employees and managers in predicting the degree of self-handicapping in the management group and the likely project implementation failures that will result from it. Unwillingness to explore all avenues of awareness—especially before a major strategy shift that affects all employees—is self-handicapping.

The bottom line is that there are a number of ways to assess a leader, not only on skills and competencies, but on his awareness of himself and his impact on other people. How well a leader knows himself, is critical in understanding self-handicapping behavior. The reason is that much of self-handicapping comes from not knowing what one is doing or denying the implications of it.

But Most of All, Be Humble

Humility is characterized by low self-focus, secure sense of self, and an increased sense of the value of others. Humility has many positive outcomes for leaders. Leader humility involves leaders modeling to followers how to grow. It produces positive organizational outcomes because followers believe that their own developmental issues and feelings of uncertainty are legitimate.[23] CEO humility has been shown to be positively associated with empowering leadership team behaviors which in turn correlates with leadership team integration. Leadership team integration then causes middle managers to have a perception of having an empowering organizational climate which is associated with their work engagement, affective commitment, and job performance.[24]

Great leaders admit that they are not the best at everything. No matter how competent a leader is, there will always be somebody better. A leader has to recognize his own faults and be grateful for what he has. Great leaders appreciate others' talents and remain teachable. Great leaders will not judge others; they know it takes team effort. They look at themselves and become aware. A great leader will allow himself and others to make mistakes; he will readily admit his mistakes. He will avoid bragging and taking all the credit. And he will be considerate in conversations, not talking down to anyone. He won't take all the credit. Being humble means appreciating the talents and qualities of others. Being humble means to move away from performance goals—the leader must stop comparing himself to others. While competition can drive people, it's nearly impossible to be humble when we're constantly striving to be the "best," trying to be better than others, or trying to avoid mistakes. Instead, try developing more healthy competitive environments where the competition is to learn more, grow, and provide more value for customers. Finally, great leaders talk less and allow others to blossom. A great leader *is best when people barely know he exists.*

Why Don't You?

Expediency

It should be obvious from reading the section "What to Do?" that it takes time and effort to plan and carry out the project of fully understanding yourself from others' (experts') eyes. So, before one even gets to the point of not wanting negative feedback, it is easy to come to a halt because of the tremendous effort required. Also, many leaders have a negative opinion of any kind of self-assessment tests and don't trust them. We all can argue lack of time for seeking information about ourselves. We can also argue that we are introverted and reluctant to ask others about our behavior or the consequences of that behavior. When the excuses to avoid self-examination start, understand that this is self-handicapping and leading you down the ERO Spiral.

Any person's thinking requires choice.[25] Thinking about oneself is not automatic and takes effort. A leader must make a choice to focus on what he is doing and why. Additionally, there are degrees of focus. He can look at an employee and recognize him, but not focus on particular features such as eye color. What is important is that lack of awareness is easy—no effort, no awareness. The easy road is to stay unaware until some obstacle hits you in the face and even then, leaders can stay unaware by wondering, "Why me?," or blaming someone or something else for all his troubles. The natural state of a person is lack of awareness.

Where do you fail to be aware due to expediency?

_____

_____

Avoidance

Some leaders focus on the positive and try to block out the negative. Grandparents are often guilty of this. They go on and on about their grand-daughter and how she has a full-ride scholarship to the top university in the state, but neglect to mention (or think about) their grandson with the drug problem. In a professional situation, we can all fool ourselves into believing we are "fully aware" of the landscape at work and ourselves—while mentally diminishing the impact of negative issues. The motivation for selective awareness is quite luring—avoiding pain. However, when we postpone (at best) or neglect totally (at worst) these issues, they have the potential of attacking us when we are least expecting and least prepared.

Where do you avoid awareness?

Apprehension

Leaders often rationalize that "I have made it this long, I can go a little longer." An example of this can be found in physical health—men do this more than women. Men will delay getting an annual physical, their prostate checked, or other health screenings because they may be afraid of the results. They keep eating unhealthy diets. But why? Perhaps it is a longing to remain forever young—with no health abnormalities or concerns. Perhaps they are afraid of the lifestyle ramifications of their eating and other bad habits. Looking at this situation from the outside, most of us would say, "Go get health screening, because the sooner you know what is wrong—the sooner you can fix it!" But when it's a leader avoiding awareness in a work situation, none of us say anything.

A leader can also play the "What if" game. He can ask, "What if I can't eat cheeseburgers?" or "What if I really do have something wrong with me?" The effect of this "What if" game can be positive or negative—depending on how a leader uses it. It can be a fruitless pursuit that only helps work up emotions and causes great stress, or on the other hand, it can help him develop contingency plans. An example of this positive approach is, "What if my director of finance gets offered a position at another company," or "What if a supplier raises their prices by 5 percent next quarter?" Both of these questions can be used to develop a "Plan B" action. But when worry occupies the majority of a leader's thinking, little room is left for maintaining awareness and taking action. A good leader is aware of his personal impact and environment and anticipates future needs by playing "What if" in the positive sense.

What do you fear that leads to lack of awareness?

_____

_____

Self-Deception

One further point is important to make here—all addictions are an attempt to become unaware, to not face some issue in life, to zone out/ fog up the brain so we don't have to deal with an issue. Addictions such as alcohol, drugs, sex, the Internet, or work decrease an individual's sensitivity to what are appropriate forms of behavior, insight, self-regulation, and self-evaluative feedback about behaviors.[26] Although initial experimentation with a drug is largely a voluntary behavior, continued drug use can eventually impair neuronal circuits in the brain that are involved in free will, turning drug use into an automatic, compulsive behavior. To move into any self-regulated form of self-awareness, an individual first must work through any compulsive needs that come from addiction. Simply dealing with the addiction raises one to the first level of awareness, but as we all know, it is not easy to beat an addiction. We are leaving recognizing and beating an addiction to others. It is a huge industry. Addiction can surely effect the overall problem of awareness.

Where does lack of awareness lead to self-deception in your life?

_____

_____

Behaviors to Change

Emotional Intelligence

Recognize

The ability to express and control our own emotions is important, but so is our ability to understand, interpret, and respond to the emotions of others. This is called *emotional intelligence*.[27] Salovey and Mayer say that there are four factors of emotional intelligence: (1) The perception of emotion, (2) The ability to reason using emotions, (3) The ability to understand emotion, and (4) The ability to manage emotions. This might involve understanding nonverbal communication from employees, feeling what you feel instead of ignoring it, or prioritizing what emotions you pay attention and react to. There is lots of information coming at you—attend to emotions along with facts. The emotions that we perceive can carry a wide variety of meanings and we must interpret the cause of them. Monitoring your emotions is a fundamental piece of emotional intelligence—your own and from others. Curb your emotional reactions and react in an understanding, supportive way when employees are emotional.

Admit

A meta-analysis comparing data from 91 studies involving nearly 8,000 participants looked at whether people actively avoid information that contradicts what they believe and why they might seek conflicting information.[28] The researchers found that people are about twice as likely to select information that supports their own point of view (67 percent) as to consider an opposing idea (33 percent). Very closed-minded individuals are even more reluctant to expose themselves to differing perspectives. Furthermore, people are more resistant to new points of view when their own ideas are associated with their values. Finally, people who have little confidence in their own beliefs are less likely to expose themselves to contrary views than people who are very confident in their own ideas. Self-handicapping starts with lack of confidence in oneself.

On the other hand, those who may have to publicly defend their ideas, such as politicians or businessmen trying to sell an idea, are more motivated to learn about the views of those who oppose them. People are more likely to expose themselves to opposing ideas when it is useful to them in some way. Great leaders do this. Not accepting differing information can be a defense mechanism to reduce anxiety generated by perceived threats. Defense mechanisms are often thought of as negative, but some can be useful. For example, utilizing humor to overcome a stressful situation can be good if not overused. In many cases however, these defenses work unconsciously to distort reality and are overused where they become truly self-handicapping.

Adjust

A leader can learn to be more emotionally intelligent. This is a good way to increase awareness—especially of other people (your employees). Here is what you should do:[29]

- Listen with intent, do not prepare a response to what another person is saying. Ask questions to clarify if needed.
- Repeat what you think you heard and ask for accuracy.

- Ask "feeling" questions—"How do you feel about this?"
- Pay attention to body language. Try to pick up with nonverbal communication doesn't match verbal communication.
- When you react to someone, react to both the facts and emotions on what is at hand.
- Examine the assumptions that you make when communicating with others. Don't assume that they understand you on the first take, or you, them.
- Do not rush to judgment or stereotype.
- Don't let stressful situations dictate how others perceive you.
- If you hurt someone's feelings, apologize quickly and directly. Don't ignore what you did or avoid the person.
- Before you do something, figure out how that action will effect others.

Key Behaviors
Here are the several things to do to work on emotional intelligence.

1. Practice before, during, and after interactions. Try to relate and understand the other person(s) situation before you start speaking, what they are feeling when you speak, and how it affected them after you speak. Write this down for several instances and reflect on its impact on your understanding of the situation.

2. Recognize and adapt to facial expressions. A lot of information can be gained through the face, instantly. Record what you learn over several encounters.

3. Take one employee you do not know well. Take out a sheet of paper and write down five things you would do if you were to show this person that you really care about him/her.

Learning to "Read the Room"

Recognize
In reading the room, we are referring to skills that allow a leader to read body language and other nonverbal communication, hearing words that aren't spoken, attending to tone, inflection, or other cues, and being able to understand what someone is really trying to say. Instinctively knowing when you have lost an audience because of lack of understanding, they are tired of something and need to move on, or are peeved with

one person dominating a discussion are critical skills for a leader. Most crowds are kind and reticent—they won't speak up. A leader has to read the nonverbal communication.

When giving presentations or in a meeting, a leader should silently practice reading the room—read faces in the audience, know when someone is about to ask a question (without verbal cues), think about what question that person is about to ask, know when the crowd is bored or when they are lost because they are confused. A good leader does these things while speaking; it is an acquired skill.

Admit

One of the authors will never forget the time he was speaking to a group of downstream oil and gas managers and kept using the term "gas station." The room got quieter and quieter and he finally realized he was doing something wrong, so he asked. After a long pause, one of the individuals said, "In our company, we *don't* have *gas* stations, we only have *service* stations." Well, the author was thinking that it had been years since we had any real service from one of their outlets, but of course, he apologized and never said the words "gas station" again. The program livened up and was successful. So, read the unspoken, and don't be afraid to ask. If it is an easy fix, fix it. If not, explain why you can't fix it right away and work around it.

Here are the 12 telltale signs that the audience is not listening.[30] These are the things a leader needs to look for in a meeting or presentation. The audience:

- Start to look down (particularly at their smartphone)
- Touch or rub their face, hands or hair
- Eyes glaze over and look at the screen (this is easy to mistake as sitting and listening intently)
- Fidget
- Yawn (often with a hand covering their mouth)
- Flick through the conference catalogue or handouts
- Make copious notes or jot down things they have forgotten to do (this can be mistaken for jotting down key points)
- Sigh heavily
- Lie back in their chair and cross their arms
- Scan across the room

- Whisper to each other quietly
- Tap their feet

On the other hand, if they like what a leader is saying, the audience will:[31]

- Sit intently listening to a leader speech
- Smile
- Flick their eyes briefly between the slides and the speaker

Adjust

In a meeting there are other subtle hints that let you know what is going on in the group. When people fail to look others in the eye, it can seem as if they are evading or trying to hide something. On the other hand, it may be a sign of low self-esteem or a cultural perception that too much eye contact can seem confrontational or intimidating.

Look at Lencioni's five dysfunctions of a team.[32] They are absence of trust, fear of conflict, lack of commitment, avoidance of accountability, and inattention to results. All five are symptoms that team leaders can learn to identify. One good indicator of team dysfunction, for example, is a boring team meeting where people don't challenge one another in discussions. Another good indicator of team problems is undiscussable back-channel conflict. Do people reserve their complaints for hallway conversations instead of voicing them during meetings?

Key Behaviors

Here are the key behaviors for reading the room.

1. Instead of mentally viewing a presentation as one way—picture it as a conversation. You are the one who is speaking, but your audience members' facial expression is the other side of the conversation—consistently monitor it.

2. If you get a facial expression that you aren't expecting—try and figure out why. Ask a question for understanding.

3. Remember that verbal and nonverbal communication work together to convey a message. Look for discrepancies between the two.

4. Take the team's temperature often. If a team has been allowed to drift for any length of time, it may take many attempts to get them back on course.

5. Always ask for questions during and at the end of a presentation.

Understanding What You Left in Your Wake

Recognize

A major sense of awareness is understanding what you left in your wake. Sometimes it is best to burn bridges. If in a love relationship that doesn't help you grow, you need to get out of it completely. If you are settling for a job you hate, realize that you have the rest of your life ahead and being stuck in a dead end job is not a good way to start it. Some employees need to be fired. But in most situations, burning bridges will come back to harm a leader. Where there is no need to burn the bridge, a leader shouldn't. Most of us know that leaving a job the wrong way could ruin a leader's reputation, make enemies in the industry, and lose an opportunity to come back to the company or position.

Admit

Careers are long; very few paths are only one way—even though we all want to keep going up and up. A leader will often need to come around again, so do not burn bridges and manage your "brand." Those who do too much self-sabotage often create an environment of confusion and these leaders eventually get exposed.[33] The proper route for an exceptional leader is to be competent, aware, and ethical. Do what you say you will and do it well. Pay attention to those around you—360 degree. By doing this, you will enhance your boss's position, build a brand of trust, and maybe even inspire.

Personal brand management is about continually elevating your leadership talent to align with the marketplace and your organization's needs. Personal branding is the ultimate individual responsibility and starts with never burning bridges. Unfortunately, most leaders still view personal branding as a self-promotion campaign rather than a leadership development requirement. The workplace is now less about loyalty to company and more about open labor markets. As such, a leader's personal brand is the ultimate identifier of what you are able to deliver and how you will behave.

A leader must be extremely mindful and disciplined about the relationships he forges. And he must also be mindful to seize opportunities to increase his brand—this can be a form of "burned bridge." We tell our students to never turn down a position or project offered that will enhance their competencies; rather take the weekend to visit with their network and thoroughly learn how to do the job before Monday. Then listen to the employees and gain their help.

Adjust
Managers build bridges by:[34]

- Being approachable and encouraging staff to be open and honest.
- Ensuring that workers feel safe and supported.
- Managing disagreement or conflict quickly. Recognizing the sources of conflict when it happens; encourage those involved in the conflict to clarify their perspective of the conflict without judgment.
- Admitting one's mistakes and learn to say sorry.
- Not gossiping or talking behind anyone's back.
- Acknowledging everyone's individual contribution and never claiming it for one's own.
- Finish all projects and carry your own weight.
- Build a network and keep it up as a two-way street.

Here is how to leave a job without burning bridges:[35]

1. Choose your next job with the long term in mind. Pay attention to nonpay issues.
2. Write a (positive) formal letter of resignation.
3. Give as much notice as possible. Make sure that you DO give notice.
4. Help find (and maybe even train) your replacement if necessary.
5. Thank your coworkers.
6. Don't use company tools or time for your transition.
7. Stay focused and tie up loose ends.

Key Behaviors
Here are the key behaviors for dealing with burned bridges with individuals:

1. Don't do it in the first place. Treat all professionally and equally.
2. If you received something and did not reciprocate or acknowledge it appropriately, do so now.
3. Say you are sorry.
4. Listen when you apologize. If the other gives feedback, acknowledge it.

5. If you have to get out of a bad situation gracefully, pass cranky customers to other providers, or offer referrals.

6. Avoid hurtful statements, anger, or accusatory remarks.

7. Stay away from social media in discussing any of the earlier mentioned statements.

Managing Up

Recognize

When someone says that a person needs to "manage up," he is often describing the self-handicapping strategy of managing impressions. We define it as doing what the leader needs to do above and beyond the tasks assigned to him so that he can enhance his boss's work. Check out, Rosanne Badowski, *Managing Up: How to Forge an Effective Relationship With Those Above You.*[36] A leader must think about managing both up and down. It is the managers who only manage up through impression management who give managing the bad reputation. Managing up means to be competent and get your job done at an exceptional level. It does not mean cutting corners with impression management techniques or flattery of the boss. That is self-handicapping.

Admit

People start to handicap themselves when their management is solely focused up, rather than up and down. While it is important to understand the needs and thoughts of one's superiors, a leader must also relay that information and provide motivation to the staff. Ultimately, satisfying the customer should be the best form of managing up.

Adjust

The following strategies will help a leader manage up:[37]

- The better a leader understands what his boss does, why, and what he cares about, the better positioned he is to deliver results, manage expectations, and avoid losing situations.

- There is absolutely nothing to be gained by making a boss look bad. So work around his weaknesses and support his success. If you have a disorganized boss, help him to be on top of things rather than whining about his lack of organizational skills.

- Make sure there are no surprises. Make your boss aware of the status of all projects and tasks. Be honest and trustworthy. And be aware of your boss's hot buttons.

- If your boss demonstrates bad behavior—don't follow suit. Often, people perform poorly because of their bad boss. Complain to your spouse all you want, but be engaged at work.

- Try to adapt or mesh your and your boss's personality styles. You can do this by using Myers-Briggs or DISC Profile.

- Stand firm when your boss yells or criticizes you. Don't necessarily confront, but keep your head held high and don't let him push you around. Controlling bosses are bullies and love those who cower, but are really afraid deep down. Aggression back will not work; assertiveness will win the day.

- Be proactive. Anticipate what needs doing and do it. At least be prepared to do it. Find important holes in your department before your boss notices them.

- Provide solutions, not problems. Never go to your boss and attempt to put the accountability monkey back on his back; have done your research and have a plan.

- Communicate in the way the boss receives information best. If he reads best, write it. If he hears best, speak it.

Key Behaviors

Here are the key behaviors for talking to the boss about a work-related problem.[38]

1. Write a plan laying out your proposed solutions, justifying your ideas.

2. Wait until the boss has the time and can listen to your ideas; then, state your desire to talk about a work-related problem.

3. Listen and be considerate of his needs and/or desires. If it is not a convenient time, ask when and where it would be convenient.

4. State the problem very succinctly and explain its effect on work activities.

5. Listen for any restatement of the problem or for an indication that the problem has been understood.

6. State your willingness to cooperate in any solution to the problem and listen openly to your boss's comments. Reflect confidence and be assertive.

7. State your preferred solution or discuss alternatives.

8. Agree on steps each of you will take to solve the problem.

9. Ask if there is a need to follow up on the solution. If so, plan a specific follow-up date.

Being Aware of Your Environment

Recognize

When a leader moves up in an organization, his level of awareness and the number of stakeholders (and therefore level of accountability) increases dramatically. Now he has to take into account customers, vendors, the board, competitors, community and governmental regulation, and the entire organization and workforce.

Admit

Some executives move from company to company seeking new challenges.[39] There are always plenty of challenges to keep one engaged for a long time. The key is to keep paying attention to your industry, business, technology, and the economy.

One of the most dangerous traps you can fall into as a leader is to fail to look beyond the current horizon for potential threats or opportunities. Visiting and learning from companies at the cutting edge of their respective industries or technologies should be a key part of a leader's ongoing professional development program. But beware of benchmarking in only in your industry; that is tunnel vision. Another is benchmarking only one indicator and ignoring potentially larger outcomes. Don't try to save $200,000 and then lose $2 million in the process. Focus, be aware, but avoid tunnel vision.

By doing these things you keep up with the changes in your industry (which is becoming very critical) and anticipate those disruptive changes over the horizon. Change is coming faster and faster. A leader can't dismiss the changes the "kids" in garages are driving. Disruptive innovation always starts as a toy or a weird idea—computers on desk tops were toys and smartphones were considered impossible at first. Everything that happens in healthcare technology today happened at Disney a generation ago. Don't be afraid to read about weird ideas on the edge. At minimum, start reading a publication in your industry.

Furthermore, the whole culture of business is changing to be more ruthless. Uber, AirBnB, and Twitter have shown they have no interest in abiding by the traditional status quo. Big companies ignore regulatory bodies, accept the small fine imposed, and write it off as a business expense. Startups exploit large company bureaucratic inertia to expand at frighteningly high speed. So, knowing what is coming down the road at you is becoming a survival necessity.

Reinventing yourself as a person doesn't mean taking baby steps.[40] It probably means diving into a new and improved program headlong. Have a game plan, address your flaws, and never stop learning. Make a list of all the things you have to change, and what you don't know. The best way to do this is to go to professional associations and look for competence models. Examples of this are shown here at https://www.k4health.org/sites/default/files/Competencies%20Assessment%20Tool%202010.pdf (Healthcare execs) or http://marketplace.pmi.org/Pages/ProductDetail.aspx?GMProduct=00101024401 (Project Management) or at one of the clearinghouses of competency models http://www.careeronestop.org/competencymodel/blockModel.aspx?tier_id=4&block_id=646&hg=Y.

Use these models in a spread sheet to identify strengths and weaknesses. Then design a plan to stay informed and moving forward.

Adjust

Although keeping up with industry news may seem to be just one more thing to add to your To-Do List, there are benefits.[41] Doing so will make you more prepared for changes, be able to spot threats and opportunities early, and help identify things like sales opportunities or better jobs. By developing expertise like this, you will earn the trust of the people around you. As a leader, this is invaluable.

Key Behaviors

Here are some hints on what to do:[42]

1. Go to conferences and seminars.

2. Scout out forums and discussion boards for your profession.

3. Pay attention to what the top bloggers in your area of expertise are writing about. Attend online webinars. Subscribe to newsletters and industry magazines. Set up Google Alerts.

4. Read books.

5. Take advantage of all of your organization's internal educational resources.

6. Talk to people in other departments about what they do.

7. Join task forces or committees to see a bigger picture.

8. Talk to customers.

Networking

Recognize

Networking is essential for a manager's continued awareness. Managers need to be involved in networking both within and outside of the institution, organization, and profession. Networking is a deliberate process of developing, nurturing, and maintaining contacts for information, leads and referrals, advice and ideas, and moral support. Networks (such as LinkedIn) provide a referral system that keeps one in touch with one's contacts and, in turn, with that contact's contacts in an ever-widening circle. Networking provides opportunities for managers to promote the development of their careers, share information, empower themselves personally and professionally, and work with others cooperatively.

Admit

Successful networking requires effort and demands that one contribute as much effort as is reaped in benefits. Networkers must clearly understand what they expect to get from and give to their network—we tell our students it is not just about getting a job. Networkers must clearly understand their own assets and weaknesses for networking, determine what kinds of contacts are needed to meet their goal, and refine a professional image (branding). Effective communication skills are an absolute necessity. Assertiveness skills enable networkers to ask for what they want, to give advice and information clearly, and to say "no" when necessary without closing the doors to future networking with a contact— burning bridges. Recognize that some requests will be refused, but do not take refusals personally. At some point you may also have to refuse a request from a valued contact.

While LinkedIn is efficient and wide-ranging, active membership in professional organizations may be the most important networking tool. Paying dues to an organization provides one with journals, newsletters, and other information. Actively participating in the work of a professional organization offers an opportunity to meet large numbers of professional colleagues from a variety of work settings and locales.

Adjust

Give feedback—a progress report—to your contacts on advice or information they have given. Keep in touch with contacts when you do not need anything from them. Nurture contacts; do not just use them. Offer your help generously, even if you have never been helped directly. It will pay off at some time. Deliver on your promises, each and every one of them. Do not burn bridges. And, remember, you do not have to like everyone in your networks. The research on self-handicapping even suggests that people will collaborate with a chronic self-handicapper even while they may wish to not socialize with him.

Key Behaviors

The key behaviors for networking are as follows:

1. Introduce yourself to a new person—"Hello, I'm David."

2. Introduce a neutral, industry-specific topic—"Did you hear the news about...."

3. At the end of the conversation, offer the person business card and ask for theirs (or tap phones).

4. If applicable, connect via an online social network—LinkedIn or Twitter—make sure your account is professional.

5. Follow up—"It was nice to meet you yesterday, by the way...."

6. After some time, offer information on an upcoming event or something to that contact. Follow up.

7. When appropriate, ask for advice or help.

Having a Home/Work Balance

Recognize

Many managers are putting in extra hours, using their smartphones to be on call, and in other ways, being owned by their work. Any search of the web will give you lots of ways to remedy this situation—build downtime into your schedule, drop activities that sap your time or energy, rethink your meetings, routes, errands, and just get moving and be more efficient. It kind of sounds like us saying, "Get rid of all self-handicapping habits." Yet, job stress equals family stress. Many companies are beginning to address overwork, not because they are public-spirited, but because it makes sound business sense to do so. So, how do we get a leader to see this? We probably won't be effective suggesting the "just-say-no" approach to overwork. The lead author has never been successful telling his son, "The stockholders won't care when you have your first heart attack." Because managers and professionals often work on open-ended projects, there's always something more they can do.

Admit

Start by making deliberate choices about which opportunities you will pursue and which you will decline, rather than simply reacting to emergencies. We suggest overcoming all of your varied self-handicapping behaviors that chew up inordinate amounts of time for no useful purpose. But deliberate choices don't guarantee complete control—emergencies do happen. *Harvard Business Review* suggests executives should define success for themselves, manage technology, build support networks at work and at home, and collaborate with partners.[43] Have a vision and know what this looks like, build a network to do it, understand the information age, and work with your family to build a system of effective interaction.

Adjust

Work-life balance is achievable, but it is something that is perpetually changing. Be flexible and realistic, have a sense of humor, and be happy when everything is in balance. If you haven't figured it out yet, money can protect time. Single-parent families experience greater stress than two-parent families. Executives can hire more services than workers. The lead author's son and his wife are executives and have two young sons. They struggled getting ready for work each morning until they hired one of the pre-school teachers to come to their house to handle one kid as they dressed. All of a sudden, life in the morning was less stressful and it did not carry into work. After a while, this helper was loading the dishwasher and many other tasks. Home life improved immensely. It works the same way in reverse. Remove the self-handicapping that does not add value at work and don't take work stress to your home.

Key Behaviors

Here are some key behaviors for having a work/home balance.

1. Remember there is no final work/home balance solution. It is always in flux and therefore must be managed daily/weekly.

2. Set up and enforce boundaries for both sides. These may have to be more like guidelines rather than laws.

3. Be aware of the needs of those at home. If they don't say anything, ask how they assess your work/home balance.

4. Use your resources to reduce stress.

Final Personal Takeaways

Action Plan for Awarenenss

Take a few minutes and complete this action plan about awareness.

Awareness Self-Handicap	What Is the Situation?	Trigger	Impact on Others	What to Do/When
What about my personal awareness of myself?		__Expedient __Avoiding __Apprehension __Self-deception		__Deliberate action____ __Self-efficacy_____ __Face it_____ __Look and listen_____
Don't know how to read the room		__Expedient __Avoiding __Apprehension __Self-deception		__Deliberate action____ __Self-efficacy_____ __Face it _____ __Look and listen_____
How will I assess the damage left in my wake?		__Expedient __Avoiding __Apprehension __Self-deception		__Deliberate action____ __Self-efficacy_____ __Face it_____ __Look and listen_____
Am I humble?		__Expedient __Avoiding __Apprehension __Self-deception		__Deliberate action____ __Self-efficacy_____ __Face it_____ __Look and listen_____
What about managing up?		__Expedient __Avoiding __Apprehension __Self-deception		__Deliberate action____ __Self-efficacy_____ __Face it_____ __Look and listen_____

Awareness Self-Handicap	What Is the Situation?	Trigger	Impact on Others	What to Do/When
How will I increase my awareness of my general environment and industry?		__Expedient __Avoiding __Apprehension __Self-deception		__Deliberate action____ __Self-efficacy_____ __Face it_____ __Look and listen_____
How will I increase my awareness of my organization?		__Expedient __Avoiding __Apprehension __Self-deception		__Deliberate action____ __Self-efficacy_____ __Face it_____ __Look and listen_____
What will I do in networking?		__Expedient __Avoiding __Apprehension __Self-deception		__Deliberate action____ __Self-efficacy_____ __Face it_____ __Look and listen_____
Developing a personal mission/vision		__Expedient __Avoiding __Apprehension __Self-deception		__Deliberate action____ __Self-efficacy_____ __Face it_____ __Look and listen_____
What will I do to support a healthy work/life balance?		__Expedient __Avoiding __Apprehension __Self-deception		__Deliberate action____ __Self-efficacy_____ __Face it_____ __Look and listen_____
Developing a personal and organizational vision		__Expedient __Avoiding __Apprehension __Self-deception		__Deliberate action____ __Self-efficacy_____ __Face it_____ __Look and listen_____

Baby Steps

This chapter has explored many actionable items related to awareness. To start you on the right path (and to avoid getting overwhelmed), here are a few baby steps for you to start practicing tomorrow.

- Identify one or two professional associations or blogs that may be helpful to you in developing needed competencies.

- Join and become a member of one professional association.
- Follow and "friend" one industry-related account on social media.
- Join one current event website or blog for up-to-date news on your industry.
- Take a "pulse" of five people around you—subordinates, peers, superiors, etc. Write down five ways to build bridges to each.
- Focus on understanding where your boss is coming from when he does certain things.
- Determine how you will have a healthy balance of managing up and down. Write it down.

Follow-up Questions

1. What are the major outcomes for a leader who is unaware of his traits and preferences?
2. Why is awareness of boundaries so important in leadership?
3. Why would a leader have aversion to taking personality tests for self-awareness?
4. How does a personal vision help with self-handicapping?

Endnotes

1. Adapted from Nilofer Merchant, "2 Ways to Skirt Self-Handicapping." http://nilofermerchant.com/2011/12/19/2-ways-to-skirt-self-handicapping/ (accessed March 25, 2015).
2. Adapted from Gary van Warmerdam, "Self Awareness." http://www.pathwaytohappiness.com/self-awareness.htm (accessed March 25, 2015).
3. Adapted from Peter Dricker, "Managing Oneself." http://hbr.org/2005/01/managing-oneself/ar/1 and Jack Zenger "Developing Strengths or Weaknesses: Overcoming the Lure of the Wrong Choice." http://zengerfolkman.com/wp-content/uploads/2013/05/Developing-Strengths-or-Weaknesses-Article-Rev-02-23-09-2.pdf (accessed March 25, 2015).
4. Personal conversation with Allen Kenyon, Memorial Hermann Healthcare System, Houston, TX.
5. See Bratton, VK., Dodd, NG., Brown, FW. (2011) "The impact of emotional intelligence on accuracy of self-awareness and leadership performance." Leadership & Organization Development Journal, Vol. 32 Iss: 2, pp. 127–149 http://www.emeraldinsight.com/doi/full/10.1108/01437731111112971 (accessed March 25, 2015).
6. Ibid.

7. See Tekleab, A. G., Sims, H. P., Yun, S., Tesluk, P. E., & Cox, J. (2007). Are we on the same page? Effects of self-awareness of empowering and transformational leadership. *Journal of leadership & organizational Studies*. http://jlo.sagepub.com/content/early/2007/12/18/1071791907311069.short (accessed March 25, 2015).

8. See WikiPedia, "Lawrence Kohlberg's Stages of Moral Development." http://en.wikipedia.org/wiki/Lawrence_Kohlberg's_stages_of_moral_development (accessed June 17, 2015).

9. Summarized from "Professional Boundaries in the Workplace." http://www.dphhs.mt.gov/sltc/services/communityservices/ProfessionalBoundariesInTheWorkplace.pdf (accessed June 17, 2015).

10. Adapted from Steve Tobak, "7 Signs You're Not as Self-Aware as You Think." http://www.inc.com/steve-tobak/7-signs-youre-not-as-self-aware-as-you-think.html (accessed April 1, 2015).

11. See Drew Hansen, "7 Steps to Increase Self-Awareness and Catapult Your Career." http://www.forbes.com/sites/drewhansen/2012/01/24/7-steps-to-increase-self-awareness-and-catapult-aleader-career/2/ (accessed June 17, 2015).

12. Ibid See note 3.

13. Summarized from David Dunning, Chip Heath, and Jerry M. Suls, "Flawed Self-Assessment: Implications for Health, Education, and the Workplace," *Psychol Sci Public Interest*, 2005, 5(3), 69–106.

14. Ibid.

15. Check out http://www.hillconsultinggroup.org/assets/pdfs/leadership-assessment.pdf or http://qiroadmap.org/?wpfb_dl=20.

16. http://www.myersbriggs.org/my-mbti-personality-type/mbti-basics/. Accessed 11 September, 2015.

17. https://www.cpp.com/products/mbti/index.aspx or https://www.mbticomplete.com/en/index.aspx. Check it out if your company does not administer it.

18 Barbara Pachter, *When the Little Things Count*, Marlowe & Co., An imprint of the Avalon Publishing Groupup, New York, 2001.

19. Summarized from NonProfit Quarterly, "A Leader's Guide to Executive Coaching." https://nonprofitquarterly.org/management/538-a-leaders-guide-to-executive-coaching.html?gclid=CK_IufyDlsACFWoR7AodsTsAyw (accessed June 17, 2015).

20. Adapted from Douglas LaBier, "Why CEOs Don't Want Executive Coaching." http://www.huffingtonpost.com/douglas-labier/why-ceos-dont-want-execut_b_3762704.html (accessed June 17, 2015).

21. Ibid.

22. Roger Durand, Phillip J. Decker, and Dorothy M. Kirkman, "Evaluation Methodologies for Estimating the Likelihood of Program Implementation Failure," *Am J Eval*, 2014, 35(3), 404–418.

23. BP Owens and DR Hekman, "Modeling How to Grow: An Inductive Examination of Humble Leader Behaviors, Contingencies, and Outcomes," *Acad Manag J*, August 2012, 55(4), 787–818.

24. AY Oul, AS Tsui, AJ Kinicki, et al, "Humble Chief Executive Officers' Connections to Top Management Team Integration and Middle Managers' Responses," *Admin Sci Quart*, March 2014, 59(1), 34–72.

25. From Landauer, J. and Rowlands, J, "Importance of Philosophy: Focus/Volition." http://www.importanceofphilosophy.com/Epistemology_Focus.html (accessed June 17, 2015).

26. Jay G Hull, "A Self-Awareness Model of the Causes and Effects of Alcohol Consumption," *J Abnorm Psychol*, 90(6), December 1981, 586-600. Also, Rita Z. Goldstein, et. al. "The Neurocircuitry of Impaired Insight in Drug Addiction," Trends in Cognitive Science, http://www.cell.com/trends/cognitive-sciences/abstract/S1364-6613(09)00146-6?cc=y?cc=y. (accessed August 14, 2014) and http://www.divisiononaddiction.org/html/handouts/chapter23.pdf, and http://onlinelibrary.wiley.com/doi/10.1002/bies.201000042/abstract;jsessionid=7725A5AB5FC0C6C2 6EE4EBFD46BFCD34.f03t04?deniedAccessCustomisedMessage=&userIsAuthenti cated=false (accessed June 17, 2015).

27. P Salovey and J Mayer, "Emotional Intelligence," *Imagin, Cogn Pers*, 1990, 9(3), 185–211.

28. See EurekAlert! Public Release, "Those Unsure of Own Ideas More Resistant to Views of Others." http://www.eurekalert.org/pub_releases/2009-07/uoia-pss062509.php and Hart Albarracin, Inge Brechan, Lisa Merrill, et al. "Feeling Validated Versus Being Correct: A Meta-Analysis of Selective Exposure to Information," *Psychol Bull*, 135(4).

29. Adapted from Susan Heathfield, "How to Develop Your Emotional Intelligence." http://humanresources.about.com/od/interpersonalcommunicatio1/qt/develop -your-emotional-intelligence.htm and Caroline Smith, "Emotional Intelligence: Developing Strong 'People Skills.'" http://www.mindtools.com/pages/article/newCDV_59.htm (accessed June 17, 2015).

30. Adapted from Presentation Magazine, "Reading the Audience—Are You Sending Them to Sleep?" http://www.presentationmagazine.com/reading-the-audience -are-aleader-sending-them-to-sleep-11740.htm (accessed June 17, 2015).

31. Check out this video for more information on reading an audience https://www.youtube.com/watch?v=8sXF7M5fkHQ

32. See Patrick Lencioni, "Teamwork." http://www.tablegroup.com/teamwork (accessed June 17, 2015).

33. Summarized from Glenn Llopis, "The Ultimate 5 Step Playbook to Managing Your Personal Brand." http://www.forbes.com/sites/glennllopis/2013/08/12/the -ultimate-5-step-playbook-to-managing-aleader-personal-brand/ (accessed June 17, 2015).

34. Adapted from Seth Godin, "Managers Should Build, not Burn, Bridges." http://www.cfcd.com.au/managers-build-not-burn-bridges/ (accessed June 17, 2015).

35. Adapted from Time Staffing, "8 Ways to Not Burn Bridges When Leaving Your Job." http://timestaffinginc.com/8-ways-to-not-burn-bridges-when-leaving-your-job/ (accessed June 17, 2015).

36. See Badowski, R, Gittines, R, "Managing Up: How to Forge an Effective Relationship with Those Above You." http://www.amazon.com/Managing-Up-Forge -Effective-Relationship/dp/0385507739 (accessed June 17, 2015).

37. See Margie Warrell, "How to Handle a Bad Boss: 7 Strategies for 'Managing Up.'" http://www.forbes.com/sites/margiewarrell/2014/01/20/6-strategies-to -hanhandldling-a-bad-boss/ and Jean Lewis, "The 5 Basic Principles on Managing Up." http://www.w2wlink.com/Articles/Basic-Principles-Managing-artid136.aspx (accessed June 17, 2015).

38. Adapted from PJ Decker, *Management MicroTraining,* 1982.

39. Summarized from Barbara Chapman, "Aspiration for Inspiration." https://www .linkedin.com/pulse/article/20140901045658-308506307-aspiration-for-inspiration (accessed June 17, 2015).

40. Summarized from WikiHow, "How to Reinvent Yourself." http://www.wikihow .com/Reinvent-Yourself (accessed June 17, 2015).

41. See Alexandra Levit, "How to Better Understand Your Business." http://quickbase .intuit.com/blog/2012/09/20/how-to-better-understand-your-business/ (accessed June 17, 2015).

42. See Eva Rykrsmith, "Keep Up with Industry Trends to Stay Relevant." http:// quickbase.intuit.com/blog/2011/08/30/how-to-keep-up-with-industry-trends-to -stay-relevant/#sthash.BFmsMu4q.dpuf (accessed June 17, 2015).

43. See Boris Groysberg and Robin Abrahams, "Manage Your Work, Manage Your Life." http://hbr.org/2014/03/manage-your-work-manage-your-life/ar/1 (accessed June 17, 2015).

5

Tunnel Vision

Chapter Takeaways

- ► Nonlinear thought increases innovation
- ► Understand the importance of prioritization
- ► Learn how to pull out of procrastination
- ► Don't interact with people only to get what you want
- ► Learn to juggle multiple projects rather than operate linearly

Tunnel vision is not seeing the big picture or only part of a project. It is a process that pulls leaders to focus on a particular outcome, and then filter all evidence through the lens provided by that outcome. This causes concentration on a single idea to the exclusion of others—all information that supports the outcome is elevated in significance, while evidence inconsistent is discounted or overlooked. Tunnel vision can be detrimental to the strategy, engagement, and problem-solving initiatives of any leader.

Leaders can have problems with tunnel vision. They sometimes think and operate linearly (one thing at a time) or get overly-involved in projects and problems and forget to see what is going on around them. They often attend to who is making the most noise. Or they get into "crises mode" and focus on a problem until it is fixed—to the detriment of all other activities. They can focus too intently on a "people problem," or even "winning" in some situations. Leaders can be so deep in the forest they can't see the trees.

One of the authors was working with a nonunion manufacturing division that was expanding. They were hiring workers from a nearby unionized company that had a major project scaling back. No one paid any attention to the number of union employees coming into one plant.

The organization also had a routine biyearly employee climate survey; all leadership and management were apprised of the results. Over 2 years, employee satisfaction was steadily declining in issues highly related to unionization efforts—grievance procedures and arbitrary management. No one paid attention to the trend because production and finance were going well. Predictably, what happened was a serious unionization drive from the UAW that disrupted the plant for 6 months. The plant stayed nonunion in the end, but all the effort needed to keep it nonunion probably could have been averted if plant leadership had seen the trees, paid attention to the mix of new hires, and actually saw and attended to the survey trends. They handicapped themselves severely with tunneled vision.

We humans have extraordinary ability to efficiently and effectively multitask.[1] Most of us can breathe, speak, think, analyze, move, and listen simultaneously without much conscious effort. We can do things on "automatic" while we think of and do other things. When we get into a crisis situation, we can instinctively dispense with trivial issues and focus on the immediate threat. The benefits of being able to focus our attention so narrowly during a crisis are obvious; however, they are precisely the things that cause the tunneled vision that hurts leadership. Leaders focusing like this in their busy work world can be self-handicapping. Priorities may get neglected. Possibilities may not be seen. Employees may be ignored.

Impact

Tunnel vision can cause failure through flawed procedures and the need to win. Go into any casino and watch people who play slot machines to see tunneled vision focused on winning. An example of flawed procedures can be found in our criminal justice system. Mistaken eyewitness identifications are the most frequent cause of wrongful convictions. In some ways the criminal justice system both teaches and perpetuates tunnel vision.[2] Police officers may shift from investigation to interrogation once they become convinced of a suspect's guilt. Prosecutors may not objectively evaluate cases or may have flawed grand jury systems. Courts place procedural obstacles in the path of defendants rather than focusing on justice. Managerial tunnel vision, which is more prevalent than most of us realizes, can also have potentially devastating results.

The reliance on tunnel vision can also be influenced by marketing consultants and others presenting narrow information, overconfidence, and don't allow enough time to see the bigger picture. Leaders often lack time for reflection and can place too much importance on one aspect of an event and fail to recognize other factors. This type of tunnel vision can lead to poor decision-making. When focusing on increasing quality, the focus on cost or access to the product or service may not be high. Often, consultants and marketing folks rely on the tunnel vision of leaders (and consumers) to focus attention on one thing and convince them of the necessity of that feature of a product or service. Politicians do the same—exaggerate the importance of particular issues and ignore others. These instances of tunnel vision can lead to mistakes in predicting future outcomes, buying equipment, engaging employees, and in any other decision activity.

Overconfidence is a perceptual distortion causing overestimates of one's own abilities. Overconfident leaders are less likely to imitate their peers, explore their environment, and more likely to act on their own private signals. Teams with some overconfident individuals can have an advantage in business, but overconfident leaders have an uneven track record—they are wrong as often as right. Entrepreneurs' perceptions of starting a business may be distorted by overconfidence; risks are discounted, funding not secured, and the enterprise fails.

Linear thinking can doom any organization over time. As an example, consider the organization that hires mostly those referred by current employees. New employees with backgrounds that match the current employees accumulate without any thought given to the future direction of the organization. Project management can also get stuck in a rut with tunnel vision. Project managers have been trained in certain methodologies to manage projects and the strict adherence to these guidelines can cause linear thinking. They then start to frame all problems in a way that limits their ability to see the innovative solution.

When tunnel vision meets strategy, there are three types of leaders:[3]

1. Those who focus inward on their own business and expect business today to be the same as tomorrow. They focus on making what they do even better.

2. Those who keep an extremely close eye on their competitors. When competitors make changes, they do too. Their customers focus on price as the product or service is the same as everyone else.

3. Those who focus on the customers' underlying needs and wants and scan the world for ideas from other industries that they can adapt to satisfy those needs.

From a business strategy perspective, it is not uncommon to see the first two types stuck in a competitive stalemate—narrowed marketing efforts or digging in against a changing business climate. The third is obviously a better approach and is characterized by lack of tunnel vision. Any leader can self-handicap by narrowing sources of information or simply being too busy to attend to anything but what is screaming for his attention. Leaders can kill potentially good ideas too early or spend good money after bad with tunnel vision. When a leader fails to see or hear a variety of input about the environment in planning future actions, he is self-handicapping (and possibly killing the entire enterprise) with tunnel vision.

Tunnel vision can affect leaders at every level and in everything they do. For example, tunneled vision (as in seeing) can even lead to diminished hearing.[4] Focusing on something intently with your eyes can lead to the audio cortex *turning down the volume*. And, tunneled hearing can, in the same way, lead to diminished vision. So, a person intently listening to a cell phone could have diminished vision. Strange but true—all leaders must watch out for tunnel vision in building strategy, working with projects, listening to employees, and driving home.

Real Issues

Tunnel vision comes from the content of leaders' training/education, lack of training on analysis/conceptualization/systemic thinking, inflexibility and over-confidence, stress, lack of time, and personality issues. While excuses play into the lack of time issues, self-handicapping in this area is mostly behavioral. *Linear thinking*, the inability to "juggle" multiple projects, and letting failures in one project bog down other projects are typically skill issues. *Conceptual thinking*—problem solving in the abstract (devoid of operational detail)—takes practice and time and most leaders don't have the training to do it. When leaders don't think they can do a good job or fear failure, they often avoid starting (*procrastination*). Preparing "to do" lists, doing more comfortable items, and doing easy things first are examples of procrastination. Some managers will *interact with people only to get what they want*. Sometimes this is just "using" behavior from a controlling leader but it may be introverted folks not feeling comfortable with interpersonal interaction. Introverts have a predisposition to close-up and not offer vulnerability or opinions on possible problems.

With tunnel vision, the excuses usually started well before one became a leader. They are what led to choosing one education over another—causing part of one's tunnel vision. They led to not getting any training or education in decision analysis, research skills, or conceptual thinking—adding more potential sources of tunnel vision. Micromanagement set in long ago. And, so on. These things made a focused individual contributor, so by the time one accepts a leadership position, these issues have already become obstacles to leadership.

Our training and education is always an issue because many managers come from specialized backgrounds. One of the authors is an industrial psychologist and sees people problems first; the other is business-finance and sees problems through the lens of money and strategy first. It is a good combination for coauthors but acting alone we may be worrisome. Because of training, a leader may see the world one way and not listen to others. We have heard leaders say, "that psychology stuff is not important;" yet, at the same time, they struggle with culture and engagement issues throughout their organization. That is self-handicapping through tunnel vision—probably caused by their training.

Linear thinking is when a leader's thoughts follow a step-by-step progression; where a response to one step is required before another step is taken. This tunnel vision may be caused by the leader not seeing the big picture or from training (such as project management). Much of business relies on the concept of logic—math, statistics, and other areas that teach deductive reasoning—but this becomes a way of thinking that often precludes looking at the big picture or bouncing around among creative ideas. Consider tasks A, B, C, D, and E that are in your "to-do list." These tasks are in that order because that is the order in which they came in. Now suppose that task "D" is a critical item that your accounting department must have completed (by you) before they can proceed to process expense reports. Without thinking "big-picture," you may go through your to-do list in the order in which it exists. When this happens, the financial costs are obvious—lost productivity in your accounting department. The nonfinancial costs include the accounting department finding a way around your work or going to a superior about your tardiness on required reports. Leaders are constantly pulled to address the next item in line—the next meeting/appointment or the person yelling the loudest; so it is easy to fall into tunnel vision and neglect big picture thinking. In this case, it can be costly to a career.

Some managers often *act as if they don't play on a larger team in an organization* or they act like they or their department is the center of the world, which is almost never true. Each of us is one small part of a larger operation. Another form of tunnel vision is *making or allowing employees to focus on the boss (management) instead of their customers*—creating a codependent workforce. Codependent workers like to feel part of a larger organization, so they become very loyal to a boss or department. This means that they are looking at the boss controlling the employees; the employees are taking care of the boss. This prevents focus on customers and mission and can be devastating to an organization.

Tunnel vision is a common occurrence in management and it can be irritating to work for a leader who sticks rigidly to preexisting concepts, rejects ideas before hearing the evidence, or can only deal with one issue per meeting.[5] These tunneled behaviors may eventually push leaders into tyranny where they try to force other people to follow their preferred route through coercion and threats. This drives out better employees and bogs the organization down.

Seasoned leaders become accustomed to doing things their way.[6] The line between supreme self-confidence and tunnel vision is very thin. Tunnel vision can lead to inflexibility and over-confidence about relationships in a leader's inner circle. Subordinates need to understand tunnel vision and work to make sure the leader gets the information needed. Without these safeguards, experience, and an optimistic demeanor, leaders can sometimes go into "crisis mode" when there is no crisis present. Their behavior may seem irrational and their tunneled strategy can lead the organization down the wrong road.

What to Do?

Making a conscious effort to scan the environment, asking, *"What am I missing?"* is the first step in dealing with tunnel vision.[7] Being too quick to reject or gloss over others' ideas is to be avoided. One way out of this is to explore information from a variety of sources.[8] Setting up Google Alerts, reading *Business Week,* and connecting with people who have different interests helps. A regular questioning habit asking "what" and "how" questions must be part of a leader's routine. Without time to fully consider all of the issues and implications, leaders can miss warning signs.

One would think those who enjoy the Internet would move to less linear thinking. Before the Internet, our research was limited to word of mouth referrals, advertising, the yellow pages, the library, and the newspaper. It was fairly linear. With the Internet, many have learned to think faster, jump around, follow links, and see a bigger, more diverse world. Yet, our own interests and search engines can still enforce tunnel vision. So, part of the solution to avoiding tunnel vision is to be willing to jump around as you solve problems. Change search engines often and follow varied links.

Certain mindsets can create and perpetuate severe tunnel vision. Mindsets are mental attitudes or dispositions that predetermine a person's responses to and interpretations of situations.[9] If a leader says, "that is not the way things are done around here," when faced with potential innovative solutions, his mindset drives his behavior and outcomes. In "Competing for the Future," Hamel and Prahalad describe an experiment that illustrates the power of mindsets.[10] Several monkeys sit in a cage that has a bunch of bananas hanging from the ceiling accessible by a set of steps. Whenever the monkeys try to climb the steps to get to the bananas, they are blocked by a blast of cold water. After a few days the monkeys give up climbing the steps. The researchers then remove the water hose and replace one of the original monkeys with a new one. Seeing the bananas, the new monkey starts up the steps. What happens? The other monkeys being social creatures pull the new monkey down before it gets blasted with water. This happens again and again until the new monkey doesn't bother to go up for the bananas either. Eventually, if you keep adding new monkeys to the group, they will all learn the rule that, "You don't grab the bananas around here." In organizations, we know that simply as, "that is not the way things are done around here." Mindsets must be explored, their connection to outcomes understood, and changed. This is not easy across an organization. It is a communication culture issue.

Leaders can also focus on what they are doing well today rather than future needs. It is too easy to slip into a mindset of, "my company is doing well today—I can ride this wave of success." Focusing too much on today's successes is a form of tunnel vision in a competitive market. Changing these mindsets is one of the strongest leverage points in an organization. Coca-Cola in 1997 when faced with limited growth options in a mature market shifted its mindset from "we sold 1 billion servings of soft drinks this year" to "we've got 47 billion servings of beverages yet to go," which was the number of worldwide beverage servings including bottled water, coffee, and tea. Now they operate in many more beverage markets than before.

The key to influencing mindsets lies in making meaningful changes to the context in which you work. You probably act differently in church than at a sporting event. You haven't changed, but the context has. Your mindset about the behavior that's appropriate in each situation is different—this is "mindset shift." There are several ways to influence people to shift mindsets—a *compelling story or vision, reinforcement of new skills, and role modeling.* Employees will often change their mindset if they understand what is being asked of them, they see some reward, and it makes sense. Employees change their behavior if they see their leaders behaving differently and it leads to good outcomes. Most of us know that role modeling is what leaders do to show employees the proper way to behave in organizations.

To avoid the handicap of tunnel vision, leaders need to:[11]

- Have an awareness of everything that is happening in their area and beyond.
- Be able to recall important information and utilize it at a later time.
- Be proactive in their approach to leadership, not just be focused on the tasks at hand.
- Have the ability to see what is on the horizon and recognize what is changing.
- Have the ability to recognize red flags early.
- Understand your mindsets and change them where required.

Do You Have Tunnel Vision?

Survey: Do I Practice Tunnel Vision or Not?
(Y = Yes, N= No, DK = Don't Know)

There are no right or wrong answers here, the more honest you are in answering, the better we can target tunnel vision.

____ I frequently find myself trying to play catch-up with several tasks that could have been completed before "nonpriority" tasks.

____ I often think through all the possible scenarios of a situation before moving forward.

____ I rarely think about the "big-picture," I just handle emergencies.

____ The task that I begin next is often dictated by how well I complete the preceding task.

____ I seem to have an appreciation that they are playing on a larger team than their department.

____ On a team, I focus on my piece of the responsibility very well.

____ I am much better seeing the details than the big picture.

____ When I get what I need from people I want to move on to the next problem.

_____ When faced with a number of tasks to complete, my prioritization skills suffer.

_____ I have a hard time juggling multiple projects.

_____ I like loyal employees.

_____ When I discuss problems with my boss I don't tend to acknowledge his/her bigger problems.

_____ My main motivation in approaching someone is often for a favor.

_____ My conversations stay focused on the job requirements.

_____ I don't always think things through.

_____ The leaders in my area tend to staff their departments with yes-men and folks that don't speak up.

_____ I focus on what is needed now over what is needed in the future.

Scores

12–17 Y's—You are greatly self-handicapping through tunnel vision.
6–11—You are inconsistent with tunnel vision.
1–5—You have only minor problems with tunnel vision.

What was your degree of fudging on these questions? When not sure, did you round up to yes?

Why Do You Use Tunnel Vision?

Expediency

Attention and multitasking are some of the largest areas of research in psychology. Studies show that if there are many stimuli present, it is much easier to ignore the nontask related stimuli. But if there are few stimuli, the mind will perceive the irrelevant stimuli as well as the relevant.[12] Further studies show that younger people are able to perceive more stimuli, but are likely to process both relevant and irrelevant information; while older people process fewer stimuli, but usually process only relevant information. Some people can process multiple stimuli very well but this relies on one task becoming automatic due to "overlearning" the skill. Thus older managers, especially where there is more experience with a task, may focus more intently. This may become habit, and when change occurs, all those tunnel vision habits can be self-handicapping.

Research has shown the promising potential of debiasing tunnel vision through education.[13] Professional accident investigators (experienced, older, lots of stimuli) tend to allocate accident causes to the worker rather than other factors. But those who receive tunnel vision education seek a greater amount of information. The tunnel vision education does not have to be complex; viewing a slide show that defines tunnel vision, provides examples, and encourages participants to consider alternative hypotheses when investigating will suffice.

This research also shows that selective processing is a big driver of tunnel vision, which can be read either as laziness or attribution error. Attribution error is placing too much emphasis on internal characteristics to explain someone's behavior, rather than considering external factors. In other words, the boss saying the workforce is doing "X" because they are "millennials" (internal), rather than looking at what *he is doing* to cause "X" to be happening (external). There is no universally accepted explanation for attribution error, but tunnel vision can be lessened with data-based consideration of multiple options (decision analysis).

Selective processing often is the norm for leaders and simply presenting multiple alternatives is not sufficient to prompt comparative processing. Without some education, and then a requirement for data-based comparison, many leaders may tunnel their investigations before choosing one solution. With tunnel vision, decision-making becomes a process of justifying the decision the leader has already made. Accordingly, it is critically important to consider evidence for multiple possibilities and evaluate them empirically. We suggest that decreasing the likelihood of tunnel vision requires some form of education on decision analysis and not just simply a strategy of increasing accountability or "trying harder" to have wider views.

What tunnel vision do you use because of expediency?

Avoidance

Many forms of tunnel vision—such as lack of conceptual thinking—take practice and time to overcome. It can take direct effort to think in new ways. This is one of the major steps in moving from management to leadership—systems thinking. Leaders who avoid this learning continue with tunnel vision. They fail to see the complexity of a system, the mix of people, finance, and operational problems, or the long-term implications of their work.[14] Being engaged in one's work will also increase the size of the picture one has (and reduce tunnel vision). Looking at the whole and not just its parts is not difficult if you ask questions. Finally, understanding that an outcome will have an impact on other people will help. All of these entail facing the issue and taking more time to avoid self-handicaps.

Tunnel vision can cause poor time management and vice versa. When we fall behind, we focus intently on how to get something done or we take the opposite approach and procrastinate. A person may feel overloaded and go from one crisis to another, which is stressful and demoralizing. Most of us know that we should use our time more effectively; people who have time management problems really have *priority* management problems. You only have 24 hours in a day no matter what you do; you can only maximize the use of it. Multitasking may help, but the key is to use more of those minutes on productive things rather than unproductive things. There is a fine line between the tunnel vision of too much focus on a narrow range and wasting time procrastinating. Both are caused by avoidance of work for some reason—fear of failure, boring tasks, burnout, etc.

What tunnel vision of yours comes from avoidance?

Apprehension

Many types of tunnel vision, like focusing on something positive as the ship is sinking—are usually associated with fear. Procrastination can be caused by fear and can drive one to think that if he procrastinates long enough, his situation will magically improve. Unfortunately the reverse is usually true. As time goes by, fears grow larger, and the procrastination causes severe obstacles. In putting off today what can be done tomorrow, a leader is often allowing small fears to self-handicap his job and life.

Acting as if they don't play on a larger team in an organization is a form of self-centeredness. Managers complete work successfully by forming alliances, mastering the politics of the office, and understanding that those above see a bigger picture and must allocate resources accordingly. Low self-esteem can make a manager overestimate his importance or use self-importance to cover his fear of failure or vice versa. Both are self-handicapping.

Finally, focusing on what one is doing well today rather than future needs can be a form of apprehension—apprehension of the future. A great leader focuses on getting better, rather than continuing to be good.[15] Many of us believe that our intelligence, personality, physical aptitudes, or hard work got us where we are *and will keep us there.* As a result, we focus on goals that are all about maintaining our position, rather than developing and acquiring new skills and competencies for the next position. People whose goals are about getting better, rather

---

than being good, take difficulty in stride, and appreciate the journey as much as the destination. And, they do not self-handicap. This goal formation is a bulwark of how self-handicapping starts or is avoided.

What tunnel vision of yours comes from apprehension?

Self-Deception

Obsessing over one concern, while neglecting other important concerns is tunnel vision. This can become "obsessive-compulsive." When leaders obsess or focus too much, they need to change their frame or widen their focus. For example, Person A is an executive and obsessing about buying a particular expensive car and is having tunnel vision about the features of the car to the exclusion of most other things. It will be a big part of his status and the message he sends to clients. In a conversation with Person B, a friend less well-off and having problems with family finances, the issues of what features to get in this car is not critical. Person A has a hard time understanding why Person B will not pay attention or help him in his time of need; he thinks he has been abandoned to face this major problem alone. He is incredulous at Person B's attitude. But it is Person A's tunnel vision causing the problem, not Person B. This is self-handicapping and it is up to Person A to understand what he is doing, reframe, and tone down his tunneled obsession with this purchase. He can do so by getting at the root of the issue—his worry about his own status—and not letting that fear drive his behavior.

If you are or know a leader that takes employees for granted, thinks they are only there to achieve his own mission, and has tunnel vision for only his goals, you know that this is very disengaging and self-handicapping. Overcoming this habit can be tricky. A leader may think it is good to focus on being constructive and goal-oriented. Instead, his subordinates think he is seeing them as "dead meat." By thinking the world revolves around him, he is putting big limits on his leadership. Employees don't want to be in these situations and won't respect leaders who do this.

Sometimes you need to make a decisive break from the past and the act of changing mindsets is a way of doing that. For instance, when bosses become controlling and abusive, they put all their employees into a fixed mindset. Instead of *attending* to customers, everyone starts worrying about the bosses' moods, being judged or being held accountable arbitrarily. Changing this mindset may entail firing the boss, but with that mindset turned around, the entire enterprise may be more customer-focused and productive.

How do leaders uncover shared mindsets and understand how they are linked to behavior? Mindsets lead to behaviors, which lead to practices, which lead to outcomes, so you have to work backward from poor outcomes to find the mindset driving the process. Because mindsets lie below what we can readily observe, they are seldom scrutinized. A technique called *laddering* (that closely resembles the five-step approach that lean organizations use to get at the root causes of performance problems) can be used to start the process of changing mindsets.[16] You work backward from the "bad" outcome to process, then to behavior, any reinforcement involved, and finally the mindset supporting all of it. Then, you determine what new mindset you need and change it. Shifting mindsets is a gradual process but tackling poor mindsets may be one of the easiest ways to change handicapping tunnel vision.

What tunnel vision you may be missing because of self-deception?

Behaviors to Change
Linear Thinking

Recognize
Linear thinking is thinking directly along a straight path, almost wearing blinders to any diversions to the path. Early business models were built around the idea that people had to follow orders and a standard way of behaving was needed to build parts in a set order of steps. We now live in an increasingly "nonlinear" age where problem solving is more dynamic, unpredictable, and competitive with less time to do it. Much of our world remains trapped in the linear paradigm, but the nonlinear thinker is *letting go, seeing what all the angles are, and if he gets lost, so be it.* Linear thinking is a severe obstacle to effective leadership today.

Admit
Examine the extent to which you are a questioner; be on the lookout for questions you ask and the ones you fail to ask.[17] Make sure your questions help solve your problems. Question the status quo; and whenever you are dealing with a complex problem, formulate the question you are trying to answer in several different ways. For team meetings, write questions out in advance for the most significant questions you think need to be addressed in a problem.

Juggling multiple projects and keeping them all in the air can't be done in linear thinking mode. The key to this is simple—organization and follow up. A young leader is likely into Excel, has perfect order in his computer files, uses iCloud and Dropbox, and has his iPad ready for note-taking. Find your tools, organize them, and use them to track your projects in a visual form. In your computer, organize folders and move appropriate items to the correct folder. Also arrange a historical order so you know the latest iteration of something.

Adjust

Nonlinear thought increases performance because the leader using it is not so certain about the starting point for any logic process. One can practice nonlinear thinking and memory expansion. Go to www .lumosity.com. Get an account, check the sections you want to work on—linear and conceptual thinking are possibilities—and work through the exercises. You may think you are beyond this kind of nonsense practice but you will gain new skills.[18] One can make presentations that are not a linear slide show. They use pictures, into which you can zoom in and out. Get a subscription to *Scientific American Mind,*[19] which is full of articles about how to be a better thinker. There are hundreds of books on thinking, creativity, or innovation. Every one of them will have some gem for you.[20]

One way to reduce linear thinking is to employ common thinking tools used in quality improvement such as brainstorming, the five why's and five how's technique, fishbone analysis, arrow diagrams, or affinity diagrams. Detailed instruction on these and more can be found at http:// asq.org/learn-about-quality/quality-tools.html.

Key Behaviors

The key behaviors to help you get away from linear thinking are as follows:

1. See the world—particularly the problem—from different and multiple perspectives.

2. Reframe and search for as many alternative ways to view the problem, situation, or environment. Write them down.

3. Take time to be more interested in the journey than the destination. Reject the traditional spreadsheet and use an arrow diagram (see ASQ website mentioned previously). Explore unusual or illogical combinations.

4. Use more of the tools of Quality Improvement in your thinking— brainstorming, fishbone analysis, or affinity diagrams.

5. Look for how other people or industries think. Try to incorporate from these explorations.

Prioritization

Recognize

By definition, when we prioritize, we direct our efforts to the most important or urgent task to be completed. As a leader, you need to get things done. But acting without prioritizing is self-handicapping. The key to prioritizing is to have a "big picture" mindset as you look at your tasks.

In a 1954 speech by President Dwight Eisenhower, he said, "I have two kinds of problems: the urgent and important. The urgent are not important and the important are never urgent." This can be be broken down into four categories with each representing a combination of urgency and importance. Important/Urgent activities are crises that are often unforeseen. These occur because of the lack of planning or just plain procrastination. Important/Not Urgent activities include networking, strategic and contingency planning, and risk analysis. Not Important/Urgent activities include all those electronic notifications that come at you constantly (email and texts), and people popping into your office to chat. Not Important/Not Urgent activities include social media, everything you do to procrastinate, chatting in the break room, and searching the Internet for non-work related information.[21] Eisenhower was suggesting that people tend to spend too much time in urgent but unimportant priorities when they really should spend more effort on not urgent but important priorities. Many of us get stuck in important and urgent tasks because of too little time in the planning tasks that are important but not urgent. All of us experience tunnel vision in different ways and at different times; we neglect the important in favor of the urgent. Tunnel vision becomes dysfunctional whenever a pervasive pattern of obsession with a single concern such as urgency overshadows importance.

Admit

Prioritizing based on importance and urgency is important and will help you think on a larger, nontunnel scale, but it isn't enough. One of the biggest problems new leaders face is that they continue thinking like a staff member, instead of a leader. They see the technical, but not the interconnections of technology, people, culture, organizational structure, etc. We need to look outward and upward when we prioritize our tasks. Not being proactive to reach out and discuss who needs what, and by when, will self-handicap not only you, but also others who are dependent on your output.

Adjust

If you focus your efforts on managing the important tasks before they become urgent, the important and urgent "crises" will diminish in number and level of urgency. Not important but urgent items are the troublemakers. They will sneak up on you and appear to be urgent but they do not align with your organizational goals. Limit your time in the not important/not urgent activities—the real time wasters. The more time you devote to time wasters, the less time you have for achieving goals.

Key Behaviors

The following are the key behaviors to help you prioritize projects and tasks:[22]

1. Collect a list of all your tasks. Don't worry about the order.

2. Identify urgent versus important for each item (see definitions mentioned previously).

3. Identify tasks that need immediate attention—by the end of the day—those that will have serious negative consequences if not done.

4. Of those labeled important, identify what carries the highest value to your business and organization. Focus on client projects before internal work.

5. Create a table with columns for the categories described above and place every activity you do for a day in this table.

6. Order tasks by estimated effort. Start on the important tasks that you think will take the most effort to complete. But if you feel like you can't focus on lengthier tasks first, finish up the shorter urgent tasks.

7. Be flexible and adaptable. Your priorities will change sometimes when you least expect them to.

8. Know when to cut. You probably can't get everything on your list.

Procrastination

Recognize

We all have a tendency to procrastinate when we don't want to think through a tough problem or when we fear not doing well. We do this simply because we don't want to get out of our comfort zone and face the challenge, but it creates tunnel vision. The ERO Spiral starts with excuses here. Take some time out and have a detailed look at yourself—with no holds barred.[23] Look at the truth about your procrastination habits and break the cycle.

Admit

Part of dealing with procrastination is facing the fear driving it. What are you avoiding? There are the big fears, but there are lots of small, subtle fears and that is what often drives procrastination.[24] Everything is hardest the first time. When things don't go your way, and they won't, shrug it off and try again. But don't put it off—that leads to cheating and hurry-up, sloppy work. If you're clinging to your comfort zone through procrastination, you are really hanging on to an idea that the world is supposed to be a safe and predictable place. That's an illusion.

Understand the benefits of failure and hedge your risk by creating a contingency plan.[25] Even if your first option fails, you can maintain the status quo with a solid backup plan. The best way to reduce fear and build confidence is taking action. You will begin accumulating experience and knowledge, at least. Take the fear out of something by researching the potential outcomes (both good and bad) so you understand the risks.

Adjust

When procrastination starts to interfere with your work performance, you usually unconsciously know it's time to stop and get on with the task at hand.[26] First, *identify the challenge*. Write down the specific task you've been putting off. That helps you focus on it. Then, *pinpoint the underlying emotions*. This step helps you see the act of dragging your heels for what it truly is—The ERO Spiral. Try to *face the emotions and define your goal*. Your goal is your beacon to keep you on track and get beyond the emotions holding you back.

Key Behaviors

Here are the key behaviors to use in avoiding procrastination:[27]

1. Break the task down to lessen the sense of being overwhelmed. Then create a detailed timeline with specific deadlines.

2. Eliminate temptation to do something else by building in accountability and rewards for progress.

3. Finish the hard stuff first.

4. Identify your fear and excuses. Be brave and honest with yourself about the cost of continued inaction.

5. Eliminate your procrastination pit-stops. Get rid of the distractions that help you procrastinate.

6. Make your intentions public. This will add pressure, but for some of us, avoiding embarrassment is a great motivator.

7. Hang out with people who inspire you to take action. Picture Steve Jobs or Bill Gates as your coworkers.

Interacting With People Only to Get What We Want

Recognize

We have all had the type of boss that talks to us nicely with great eye contact until he gets what he wants and then his eyes glaze over and he is eager for us to disappear. We are dead to him because he got the transaction done, and he has no interest in us as people. Is this you? The issue of interacting with people only until you get what you want from them is mostly a discussion of defeating your own dysfunctional behavior. We are talking about shutting off all caring about an employee when you have what you want.

The band, *Bullet for My Valentine*, in their song, "Alone," may have worked for a boss (or known a girlfriend) like this because they wrote these lyrics:[28]

No more I'm taking this hatred from you

You make me feel dead when I'm talking to you

You'll take me for granted when I'm not around

So burn all your bridges 'cause I'm not going down

Admit

This sums up how some leaders behave and how their subordinates feel. Examine why you treat employees this way; if this comes from disrespect or control, you have larger issues to deal with, like micromanaging. Control freaks are so focused on their control, they act like this. Those of us who are introverted find it hard to interact with subordinates in empowering ways. Regardless of the reason, start by resisting the urge to judge or assume.[29] It is easier to offer someone compassion if you try to understand where they're coming from. Paying attention can be a form of endurance; it requires practice and training.[30]

Adjust

When you listen to others, you validate their need to be acknowledged and understood. We all want to know that we matter, that we are important; and when we find someone who shows interest in what we have to say, we tend to like them. We are not asking you to pretend to be interested in subordinates in hopes of being liked, but rather to pay attention to your subordinates to respect them. They all have something to contribute and it is your job to align that to the mission. By definition, the leader has to hold his subordinates' needs in mind and de-emphasize his personal needs. A good manager is continually asking, "What can I do to empower my employees?" This question can nudge us out of our need to focus on the goal rather than the people. In addition to improving your personal and professional relationships, listening also helps prevent misunderstandings and facilitates cooperation. Most importantly, it helps you avoid the kind of nonverbals that will really turn your coworkers against you.

Finally, it is easier to form a negative opinion of people when you're at a distance and you view them in the abstract. Leaders that don't know their subordinates names do this. If you don't know a coworker's story, it is easy to view them as objects. Discouraged or disengaged leaders can be wary about the whole idea of getting close and knowing people. This will cause the same phenomenon.

Key Behaviors

The following are the key behaviors for being effective in this regard:[31]

1. Shift your attention and focus on the speaker. Give them the impression that you're enthusiastic about talking to them until the conversation is done.

2. Get out of your problems or planning ahead and listen to them. Ask open-ended questions about their interests.

3. Ask questions rather than tell. Be respectful of their opinions and how they feel.

4. Try active listening to shift focus—Repeat what they are saying in your head, summarize what you heard, and look for the message—their key words.

5. Give the impression that you are on the same team. Use words like "we, us, we're, our, and ourselves" to instantly build a bond.

6. Mimic the other personal facial expressions and body positions. Mirroring will allow you to feel what they are feeling.

7. Keep what you say short and to the point. When you go on and on about something, people tune you out.

Focusing on Your Current Success Rather Than the Future

Recognize

Success can breed failure by hindering learning.[32] Celebrating accomplishments is more fun than focusing on how we can grow; however, while celebration is warranted, don't celebrate too long—there is a *kid in a garage* somewhere looking to dethrone you! Current success does not guarantee future success in any industry. There are always people looking to provide higher-benefit goods or services to customers at lower costs (adding value). Tunnel vision, by definition, puts blinders to innovation and focuses on the here and now. While having tunnel vision may not doom your team or company in the short run, it will almost certainly dim its future potential.

When leaders conclude that their talents or strategy are the reasons for success and give short shrift to the part that environmental factors, employees, and random events may have played in it, they commit *fundamental attribution error*. *Overconfidence bias* occurs when success increases their self-assurance and belief that they don't need to change anything. A third impediment is the *failure-to-ask-why syndrome*—the tendency not to investigate the causes of good performance systematically. These types of tunnel vision can be devastating.

Admit

One of the things executives miss with this type of tunnel vision is *disruptive innovation*.[33] Disruptive innovation creates new markets and customers by looking for a better value proposition. Disruptive innovation often looks like the creation of toys or gadgets when it begins—remember desktop computers were something purchased for your kids because of the low-computing power. Folks with tunnel vision run the risk of not seeing these new markets emerge. Consider the following example—Google's Chairman, Eric Schmidt said, "missing the rise of social media was the biggest mistake that he made."[34] Google initially paid little attention to Facebook but ended up locked in a battle for online and mobile advertising dollars with Facebook.

Adjust

Missing disruptive innovation is the result of not putting yourself in the shoes of your customers and looking for different ways to fill their needs and desires. The first step is to understand what *they want* out of your product and their *motivation* to purchase the product. Not what you *think* they want. Once you understand the motivation behind their purchasing your product, you can then tailor the product or service to better fit their needs or look for something that does. Ask what these customers want or need that they don't know or acknowledge yet. That is what Apple did with iPods and iPhones. Understanding *disruptive innovation is knowing what the consumer wants, before the consumer knows he wants it.* Every leader needs to pay attention to the future in this very fast world. While steam and gasoline engine power doubled every 70 years, in the new age of computers and the web, power is doubling every 2–3 years. *Celebrate your success, but know your future.*

Key Behaviors

Use the following worksheet to help explore your disruptive innovation:

What you do now?	What customers want?	What is their motivation to get it?	What are their future needs they do not know they want yet?	What is out there that may satisfy this need in the future?	What will you do about it?	How?

Key Behaviors

The key behaviors to help you stop focusing on your success now and get your thinking into the future are as follows:[35]

1. Set up a "vision" bulletin board for you (or your team). Clip articles or pictures and add them to an overall picture on the board to show what your customers want you or your product or service to look like in the future.

2. Decide who they are and get the negative people out of your life. You become who you surround yourself with and negative people live their lives in the past. If you surround yourself with those who are focused on the past, you too will do the same.

3. Celebrate success but examine it. When a win is achieved, investigate what led to it with the same rigor and scrutiny it might apply to understanding the root causes of failure. Hold "after-action reviews" like the military does after combat.

4. Watch your time horizons. When the time lag between an action and its consequences is short, it's relatively easy to identify the causes of performance. In many cases, this cycle is too long for leaders to make all of the necessary connections.

5. Forget replication of success; experiment for the future. When things go well, our biggest concern is how to make sure we can repeat the success. Instead, dig into root causes of future success and build systems for that.

Final Personal Takeaways
Action Plan—Tunnel Vision
Take a few minutes and complete the action plan about tunnel vision.

Tunnel Vision Self-Handicap	What Is the Situation?	Trigger	Impact on Others	What to Do/When?
Changing your mindsets		__Expedient __Avoiding __Apprehension __Self-deception		__Deliberate action____ __Self-efficacy_____ __Face it_____ __Look and listen_____
Get beyond linear thinking		__Expedient __Avoiding __Apprehension __Self-deception		__Deliberate action____ __Self-efficacy_____ __Face it_____ __Look and listen_____
Learn to juggle projects		__Expedient __Avoiding __Apprehension __Self-deception		__Deliberate action____ __Self-efficacy_____ __Face it_____ __Look and listen_____
Think long term		__Expedient __Avoiding __Apprehension __Self-deception		__Deliberate action____ __Self-efficacy_____ __Face it_____ __Look and listen_____

continued

Tunnel Vision Self-Handicap	What Is the Situation?	Trigger	Impact on Others	What to Do/When?
View situations from different perspectives		__Expedient __Avoiding __Apprehension __Self-deception		__Deliberate action_____ __Self-efficacy_____ __Face it_____ __Look and listen_____
Practice conceptual thinking		__Expedient __Avoiding __Apprehension __Self-deception		__Deliberate action_____ __Self-efficacy_____ __Face it_____ __Look and listen_____
Engage in "what-if" thinking		__Expedient __Avoiding __Apprehension __Self-deception		__Deliberate action_____ __Self-efficacy_____ __Face it_____ __Look and listen_____
Create a map of the variables for a project and their interactions		__Expedient __Avoiding __Apprehension __Self-deception		__Deliberate action_____ __Self-efficacy_____ __Face it_____ __Look and listen_____
Analyze group influences on your thinking		__Expedient __Avoiding __Apprehension __Self-deception		__Deliberate action_____ __Self-efficacy_____ __Face it_____ __Look and listen_____
Choose a problem to work on when you have free moments		__Expedient __Avoiding __Apprehension __Self-deception		__Deliberate action_____ __Self-efficacy_____ __Face it_____ __Look and listen_____
Better prioritizing		__Expedient __Avoiding __Apprehension __Self-deception		__Deliberate action_____ __Self-efficacy_____ __Face it_____ __Look and listen_____
Deal with procrastination		__Expedient __Avoiding __Apprehension __Self-deception		__Deliberate action_____ __Self-efficacy_____ __Face it_____ __Look and listen_____

continued

continued

Tunnel Vision Self-Handicap	What Is the Situation?	Trigger	Impact on Others	What to Do/When?
Ignoring people after you get your way		__Expedient __Avoiding __Apprehension __Self-deception		__Deliberate action____ __Self-efficacy_____ __Face it_____ __Look and listen_____
Understanding your place in the bigger picture		__Expedient __Avoiding __Apprehension __Self-deception		__Deliberate action____ __Self-efficacy_____ __Face it_____ __Look and listen_____
Employees focusing on you, not the customer		__Expedient __Avoiding __Apprehension __Self-deception		__Deliberate action____ __Self-efficacy_____ __Face it_____ __Look and listen_____
Focusing on your current success not the future		__Expedient __Avoiding __Apprehension __Self-deception		__Deliberate action____ __Self-efficacy_____ __Face it_____ __Look and listen_____

Baby Steps

Remember that baby steps can be a foundation for everything else. Achieving goals requires taking small steps first and success in baby steps reinforces success in subsequent steps.

The baby steps for this chapter are as follows:

- Use the ladder technique (see below) to examine a particular mindset's hold on you.
- Practice diagramming a problem to show you how complexity increases when you look at a problem different ways.
- Explore the website Mindtools.com, create an account, and get started.

The key behaviors to use in diagramming your mindset are as follows:

1. Start with determining your mindset toward one issue. Use the ladder technique and in the center list these things:

a. What is the challenge

b. How I deal with obstacles

c. How I view effort

d. How I handle criticism

e. How I view success of others

2. Then on the left side, list what you do. Be honest. For example, let's us use the following exercise.[36]

I avoid exercise	**The Challenge**
When I have to, I give up	**Obstacles**
I think it is a waste/fruitless	**Effort**
I ignore it/am defensive	**Criticism**
I am jealous/threatened	**Success of others**

3. What you have is your current mindset toward exercise (and maybe losing weight). Now, on the right side, list what you think would be a better mindset. For example:

I avoid exercise	**The Challenge**	I seek/embrace it.
When I have to, I give up	**Obstacles**	I persist until successful.
I think it is a waste/fruitless	**Effort**	I think it is the path to mastery.
I ignore it/am defensive	**Criticism**	I learn from it/I take action.
I am jealous/threatened	**Success of others**	I find lessons.

4. This exercise was just about diagramming and discovering a mindset, so you are done with your baby step. However, you should now make a list of how you will change your context to find the mindset on the right hand side.

5. Over the next week or so, use this technique to draw a quick picture or diagram of each of your mindsets toward your:

a. Employees or team

b. Company

c. Project

d. Career

An influence diagram is intended to document an overview of a problem. It shows the variables and their relationships. By capturing the dimensions of a problem, it makes the elements that need to be analyzed visible as one picture. It encourages a broader view of a problem. The key behaviors for diagramming a problem are as follows:[37]

1. Select an appropriate result or outcome measure. Draw a square corresponding to it on one side of the paper.

2. Identify the decision variables and the external influences which may affect the result. Place rectangles corresponding to decision variables circles for external influences around the perimeter of the paper. If the problem is quite complex, use post-it notes for each of the variables so you can move them around.

3. Starting with a result/outcome measure identify major variables that would influence it. Try to have only two nodes connect to another node. Continue this process till all external influence and results nodes are connected to at least one decision or intermediate variable.

4. Check the diagram by looking at nodes that are not connected and ask yourself if a connection should exist? If it should, draw an arrow connecting the nodes.

5. Using a + or − indicate the influence of each variable on the adjacent variable.

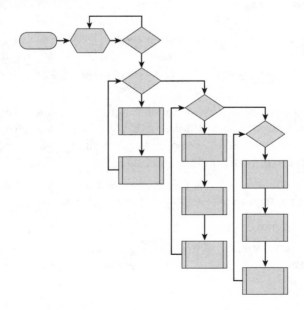

The key behaviors for exploring *Mindtools* are as follows:

1. Go to http://www.mindtools.com/
2. Create an account and log in.
3. Answer the questions that will guide your learning in the website.
4. Getting go on your practice.

Follow-Up Questions

1. What makes you procrastinate? How will you recognize, admit, and adjust?
2. In your own experience, what happens when someone has "transactional interactions" with others on a regular basis?
3. What projects do you have to juggle right now? What are their key deadlines?
4. What mindsets need to be changed in your organization or life? How would you go about changing them?

Endnotes

1. Summarized from Out of the Fog, "Tunnel Vision." http://www.outofthefog.net/CommonBehaviors/TunnelVision.html (accessed September 25, 2014).
2. Summarized from Innocence Project, "Tunnel Vision." http://www.innocenceproject.org/docs/TunnelVision_WEB.pdf (accessed September 25, 2014).
3. Summarized from Paul Simister, "Tunnel Vision of Funnel Vision." http://businesscoaching.typepad.com/the_business_coaching_blo/2007/10/tunnel-vision-o.html (accessed September 25, 2014).
4. Summarized from Situational Awareness Matters!, "Understanding Stress—Part 5: Tunnel Vision." http://www.samatters.com/understanding-stress-part-5-tunnel-vision/ (accessed September 25, 2014).
5. Summarized from Changeboard, "Leaders—Resistant to Change? Avoid Tunnel Vision." http://www.changeboard.com/content/3394/leaders-resistant-to-change-avoid-tunnel-vision/ (accessed September 25, 2014).
6. Summarized from University Business, "A Proactive Approach to Preventing Train Wrecks, Landmines, and Derailment." http://www.universitybusiness.com/article/peripheral-vision (accessed September 25, 2014).
7. Ibid. Also see Notes 1 and 4.
8. See Michele Martin, "Four Strategies for Combating Career Tunnel Vision." http://www.michelemmartin.com/thebambooprojectblog/2011/08/four-strategies-for-combating-career-tunnel-vision.html (accessed September 25, 2014).
9. From S Keller and C Price, *Beyond Performance: How Great Organizations Build Ultimate Competitive Advantage*. John Wiley & Sons, 2011.

10. Gary Hamel and CK Prahalad, *Competing for the Future*, Harvard Business Press, 1996.

11. Ibid. Also see Note 6.

12. Summarized from Wikipedia, "Attention." http://en.wikipedia.org/wiki/Attention (accessed September 25, 2014).

13. CL MacLean, E Brimacombe, and L Stephen, "Investigating Industrial Investigation: Examining the Impact of A Priori Knowledge and Tunnel Vision Education," *Law Hum Behav (American Psychological Association)*, 2013, 37(6), 441–453.

14. Summarized from The Happy Manager, "Leadership Quality." http://www.the -happy-manager.com/articles/leadership-quality/

15. Summarized from Heidi Grant Halvorson, "Nine Things Successful People Do Differently." https://hbr.org/2011/02/nine-things-successful-people/ (accessed September 25, 2014).

16. Ibid. Also see Note 9.

17. Adapted from Dr. Linda Elder and Dr. Richard Paul, "Becoming a Critic of Your Thinking." http://www.criticalthinking.org/pages/becoming-a-critic-of-your -thinking/478 (accessed September 25, 2014).

18. Prezi.com

19. http://www.scientificamerican.com/magazine/mind/

20. For reviews of books in this area, check out http://www.criticalthinking.org/. They also have articles on better thinking.

21. Dwight D. Eisenhower (August 19, 1954), *Address at the Second Assembly of the World Council of Churches*, Evanston, Illinois. http://www.presidency.ucsb.edu/ ws/?pid=9991 (accessed March 31 2015). Note that Eisenhower does not claim this insight for his own, but attributes it to an (unnamed) "former college president."

    Also see https://www.mindtools.com/pages/article/newHTE_91.htm (accessed March 31 2015) for more information

22. Summarized from Tatyana Sussex, "How to Prioritize Work When Everything is #1." http://www.liquidplanner.com/blog/how-to-prioritize-work-when -everythings-1/ (accessed September 25, 2014).

23. Adapted from Lifehack, "How to Break Out of Your Comfort Zone." http://www .lifehack.org/articles/lifehack/how-to-break-out-of-your-comfort-zone.html (accessed September 25, 2014).

24. Adapted from WikiHow, "How to Step Out of Your Comfort Zone." http://www .wikihow.com/Step-Out-of-Your-Comfort-Zone (accessed September 25, 2014).

25. Adapted from Pick the Brain, "7 Ways to Overcome the Fear of Failure." http://www .pickthebrain.com/blog/overcome-fear-of-failure/ (accessed September 25, 2014).

26. Adapted from Jude Bijou, "What to Stop Procrastinating Here are 10 Ways to Do IT." http://www.businessknowhow.com/growth/procrastination.htm (accessed September 25, 2014).

27. Summarized from Unstuck, "How We Procrastinate (and may not even know it)." http://www.unstuck.com/how-we-procrastinate.html and Margie Warrell, "Why You Procrastinate, and How to Stop it Now." http://www.forbes.com/sites/ margiewarrell/2013/03/25/why-you-procrastinate-and-how-to-stop-it-now/ (accessed September 25, 2014).

28. Michael Kieron Paget, Michael David Thomas, Matthew Tuck, et al. *Bullet For My Valentine*, album *Fever*, song *Alone*, 2010. See http://www.songlyrics.com/bullet-for-my-valentine/alone-lyrics/#6VmflwIYebWZoKll.99

29. Adapted from Lori Deschene, "10 Ways to Deal with Negative or Difficult People." http://tinybuddha.com/blog/how-to-deal-with-negative-people-or-difficult-people/ (accessed September 25, 2014).

30. Adapted from Tina Su, "How to Really Listen to Someone." http://thinksimplenow.com/relationships/how-to-really-listen-to-someone/ and Karin Gonzalez, "How to Get Someone to Listen to You." http://www.ehow.com/how_5115759_someone-pay-attention-listen.html and Henrik Edberg, "7 Common Habits of Unhappy People." http://www.positivityblog.com/index.php/2011/10/05/7-habits/ (accessed September 25, 2014).

31. Ibid.

32. Summarized from Francesca Gino and Gary Pisano, "Why Leaders Don't Learn from Success." https://hbr.org/2011/04/why-leaders-dont-learn-from-success (accessed September 25, 2014).

33. See Wikipedia, "Disruptive Innovation." http://en.wikipedia.org/wiki/Disruptive_innovation (accessed September 25, 2014).

34. See Gerrit De Vynck, "Google Chairman Says Mistake was Missing Social Networks." http://www.bloomberg.com/news/2013-12-31/google-chairman-says-mistake-was-missing-social-networks.html (accessed September 25, 2014).

35. Summarized from Ryan Avery, "How to Get Over the Past and Focus on the Future!" http://ryanavery.com/how-to-get-over-the-past-and-focus-on-the-future/ (accessed September 25, 2014).

36. Summarized from Michael Graham Richard, "Fixed Mindset vs. Growth Mindset: White One Are You?" http://michaelgr.com/2007/04/15/fixed-mindset-vs-growth-mindset-which-one-are-you/ (accessed September 25, 2014).

37. Summarized from R.E. Marks, "Decision Analysis: Games Against Nature." www.agsm.edu.au/bobm/teaching/SGTM/id.pdf (accessed February 13, 2014).18Prezi.com

6

Engagement

---

ngagement is an emotional and intellectual commitment to put forth extra discretionary effort for the job or organization.[1] It is, quite simply, passion for the work. Employee engagement has become an important topic for senior executives, who have been told that a highly engaged workforce can increase innovation, productivity, and performance while reducing cost of hiring and retention. A *Harvard Business Review Analytic Services Report* found that most leaders understand the importance of engagement;[2] however, three-quarters of those surveyed said that most employees in their organizations are not highly engaged. Even then, executives were much more optimistic than their managers about the levels of employee engagement in their company. Clearly, leaders see a need to improve employee engagement, but have yet to develop tangible ways to do it. Therefore, we think employee engagement is something all our readers will face if not already doing so.

Before we go on, we want to make sure we separate workaholism and work engagement.[3] Workaholics are psychologically "pushed" to their work, while engaged employees are pulled to their work. Workaholism is the tendency to work excessively hard and be obsessed

---

with work while engagement is the tendency to work hard to create better things. Workaholics work harder than required in order to be a hero and are unwilling and unable to disengage from work (performance goals). Workaholism can cause negative outcomes; in contrast, work engagement seems to be more positive and fulfilling. Engagement is associated with high levels of energy, mental resilience while working, willingness to invest effort in one's work, and persistence (mastery goals). While both increase productivity, workaholism hurts the individual—is self-handicapping—where engagement does not.

Impact

Research on work engagement outcomes is very limited, but all of it points in the same direction—engaged employees cause better things to happen. The more engaged workers tend to be senior level, have a college education, earn $50K+, and be under the age of 30 or over 50.[4] Comparatively, less engaged or disengaged employees are most often 40–49 years old, the most highly educated, lower-level income employees, newer employees, client-facing and clerical staffers, and those working in government, military, education, and manufacturing sectors. *Many leaders, therefore, manage disengaged employees in some of the most critical positions required for the organization to be innovative and customer-focused.* The *Harvard Business Review Analytic Services Report*, which included about 1.4 million employees in 192 organizations, across 49 industries, and in 34 countries, showed that employee engagement is strongly related to lowered absenteeism and turnover, reduced safety incidents, less shrinkage, and was related to higher customer satisfaction, productivity, and profitability.[5]

There are several signs that indicate a *disengaged* workplace.[6] Feeling left out of the loop on important information, little to no feedback about one's performance, bosses or colleagues taking credit for others accomplishments are signs of a disengaging culture. Leaders saying "you're lucky you have a job," a high turnover rate among employees, cliques dominating the office, meetings a waste of time, confusion, arbitrary deadlines or lack of focus prevailing in an office are further symptoms of larger problems causing disengagement. Peter Drucker said, many times, "Most of what we call management consists of making it difficult for people to get their work done." Leaders can create their own disengaging culture fairly easily; this is self-handicapping.

The Real Issues

It seems clear that employee engagement helps organizations, but engagement is one of those things that leaders often get mixed up in their head—Do they *make* employees engaged or do they *let* them be engaged? Commanding engagement will not work; only an individual can choose to engage in their job. Managers can only get out of the way and create the conditions to help employees open up, trust, and engage. "Being in the way" of engagement incorporates a whole range of claimed and behavioral handicaps.

Most new employees show up wanting to be engaged—most of us go to work wanting to do something worthwhile, have fun, and be proud of what we do. We all want to be engaged. If leaders can give employees a clear, worthy mission, the ability to own their jobs, and an atmosphere where engagement is "the thing to do" rather than gripe and complain about what the company or boss is doing to them—they will have gotten out of the way and allowed engagement to occur. None of this will start with a memo. It would help your talent management efforts to find those with mastery goals. The excuses leading to these types of reduced effort are what lead managers down the ERO Spiral.

We were told a story about a department director who was somewhat of a control freak. She had three staff people (an analyst and two clerical) reporting to her and the department did fairly well in accomplishing its work. One day the director was assigned to a 2-year corporate project that required travel. The analyst began to work more closely with the other two staff members, teaching, guiding and basically running the day-to-day operations, only asking for guidance as needed from the director. Over time, the director noticed how smoothly things were running and promoted the analyst to manager. All three staff members were proud that they had basically taken over control of the day-to-day operations of the department and created a new culture. The director was smart enough to see what happened when she got out of the way. The director now had the time to reflect on strategic issues and learned to ease off on the control freak mentality. The department operated at a higher, more engaged level with four people full-on.

A major issue stopping employees from being more engaged is whether their boss is engaged and shows it consistently. We had an executive tell us a story of a new leadership job he accepted in a start-up. He went to work eager to contribute (like all of us) and at day seven he had to fly half way across the country with his boss to see a client. The CEO sat in first class while he sat in coach. The issues were: (1) They were spending start-up investor money, and (2) He knew nothing about the client or processes. The boss could have spent a 3-hour flight helping and getting to know this new employee (in coach). When they got there and met the other members of the team presenting to the client, they had a party with plenty of liquor (paid for by investors) and lots of bad-mouthing the client. This was all very discouraging and disengaging to this new executive. The story ends well because this executive saw his mistake and knew this was not a company where he could contribute within his management style. Furthermore, he had the courage to resign—after 2 weeks. He is now a CEO who understands engagement in "the trenches."

A manager may not be able to control those above him, but he can buffer it before it hits his employees, or like the executive mentioned previously, have the courage to find a place where he can be engaged and allow engagement. When we go to work, we have three choices: (1) Accept what we have been given, (2) Change what we have been given, or (3) Leave. If you feel disengaged, do something about it—change the work or leave it. If the leadership is inconsistent and controlling, if the recognition is not there, if the work is not meaningful, the manager is still in charge of his area and he can work on changing it for both himself and his employees.

Finally, there is evidence that communication style affects engagement.[7] People who share the same communication style as their boss may be as much as 18 percent more engaged than people with differing styles. If you are a "big picture" communicator and your boss is more "methodical"—a "process-driven" communicator—he may want to walk through things step-by-step with nitty-gritty detail, while you avoid detail and connect lots of dots in a big picture of the problem. Conflict could occur and you would feel less engaged in your work. In these circumstances, it would be your job to align your communication style more toward your boss's comfort zone or initiate a conversation about it where you both can move toward the middle.

What the Manager Should Do for Himself

1. Make a list of the things that are causing you to be disengaged.

2. Review and categorize the list—uninteresting work, inconsistent or dysfunctional leadership, lack of support, lack of recognition, lack of trust and open communication culture, lack of vision, etc.

3. Place a strategy next to a category. For instance, if you have uninteresting work, you might request a meeting with your boss

and ask for a challenging project you would find interesting[8]—preferably something that would stretch your abilities and it is not directly tied to your role.

4. Choose to go out and meet people. Visit other areas of your company. Join professional associations. Network and bench mark what others are doing. Check with the human resources department about other positions.

5. Make a conscious choice to become engaged in your work. Engagement will require an increased amount of energy and effort on your part. Just try to put more effort in. Sounds crazy, but it works.

6. If your work is too stressful, reassess your workload and how much time is required for each task. Consider what items you could delegate or talk to your boss about letting go of.

7. If it is lack of support, have a heart-to-heart discussion with your boss on where you are right now and what you need (emotional support, equipment, or pay). Unspoken expectations are large contributors to employee disengagement. Once these expectations are spoken—even if they cannot be met, engagement levels go up.

8. Revisit your personal vision and career path. When is the last time you considered doing something new? Are there opportunities to job shadow in your organization? Discuss these options with your leader.

9. Let go of any negative opinions about your employees, boss, or the organization. Stop hanging out with the negative people. Then, you may start magically getting happier.

   Read Martin Seligman's, *Learned Optimism*.[9]

10. Offer constructive suggestions. Tell your boss about ideas you have to make your work more efficient. Demonstrate how the added cost will payoff in terms of your productivity.

11. If the issue is lack of trust or inconsistency, ask yourself who might be able to fix that. Talk to them. If you absolutely have no control over these, consider a new position internally or a new organization in which you can engage. A change of scenery is usually engaging.

12. Promote the organization at work and in your day-to-day life. Share the company's vision and values in your conversations with

coworkers and customers. Being an advocate for the business is a way to feel good about the job you do and the positive results that come from it.

13. Take up a cause. Championing something you actually care about can connect you almost instantly to your work. Volunteer for Habitat for Humanity or many other worthy organizations.

14. Get to know your employees, their goals, stressors, what excites them and how they define success. No need to start counseling your staff, but show an interest in their well-being.

15. Most importantly, get off the dime. Depression will not help; movement does. Do something![10]

What to Do for Employees

Employees are vastly more satisfied and engaged when they have opportunities to regularly renew and recharge at work, feel valued and appreciated for contributions, have the opportunity to focus on their most important tasks—are not overwhelmed by "bureaucracy," are able to define when and how they get their work done, do what they do best and enjoy most, and feel connected to a higher purpose at work.[11] Many of the following recommendations may sound like common sense, but you'd be surprised how many leaders neglect to use these to open an engagement culture with those who are receptive:[12]

1. *Communicate*—Personal communication and regular meetings can all be used to increase engagement of your employees. Ask questions, find solutions, and increase the amount of information that reaches them—clarify roles and objectives.

2. *Find Out What Employees Need to do Their Jobs*—Give it to them. Don't assume employees have all the tools, training, and support they need. Find out.

3. *Involve All Employees in Planning and Decision-Making*—Their work becomes their baby and something to master. Whenever possible, use their ideas.

4. *Provide Positive Feedback*—When good things are seen, provide positive feedback to encourage more of the same. When asked, most employees will say they don't get enough positive feedback—only negative. Provide constructive feedback to help employees self-correct.

5. *Say "Thank You!"*—Find good things to say to your employees.

6. *Make Work Fun*—People get more done when they enjoy themselves. Remove all items of work that do not add value.

7. *Act Fairly and Create Trust*—Respect and trust your team and you will get the same in return. If you make a mistake, apologize and admit you were wrong. Enforce accountability at all levels.

8. *Pay Attention to Your Work Culture*—Are people laughing *with* each other or complaining about the company? Stop discussions that are negative and keep success stories alive.

9. *Reward and Recognize Engaged Employees*—This is another reason why getting to know your employees is so important. Remember that reciprocation is a big driver of engagement.

10. *Be Consistent*—If you start an initiative and then drop it, your efforts will backfire—people get exhausted and exasperated from work initiatives that engage their passion and then fizzle.

11. *Reduce Ambiguous Behavior*—Confusing or ambiguous behavior of supervisors is a major source of tension in organizations.

12. *Find Ways the Organization Can Support Your Department*—Are there incentive programs for engagement? Will the executives help you recognize people?

13. *Finally, Create an Atmosphere That Is Focused on a Worthy Mission*—NOT on avoiding mistakes, following procedure and policy, doing what you say, or avoiding embarrassment.

If you can do these things consistently over time, you will find your employees shifting from performance to mastery goals, owning what they do, and eliminating their own self-handicapping. That is true employee engagement.

Are You Engaged and Do You Show It?

Like most self-handicapping, you have to get your house in order before you work on helping others. One reason you may not be willing or able to help your employees engage is you not very engaged. Take the following survey and see where you stand. Be honest, only you will see it.

Survey: Am I Engaged or Disengaged?[13]

(Y = Yes, N= No, DK = Don't Know)

_____This company is consistent when administering policies concerning employees.

____ I readily volunteer to take on new challenges or projects.

____ My boss understands my development needs and career goals.

____ I am paid fairly for the work I do.

____ I have the opportunity to use my strengths in the work I do on a daily basis.

____ My boss respects me.

____ I have the support and resources I need to do my job to the best of my ability.

____ My salary is competitive with similar jobs I might find elsewhere.

____ My boss deals with performance issues quickly and effectively.

____ Building relationships and collaborating with others in the company is encouraged.

____ I have an opportunity to participate in the goal-setting process.

____ When I do a good job, I receive the praise I deserve.

____ I have a clear understanding of what success in my role looks like.

____ I talk positively about my organization and the products/services we provide.

____ I have all the information I need to do my job effectively.

____ Open communication is encouraged in this organization.

____ I have a sense of ownership over my work.

____ I steer clear of gossip and negative talk of others on my team.

____ Doing my job well gives me a sense of personal satisfaction.

____ I have adequate opportunities for professional growth in this organization.

____ My work is challenging, stimulating, and rewarding.

____ I respect the senior leaders of this organization.

____ The organization values the contribution I make.

____ I can disagree with my supervisor without fear of getting in trouble.

Scores

20–24—You are very engaged.

10–19—You are somewhat engaged.

1–9—You are not very engaged.

We believe employees are smart people and a manager probably can't fake engagement for long. But we all have bad days. *Remember, inconsistency is the same as no engagement.* Engagement is an everyday thing.

Why Don't You Create Engagement?

Expediency

When a person is not interested, he often chooses what is easy or requires less time. He delegates most of the work and is not liked because employees responsible for picking up the slack are resentful and unhappy. Indecisiveness or trying to please everyone will do the same. The best leaders show their employees that they can be counted on to contribute to the mission and make decisions. Employees may not always agree with the direction, but it is much easier to follow an engaged leader. A disinterested leader vacillates, changes his mind often, and moves the group in new directions based on new feedback at the drop of a hat.[14] These leaders alienate employees who are asked constantly to start, restart, and change direction.

Remember, the best leaders are unseen and engagement for a leader may look like laziness to an employee. A brilliant leader may look lazy because he is selective.[15] Once a leader understands that very few actions and decisions have a disproportionately huge impact on his career and firm's fortunes, he naturally searches for those few big breaks. Warren Buffet says, "Don't sweat the small stuff, because small drives out big." Great leaders reflect, build strategy, and look for the disruptive innovation. "We do not normally associate idleness with determination, but the determination to find a much better solution involving much less effort can look like laziness."[16] When your mind is in the strategy clouds, don't forget the perceptions of your employees.

What issues cause you to disengage or not help employees engage that are due to expediency?

_____

_____

Avoidance

In the first chapter, we showed you Gallup's findings that great leaders *motivate* employees, engage them, are *assertive,* drive outcomes, overcome resistance, create *accountability*, build *trust* and transparency, and *make decisions* that are based on productivity, not politics.[17] *These are the things that create engaged employees.* We have suggested that so few managers do all of these things because of habitual self-handicapping. Managers giving excuses, creating barriers to success, managing up, and shying away from accountability do not help open up employee engagement. If a manager spends time self-handicapping his performance, he is not engaged. Why would employees take on accountability and engagement when their boss is not?

Motivating an employee, being assertive, or holding employees accountable often requires the manager to confront the employee. When leaders face any crucial conversation like this, they can do one of three things: (1) Avoid it, (2) Face it but handle it poorly, or (3) Face it and handle it skillfully. The first two choices are disengaging for employees. Mastering high-stakes discussions will engage employees. The authors of *Crucial Conversations* call for a "shared pool of meaning," where everyone is encouraged to share their ideas.[18] The leader should strive for employees to engage in conversations about their problems. Conversations about engagement should be open and free. Managers who are skilled at crucial conversations know what they want from any conversation and do not become unfocused. They listen for how they can get out of the way of employee's engaging and owning their work. These conversations begin to fail because employees feel unsafe and resort either to silence or resistance; both of these are engagement killers. The skilled leader recognizes these as signs to find out why employees do not feel safe in a conversation about engagement.

Furthermore, there is a widely held assumption among managers that showing any vulnerability will make them look weak to the pack.[19] But an organization like this in which managers don't feel free to be open or make mistakes can be corrosive to engagement. Trust and teamwork are eroded. This can lead to individuals simply withdrawing from their work. Managers who avoid their responsibility to the employees open up to them. They are careful about it, but understand that employees are more engaged when the boss is human and is working for the same goals and outcomes.

What issues are you avoiding that are causing problems with engagement?

Fear

Most people are somewhat hesitant about any group they join and do not want to be consumed by it. This ambivalence seriously hampers the natural tendency people have to engage in their work so they alternate pulling away and moving toward the job to keep a balance. In making these decisions, people continually ask the following questions:

- How meaningful is it to commit myself to this group or performance?
- How safe is it for me to do so?
- How available am I to do so?
- How much reciprocity exists? Will I get burned in the end?

In situations where the individual is more psychologically available to commit, the group or organization will reciprocate, and when the boss has created an open, trusting environment, engagement will likely occur. Of course, work conditions and individual differences affect how these are perceived by an individual. One study showed that this type of ambivalent fear led to lower work engagement, but only in jobs that were high in demands of the individual.[20]

Job insecurity can cause burnout and lower work engagement. It contributes to burnout and lower work engagement because it erodes the notion of reciprocity, which is crucial in engagement. Employees must be rewarded and recognized for engagement. It cannot be a one-way street.

What issues do you fear that are causing engagement problems?

Self-Deception

Any manager can unconsciously do things to disengage employees. We know of an executive who was worried that employees working at home were not engaged. There were few metrics to know if folks were engaged and productive while working from home—that was the real issue. So this leader decided to start slowly creating requirements for the workers to have to do more and more of their work in the office. This was a piecemeal strategy designed so the employees did not notice the changes. They did, of course; and as time progressed they were resentful and less productive. Few said anything or quizzed the leader about his motivation. They just disengaged and did what was required.

Most employees want and need to feel connected to, and to trust, their peers and bosses. For people to take personal risks—such as full commitment to a job—they need emotional support. They want to feel like someone has their back. Failing to keep employees informed or to take an interest in them, avoiding helping employees, failing to recognize their achievements, taking them for granted, and blaming them when things go wrong are possible unconscious behaviors of leaders that are very disengaging. Look for these—ask your employees. Lack of concern for subordinates and the conviction by those subordinates that their leader is primarily motivated by self-interest will bring engagement to a standstill.

What issues you may be seeing could be causing engagement problems?

Behaviors to Change

Lack of Empathy and Emotional Support

Recognize

Let's look at the issue of giving employees what they want and need emotionally. Employees do not separate emotion from work. An experienced leader is aware of others' emotions and is able to use that awareness to develop stronger relationships with employees. Even if delivering bad news, they are able to cushion the impact by letting employees know that they are aware of how they might be feeling. For more on this, we suggest Daniel Goleman's, *Emotional Intelligence: Why It Can Matter More Than IQ*, Bantam Dell, New York, 1994.

Admit

Managers need to be aware of their own emotions to do this. Leaders who are oblivious to their own emotions and how they impact others will have a hard time being supportive of others. They need to know what they feel and have an awareness of how their words and actions affect employees. That won't happen unless they examine whether they like people, and specifically, their employees. Experienced leaders are also aware of strong emotions and avoid speaking out of anger and frustration. If they feel the urge to give in to strong emotions, they give themselves a time out, waiting until their emotions have leveled off, and they have had a chance to think about the situation.

Adjust

Here are some hints.[21] Practice one a week until you start to see employees' emotional needs and begin to respond to them in different ways. Empathy is just one step toward helping employees engage, but a big one.

- Note your emotional reactions to events throughout the day. It's easy to put your feelings about what you experience on the back burner and let it build up.

- Pay attention to your body. Instead of ignoring your emotions, start listening to them. Observe how your emotions and behavior are connected. You can't help what emotions you feel, but you can decide how you want to react to them.

- Avoid judging your own emotions and thereby suppressing the bad ones. All the emotions you have are valid, even the negative ones, so notice patterns in your emotions.

- Practice deciding how to behave rather than reacting—deliberate action. Be open-minded and agreeable and take the time to deal with conflicts in a calm and self-assured manner.

- Read people's body language. Make a point of trying to read between the lines and pick up on people's true feelings by observing their facial expressions and other body language.

- Attend to the effect you have on others. Practice being emotionally honest. If you say you're "fine" and have a scowl on your face, you're not communicating honestly. That works against trust and empathy.

- Be more light-hearted at work. Don't live in the past or hold grudges. Success lies in your ability to rise above failure and go forward. Don't dwell on problems and don't hang around negative people.

- Be assertive; don't say "yes" unless you really mean it.

While you work down this list, add one more act—*practice random acts of kindness to your employees*. Help someone, sponsor them, introduce an employee to more challenge, donate to their favorite charity, or mention good things they do to your boss. Do something unexpected and then see how you feel and watch for their reactions. Don't ask or expect reciprocation. Then do it again. Check out the "Random Acts of Kindness Foundation" at https://www.facebook.com/therandomactsofkindnessfoundation.

Key Behaviors

Your emotional support key behaviors are as follows. Before you go out to try these out, go to the Internet and research "empathy."

1. Focus on the person. Give them all of your attention and eye contact.

2. Remove yourself from the problem. Understand your boundaries in the situation and do not become a solver. Leaders do that and it takes away from empathy.

3. Calm yourself down—it will help the other person.

4. Be patient and listen. Find out what they are feeling. This is especially important if this is uncomfortable for you.

5. Process the event. Let them talk and help them move to realistic expectations.

6. Make positive comments about their worth to you and the organization.

7. Inspire action on their part. Only they can solve the problem.

8. Be willing to seek help from human resource if you cannot help them work through this quickly. Go back to step 2.

Failure to Offer Feedback or Ask for It

Recognize

Ask yourself or any of your employees, "Have you had too much positive feedback today?" Of course, you will hear, "No!" To maximize motivation and to minimize misinterpretation, leaders must learn the effective use of feedback. There are three levels of feedback:[22]

1. about work processes

2. about how one's behavior influences processes

3. about relationships, communications, and leadership

Most leaders can ask or give feedback about work processes with confidence, but feel discomfort in the "squishy" topics such as relationships. Feedback about relationships and communications can be tough; listening to others' views when seeking feedback may cause defensiveness. But the payoff comes when a leader discovers what behaviors or incidents have led his employees to their conclusion about him. They then have a chance to understand others' reactions and can determine whether to change or not. Understanding the basics of feedback is a very important first step in creating an environment that helps employees engage.

Admit

Do you ask how *you're* doing in your employees' eyes? It is not easy for leaders to request employee feedback and it can be even more challenging for an employee to give the boss an honest response. But, develop this skill and model it for your employees; it will open the door for engagement.

Busy supervisors often do not take the time to give positive feedback.[23] They assume employees fully understand everything needed to do a good job and that is precisely what they should be doing. Yet, the importance of praise and positive feedback in motivating employees cannot be overstated. Effective leaders provide immediate, specific, and sincere praise on a regular basis to their employees.

Adjust

When giving negative feedback start your feedback by identifying the issue. It is often helpful to begin the statement with an "I" message. Such as "I have noticed . . . " or "I have observed . . . " Expressing concern about substandard performance lets employees know you care about them as individuals. If employees know you care, they are more likely to engage. Feedback works best when it is given face-to-face, privately, and timely. Here are some pointers for giving feedback:

- Be specific; relate the feedback to an outcome. Give examples.
- Express concern when giving feedback on negative situations.
- Be direct and sincere. Get to the point—mean what you say and say what you mean.
- Give feedback directly, not through messengers.
- Give timely feedback, without delay.
- Distribute feedback equally—when things go wrong and when things go right. This is not easy to do.

Here are further feedback ideas that might be very effective.[24]

- Write a thank-you note to your hard working employees.
- Put together a slideshow of your staff's accomplishments or your client's feedback, and then keep it on display in a shared conference room or during your team meeting.
- Recognize your engaged employees with unexpected perks such as treats in the break room, extra paid time off, or a visit and a handshake from your vice president or chief executive officer.

Though these kind of small appreciation techniques may sound silly, they make a big difference. Just look at the expression on your employee's face, when they meet the vice president or chief executive officer of your company.

Key Behaviors

The key behaviors for giving praise are as follows:

1. State clearly what the employee did that deserves recognition.

2. Express your personal satisfaction with the employee and his performance. Be sincere.

3. Explain why it is important to continue in this manner.

4. (Optional) Ask what you can do to help him continue the good performance.

Asking for feedback, like learning to give feedback, is not always easy. Asking for feedback can be awkward because you are vulnerable—you may have to hear something you don't like. Hearing nothing is often interpreted as negative. Employees may be reluctant to open up and will just say, "there are no problems." Many of us have never learned the skill of eliciting the views others hold about us. Yet the benefits of acquiring and acting on this information are extensive. It can clear up misunderstandings. It can help identify areas needing improvement. It builds trust.

Key Behaviors

The key behaviors for asking for feedback are as follows:

1. Have a clear idea about why you are asking for feedback. You should be able to discuss how you will use the data.

2. When you ask for feedback and they get hesitant don't get impatient or critical. Don't get offended. People are rarely candid the first time out.

3. Start with a disclosure, "I've heard from some that I have a bad habit of making poor decisions. What do you think about how I make decisions?"

4. Ask about reluctance directly—"Sam, you seem to be cautious about sharing your opinions. Can you tell me what that's about?" These questions are intended to reduce the natural defensiveness of the person asked for feedback.

Practicing these key behaviors will gradually build trust and confidence so that you can constantly ask how you are doing in your employees' eyes.

Acting Arrogant

Recognize

A belief many experienced leaders have is that their capabilities got them there and will get them further. This goes along with the feelings that they only need themselves and do not need to engage others, understand their feelings, or network. Over time, this can bleed into assuming all problems stem from peers or employees. It is easy to dump your problems on Generation "This" or Generation "That;" this will kill employee or team engagement quickly.

Another twist is the inexperienced manager who is new to the job. Often, managers who are uncertain about their capabilities will act like the know everything rather than lay back and learn the "lay of the land." This attitude coming from the leader's insecurity can disengage employees. It is also a double-sided coin—this new leader's boss has to be careful to not disengage him with sloppy feedback. Statements like "you are trying too hard" and "you are compensating for your age" without empathy for the insecurity, and hints on how to behave, will end up disengaging the new leader right along with his employees.

Admit

Ask yourself these questions to see if arrogance may be getting in your way of helping your employees engage:

- Are you certain about things a lot?
- Do you think you have to get things done by yourself?
- Do you become inpatient with employees when they don't get it?
- Do you sometimes talk down to employees?

Regardless of what you are feeling (insecure, unrewarded) remember to always give credit to others.[25] Being generous with giving credit does not take away from what you contributed. Offer meaningful compliments to others in the team or ask questions that allow others to supply information. And if you make a mistake, admit it. Remembering other people's names will also lessen any perceptions that you are arrogant. You can use yourself as an example of poor behavior and laugh at yourself. All of this adds up to not taking yourself too seriously and showing empathy for others. Learning to communicate assertively also helps because the likely alternative is aggressive communication. This will be considered arrogance.

Adjust

Being arrogant for any reason means that you probably have given more orders than made collaborative decisions with your workforce. *You could just stop giving commands and see what happens.* But be careful—if you have been running things through command and control, you may find further problems. You *telling* your workforce what to do means they have not had to *learn* what to do on their own. They didn't have to own their own competence and jobs—you owned it. So if you all of a sudden stop giving commands, your employees may not be ready to step up and take over.

You must initiate procedures to help your employees want to be competent. We have all heard that we should create a learning organization. This is where the rubber hits the road. If you make employees responsible for being competent and owning their jobs, most employees will engage more. Help those who don't engage to leave easily—*once you know it is them and not something you are doing.* The engagement of those who are willing can be focused toward continually learning their craft. If you provide a clear mission and vision they accept, keep it front and center, and refrain from taking over, they will understand that they must continually improve themselves to drive the mission.

There are many other reasons employees think you are being arrogant. Always ask yourself about your intent and the outcomes of the communication. Sometimes people let factors such as race, gender, marital status, age, or disabilities factor into a conversation that can cause a person to assume that you have an "attitude." Some people tend to take things personally regardless of what is said or how it is said. Finally, some people see assertiveness as aggression. These problems are not your problem until you become a leader. Then, you have to be the adult and remove the barriers to engagement. One of the hardest things to master in the workplace is how to vary your communication style, so that you can communicate effectively with a range of different people. To work around these problems, be genuine and assertive.

Key Behaviors

Here are some key behaviors to follow when you feel insecure. Before trying these, go to Chapter 8, Communication Culture, and review the section on assertiveness. Do not start speaking unless you can do it in an assertive way.[26]

1. If you have to talk about yourself, state the true facts quickly and move on to the mission. Do not do it to impress other people or to make yourself feel better.

2. Use "we" instead of "I" in what you say about the mission.

3. Admit your insecurities. Showing vulnerability in public is actually a sign of strength, especially when you share your feelings so that you can help others who are feeling the same doubts that you've felt.

4. Do not criticize what other people have done or said. Stick to the mission.

5. Give sincere compliments to others whenever they have contributed to the outcomes. They are the center of the universe, not you.

6. Let your actions do the talking for you.

Viewing Everything as a Transaction, Rather than a Partnership

Recognize

There are two components that contribute to employee perceptions about your communication.[27] These are: (1) The transaction—getting the work done or the problem solved, and (2) The "softer side"—the interpersonal interaction between two people. Not only do employees want their problems resolved and questions answered, but they want to be treated fairly and nicely. They want to hear enthusiasm about their work from their boss. All of this increases engagement.

Admit

We have all had the type of boss that talks to us nicely with great eye contact until he gets what he wants and then his eyes glaze over and he is eager for us to disappear. We are dead to him because he got the transaction done, and he has no further interest in us as people. Every single interaction between you as a leader and an employee represents an opportunity to increase engagement. Asking how someone is doing, getting to know their needs, etc, may take a bit more time (and even conflict with your personality) but it does not take away from the transaction. Get the transaction done and add an element of engagement building in every conversation. Email makes communicating with employees convenient, but it is no substitute for you being visible and talking to your employees. Even texting is more personal. Have a real relationship with your employees.

Adjust

In business, the focus is all about the transaction with very little time or content devoted to the interaction aspect. Change this. This is particularly true with a younger workforce that has fewer life experiences, more use of electronic communication, and a greater need for support in their work—they still want engagement. All conversations, even when the answer is no, should have a positive tone. Remember to give feedback, recognize engaged employees, be fair to all, and talk to your employees as partners. Great leaders walk around and inject interpersonal interaction in everything they do. They know it is what drives success.

Key Behaviors

The key behaviors for partnering are as follows:[28]

1. Write down all the positive benefits of working with an individual. This will remind you of the value each person adds to your organization or team before you take any action toward him.

2. Think about what you can do for the other person rather than what you can get from him.

3. Approach the individual assertively while developing rapport with him. You can establish rapport by asking about his concerns or issues and trying to address them.

4. Identify and understand his approach to problems and problem-solving strategy.

5. Communicate honestly and openly about both your and his expectations.

6. Under-promise and over-deliver on commitments you make.

Talking About Others Behind Their Back

Recognize

Talking about other people may make a manager feel better, but it can undermine him in the eyes of employees and peers. It can also create conflict and mistrust among staff. The reasons for doing this include disrespect for the individual, a negative and disengaged culture, and to show everyone how much he knows about everything and everyone—insecurity. This is jumping into the ERO Spiral right at the obstacle stage.

Admit

A good way to stop doing this is simply to refuse to be drawn in. Do not respond to comments about an absent person. Stay out of the "gripe groups"—the negative folks. It helps get to know your staff as human beings—learn their names.[29] Praise in public; criticize in private face-to-face meetings only. Recognize that some staff members may not fit in with the prevailing culture; stop talking about them. Remove employees who are toxic to the workplace, no matter how good they are technically. Your organization will go on and be healthier for it. If employees or peers are talking about you, don't reciprocate by doing the same thing. Confront the person and say, "If you have a problem with me, let's resolve it now, because we need to work together." Check out Patterson, et al, *Crucial Confrontations*.[30]

Adjust

If you are the leader who wants to reduce or eliminate workplace gossip, take a look at yourself first. If you treat your employees like adults and don't talk behind their backs, they are more likely to act the same way. If your employees believe they can't talk to you, they will merely complain to each other or make stuff up. If you don't confront this, they have no incentive to stop gossiping. So confront gossipers in private and focus on the issue or behavior rather than on the person. If you feel you can't avoid gossip, try to verify the information you're hearing. By asking about details, you are subtly forcing the group to tacitly acknowledge the lack of credibility of that information. You can also simply ask the group what they think might be a solution.

Key Behaviors

The key behaviors for staying out of gripe sessions and away from griping coworkers are as follows:[31]

1. Get to know your team members. Discover the things they actually do like and talk about those things.

2. Determine your motives. Do you want to join a gripe session to make yourself look good by putting colleagues down or are you doing it as a way of getting people on your side—gaining power. Develop a strategy to overcome these thoughts.

3. Interact daily with colleagues who have an optimistic outlook— positive encounters will help you keep your spirits up when working with negative types.

4. Understand the motives of chronic complainers (see step 2). Turn the focus back on the complainer, asking what they plan to do differently the next time. When people say "we," ask who we is.

5. Draw your own conclusions and have the courage to state them. Those doing the griping are probably doing it unconsciously without understanding their own triggers.

6. Ask "What's the problem? What's the solution? What's the next step?" Turn the discussion around to a "problem identification and a solution" session with "What" and "How" questions."

Final Personal Takeaways

Action Plan—Engagement

You know what should be done and what is disengaging your employees, so what will you do about it? Complete the action plan.

Engagement Self-Handicap	What Is the Situation?	Trigger	Impact on Others	What to Do/When?
Do the little things that I know I should be doing (list mentioned previously)		__Expedient __Avoiding __Fear __Self-deception		__Deliberate action____ __Self-efficacy_____ __Face it_____ __Look and listen_____
Don't get to know my employees—have negative opinions		__Expedient __Avoiding __Fear __Self-deception		__Deliberate action____ __Self-efficacy_____ __Face it_____ __Look and listen_____
Have not communicated a clear vision that motivates		__Expedient __Avoiding __Fear __Self-deception		__Deliberate action____ __Self-efficacy_____ __Face it_____ __Look and listen_____
Can't give employees what they want and need emotionally		__Expedient __Avoiding __Fear __Self-deception		__Deliberate action____ __Self-efficacy_____ __Face it_____ __Look and listen_____
Don't constantly ask how I am doing in my employees' eyes		__Expedient __Avoiding __Fear __Self-deception		__Deliberate action____ __Self-efficacy_____ __Face it_____ __Look and listen_____
Don't reward and recognize engaged employees		__Expedient __Avoiding __Fear __Self-deception		__Deliberate action____ __Self-efficacy_____ __Face it_____ __Look and listen_____

Engagement Self-Handicap	What Is the Situation?	Trigger	Impact on Others	What to Do/When?
Do not involve employees in planning and decision-making		__Expedient __Avoiding __Fear __Self-deception		__Deliberate action____ __Self-efficacy_____ __Face it_____ __Look and listen_____
Don't practice random acts of kindness		__Expedient __Avoiding __Fear __Self-deception		__Deliberate action____ __Self-efficacy_____ __Face it_____ __Look and listen_____
Don't always act fairly, openly, and create trust		__Expedient __Avoiding __Fear __Self-deception		__Deliberate action____ __Self-efficacy_____ __Face it_____ __Look and listen_____
Don't make work fun and enjoyable		__Expedient __Avoiding __Fear __Self-deception		__Deliberate action____ __Self-efficacy_____ __Face it_____ __Look and listen_____
Not consistent and assertive		__Expedient __Avoiding __Fear __Self-deception		__Deliberate action____ __Self-efficacy_____ __Face it_____ __Look and listen_____
Engage more myself		__Expedient __Avoiding __Fear __Self-deception		__Deliberate action___ __Self-efficacy_____ __Face it_____ __Look and listen_____
Lack of empathy and emotional support		__Expedient __Avoiding __Fear __Self-deception		__Deliberate action____ __Self-efficacy_____ __Face it_____ __Look and listen_____
Failure to offer feedback and ask for it, or provide enough positive feedback		__Expedient __Avoiding __Fear __Self-deception		__Deliberate action____ __Self-efficacy_____ __Face it_____ __Look and listen_____

Engagement Self-Handicap	What Is the Situation?	Trigger	Impact on Others	What to Do/When?
Acting arrogant		__Expedient __Avoiding __Fear __Self-deception		__Deliberate action____ __Self-efficacy_____ __Face it_____ __Look and listen_____
Viewing everything as a transaction, rather than a partnership		__Expedient __Avoiding __Fear __Self-deception		__Deliberate action____ __Self-efficacy_____ __Face it_____ __Look and listen_____
Talking about others behind their back		__Expedient __Avoiding __Fear __Self-deception		__Deliberate action____ __Self-efficacy_____ __Face it_____ __Look and listen_____
Not adding value for customers		__Expedient __Avoiding __Fear __Self-deception		__Deliberate action____ __Self-efficacy_____ __Face it_____ __Look and listen_____

Baby Steps

The baby steps for this chapter are as follows:

- Look everyone in the eye when you are talking to them—all day.
- Get to know one of your employees beyond work behavior.
- Write down who of your employees are: (1) very engaged, (2) moderately engaged, and (3) not engaged.
- Write a list of what may be disengaging one or two of the folks in category 2.

Here are the key behaviors for eye contact:[32]

1. Relax yourself. The more you think about it, the more self-conscious you'll become.

2. Just look directly into the person's eye in a relaxed manner. Avoid staring. Concentrate on one eye, if needed. But don't switch from left to right.

3. Really listen to what that person is saying and you won't worry about eye contact.

4. Try not to look away instantly when something else calls for your attention.

5. Do not attend to how they are dressed or groomed.

6. Be open and caring. Hostile eyes or false smiles will probably make the person try to end the conversation.

Here are the key behaviors for getting to know an employee:

1. Walk around and ask them questions. Not "What are you doing?" or "Why are you doing that?" but "Is there anything that would make that easier?" or "How was your weekend?"

2. Ask to shadow an employee and help them get the job done. Talk while you work.

3. Walk to meetings on different routes through the building and talk to one employee each time.

4. Eat breakfast or lunch with them.

5. Ask them something out of character like "What would you do if I put a live octopus on your desk?"

Follow-Up Questions

1. What are some ways that you disengage your employees?

2. How will you take baby steps to create a culture of engagement?

3. How would a more engaged staff help your organization?

4. What if, instead of rolling out complicated programs to address engagement, employers tapped into simply allowing more employee feedback and discussion?[33]

Endnotes

1. S Kular, Gatenby, M., et. al. "Employee Engagement: A Literature Review," Kingston University Working Paper Series No. 19, 2008. See http://business.kingston.ac.uk/sites/default/files/6_rp_emplyengag.pdf (accessed February 8, 2015).

2. Visit Harvard Business Review, "The Impact of Employee Engagement on Performance." http://www.yorkworks.ca/default/assets/File/analyst-insights-HBR_Achievers%20Report_TheImpactofEmployeeEngagementonPerformance(1).pdf. Also see AM Saks, "Antecedents and Consequences of Employee Engagement," JMP, 2006, 21(7), 600–619, http://cinik.free.fr/chlo/doc%20dans%20biblio,%20non%20imprim%C3%A9s/maintien%20dans%20l'emploi/atcd%20et%20cons%C3%A9quences%20de%20engagement.pdf (accessed February 8, 2015) downloaded.

3. See Dan Defoe, "'Engaged Workaholics'—'Do I really want to be a member of this group' and other questions." http://www.psycholawlogy.com/2012/05/01/engaged-workaholics-do-you-really-want-to-be-a-member-of-this-group/ (accessed February 8, 2015).

4. See Dale Carnegie Training, "What Drives Employee Engagement and Why It Matters." http://www.dalecarnegie.com/assets/1/7/driveengagement_101612_wp.pdf (accessed February 8, 2015).

5. See Gallup, "Engagement at Work: Its Effect on Performance Continues in Tough Economic Times." http://www.gallup.com/strategicconsulting/161459/engagement-work-effect-performance-continues-tough-economic-times.aspx (accessed February 8, 2015).

6. Visit Melody Wilding, "7 Signs Your Workplace is Toxic." http://psychcentral.com/blog/archives/2014/11/13/7-signs-your-workplace-is-toxic/ (accessed February 8, 2015).

7. See Leadership IQ News markmurphy@leadershipiq.com

8. See Tara Powers, "Are You Engaged or Disengaged? Take this Survey." http://mamameansbusiness.com/2013/01/are-you-engaged-or-disengaged-take-this-survey/ and Catherine Lovering, "How to Get Engaged in Your Work." http://smallbusiness.chron.com/engaged-work-25587.html (accessed February 8, 2015).

9. Martin Seligman, *Learned Optimism*, Alfred A. Knoph, New York, 1991.

10. For further information, read Loehr and Swartz, *The Power of Full Engagement: Managing Energy, Not Time, Is the Key to High Performance and Personal Renewal,* Free Press, New York, 2003; Marquet's, *Turn the Ship Around,* Portfolio, New York, 2013; or the more scholarly book by Bakker and Leiter, *Work Engagement: A Handbook of Essential Theory and Research,* Psychology Press, New York, 2010.

11. See Tony Schwartz and Christine Porath, "Why You Hate Work." http://www.nytimes.com/2014/06/01/opinion/sunday/why-you-hate-work.html?_r=0 (accessed February 8, 2015).

12. This list is abstracted from the following: JoAnna Brandi, "9 Ways to Keep Employees Engaged." http://www.entrepreneur.com/article/77158 and, Eric Friedman, "10 Steps to Keeping Employees Engaged and Motivated." http://blog.eskill.com/employees-engaged-motivated/ (accessed February 8, 2015). Also see J Goodman and C Truss, "The Medium and the Message: Communicating Effectively During a Major Change Initiative," *Journal of Change Management,* 2004, 4, 217–228. Sirota Survey Intelligence summarized in *"The Enthusiastic Employee: How Companies Profit by Giving Workers What They Want,"* 2007. *Incentives, Motivation and Workplace Performance*: Research & Best Practices, the International Society of Performance Improvement 2002.

13. Developed with help from Custom Insight, "Employee Engagement Survey." http://www.custominsight.com/employee-engagement-survey/sample-survey-items.asp and Tara Powers, "Are You Engaged or Disengaged? Take This Survey." http://mamameansbusiness.com/2013/01/are-you-engaged-or-disengaged-take-this-survey/ (accessed February 8, 2015).

14. Summarized from Susan Heathfield, "10 More Dumb Things Managers Do." http://humanresources.about.com/od/badmanagerboss/a/10-more-dumb-things-managers-do.htm (accessed February 8, 2015).

15. Summarized from Richard Koch, "In Praise of Lazy Managers." http://www .forbes.com/sites/forbesleadershipforum/2013/09/27/in-praise-of-lazy-managers/ (accessed February 8, 2015).

16. Ibid.

17. See Randall Beck and James Harter, "Why Good Managers Are So Rare." http:// blogs.hbr.org/2014/03/why-good-leaders-are-so-rare/ (accessed February 8, 2015).

18. Grenny Patterson, McMillan Switzler, *Crucial Conversations: Tools for Talking When Stakes Are High*, McGraw-Hill, New York, 2002. Also see http://www.amazon.com/ Crucial-Conversations-Tools-Talking-Stakes/dp/0071401946

19. Visit Monica Parker, "Embracing Vulnerability at Work is the Key to Employee Engagement." http://www.theguardian.com/sustainable-business/embrace -vulnerabilty-workplace-employee-engagement (accessed February 8, 2015).

20. AD Matthew, T Clark, NJ Loxton, "Fear, Psychological Acceptance, Job Demands and Employee Work Engagement: An Integrative Moderated Meditation Model," *Pers Indiv Differ*, 2001, 52, 893–897.

21. Adapted from WikiHow, "How To Develop Emotional Intelligence." http://www .wikihow.com/Develop-Emotional-Intelligence (accessed February 8, 2015).

22. See Daniel Oestreich, "Asking for Feedback." http://www.unfoldingleadership.com/ downloads/AskingforFeedback.pdf (accessed February 8, 2015).

23. Adapted from PJ Decker, *Management MicroTraining*, 1982.

24. From Bhavin Gandhi, "5 Practical Ways to Show Your Employees that You Care." http://bhavingandhi.com/2013/08/13/5-practical-ways-to-show-your-employees -that-you-care/ (accessed February 8, 2015).

25. Summarized from Gretchen Rubin, "Twelve Tips to Avoid Seeming Like an Arrogant Know-It-All Jerk." http://www.huffingtonpost.com/gretchen-rubin/twelve -tips-to-avoid-seem_b_77587.html and WikiHow, "How to Be Assertive Without Being Arrogant." http://www.wikihow.com/Be-Assertive-Without-Being-Arrogant and The Workplace, "How Can I be Assertive Without Being Rude or Offensive." http://workplace.stackexchange.com/questions/6853/how-can-i-be-assertive -without-being-rude-or-offensive (accessed February 8, 2015).

26. With the help of WikiHow, "How to Brag Without Being Arrogant." http://www .wikihow.com/Brag-Without-Being-Arrogant (accessed February 8, 2015).

27. Summarized from Quality Assurance & Training Connection, "From Transactions to Interactions: 25 Workforce Strategies to Support Extraordinary Customer Experiences." http://www.qatc.org/wp-content/uploads/2014/01/Transactions-to -Interactions-Paper.pdf (accessed February 8, 2015).

28. With help from Dana Sparks, "How to Deal With Coworkers Who Don't Do Their Part in the Project." http://www.ehow.com/how_8188197_deal-coworkers -business-partners.html (accessed February 8, 2015).

29. Summarized from Vinay Kumar and Joe Isaacs, "16 Ways to Show Staff You Care." http://www.asaecenter.org/Resources/ANowDetail.cfm?ItemNumber=137298 and Calvin Sun, "10 Tips for Dealing With Workplace Gossip." http://www.techrepublic .com/blog/10-things/10-tips-for-dealing-with-workplace-gossip/ (accessed February 8, 2015).

30. Patterson, Grenny, McMlian, and Switzler, *Crucial Confrontations*, McGraw-Hill, New York, 2005.

31. With the help from Sue Shellenbarger, "Whine-O-Whine: How to Cope with Chronic Complainers." http://blogs.wsj.com/atwork/2012/09/12/whine-o-whine-how-to-cope-with-chronic-complainers/ and Luke Roney, "Don't Let Unhappy Co-Workers Sour You New Job." http://money.usnews.com/money/blogs/outside-voices-careers/2013/08/23/dont-let-unhappy-co-workers-sour-your-new-job (accessed February 8, 2015).

32. Adapted from WikiHow, "How to Look People in the Eye." http://www.wikihow.com/Look-People-in-the-Eye (accessed February 8, 2015).

33. Summarized from Michael Papay and Alexandre Santille, "Disengagement at Work is a Costly and Frustrating Problem. Treating Employees as Humans—Not Experiments – Makes Fixing it a Little Simpler." http://blog.waggl.it/2014/10/the-most-logical-yet-underrated.html??utm_source=streamsend&utm_medium=email&utm_campaign=fc-blog-oct (accessed February 8, 2015).

7

Analysis and Decision-Making

Chapter Takeaways

- ► Good analysis does not substitute for a poor frame
- ► Recognize biases in framing and forming alternatives
- ► Know when to decide—avoid "paralysis by analysis"
- ► Learn when to share decision-making
- ► Understand the "wisdom of the crowd"
- ► Knowing when you don't know what you don't know

All leaders make decisions. Decision-making can involve complex analysis or be as simple as flipping a coin. Either way, there are lots of issues that can prevent us from deciding well. Let's look at the parts of the decision process where problems can occur:

- *Problem*—Choosing and defining the problem to solve
- *Alternatives*—Finding good and unique alternatives to choose from
- *Evaluate Alternatives*—Getting quality information to compare alternatives
- *Make a Decision*—Choosing an alternative based on knowing risk and uncertainty
- *Monitor the Decision*—Implementation and monitoring of results

A mistake in any of these areas will lead to poor problem solving. There are many ways to self-handicap in the problem-solving and deciding process—most are behavioral. Decisions can be made emotionally and

---

without considering enough alternatives or information. Leaders can also make poor decisions because of tunnel vision, trying to appease everyone, or avoiding decision-making because of fear of accountability. Managers make hundreds of decisions a day and cannot analyze all of them well.

A good decision is one that incorporates what an individual or a group knows, where they assess the probability of success for each available outcome, and they stay within the frame of their attitude toward risk. A bad decision is a decision that violates what they want or can afford. For example, buying a lottery ticket can be a good decision if one spends just a dollar or two and he is lucky enough to win, but it becomes a bad decision when one spends much more than he can afford and loses. The individual is relying on luck to beat enormous odds.

Analysis of alternatives is required in most decisions. It can be as simple as standing in a store and looking at four different ladders, analyzing their attributes, and then deciding which one to buy. In business strategy planning, it can take months to accomplish and include large teams of people. In his book, *Introduction to Decision Analysis*, David Skinner breaks this process into three areas: (1) *Structuring*, (2) *Evaluation*, and (3) *Agreement*.[1] *Structuring* involves identifying the problem, assessing the business situation, and generating creative alternatives. During the *evaluation* phase, quantifying the risk and return and determining the value of new information (to determine when to stop evaluating and start deciding) are done. The *agreement* phase is where the course of action is chosen, appropriate resources are allocated, and it is implemented. Having the decision-making body and the project or implementation team work together during this process helps produce more compelling decisions and better implementation.

Impact

Companies, teams, and individuals can all have problems in decision-making—leaders avoiding accountability, changing business models and politics, complexity of problems, decision teams misunderstanding framing (the definition of the problem), risk and uncertainty, and the inability to generate and analyze appropriate alternatives against meaningful criteria. Decision-making becomes difficult in several instances. These are as follows:[2]

- When the real decision-maker is hidden (not on the team) or there are multiple decision-makers

- Objectives are not established and framing is not understood
- Uncertainty and risk are misunderstood
- Unique options are not developed or analyzed
- No clear definition for success is established

The traditional approach to decision-making involves a leader analyzing a situation, proposing a solution based on his assumptions and past experience, and then a team does the cost/benefit analysis, builds a business case, and presents that case to the decision-maker who uses it to justify the decision he has already made. This is very common and you have probably seen it in operation. This approach either hardwires the needs of the politically powerful if the team's result is the same as the decision-maker's or results in endless challenges or requests for more information in order to avoid a decision or any commitment if it does not. This is called *analysis paralysis* and is often used by those above to avoid accountability.

These decision strategies are why so many projects fail in business. Failure to successfully implement change initiatives in organizations is widespread, commonplace, and costly. The average failure rate is 73 percent and has been reported as high as 93 percent.[3] Projects are abandoned about 30 percent of the time and joint ventures are said to fail 61 percent of the time. Poor decision-making in many industries such as healthcare and auto manufacturing can kill people. When so much is known about how to improve decision-making, how to successfully choose a project with a high-expected economic return, and how to apply change management processes to improve implementation, why then do failures persist in such great numbers? The answer is lots of self-handicapping, but it all starts with poor decision analysis and decision-making. Not understanding the process, not framing a problem well so that the wrong problem is solved, continued use of problem solving to avoid accountability, and avoiding risk or uncertainty are all self-handicapping.

There is clear evidence that the decision process used influences decision-making effectiveness and results.[4] Managers who collect information and use decision analysis methods make more effective decisions and have better results than those who do not. Managers who use power and hidden agendas tend to make poorer decisions and their results are inferior to those using a decision analysis process. A company's decision process matters.

Your decisions can always have a large impact—on you, your employees, and your career. Decision-making is an important determinant of your health and well-being across your lifespan—overeating is associated with many diseases. Poor decision-making can upset coworkers with constant mistakes that affect them. Moving up and gaining greater status and responsibility in business are usually based on your ability to conceptualize issues, make decisions, and solve problems. Do it poorly and you will not progress. The key principle remains the same—poor decision analysis leads to bad decisions that can make proper implementation impossible.

The Real Issues

Leaders often self-handicap by not asking the right question—not framing a problem correctly. Framing is how we structure a decision in our minds so we can look for alternatives that fit within that frame. This self-handicapping can result from *not knowing what you don't know* or not paying attention to what you *do* know. Not considering the assumptions being made in framing is clearly self-handicapping in decision analysis and can cause leaders to dive into action without understanding the problem or the range of solutions. We will say this repeatedly—*good analysis will never make up for a poor frame.*

Considering multiple alternatives and not evaluating any of them until the generation process is completed can significantly enhance the value of a final solution. A common mistake in problem solving is that alternatives are evaluated as they are proposed. With this, *satisficing* occurs—you choose the first alternative that comes along that is satisfactory. It is better to develop a range of alternative solutions, define success, fully evaluate all alternatives, and then choose the best one—that is *optimizing* your decision-making. Here is a simple trick. Do not start developing alternatives by opening Excel, start with Word. Too many times people want to get to the "answer" (Excel) rather than generate solutions (Word). Not understanding how to calculate uncertainty and evaluate one's attitude toward risk are major issues in evaluating alternatives.

Making decisions for instant gratification, impulse, selfishness, or to please others—focusing on feelings, rather than facts can all be self-handicapping. Making decisions based on what you want before what is right for the institution and its mission can clearly have negative outcomes for all involved. Ethical judgment requires four distinct psychological processes: (1) moral sensitivity, (2) moral judgment, (3) moral intention, and (4) moral action.[5] Moral sensitivity is a person's ability to recognize that a situation is a moral decision. Moral judgment refers to evaluating which solutions have moral justification. Moral intent is the intention to choose a moral decision over another solution. Moral action refers to an individual's courage, determination, and the ability to follow through with the moral decision. Moral sensitivity is where most people shoot themselves in the foot. For example, not seeing that those who pay you or what is right for a customer take priority or not sharing all of the information you have on an issue so that you are seen to be more valuable to an organization are issues of poor sensitivity. This leads to many decisions being made for selfish reasons.

Other self-handicapping seen in decision-making includes the following:

- a lack of data and alternatives generated by a team
- relying too heavily on recent information or events
- overconfidence
- avoiding using the wisdom of the crowd (decisions made by the elite rather than creating a trusting communication culture)
- knowing when to decide rather than doing continued research (this can lead to perpetual study of a problem rather than reasoned action—analysis paralysis)
- being mired in too much data to make a decision

Information, by its very nature, consumes attention. The more data we have, the more it consumes our processing ability. The more we move data around, the less we have time and ability to think, ponder, and process. There are many ways to self-sabotage decision-making knowingly or unknowingly.

How Is Your Problem Analysis?

Survey: Do I Do Poor Analysis or Not?
(Y = Yes, N = No, DK = Don't Know)

____ Neglect building a mental framework of the decision

____ Do not typically ask for help or a second pair of eyes to avoid biases

____ When I attain valuable information, I don't always pass it along to others for them to use

____ Make decisions on impulse

____ Make decisions aimed at pleasing my boss

____ Surround myself with "yes-people"

___ I understand framing in decision-making

___ Many managers here make decisions based on *their* needs rather than the mission/customer

___ Delay releasing data so I look valuable

___ Usually do not rely on the wisdom of the crowd

___ Often have paralysis from analysis in my team

___ Management does not know how to create boundaries for a decision so the team is all over the place in deciding

___ Most of my decisions are based on good data

___ Sometimes make decisions for my own short-term gratification

___ I rarely question myself regarding what I don't know

___ Prior experience with someone will alter your job progression/promotion—regardless of your qualifications

___ Avoid making a decision by asking for more data/time when you know it won't alter the decision

Scores

13–17 Y's—You are greatly self-handicapping your decision-making.

6–12—You are inconsistent on your approach to good analysis and decision-making.

1–5—You are a good decision analyst and maker.

Now, we have the same question: What was your degree of fudging on these questions? When not sure, did you round up to yes?

What to Do?

Framing

Framing is how we structure a decision in our minds and for others to see. No amount of analysis or comparing alternatives can make up for poor framing. Russo and Schoemaker, in their book *Decision Traps* suggest that everyone must do things to simplify their world because you can never consider all of the information that might be relevant.[6] So, we adopt mental frameworks that simplify and structure the information coming in about a problem.

Stop and think about deciding what car to buy. You own a 10-year old car, which has roughly 150,000 miles on it. It was a good car, but now the repair bills are too high. You have no emotional pull toward any car; you view it as strictly a tool to get from A to B. How do you begin the car-buying decision process? Do you automatically go to a randomly chosen lot to look at cars? Of course not! If you are like most people, you frame your decision based on what you emotionally want, can afford, and/or you actually need at that particular time. You may be after a reliable, fuel efficient sedan that has good 5-year resale value. If you have a large family—it may be a larger SUV-type vehicle. You may be going through a mid-life crises and want a sports car. You begin your process with the outcome in mind. These characteristics go into forming the *frame* of your decision. Once this framework is in place, you can then start accumulating alternatives from within the frame which would be evaluated for a decision. *Here is the dilemma: Because of this, any frame leaves us with only a partial view of the problem.*[7]

Suppose the opposite—you do not have a frame, and decided to go to the car lot. Your decision could be easily manipulated by the salesman because you had no characteristics to tell him you wanted in your new car. Of course, then you wouldn't have to blame yourself for the poor result—you would blame the salesman—which is self-handicapping. *Frame blindness* is setting out to solve the wrong problem because you have created a poor mental framework and lose sight of your objectives.

Framing in a business-setting is similar. Suppose you are trying to decide who should be included to be a mentor in your organization's mentorship program. In order to frame this situation, you must decide what characteristics you are seeking in a mentor, but because you are human, the frame has potential to have flaws or be biased. To understand the importance of framing, try this on your employees: Ask them to brainstorm "ways to increase their productivity." You may not get much. Then try, "ways to make their jobs easier." It is likely you will be inundated with suggestions.[8] Framing is important and is the first self-handicap to avoid in the problem-solving process.

Have you ever been in a team meeting where "one thing led to another" and 45 minutes from when you started you were on a completely different subject and coming up with a solution for something completely different from where you started? This is "solution creep"—when "a problem starts small and then keeps expanding and the boundaries shift until the boundaries are too large for the team to manage."[9] The effect of this is a lack of focus on what is truly the important decision to make. In your framing, keep the scope of your analysis appropriate to the situation at hand. It's better to make a good decision on a small scale than make an irrelevant one on a larger scale. *A problem well framed is a problem half solved.*

Beyond Framing

After a problem is framed, one has to gather information and possible solutions, come to a conclusion/chose an alternative, and audit the results.[10] Russo and Schoemaker, in their book *Decision Traps* propose several decision traps beyond having a problem properly framed.[11] All are self-imposed:

- Assuming that with a lot of smart people involved in a team, good choices will automatically follow.

- Not adequately examining the assumptions being made in the analysis process.

- Believing you can keep all the information in your head rather than follow a systematic procedure to make a final choice.

- Failing to interpret feedback correctly because you are protecting your ego.

- Failing to keep systematic reference records or otherwise auditing your decision process.

While likely to outperform individuals, groups are not superhuman. Conflict can arise as well as other biases, such as groupthink. Groupthink is allowing a group's internal cohesiveness to dominate the decision-making process.[12] Ideas that conflict with the group's preconceptions get little attention. Because of this, group facilitation is often required for effective group decision-making. If you find yourself in a mismanaged decision-making group, make sure you understand the leader's frame, try to communicate to the group or group leader—regardless of any pressure to the contrary—that you believe the frame may not be appropriate, and try to stay tactful and positive.[13]

Analyzing Decision Alternatives

Making a decision implies that there are alternative choices and you have a method for evaluating them.[14] A wide range of possible solutions allows you to choose the best—a choice from one possible solution is not a choice. One of the errors commonly made in generating alternatives is to create iterations of alternatives already listed. Skinner calls this "variations on a theme." When this occurs, it is time to quit and start analyzing the alternatives generated.

There are many techniques for generating alternatives. For example:

- **Brainstorming** can be done individually or in a group and requires participants to be free to "think out loud" and blurt out as many ideas as possible.

- **Surveys** economically tap the ideas of a large group of respondents.

- **Public Posting** of the problem to generate a wide array of solutions from more than direct stakeholders.

When evaluating alternative courses of action, if an alternative is not doable, then it is not an alternative and should not be considered. Only the differences between alternatives that are relevant should be discussed and evaluated. And that is true for future events;[15] the results of alternatives used in the past are known, so only the future should be evaluated. Therefore, alternative evaluation involves subjective and uncertain assessments because it deals with future events. Issues like product sales, forecasts, or the actions of competitors are often very difficult to determine because of uncertainty.

When evaluating alternatives you are always dealing with uncertainty, ambiguity, and risk, as well as deciding when to stop gathering more information. Nearly all important decisions we make involve *uncertainty* which is a lack of a clear understanding of the future. It is something that is unknown or not perfectly known. *Ambiguity* is a lack of clarity about goals and outcomes that impact the value and choice between alternatives. *Risk* is the severity of the consequences of a decision. Ambiguity can be resolved before a decision has to be made, whereas uncertainty and risk can only be resolved over time and after the decision is made.

Sorting out the ambiguities from the uncertainties will begin to structure the decision process. Ambiguities include the criteria used to evaluate alternatives, what outcomes will determine success of the project/strategy, what experts to use and what to ask, and who should be involved in the decision and implementation. Uncertainty includes the likelihood that a project will make money, how long before there is a return on investment, and what is the real value of the deal/project anyway. There is uncertainty about which prize to play for in any game. Uncertainty can be measured in evaluation of alternatives by asking experts to state their level of confidence (I am 80 percent sure it will happen; I am 20 percent sure it will happen). This is done in your weather forecast every evening. When rain is forecast at 50 percent or greater, you may decide to carry an umbrella. At 100 percent, you may choose to stay home. Attitude toward risk can also be measured and factored into alternative evaluation.

Most traditional decision-making processes are not equipped to adequately deal with ambiguity and uncertainty.[16] Uncertainty in problem solving means you are risking value—you do not know the future and cannot say what will add value in the future, while ambiguity means you are risking time—indecisiveness and avoiding accountability are each a waste of valuable time. What is even worse is to fall into the habit of *dealing with neither*. Where uncertainty leads to intuitive "gut feel" decisions by leaders, ambiguity often leads to one person making a power play or the team deciding to "just do it" to move things along. Being in a state of uncertainty and ambiguity simultaneously will lead to *analysis paralysis* where no decision is made. Complex decision analysis models such as that proposed by Skinner deal with these issues and the enhanced problem-solving process produces better decisions and better outcomes.[17] But is not simple or quick—there is a tradeoff.

Uncertainty is a fact of life in business. Many leaders tend to ignore uncertainty rather than deal with it; much less use it to their advantage. Every analysis made requires us to make some assumptions about the risks involved. The key is whether you are making explicit assumptions using probability, or making uninformed guesses. While there are some situations where a team may have all the information, most decisions require the subjective opinions and information from experts. Experts have the ability to make clearer distinctions between alternatives. If the identified expert cannot provide these powerful distinctions, then you need to find another expert. Most analyses are a refinement of information already known—budgets, operating expenses—but you can use probability judgments from experts to reduce uncertainty. [18]

Quit Stalling—Decide Already!

Once the alternatives have been generated and evaluated for uncertainty and risk, the next step is analyzing the value of new information in the decision.[19] Often when a group is involved in making a decision there is a diffusion of accountability—no one wants to stand up and say, "let's decide." This is giving in to the ambiguity of the situation—"analysis paralysis"—and it is the leader's responsibility to eliminate this—without bias or personal gain. This is done by calculating the value or lack of value of new information. When you gather information for the first time on a situation, many good things happen—you become more educated on the topic, you feel as if you can make a more informed decision, etc. But then, there is a little voice in your head that says, "If this data is good, even more should be better, right?" You go out and gather more data, and more, and even more. There is such a thing as having too much data; there is also a point when more data adds no new knowledge. Meanwhile, back on the ranch, people are waiting for you to make a decision. Will having more marginal data significantly change your decision? Nine times out of ten—no. If new information will not change your mind then it has no value and you should just make the decision.

People like to pretend that a situation is more complex than it really is. As a leader, one of your tasks is to simplify the complex (as much as possible).[20] The leader must work to reduce ambiguity in the process; sometimes a team can wallow in the chaos of a problem situation. Look at the data that you have already collected. Is the data collected directly related to the decision at hand? Does it relate to the objectives and strategies of the organization? Is it adding value?

Why Don't You

Why Don't You Frame a Problem Well?

Expediency in Framing

Sometimes untying the handicap of poor framing can be as simple as not accepting the first frame that comes to mind.[21] It is best to try to determine if the frame needs to be broadened. Members of a team can individually construct their own frames. Once this is complete, they can share and see how similar or different their frames are. If alone in the decision, one can follow the same spirit as multiple frameworks—try to construct frameworks that are based on different perspectives to the situation—boss, customer, and employees. Saving time in framing is always self-handicapping.

People's emotional responses to events are quite often influenced by "what might have been." If you won too many trophies as a kid, you may expect to be the winner every time you try—an issue with some millennials. This kind of a frame will make you feel like a real loser when you come in second. If you were thinking about how great it would be to just "place," then second is good, not horrible. If in your organization whatever problem you and the team are facing is the most important and critical ever, slow up and get dispassionate in your problem solving as much as possible.

We often want to rush through framing. We want to jump right into finding solutions. This is like driving without checking the map first or asking for directions—something many of us men do routinely. Rushing into decision-making without the preliminaries of good problem format is reduced effort that is self-handicapping. It is best to solve the right problem and stay out of the ERO Spiral.

Even in slow mode, some leaders simply don't know enough about the complexities of problem solving to do a good job. The authors think part of the fault is on schools who teach problem solving as a simple 5–8 step process in one lecture in one course. They often compound this by making all problems financial or focus on past data. We think problem analysis is such a complex and important task deserves its own class. Please realize that unless you have been through more extensive training in decision-making and analysis, you probably should go seek more information. We suggest *MindTools* (http://www.mindtools.com/pages/main/newMN_TED.htm), Skinner, *Introduction to Decision Analysis*, Probabilistic Publishing, 3rd ed., Gainsville, FL, 2009, and *Tools for Decision Analysis* (http://home.ubalt.edu/ntsbarsh/business-stat/opre/partIX.htm). Click on "problem solving" and "decision-making."

What poor framing of yours comes from expediency?

Avoidance in Framing

Perceptual biases occur when we are in avoidance. A few biases to eliminate when framing a situation are—conformation bias, the mere-exposure effect, and the halo effect. Revisiting the car-buying example—do you favor one brand of car because you intrinsically believe that car is better? In other words, did your father continually define FORD as, "First on race day" or "Fix or repair daily" as you were growing up. That would cause a confirmation bias. *Conformation bias* nudges you to construct your framework to favor information that confirms your beliefs. For example, it may artificially lesson the importance of gas mileage because of your belief that a certain car brand is better. Because of this, you may be overconfident in your decisions. Surrounding yourself with people that want to agree with you all the time, or "yes-men," can have this effect. If you don't have people to catch your biases, you run the risk of being overconfident in your decisions.

The *mere-exposure effect* is when you prefer things because you are familiar with them. Managers evaluating two alternatives (of similar utility) who pick the one that they are most familiar with commit this error. Suppose two of your staff members are in line for a mentorship—Jan and Sue. Jan is slightly more qualified for the mentorship, but you are familiar with Sue's work and she is in your "in-group." Because you have had prior experience with Sue—you choose her over the more-qualified Jan. This can be a severe problem in employee selection. When interviewing candidates, one candidate may look and act just like you—same experiences, same attitudes, and maybe even went to the same school you did. This candidate will feel very comfortable and you are likely to select him over other potentially more qualified candidates.

Lastly, the *halo effect* is a bias in which an overall impression of a person on one dimension (important to you) influences other sub-characteristics. Many managers have a staff member who in their eyes can do no wrong. When time comes for the annual performance review, the manager will give high ratings on all factors regardless of actual performance because he trusts the individual and any problems with this period are really only an aberration. This is halo and it is difficult to see when it occurs.

By definition, when you bias your own decisions, you are ignoring or avoiding pieces of information—consciously or subconsciously.[22] In order to minimize this problem, recruit others to take the opposite view that you are taking. This "devil's advocate" approach may present evidence that you either neglected or devalued. Of course, you both have to be open to this.

What poor framing of yours comes from avoidance?

Apprehension in Framing

Managers often miss the basic premise of framing. A tightly structured frame will generate energy; a wide-open one will drain it. Creative people won't stay in a frame and those seeking to avoid accountability cause trouble with wide open frames because they keep others fearful and not speaking up. A solution is for everyone to write problem statements summarizing the challenge and likely outcomes. Have everyone in the team write one and compare. Then rewrite them until everyone in the team agrees that the statement describes success as well as the most likely outcome of doing nothing. This hones the frame and keeps one leader or outspoken person from dominating. That strong decision-maker can be focused on an idea based on superficial, unreliable, or inaccurate information. This is called *anchoring*. Without others' opinions, anchoring causes rushing too fast into decision-making and skipping problem solving.

One important thing to learn is that framing radically changes how we perceive risk and this can be self-handicapping. Tversky and Kahneman showed that people will value a certain gain more than a probable gain with an equal or greater expected value and the opposite is true for losses.[23] For instance, imagine that the United States is preparing for the outbreak of an unusual Asian disease, which is expected to kill 600 people. Assume that the exact scientific estimates of the consequences of the two programs proposed to fight the disease are as follows:

> **Program A:** If Program A is adopted, 200 people will be saved (72 percent).

Program B: If Program B is adopted, there is one-third probability that 600 people will be saved, and two-third probability that no people will be saved (28 percent).

The majority of people (numbers in parentheses) in this problem were risk averse—the prospect of saving 200 lives with certainty was more promising than the probability of a one-in-three chance of saving 600 lives. Yet each proposal has the same expected result.

A second group of respondents were given the same story, but were provided with different program options.

Program C: If Program C is adopted 400 people will die (22 percent).

Program D: If Program D is adopted there is one-third probability that nobody will die, and two-third probability that 600 people will die (78 percent).

The majority of respondents in the second problem chose risk taking—the certain death of 400 people is less acceptable than the two-in-three chance that 600 people will die. *Gains and losses are evaluated from a subjective reference point and this point of view can be manipulated by how the problem is presented.* Haphazard presentation of a frame or manipulated presentation are both very self-handicapping.

A similar effect is the "sunk-cost fallacy"—continuing to fund a failing project. People are generally reluctant to accept a sure loss, and are therefore, willing to make unsound bets in the hopes of breaking even. They keep "throwing good money after bad." Where this is important in framing is that leaders let their sunk costs become part of the frame and therefore part of the problem-solving process. Sunk costs are just that—gone. They have no bearing on any future decision and should not be worried about or used in framing.

What poor framing of yours comes from apprehension?

_____

_____

Self-Deception in Framing

A decision-maker who is overconfident may find it difficult to seek advice and consult others. Overconfidence stems from previous decisions that had only positive outcomes. It also is caused by giving managers a set of numbers or test results—numbers create anchoring in teams. The use of probabilities and bringing in the soft issues (such as what people will do) into the equation will also cause it. Your tools to avoid overconfidence should be the concept of expected value (the sum of the probabilities associated with an event or set of events times the value of each event) and decision trees (see the learning opportunities mentioned earlier for more on this). Managerial optimism can result in all kinds of flawed and risky decisions. Optimism and confidence can both be carried to excess in framing.

Mindsets are used all the time to bias people's thinking and decision-making—beyond manipulating their sense of risk—on purpose. This is a form of self-deception. Think of the term "tax relief" as used by a politician.[24] Said over and over again, it produces an image of taxes being an affliction that needs relief—just give it a pill and all will be better. And the pill giver becomes a hero. Then we get, "tax relief will create jobs," which quantifies the relief so it can be measured. After a while, you would have to be very mean spirited—almost a crazy—not to support "tax relief." If leadership's aim is to drive employee opinion, biasing like this may be a regular feature of organizational communication—as it is in politics every day. It becomes a cultural artifact and very self-handicapping.

Another thing many managers don't realize is that smaller, shorter frames cause problem solutions to come faster. If you can find a faster way to fail, recover, and try again; it helps break self-deception in framing and problem solving. If the problem you are trying to solve involves creating a "one pill" cure for all cancer, you are solving problems way too large and requiring too much time.

Here's what to remember:[25]

- **Be Aware of Your Frame**—Write down the issue being addressed. Determine the boundaries that you are using and what you may have left out. Ask if there are other possible frames. Ask yourself what the assessments are to measure success.

- **Select Your Decision Frame**—Don't let it select you. Generate alternative frames, evaluate them, and select the most appropriate one. Define your frame in more ways than one. Do not be unduly influenced by the frame of others.

- **Feel Free to Reframe When You Find Yourself Using an Inadequate Frame**—Challenge the frame that you are using by seeking other opinions in brainstorming or thinking in different ways.

- **Understand Others' Frames**—Good communicators align their message with their listeners' frames and salespeople try to figure out which frame is being used by a customer for a purchasing decision.

  And remember, no amount or quality of alternative generation or analysis can make up for a poor frame.

What poor framing of yours comes from some form of self-deception?

_____

_____

Why Don't You Generate and Analyze Alternatives Well?

Expediency in Analysis

Lack of tools to analyze alternatives can never be used as an excuse for doing it poorly because MindTools lists and describes 40 different tools.[26] Managers are often good at fooling themselves about feedback and fail to interpret the evidence for what it really says. Believing they can keep all the information straight in their heads rather than following a systematic or statistical procedure when comparing alternatives will always lead to trouble. Relying on experience alone rather than expert opinion can cause poor analysis.

Intuition, rules of thumb, tradition, and experience are no longer sufficient for analyzing decisions made by today's managers. There is a need for much more complex decision-making at all levels in organizations. That need is filled by decision analysis which is a technique that provides quantitative support for the decision-makers. Our intent is not to teach you decision analysis here but to have you see that lack of understanding it is self-handicapping. We refer you to the links and books listed previously.[27]

What poor analysis of yours comes from expediency?

_____

_____

Avoidance in Analysis

Many leaders want to *please the boss* and make decisions that would look good to him. Because of that, they can bias alternative generation, evaluation, and the final decision. Managers go along with their bosses because no one wants to be labeled a "non-team player." This can lead to decisions being made where all the moral ground is wrong. Sometimes managers are self-centered and make decisions for themselves over the organization. This is a tough one for two reasons: (1) If a manager is self-centered and blind to organizational goals and rules, usually the best solution is to simply get rid of the person. Yet, sometimes you can't get rid of them—a physician who is a top admitter in a hospital, tenured in education, or being a top executive. (2) Most of us don't want to be the person to turn someone else in and get them punished or fired.

Illegal activity can jeopardize a department or an organization. Self-centered management can rob an institution of its goals and finances so that eventually competitors overtake it. Allowing this kind of management to bias problem analysis is self-handicapping.

If you find that you have to talk yourself into something, it is usually a less ethical decision. Think about how you will feel when you are retired—will you know you did some good for society?

Following these simple guidelines will likely prevent someone from accusing you of making selfish or unethical decisions.[28] Ask yourself:

- Does this decision help the people in my organization?
- Does this decision help the organization?
- Does this decision help the organization's customers?
- Can you defend the merits of this decision for all stakeholders involved?
- Does this decision provide any unfair advantage to any group or person?
- Do I feel any need to hide this decision?
- Does this decision ultimately give the organization credibility and health?

An organization with a culture of "yes people," perpetuates this problem because no one is challenging decisions. There is little diversity of opinion. Yet, diversity of opinion is where all of the solutions to untying biases, making decisions on impulse, and poor framing begin. The likelihood of you making a decision on impulse is lessened when you have others taking the contrarian viewpoint on situations. Biases can be lessened by having multiple viewpoints to counteract halo effects and confirmation biases. Diversity of opinion can also prevent poor framing. By having diverse people on the team to create and edit frameworks, and analyze alternatives, we get a more accurate perception of reality.

What poor analysis of yours comes from avoidance?

_____

_____

Apprehension in Analysis

Risk affects framing, but it also affects analysis of alternatives. Everyone has an attitude toward risk taking—even after framing—neutral, averse, and risk seeking. The work of Tversky and Kahneman is important in analysis, as it is in framing, because it showed that people's attitudes toward the risks concerning gains may be quite different than their attitudes toward risks concerning losses.[29] When given a choice between getting $1000 with certainty or having a 50 percent chance of gaining $2500, those who are risk averse will choose the certain $1000. Risk seeking people, when confronted with a certain loss of $1000 versus a 50 percent chance of no loss or a $2500 loss often choose the risky alternative. This is not necessarily irrational but it is important for analysts to recognize that attitude toward risk affects how people analyze alternatives.

When a team decides to collect more information or form a subgroup to do more study, it can be a self-handicap of fearing accountability. Skinner provides a set of statistical and graphical steps to determine the value of new information, but anyone can *look at additional data being generated and make a subjective calculation that it is not adding value.*[30] Without statistically calculating the worth of information a team can still:

- Acknowledge that it is just about exhausted the search for alternatives and it may be time to decide.
- Poll the members to see if there are any other alternatives or sources of new information to help choose an alternative.
- Determine if alternatives coming in are actually new.
- Informally calculate what new information might add.

Why do we not do these things? The answer for risk averse individuals—it may be that asking for more data postpones stepping outside of their comfort zone or being accountable. To the average person, being judged on the outcome of a decision is a scary thing—so why not delay it if it does not hurt the department? Sometimes things just go away if a decision can be avoided.

What poor analysis of yours comes from apprehension?

Self-Deception in Analysis

Fear of failure or loss of control are fears that cause decision-makers to consider the wrong kinds of alternatives or to rely too heavily on the status quo. These often move into a self-deception that doing nothing is a safer course of action. Certainly, the status quo should always be considered a viable option, but adhering to it out of fear or spent costs will limit options and compromise effective decision-making. These issues are why you hear so much discussion of "exit strategies" in international politics. An *exit strategy* is a means of "leaving one's current situation, either after a predetermined objective has been achieved, or as a strategy to mitigate failure."[31] At worst, an exit strategy will save face; at best, it will peg a withdrawal to the achievement of an objective that is worth more than the cost of continued involvement." Every decision team should have an exit strategy for analysis.

Most leaders think from the lens of their background. For example, if a problem is being worked by production and finance types, they may not think heavily in people problems and most alternatives will be production processes and tools or financial remedies. Yet, when the decision is made and it moves into implementation, the likelihood is very high that "people problems" will be what causes failure (because they were not adequately reviewed in the decision phase). Analyze your team and determine which viewpoint is missing. Focus toward that or find someone to represent that viewpoint. Use the *product, planning, potential,* and *people (4Ps)* as the basis for gathering different perspectives.

Remember "variations on a theme"—that is, breaking alternatives down into different versions of the same thing. This can be self-deception if you are adding alternatives to compare, but in reality, you are adding little value. Leaders should try to bring creativity, deeper thinking, and different perspectives to a problem analysis, but watch where this leads. MindTools is a great source for tools to help generate alternatives.[32]

We have not discussed it in this book, but *appreciative inquiry* forces you to look at a problem based on what's "going right," rather than what's "going wrong."[33] What is common to most of us is to approach an issue as a "problem," focus on the things that aren't working, and generate alternatives to fix it. Appreciative inquiry tries to shift to a positive perspective, look at the things that are working, and build on them. In some situations this can be very powerful. It builds on some of the same logic as *Strength Finders* that we suggest in Chapter 4, Self Awareness. Appreciative inquiry can cut through some self-deception.

Creativity in problem solving can produce innovative solutions, but can also be self-deceiving.[34] When we search for other people's ideas, search literature, adapt, change, or combine ideas for a particular problem, we can get too enamored with our creativity. Generating alternatives often requires an open atmosphere so that divergent or lateral thinking, inspiration, and innovation can occur and it is okay to jump back and forth between analytical problem solving and creative, imaginative and wild thinking. But, don't go too far. For more on creativity in problem solving, go to http://www.mindtools.com/, and at the bottom of the homepage, click on "practical creativity."

What poor analysis of yours comes from self-deception?

Behaviors to Change

Not Knowing What You Don't Know

Recognize

What we don't know may be as important as what we do know. There are no simple solutions for these situations, but recognizing that the problem exists is the first step.[35] To think or pretend you know something when you do not is self-handicapping. It can be undiscussed—when a young manager goes on about something he knows little about, few will jump in and correct him. This can be embarrassing—mostly, the group rolls their eyes and makes fun of him later when he is not around. Another example is when leaders associate with people that have the same backgrounds and make the same assumptions without exploring the consequences of the assumptions made in framing or analysis.

To make it even worse, not knowing what you don't know is a habit for some people. It is self-delusion and can be very handicapping. Keep forcing yourself to ask a series of "what if" questions that make you think about new possibilities. Keep questioning yourself and your organization. Look at the opinions on the periphery of your team—that is where the dissenting views are—you may have to force yourself to do this. Business is in a constant state of change and the change that is counter to what is comfortable is often ignored. Reading about "disruptive innovation"[36] at christenseninstitute.org will be helpful.

Admit

Overconfidence will delude anyone into believing they know more than they actually do. Daniel Willingham explains why many students think they've studied well[37]—and then later bomb the examination. The difference is that students confuse familiarity with recollection. Being able to recognize the correct answer is not the same as being able to reproduce the correct answer with no prompt. Smart learners understand that feelings of familiarity are often deceptive and they use tools to better understand what they know and don't know more accurately. The simplest of such tools is self-testing where the complete answer is replicated. Teaching others and reciting explanations out loud are also ways to help see how much you understand about an idea. Articulation is a difficult task, so a weakness in your knowledge gets exposed quickly. We suggest training others—you cannot teach what you yourself do not understand.

Adjust

Russo and Schoemaker, in their book *Decision Traps*, suggest two traps having to do with not knowing what you don't know.[38] These are: (1) Failing to collect key information because you're too sure of your assumptions and opinions, and (2) Using shortsighted shortcuts in decision-making—relying inappropriately on "rules of thumb" or anchoring too much on readily available or convenient information. Virtually all people put too much trust in their own opinions; always ask for other experts' opinions. People also have a fondness for evidence that confirms, rather than challenges, their current beliefs. Have the discipline to seek information that may disconfirm your opinions. If you look for it and can't find it, you have reason to be confident; if you don't look for it, you could be wrong. Explicitly developing a good frame for your decision is a partial antidote to overconfidence in your judgment. Remember the old saying, "The more you learn, the more you realize you don't know."

Key Behaviors

Here are the key behaviors for what you don't know:

1. Be humble, ask 5 "what if" questions outlined in Chapter 1.
2. Always question your frame and analysis tools.
3. Do not pretend to know—if you can't recreate it, you don't know.
4. Question yourself and your organization.
5. Seek information that disconfirms your opinion.
6. Only then, say you *may* know.

Being Risk Averse

Recognize

There's an old saying that money managers use—"be risk diverse, not risk averse."[39] That is because you cannot make any money without taking *some* risk, but excessive risk can be disastrous. In reality you should aim to be risk neutral with an even mix of high-risk and low-risk investments—we have all heard we should "diversify our portfolio." What is often self-handicapping in problem solving is a manager or team that is consistently risk averse. This pushes the team toward the status quo and avoids possible innovative and creative solutions. Your aim in decision-making should be to be risk neutral. A team should be balanced with risk-friendly and risk-averse individuals, and the leader must make sure all are heard. Higher risk does not mean putting all your eggs in one basket or gambling—the definition of a good decision included "what you can afford."

Admit

Tory Higgins suggests managers are risk averse because they tend to see their goals as opportunities to maintain the status quo and keep things running smoothly.[40] Higgins calls this a prevention focus—a fear of being optimistic, making mistakes, and taking chances. These performance goals are a major factor in self-handicapping. While prevention-focused people are more likely to behave ethically and honestly, they do not focus on opportunities to make progress or be innovative. Even worse, when the status quo becomes unacceptable—when actually in danger of loss—and when a risky option is the only way to eliminate that loss, managers can put all their eggs in a very risky basket with high potential for even greater loss.

Adjust

If you feel you are risk averse, make a list of things that you would want to do if you weren't so risk-averse, and try to do one a week. It can be anything from trying a new place for lunch, doing something completely different on weekends, talking to a strange person, or visiting a department of the company where you have never been. And, stop describing yourself as "risk averse." That will be your first baby step. Remember that self-talk will drive behavior. Be courageous and start with little risks. You can become risk tolerant. Part of that process is to see beyond the risk to the possible rewards and the other is to see the obstacles so you can plan for them. You can take a short quiz and determine your investment risk tolerance at http://money.cnn.com/quizzes/retirement/risk-tolerance/index.html.

Key Behaviors
Here are the key behaviors for overcoming being risk averse:

1. Make a list of where you act in a risk averse way.
2. Pick one or two you may wish to change—your baby step.

3. List why you are risk averse—your fears.
4. Look beyond the risk and list the positive outcomes.
5. List the obstacles to those outcomes.
6. Develop a plan to manage or overcome those obstacles.
7. Take the risk and monitor the results.

Sharing Decision-Making

Recognize

Without data from the people a decision will impact—results will often fail. Meet Cindy who is the branch manager at a bank. One day, higher administration within the bank told Cindy to implement a new policy mandating that they increase their loan production via cold calls. Several weeks later, an influx of resignation letters from the branch tellers came in. The decision that was made by the administration did not take into consideration the feelings (and fears) of those the decision would affect (tellers enjoyed the service aspect but not cold-call selling). Leaders do not always inherently know individual processes, implications, or workflows of the population in which a decision is meant to impact. The outcome of these missteps typically results in creating, at best, more rework and, at worst, a more problematic situation.

Admit

For these situations, there is no special tool to use. It only involves getting people at different levels of management involved in the decision-making process. Specifically, you should aim to involve the people that will be affected the most by the decision. You never really know how things work on a microscale until you ask or involve those people. Ideas, thoughts, and concerns arise that you haven't thought about before.

Adjust

One of the best ways to decide how your people should be involved in the decision-making process is to use the Vroom and Yetton Normative Model.[41] Taking people away from their work to participate in decision-making creates empowerment, but when unnecessary it is costly. The Vroom-Yetton Model enables a leader to determine at which level of involvement to engage employees. Understanding the degree of participation you need from your employees is affected by four main factors:

1. Decision quality is the information needed to make the decision available to the manager. Is there a "right" solution?

2. Subordinate commitment is how important is it that your team and others buy into the decision?

3. Employee motivation is if the decision is delegated, will the team make a decision acceptable to the leader?

4. Time constraints are how much time do you have to make the decision?

Key Behaviors

This model identifies a series of questions (Figure 7.1 is a simplified version of these) about the nature of the problem; the answers can be used to choose among five leadership styles. The styles range from little time used (top) to much time devoted (bottom). The leadership styles are as follows:

1. *Tell* (A1)—The leader uses the information he has and makes the decision.

2. *Sell* (A2)—The leader seeks specific information and once he has it, makes the decision (*Sell*).

3. *Consult* (C1)—The leader individually ask employees their opinion, however, he still makes the decision.

4. *Join* (C2)—The team gets together as a group to discuss the situation, and offer suggestions, but the leader still makes the decision.

5. *Delegate* (G2)—The leader and the team makes a decision together and his role is as a facilitator.

To use Figure 7.1, identify the problem situation in which you are trying to decide the level of involvement. For each of the yes/no questions, your answer will take you through the decision tree to the appropriate leadership style(s).[42]

The idea behind the Vroom-Yetton Model is that no one leadership style or decision-making process fits all situations. The leader must analyze the situation based on time, employee buy-in, and decision quality to decide which style best fits the situation. Try the model out now—choose an upcoming decision at work and follow the diagram. After using it for a while, you'll quickly get a feel for the right approach to use in most situations and it will become second nature quickly.

Other hints on empowering employee participation in decision-making include the following:[43]

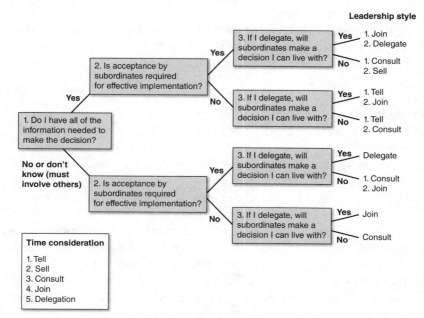

Figure 7.1 Vroom and Yetton Normative Model

- Establish decision-making parameters for various levels of employees. Not all employees should have equal authority for every single decision.

- Training sessions work—your employees can't be empowered if they're not properly trained on all aspects of the business and making decisions about it.

- Teach your employees the lifetime value of a customer. A big part of this training involves educating your employees about how much business a customer has given or could give the company in the future.

- Trust is the foundation for any type of functional relationship.

- Reward your employees for contributing valuable information.

The Wisdom of the Crowd

Recognize

Think about your history of decision-making; once a decision was made, did it ever fail during the implementation phase? If so, there may have been information missing in the framing or analysis of the decision or the ground troops felt devalued. Ultimately, these are self-handicapping all around and often cause implementation failure. In order to get the best data to support your decision analysis, you need to involve the people closest to the impact of the decision and those who are in charge of implementation.

Admit

While it would be easy to say that the decision-making team and the implementation team must be at the same table—this is not enough. The implementation team's voice has to be heard on specific issues. The implementation team can provide valuable information as to expected time to completion, confirmation of financial costs, alternatives to project structuring, and resistance. These are the factors that cause project failure. An example of failing to involve all players can be seen in numerous hospitals and healthcare systems with their implementations of electronic medical records. While counted as a solution to help curb medical costs, improve quality, and better coordinate care—often there is insufficient funding for implementation, key people are not trained, physicians are not involved, and other vital elements are missed. Implementation is made more difficult.

The "wisdom of the crowd" is a process to elicit opinions of a group of lower power individuals rather than a single individual or an elite crowd. This concept is based on James Surowiecki's book, *The Wisdom of Crowds*.[44] Surowiecki argues that crowds are better than experts at diagnosing and solving problems. But, not all crowds are equally wise. To be wise, crowds have to meet four necessary conditions: (1) *Diversity of opinion*—each person should have private information, (2) *Independence*—people's opinions are not determined by the opinions of those around them, (3) *Decentralization*—people specialize and draw on local knowledge, and (4) *Aggregation*—some type of mechanism exists to arrive at collective judgments (like an anonymous survey). There is considerable value in using the "wisdom of the crowd" for predicting the likelihood of implementation or strategy failures. Each person has unique information about the subject matter and lower level employees, often not heard, have specialized knowledge.[45] By taking into account the average opinion of the crowd—those in the know and who must implement—a better decision can be reached. Some recent popular examples of tools that use the wisdom of the crowd include Wikipedia and Yahoo Answers.

Another popular example of the wisdom of the crowd can be seen on TV every weekday. For decades, the "Price is Right" has been captivating audiences in the United States and around the world. When a contestant goes onstage and the price guessing game is presented to them—what happens? A great majority of them look at the audience intently to get their opinion on whether a pair of men's and women's matching watches is above $200, or maybe $300, or maybe even $500. What does this tell us? It tells us that no matter how large the ego of the contestant is onstage, or how much he knows, when he has 300 opinions in the audience, why not let them weigh-in? Even if the contestant has a pretty good idea about how much a new flat screen TV is, it would be nice to get confirmation from those other audience members. Relating this to the workplace, by using the wisdom of the crowd, you could predict success or failure of a decision, or use the crowd as confirmation of leadership's opinions about alternatives being analyzed.

Adjust

Decker and his colleagues showed that there are over 60 "critical failure factors" that can help predict implementation success or failure in complex projects.[46] Assessing these factors as markers for failure using the wisdom of the crowd can reduce project/strategy implementation failure and the resulting costs of interventions to correct problems in implementation. Potential failure can be predicted by measuring employees' and managers' aggregate assessments about the presence or absence of factors, which could cause failure of a project or strategy. The simplest operationalization of this is to implement a survey administered using a web-based survey tool. This data collection should be confidential and anonymous, allowing each vested individual to employ his unique perspective, independent of other's opinion, and allow for aggregation by group in order to gain a collective wisdom about potential "critical failure factors" in a project or strategy. Examples of failure factor questions are presented below. The results can be graphically depicted in a bar chart or radar diagram.

- *Hard Work/No Fun*—I don't think people here like all the extra, added work that comes with a new change effort.

- *IT Not in Place*—It seems like IT never keeps up with new changes here.

- *Employee Resistance*—I expect the employees to resist any new strategies we try to implement.

- *Performance Indicators Not Aligned to Change*—The metrics measured in our organization are usually not the ones needed to support change efforts.

We argue strongly for engagement and open communication in other chapters, and this is more of the same. We strongly believe that your crowd at work is a wise crowd if handled properly and it should always be used to help determine solutions to problems that rely on their help to implement. To do anything else, given the ease of collecting this information, is clearly self-handicapping.

Key Behaviors

The key behaviors for using the wisdom of the crowd are as follows:

1. For a given project, program, or strategy to be implemented, determine the crowd that would have a diversity of private opinion about it—typically managers and employees.

2. List the failure factors that could be an issue. If in doubt, include all (see Note # 44).

3. Make sure each in this crowd has local, direct knowledge of the organization and project.

4. Make sure their opinions will not be determined by the opinions of those around them—usually done by an anonymous, confidential survey.

5. Determine the statistics used for aggregation. It can be as simple as the percentage of those saying, "strongly agree" to "strongly disagree."

6. Determine how you will feed the aggregated data back to the participants.

7. Collect the data.

Final Personal Takeaways

Action Plan—Decision Analysis

Let's see what you want to do about these poor analysis actions.

Decision Analysis Self-Handicap	What Is the Situation?	Trigger	Impact on Others	What to Do/When?
Defining a frame objectively and thoroughly		__Expedient __Avoiding __Fear __Self-deception		__Deliberate action____ __Self-efficacy_____ __Face it_____ __Look and listen_____

continued

Decision Analysis Self-Handicap	What Is the Situation?	Trigger	Impact on Others	What to Do/When?
Select a decision frame and try other frames to help make sure it is a good frame		__Expedient __Avoiding __Fear __Self-deception		__Deliberate action____ __Self-efficacy_____ __Face it_____ __Look and listen_____
Reframe when you find yourself using an inadequate frame		__Expedient __Avoiding __Fear __Self-deception		__Deliberate action____ __Self-efficacy_____ __Face it_____ __Look and listen_____
Understand other's frames		__Expedient __Avoiding __Fear __Self-deception		__Deliberate action____ __Self-efficacy_____ __Face it_____ __Look and listen_____
Keeping information in your head rather than a systematic procedure		__Expedient __Avoiding __Fear __Self-deception		__Deliberate action____ __Self-efficacy_____ __Face it_____ __Look and listen_____
Assuming group automatically makes good choices		__Expedient __Avoiding __Fear __Self-deception		__Deliberate action____ __Self-efficacy_____ __Face it_____ __Look and listen_____
Generating and analyzing alternatives		__Expedient __Avoiding __Fear __Self-deception		__Deliberate action____ __Self-efficacy_____ __Face it_____ __Look and listen_____
Assessing uncertainty and risk		__Expedient __Avoiding __Fear __Self-deception		__Deliberate action____ __Self-efficacy_____ __Face it_____ __Look and listen_____
Being risk averse		__Expedient __Avoiding __Fear __Self-deception		__Deliberate action____ __Self-efficacy_____ __Face it_____ __Look and listen_____

continued

Decision Analysis Self-Handicap	What Is the Situation?	Trigger	Impact on Others	What to Do/When?
Failing to interpret feedback correctly		__Expedient __Avoiding __Fear __Self-deception		__Deliberate action____ __Self-efficacy_____ __Face it_____ __Look and listen_____
Failing to keep systematic records		__Expedient __Avoiding __Fear __Self-deception		__Deliberate action____ __Self-efficacy_____ __Face it_____ __Look and listen_____
Deciding when to decide		__Expedient __Avoiding __Fear __Self-deception		__Deliberate action____ __Self-efficacy_____ __Face it_____ __Look and listen_____
Making decisions for all the wrong reasons		__Expedient __Avoiding __Fear __Self-deception		__Deliberate action____ __Self-efficacy_____ __Face it_____ __Look and listen_____
Not knowing what you don't know		__Expedient __Avoiding __Fear __Self-deception		__Deliberate action____ __Self-efficacy_____ __Face it_____ __Look and listen_____
Not sharing decision-making		__Expedient __Avoiding __Fear __Self-deception		__Deliberate action____ __Self-efficacy_____ __Face it_____ __Look and listen_____
Using the Vroom and Yetton Normative Model		__Expedient __Avoiding __Fear __Self-deception		__Deliberate action____ __Self-efficacy_____ __Face it_____ __Look and listen_____
Trying out the wisdom of the crowd		__Expedient __Avoiding __Fear __Self-deception		__Deliberate action____ __Self-efficacy_____ __Face it_____ __Look and listen_____

continued

Baby Steps

The baby steps for this chapter are as follows:

- Frame a problem three different ways and ask yourself what are the differences.
- Determine whether you are risk averse.
- Using the Vroom and Yetton Model, determine the style you will use in a complex decision.

The key behaviors to use in framing a problem are as following:

1. Choose a problem.
2. Rephrase the problem. Reword it several times in different ways. Take single words and substitute variations.
3. Increase your awareness of the problem by looking at it from different perspectives.
   a. Consider the concern ethically or legally.
   b. How would we have framed this X weeks ago?
   c. If we were unwilling to take a risk how would we define the problem?
   d. If money were no object, how would we define the problem?
   e. Invert the situation and see how you feel about it.
4. Rewrite it from different stakeholders' perspectives. How would our employees or a client frame this?
5. List and challenge any assumptions. Test each assumption for validity.
6. Ask how much the problem changed as you adjusted your frame.

You can determine your level of risk seeking/aversion by taking a test at http://www.humanmetrics.com/rot/rotqd.asp or http://testyourself.psychtests.com/testid/2122. The latter will take longer and you only get the snapshot without paying a small fee for the complete report.

All you need for the Vroom and Yetton Model is already provided. Choose a problem and follow the decision tree to determine what style you should use.

Follow-Up Questions

1. Good analysis does not substitute for a poor frame. Why?
2. Are you in a paralysis from analysis state now? How will you move on?
3. How can you use the wisdom of the crowd?
4. How do you know when to share decision-making?

Endnotes

1. DC Skinner, *Introduction to Decision Analysis*, Probabilistic Publishing, Gainesville, FL, 2009, 3rd ed. See http://www.amazon.com/Introduction-Decision-Analysis-3rd-Edition/dp/0964793865 (accessed October 23, 2014).

2. Ibid.

3. PJ Decker, R Durand, CO Mayfield, et al. "Predicting Implementation Failures in Organization Change," *Journal of Organizational Culture, Communications and Conflict*, 2012, 16(2), 39–60.

4. JW Dean and MP Sharfman, "Does Decision Process Matter? A Study of Strategic Decision-Making Effectiveness," *Acad Manage J*, April 1996, 39(2), 368–396.

5. See Sarah Lincoln, Elizabeth Holmes, "Ethical Decision Making: A Process Influenced by Moral Intensity." http://www.usna.edu/Ethics/_files/documents/ethical%20decision%20making%20and%20the%20influence%20of%20moral%20intensity.pdf (accessed October 23, 2014).

6. JE Russo and PLH Schoemaker, *Decision Traps*. New York, NY: Simon & Schuster, 1989.

7. Ibid.

8. From WikiHow, "How to Define a Problem." http://www.wikihow.com/Define-a-Problem (accessed October 23, 2014).

9. Ibid. Also see Note 1.

10. Ibid.

11. Ibid. Also see Note 6.

12. Ibid.

13. We highly recommend Peter Scholtes, Brian Joiner, et. al., *The Team Handbook*, Joiner Associates, Madison, WI, 2003, for further reading on team functioning and decision-making.

14. From WikiHow, "How to Define a Problem." http://www.wikihow.com/Define-a-Problem (accessed October 23, 2014). Also see Note 1.

15. Ibid.

16. Ibid.

17. Ibid.

18. Ibid. Also, See DC Skinner Skinner, *Introduction to Decision Analysis*, Probabilistic Publishing, 3rd ed., Gainsville, FL, 2009 or visit http://home.ubalt.edu/ntsbarsh/business-stat/opre/partIX.htm#rutility for the process of using decision trees to calculate uncertainty. For a simple illustration visit https://www.aasv.org/shap/issues/v1n4/v1n4p17.pdf

19. Ibid.

20. We suggest reading Trout's, *The Power of Simplicity, McGraw-Hill, New York*, 1999.

21. From FBI, "June 2010 Bulletin." http://www.fbi.gov/stats-services/publications/law-enforcement-bulletin/june-2010/good-decisions (accessed October 23, 2014).

22. From Robert Wolf, "How to Minimize Your Biases When Making Decisions." http://blogs.hbr.org/2012/09/how-to-minimize-your-biases-when/(accessed October 23, 2014).

---

23. A Tversky and D Kahneman, "The Framing of Decisions and the Psychology of Choice," *Science*, New Series, January 30, 1981, 211(4481), 453–458.

24. From California State University Northridge, "Framing and Framing Theory." http://www.csun.edu/~rk33883/Framing%20Theory%20Lecture%20Ubertopic .htm (accessed October 23, 2014).

25. Ibid. Also see Note 6.

26. See MindTools, "Decision Making: How to Make Better Decisions." http://www .mindtools.com/pages/main/newMN_TED.htm#choosing (accessed October 23, 2014).

27. Ibid. Also see Note 1.

28. Adapted from Creative Problem Solving, "Generate Creative & Logical Alternative Solutions." http://www.problemsolving.net/stage05.html (accessed October 23, 2014).

29. Ibid. Also see Note 21.

30. Ibid. Also see Note 1.

31. John Hawkey, "Exit Strategy Planning: Grooming Your Business for Sale Or Succession," Google Books. *Google Books.* (retrieved September 8, 2014).

32. See James Manktelow and Amy Carlson, "How to Make Decisions: Making the Best Possible Choices." http://www.mindtools.com/pages/article/newTED_00.htm (accessed October 23, 2014).

33. See Keith Jackson, "Appreciative Inquiry: Solving Problems by Looking at What's Going Right." http://www.mindtools.com/pages/article/newTMC_85.htm (accessed October 23, 2014).

34. Ibid. Also see Note 26.

35. Some from D6Family, "Selfish Decisions." https://www.d6family.com/articles/ selfish-decisions (accessed October 23, 2014).

36. See Clayton Christensen Institute for Disruptive Innovation, "Disruptive Innovation." http://www.christenseninstitute.org/key-concepts/disruptive-innovation -2/?gclid=CMX9oMrdu8ECFeVaMgodmHQAQA (accessed October 23, 2014).

37. From University of Arizona, "Knowing What You Don't Know." http://ag.arizona .edu/futures/shortcourse/knowingyourself.html and Wayist Mysticism. http://www .wayist.org/ttc%20compared/indexchp.htm (accessed October 23, 2014).

38. Ibid. Also see Note 6.

39. From Brian Bloch, "Be Risk Diverse, Not Risk Averse." http://www.investopedia .com/articles/stocks/10/risk-diverse.asp (accessed October 23, 2014).

40. From Heidi Halvorson, "The Hidden Danger of Being Risk-Averse." http://blogs .hbr.org/2013/07/hidden-danger-of-being-risk-averse/ (accessed October 23, 2014).

41. Adapted from The College of St. Scholastica, "Vroom-Yetton-Jago Normative Decision Model." http://faculty.css.edu/dswenson/web/LEAD/vroom-yetton.html and Keith Jackson, "The Vroom-Yetton-Jago Decision Model: Deciding How to Decide." http://www.mindtools.com/pages/article/newTED_91.htm and VH Vroom and AG Jago, *The New Leadership: Managing Participation in Organizations.* Englewood Cliffs, NJ: Prentice Hall, 1988.

42. PJ Decker and J Breaugh, Chapter 4, "Leading and Managing, in Sullivan and Decker," *Effective Leadership and Management in Nursing*, Addison-Wesley, 1997. See also Keith Jackson, "The Vroom-Yetton-Jago Decision Model: Deciding How to Decide." http://www.mindtools.com/pages/article/newTED_91.htm (accessed October 23, 2014).

43. Adapted from Anne Houlihan, "Empower Your Employees to Make Smart Decisions." http://www.myarticlearchive.com/articles/7/084.htm and Bloomfire, "5 Ways to Encourage Knowledge Sharing Within Your Organization." https://blog .bloomfire.com/posts/522359-5-ways-to-encourage-knowledge-sharing-within -your-organization/public (accessed October 23, 2014).

44. J Surowiecki, *The Wisdom of Crowds*. New York, NY: Anchor Books, 2005.

45. SKM Yi, M Steyvers, MD Lee, et al., "The Wisdom of the Crowd in Combinatorial Problems," *Cognitive Sci*, 2012, 36, 452–470.

46. Ibid. Also see Note 3.

8

Communication Culture

Chapter Takeaways

► A positive communication culture is dependent on trusting relationships

► Assertive managers are more effective

► Learn how to actively listen

► Blame is the ultimate obstacle in communication

Leaders lead through communication, but breakdowns in communication do occur and usually lead to problems. Imagine sitting in a conference room and someone is giving a traditional PowerPoint presentation—only with lots of text on each slide. Furthermore, the presenter watches the projector screen and reads each slide. As a spectator, you would most likely not be enthralled by the content or the presenter. While good slides would have helped this situation, a more effective presentation method would be to hold a conversation—involve the audience, ask them questions, and invite discussion. This would create a totally different atmosphere than the one-way, bland PowerPoint presentation. The question here is why don't we do this as presenters?

One reason is that it is uncontrollable and therefore scary. Communication is a process of exchanging verbal and nonverbal messages and should be a continuous two-way process. PowerPoint presentations break that cycle and become one-way. A prerequisite of communication is a message conveyed through some medium to the recipient. It is essential that this message get to the recipient and be understood in the same terms as intended by the sender. Too much information, poorly framed messages, inappropriate channels, and incomplete feedback

---

from the recipient to the sender on how well the message is understood and accepted can all be self-handicapping.

Most self-handicapping in communication occurs by not developing an open and trusting communication culture. Picture a meeting where the boss comes in a few minutes late and starts talking about a critical issue and he doesn't allow for questions (during or after). At the end of the meeting, several people try to pose questions but the boss says "no questions now" and immediately walks out of the room. More than likely, the employees are even more concerned than they were before the meeting. Without a chance to clarify concerns or ask questions, the employees' thinking will evolve to the worst-case scenario. Their concerns and apprehensions are magnified. This form of presentation creates a negative communication culture which is an obstacle to employee performance.

Individuals at work interact with one another—leaders and employees—and create many cultures throughout an organization. Most workers belong to an organizational group and hold common ideas about how to deal with recurrent problems and uncertainties—organizational subcultures. *People create and perpetuate social order through these cultures.*[1] Communication causes cultures to form and those cultures than drive future communication. Cultures are sets of beliefs, values, and norms that are emotional and resistant to change. Most analysts agree that there are six major characteristics of cultures. They are: (1) Collective, (2) Inherently symbolic, (3) Emotionally charged, (4) Dynamic, (5) Historically based, and (6) Inherently fuzzy. Cultures cannot be produced by people acting alone; it is the *interaction* that defines culture. How communication works or does not work across cultures is a key to how organizations function. Communication culture is the glue that holds teams and organizations together. This glue can be a driver or an obstacle to performance.

Belonging to a culture involves believing what others believe and doing as they do—at least part of the time. If leadership is chaotic, untrustworthy, abusive, etc. the likely culture for employees will be keeping one's head down, not speaking up, avoiding trouble and punishment, and "just doing one's job." Upward communication of concerns or fears will be unlikely. While the employees will not like the style of this leadership group or its impact on them, *it still creates a social order for the employees that protects them from the potential greater chaos that emanates from this leadership.* It creates the communication culture—keeping out of sight and being close-mouthed. Great leaders do everything they can to foster an open communication culture because they know that communication drives all aspects of their organization.

Leaders need to assess their organization's subcultures—some subcultures are good; some are dysfunctional. But, some leaders think about culture as simply another managerial tool at their disposal. Yet, organizational cultures cannot be manufactured or changed at will. It usually takes enormous effort to change negative cultures and how communication occurs in an organization. The glue of communication culture is holding it all together and those that want structure and peace are loath to let go of what they are doing. Even so, if communication does not work, great leaders do something about it—to do otherwise is self-handicapping. Leaders who effectively manage communication culture adopt methods that enable them to get closer to employees, promote dialogue, engage employees, and align their communication with organizational strategy.

Impact

Stories of companies failing because of poor communication culture are legion.[2] Research into the problems that led to Enron's collapse pinpointed several "communication-based leader responsibilities" that senior managers failed to meet—responsibilities such as "communicating appropriate values" and "maintaining openness to signs of problems." Most leaders understand the consequences of poor financial management, but not all leaders appreciate the risks that come from a poor approach to communication culture. The blowout of the Deepwater Horizon offshore oil rig, in April 2010, resulted in a massive crisis for BP and its partners. Among the key factors that contributed to the disaster were "poor communications" and a failure "to share important information."[3]

More than half of change programs fail to meet their objectives and this is often attributed to managers being unable to deal with employee resistance to needed changes. Poor communication is often cited as the main cause of failure for IT projects. Inadequate communication is a major factor in many accidents and safety incidents; the root cause of errors in hospitals that harm patients is often due to communication failure. Employee stress from poor relationships is a key driver of company law suits. Putting in place collaborative communication systems and processes for resolving conflict assists greatly in reducing the high cost of law suits.[4]

We have all seen instances of poor communication; many of us have worked in environments where there was a culture that did not allow any questioning of leadership actions or employees voicing their fears and concerns. We have seen organizations where there was such a massive flow of communication it could not be prioritized and analyzed into any meaningful information; managers manipulating communication for their individual gain; and situations where lack of communication caused problems. Poor communication is one of the largest areas of self-handicapping in business organizations and comes mostly from reduced effort and excuses.

Any organization must be managed like a healthy family; otherwise, it will become a dysfunctional one. A team that cannot define employees' responsibilities and manage accountability fairly, provide no "nurturing" to soothe fears, cannot find ways to get around the rules when special situations arise, or create trust between members is not going to have a healthy communication culture. We all judge the relationships we have on the basis of the communication that occurs within them. Research shows that people who communicate more intimately have "better" relationships.[5] Yet, business conversations are traditionally expected to stay "on task" and focus on the "facts and figures" that are needed to get the job done. Managers are expected to give presentations and write memos. Yet, the very characteristics of communication that make a business conversation efficient, productive, and appropriate might be taken as signals of dislike, distrust, or dysfunction in a purely social conversation.

The most successful way of communicating in a workplace is to *treat each other as both friends AND as task partners.* In this type of communication culture, people are kind to each other, but at the same time they expect each other to carry out their jobs. People go along with each other's preferences and are tolerant, but at the same time they give each other criticism when something is not going well and hold each other accountable. This constant balance between social and business relationships is not simple, but neither is it impossible. It is self-handicapping at either extreme—too much friendly intimacy or none at all. "Heartless" communication does not engage employees, illuminate problems in the workforce, allow people to express worries and ideas, or help create a "trusting" culture. Too much friendly intimacy can be anything from a time-waster to illegal.

Poor communication can also cause conflict. Misunderstandings and unrealistic expectations can be irritating and if left to fester, usually cause some form of conflict. While a leader can't always prevent conflict, if a conflict does flair up, he can minimize its severity by dealing with it quickly.[6] It is absolutely essential to understand other's motivations about the situation and help them find a way to achieve their goals. Finally, every aspect of communication is influenced by ethnic and cultural differences. The choice of medium used to communicate—electronic technology versus face-to-face communications, the use of personal bonds versus formal agreements, nonverbal communication, and how time is thought of and used can all differ across national boundaries and be important to successful communication. Not attending to these cultural differences can be self-sabotaging; research to determine differences before communicating with members of another culture can eliminate self-handicapping communication culture.[7]

The Real Issues

Relying on misinformation or no information, allowing unresolved conflict, lack of meaningful or trusting relationships, a culture that is not conducive to interaction or voicing fears, and inappropriate team dynamics are all forms of poor communication culture. Communicating poorly also can cause poor talent management, poorly engaged employees, and virtually every other class of self-handicapping described in this book. It is critical that a leader not self-sabotage communication as it is the foundation for most of leadership.

Like most self-handicapping, communication self-handicapping starts with excuses—"I don't have time for small group meetings, I will just do a presentation. My managers will work out the employee problems." That leads to a culture of presentations because it saves the leader's time. And it keeps on because the employees don't say much. They just accept that as the communication culture and hunker down. But over time, this becomes a huge obstacle to performance—the employees disengage and problems are not brought to the surface. The ERO Spiral is easy to see in this case. In other cases, it starts with apprehension and fear—"I am afraid that the employees aren't going to like this. I don't want to have to put up with all their whining and gripping about it. I'll put it in a memo or presentation—no open meetings." The same obstacles are created but they come from deeper within the thinking of the leader, which are likely not acknowledged by him.

There are many reasons leaders self-handicap in communication. Probably the most common is to avoid difficult interpersonal situations. Another is lack of time; meeting with people individually or in small groups is much more time-consuming than giving a one-way presentation with PowerPoint slides and no questions. Empathy takes time and you never know what is coming your way from the employees. It is common for students in business schools to be required to give presentations with PowerPoint in every class. When they get out into the "real world," their preferred mode of communication is presentation of concepts (like back in school) rather than one-on-one problem solving. These engrained habits do not promote openness, trust, or listening. Most importantly, they do not allow employees to voice their fears and concerns about a situation—which can be critical information to an organizational change process. Presentations have their place in organizations, but the leader must not use them as a crutch for expediency, avoiding employee concerns, or fear of getting too close to people problems—that is self-handicapping.

Several more manifestations of culture are important. Much of culture is taken for granted and goes unexamined since it is learned unconsciously. Furthermore, cultural communication is often symbolic which makes it inherently imprecise and hidden from the uninitiated— things often stand for other things. In healthcare, lab coats, garment color, names embroidered on garments, and where stethoscopes are carried all indicate power and status to those who know how to read the signs. Also, organizations must often assimilate new groups and technology to deal with their changing environments and these new mergers or acquisitions carry with them cultural baggage that will affect existing cultures. Clear communication is critical at these times as this can kill a merger. It takes something out of the ordinary, something that makes a specific element in the culture salient, to make people become aware of what is ordinarily latent. In any attempts to make enterprise-wide strategy changes or mergers, this is critical. At these junctures, cultures should not be "dysfunctional"—in that they can make employees unwilling to change what they do, color the interpretation of information and events, or encourage behaviors that do not help the organization.

Do You Practice Poor Communication?

Survey: Do I Practice Poor Communication or Not? (Y = Yes, N= No, DK = Don't Know)

_____I don't really encourage my employees to express their fears and doubts enough.

_____ I wish I was better at being consistent and creating trust with all of my employees.

_____ I probably don't understand how to work with organizational culture very well.

_____ I am somewhat unwilling to share personal stories to better connect with staff.

_____ I don't always understand the appropriate vehicle to communicate.

_____ I can be defensive or sometimes can't take constructive feedback.

_____ I pretty much use email or texting for all communication.

_____ I would rather make a presentation than sit down with small groups of employees and find a good solution.

_____ I am a poor listener—my employees' problems bore me.

_____ I can get defensive in conversations.

_____ I suspect there are some undiscussables in my area. There are a lot of issues here that are under the table and no one talks about them openly.

_____ I can't take constructive feedback.

_____ I don't know all of my employees' names.

Scores

10–13 Y's—You are greatly self-handicapping your communication culture.

5–9—You are inconsistent on your approach to communication culture.

1–4—You are a good communicator.

What to Do?

Review of the Basics of Communication

The intent of this chapter is not to teach basic communication; it is to promote developing a communication culture that is not an obstacle to excellence. Even so, let us quickly review communication and how to increase communication in organizations.[8] Oral communication is generally recommended when the communication matter is temporary or building rapport and trust is significant. Written communication is used where a record must be kept and there is more formality needed (Table 8.1).

Table 8.1   Advantages and Limitations of Oral and Written Communication

Oral Communication		Written Communication	
Advantages	**Limitations**	**Advantages**	**Limitations**
• High level of understanding and transparency = interpersonal • Flexible, allows for rapid changes • Spontaneous feedback, quick decision-making • Best for problem resolution—easy to put an end to conflicts or disputes	• Possible misunderstandings if information isn't complete • Requires attentiveness and receptivity • Can't be used as legal records except in investigation work	• Establish principles and policies • Keeps record • Records delegation assignments • Precise and explicit	• Costs—time and resources • Nonspontaneous response • Requires great competency in language and vocabulary

Nonverbal Communication

Nonverbal communication comprises feelings, emotions, attitudes, thoughts projected through body movements, gestures, eye contact, touching, the measurable distance between people as they interact, time (running a few minutes late to a meeting), variations in pitch, speed, volume, and pauses, and physical appearance. Nonverbals convey information that reinforce what is said, provide additional feedback, and even signal to others one is finished speaking.[9] Eye contact is an important aspect of nonverbal behavior; looking at someone lets them know that one is concentrating on the content of their speech. Little eye contact can indicate disinterest. Posture also indicates interest or emotions, and intentions. Two forms of posture have been identified: (1) Open and (2) Closed. Closed means arms folded, legs crossed or positioned at an angle to the other person. Finally, every culture has different levels of physical closeness which are expected or tolerated. When someone violates an "appropriate" distance, people may feel uncomfortable or defensive.

To improve on nonverbal interpretive skills, focus on the most useful cues for a given situation. Movements that are unusual for a particular person are more meaningful; for example, when someone who ordinarily has very relaxed fingers and hands begins tapping a finger. Discrepancies between verbal statements and nonverbal behaviors are also significant. Nonverbal cues are indicators of masked or hidden emotions or thoughts. For example, someone who speaks to his boss with a shaky voice but with confident words is indicating discomfort with the situation or fear of the boss. Nonverbals can become a barrier to effective communication—they must match the verbal message. *Remember, what we say is often less important than how we say it*—as words are only 7 percent of our communication.[10]

Barriers to Communication

A leader must discover the various barriers to communication, analyze the reasons for their occurrence, and take preventive steps to avoid them. There are several barriers that affect the flow of communication in an organization. These are as follows:

- *Perception*—Perception is generally how each individual interprets the world around him. An employee's perception is more important than your "truth."

- *Language Differences*—Linguistic differences cause the same word to mean different things to different individuals. All professions have their own lingo—just make sure others know it.

- *Information Overload*—Leaders and employees are surrounded with too much information. Consequently, information is often misinterpreted, forgotten, or overlooked.

- *Inattention*—At times we listen, but not hear. Thus, urgent problems can distract us from hearing a subordinate explain his problem—even poor hearing on the part of one of the parties— some of us need hearing aids.

- *Emotions*—If the receiver feels that the communicator is angry he interprets the information differently than if the communicator is happy.

- *Complexity in Organizational Structure*—Greater the hierarchy in an organization, the chances of communication getting mislaid or distorted is greater.

- *Poor Retention*—Human memory cannot function beyond a limit. One cannot always retain what is being said—this leads to communication breakdown.

Ask questions to find out how someone interprets your message. Ensure that employees have command over both written and spoken language.

Use simple and clear words; ambiguous words and jargon should be avoided. Listen attentively and carefully; there is a difference between "listening" and "hearing." During communication one should make effective use of body language—do not show emotions as the receiver might misinterpret the message being delivered. Reduce the number of hierarchical levels and signatures needed in communication. Reduce overload; delegate email to an assistant or use texting for critical interactions. Properly select the medium of communication. Simple messages should be conveyed orally, written communication should be encouraged for delivering complex messages. Finally, be transparent. When leaders practice transparency, employees are not afraid to be transparent either. This facilitates an honest dialogue up and down the organization.

Transparency

A *Harvard Business Review* survey revealed that more than half of all managers don't trust their leaders.[11] When people experience such distrust, they describe their working environment as threatening, divisive, unproductive, and tense. In contrast, when working in a trusting environment, people report the experience as fun, supportive, motivating, and productive. Companies that foster a culture of transparency and trust clearly have a competitive advantage for sustainable success.

So, why wouldn't leaders remove this self-handicap to promote openness and a free flow of information? Why can't people communicate upward and do so honestly? Most employees want to be a part of a workplace culture that puts a premium on delivering the truth.[12] They want their leaders to share where the company is headed so they can plan and protect themselves. Most people now realize they need to look out for themselves in their careers.

Transparency issues can involve a leader who won't listen to employees, as well as employees who won't speak up. The reason most leaders are not transparent is because they believe they will be viewed as less authoritative, have less power or control, or they have a habit of being very tight with information—which was learned over time in a more dysfunctional earlier work environment. One of the most powerful questions you can ask yourself is, "Do I lead by inspiring transparency and trust?"

Here is what leaders *should do*:[13]

- Treat others as you would want to be treated. Treat everyone with respect.

- Make time to listen to employees' questions and suggestions. It's important to communicate that you, in fact, want to hear from employees. Don't tell your stories.

- Show that you have heard employees' opinions and use some of them. Listening during one-on-one communication is vital.

- Greet employees when seen. Remember their names. Walk to meetings on different routes so one can see more of them.

- Give compliments; recognize employees for their contributions. Everyone likes being told something looks good.

- Make an effort to get to know employees beyond their role. Find emerging talent. Make emotional connections—ditch the small talk and get out of communication autopilot.

- Be authentic. Let people know who you really are—talk about vulnerabilities, problems, and failures.

- Ask for help. As much as people like giving help, it's still kind of scary to ask for it. But, most people like to help.

- Provide small meetings for information and opinion exchange. Do not use PowerPoint presentations exclusively.

- Dress up (or down). Our clothes are the physical armor that stands between us and others we encounter. You can open others up or close them down by how you dress.

- Give employees an open, standing invitation to approach you with questions, concerns, complaints and comments at any time and honor it.[14] Specify 20 percent of your week as open time.

- Distributing a daily or weekly memo about projects, announcements, and deadlines keeps employees and leaders on the same page.

- Send all messages across multiple channels. And make important messages repetitive—it takes three times.

Why Don't You?

Expediency

As with any other category of self-handicapping, you have to ask yourself how much of this is due to taking the expedient route, versus avoiding problems, apprehension, and so on. Much of the handicapping we do in basic communication is expedient. Much of what we do in creating or contributing to the communication culture in our area is due to the apprehension we carry around about disclosure, how close we allow others to come to our "inner being," shyness, shame, and other deeper issues. None of this is bad; it is just you. But if you are or want to be a leader—you may have to face these fears and get beyond them. Great leaders help create or change communication cultures to be more open and trusting and promote maximum exchange of information. Understanding that you are a big contributor to the culture in your area may help you face those fears, work to overcome them, and practice new ways of operating.

There are lots of reasons for not opening up; you will have to examine yourself to find out why you don't. If the answer is lack of training, we have some suggestions. If you find it difficult to open up and be vulnerable in personal disclosure, read Smith, *When I Say No, I Feel Guilty* or Antony and Swinson, *Shyness and Social Anxiety Workbook: Proven, Step-by-Step Techniques for Overcoming Your Fear.*[15]

What communication handicaps do you use because of expediency?

Avoidance

If you view your coworkers as judgmental and mean-spirited, then sharing your vulnerabilities is a high-risk move. Furthermore, you may have had some exposed weaknesses used against you in the past. Maybe things went on at home that you (and the family) were wary of anyone finding out about. Shy people are sometimes overly guarded and not open.[16] We all can find reasons to avoid close communication.

Usually as people get to know each other, they start opening up and sharing more and more of their vulnerabilities. Shy, introverted leaders need to use baby steps and start with mild disclosures. If these are met with acceptance and understanding, they reveal more. The expectation is that if one person reveals something about themselves the other will match it. Some people can be reluctant to start this process and make these kinds of personal self-disclosures that help deepen relationships. Just remember that the leader is the adult in this relationship by definition and must start the baby steps toward openness.

What communication handicaps do you use because of avoidance?

Apprehension

Many leaders have some level of apprehension when connecting with other people. They sometimes feel others will judge them or dislike them. This fear holds many of us back from being open and is the greatest source for communication self-handicapping. Yet, if leaders don't share some of themselves, the employees won't trust them. Leaders will need to push that fear aside and not worry so much about what others might think or say or do. When leaders open up and are authentic, they are usually surprised by how much people accept them and open up. Judging or blaming others can also prevent openness.

Being too guarded and self-protective is a self-defeating strategy in most leadership situations.[17] Secretiveness can sometimes bring more attention than it helps avoid. Remember, in the absence of data about a leader, employees will make up their own. When leaders try to act like there's nothing wrong with them, they become distant and not relatable. Of course, it may help keep some personal information under wraps; there are always those who will try to use a leader's issues against him. Figure out what information about yourself you are most and least comfortable sharing with people. You can practice opening up by sharing small things about yourself to strangers. If a particular secret is holding you back socially, consider getting it out in the open. Doing this takes away the power your secret has over you.

What communication handicaps do you use because of apprehension?

Self-Deception

Self-betrayal leads to self-deception. People can, in essence, betray themselves by acting contrary to what they believe or are "supposed" to believe. A person may know that they should save for retirement, but the time comes that they want a big screen TV. By buying the TV instead of saving, they betray their own belief about saving for the future. This betrayal becomes self-deception when they begin to believe that the contrary behavior is the way things should be. "It is the American way to consume and own big TVs! Who wouldn't do this?" They begin to see the world in a way that justifies their self-betrayal. Over time, their view of reality becomes distorted and they may be unable to focus on their responsibility for the consequences of their behaviors. And then the obstacle always appears—retirement with no savings. Managers follow this self-handicapping process all the time. "It is not something I am doing, it is just these darn 'millennials' who don't appreciate that hard work will insure the future."

If a leader is in the habit of judging others, he will be judged. Self-handicapping can revolve down from excuses to a level of self-deception where it is all someone else's fault. Then the blame is habitual. Labeling employees in this way takes away opportunities for meaningful interaction. Leaders in this "box" need to look and listen to the world around them and find ways to communicate with others and truly connect without judgment or blame. Finally, leaders that consider themselves a part of the team, and not just as someone who looks over the team, grow stronger relationships with their employees.

Leaders may think that they are good communicators if they can transfer an idea or thought to another person or they can stand up in front of a group and speak.[18] Often they attend to some components of communication and do not "hear" when people give unflattering feedback about their communication. Additionally leaders often do not place a high priority on communication skills compared to professional skills. They are deceived into believing that they can "wing it" when it comes to communicating. This is just one example of self-deception learned early that continues as leaders move higher within the work environment.

Leaders must be willing to assume responsibility for all communication even when they feel that the responsibility should be shared or that someone else should make the initial effort. Leaders need to drop their defenses and protective mechanisms, to become more open and trusting, thus facilitating communication. Lastly, leaders must be willing to acknowledge and change past routines and behaviors that have hindered skilled communication. In other words, they must get out of the "box" to communicate in a way that does not cause self-handicapping obstacles. As leaders achieve a heightened awareness of self-deception, and move toward becoming skilled communicators, they should view themselves as accountable for their work environment.

How does self-deception affect your communication efforts?

Behaviors to Change
Saying "I'm Sorry"

Recognize
The first place to practice vulnerability and openness is being willing to apologize—to say, "I'm sorry." We all need to openly apologize because we all make mistakes that hurt people whether intentional or not. It isn't always easy to apologize. It takes courage, makes you vulnerable (one

reason that you should do it), and you have to get above embarrassment to face up to your actions. Yet, it is the most effective way to create or restore trust.

Admit

Not apologizing can damage relationships and harm your reputation. No one wants to work for a boss who doesn't "own up" and apologize for his mistakes. There are many reasons why you should make a sincere apology when you've hurt someone. These are as follows:[19]

- To open a dialogue between yourself and the other person
- To acknowledge that you engaged in unacceptable behavior
- To admit that the situation was your fault and restore dignity to the person you hurt
- To take accountability for your actions

There are many possible reasons for *not* apologizing—feeling superior, not wanting to be vulnerable, not realizing what was done or that it was inappropriate, or not doing it right away and then being too embarrassed to do it later. All these excuses lead you into the ERO Spiral.

Adjust

One of the best places to find help in all management skills is Mindtools (www.mindtools.com) and they have a great page on apology. (http://www.mindtools.com/pages/article/how-to-apologize.htm)

Key Behaviors

Here are the key behaviors for apologizing:

1. Apologize as soon as you realize that you've wronged someone.
2. Say "I'm sorry," or "I apologize" sincerely to express remorse. With full eye contact.
3. Admit responsibility for your actions.
4. Make amends if possible. Don't give empty promises.
5. Say you will not do it again.

Reassuring the other person that you're going to change your behavior helps rebuild trust. Explanations and excuses can weaken your apology. Keep in mind that the other person might not be ready to forgive you for what happened. Give that person time to heal, and don't rush him through the process. Finally, keep in mind this caveat—in some countries, an apology is seen as an admission of liability or guilt.

Listening

Recognize

Listening can be very difficult especially in today's fast paced world. Maybe you are thinking about the football game last night, worrying about your 401k, or weighing lunch options. Maybe you have heard it before—ten times before. Maybe you made up your mind how to proceed on the first sentence. Worst of all, maybe you have gotten what you wanted from this person and you are thinking, "I just wish they would go away now." Allowing these mental distractions is self-handicapping.

Admit

Vulnerability, openness, creating or rebuilding trust all require one to pay attention and listen. That simply means stop talking and try to hear what is being said. It means caring about the speaker and his issues. Because the brain does not use all of its capacity when listening, a leader's mind may drift to thinking of answers or explanations rather than listening to the message at hand. Make sure that employees and others who approach you feel that you are fully available and listening to them.[20] It will build engagement.

Adjust

Nonverbals are important. Establishing eye contact with the person you are listening to establishes rapport and allows you to focus on the person; it helps you avoid distractions and pay attention more fully. Recall the information that you hear and paraphrase it, but don't do a lot of restating what is said out loud—that can be irritating (think about your last call to a technical support center). You can also encourage an individual by nodding your head, smiling, or leaning in slightly. Ask open questions.

Because a listener can listen at a faster rate than most speakers talk, there is a tendency to evaluate too quickly. That tendency is perhaps the greatest barrier to effective listening. Also, time spent explaining or defending your decision or position is a sure sign that you are not listening.

Key Behaviors

The key behaviors for listening are as follows:[21]

1. Look at the speaker directly and put aside distracting thoughts.
2. Stop talking—do not interrupt, talk over the person or finish their sentences for them.
3. Don't doodle, shuffle papers, look out the window, or pick your fingernails. Give good eye contact.

4. Don't mentally prepare a rebuttal as the other person is speaking.

5. Use your own body language and gestures to convey your attention.

6. Help the speaker feel free to speak. Encourage the speaker with small verbal comments like "yes" and "uh huh."

7. Clarify what you are hearing with phrases such as "What I'm hearing is" or ask questions to clarify certain points.

8. Look at issues from their perspective. Let go of preconceived ideas. Be patient.

Developing and Maintaining Trust

Recognize

Many different definitions of trust can be found; yet, there are three elements required in trusting another person.[22] These are: (1) Their *ability or competence*, (2) Their *benevolence*—the willingness of the person to do good, and (3) Whether the person has a *core set of values* to guide behavior. *It is not enough to just be a good person in order to earn trust; one also needs to be competent and able to deliver on one's promises.* The greater the trust and the lower the perceived risk in any context, the more likely that open communication will occur.

Covey suggests trust is the most fundamental component to all business relationships, including those within and between businesses.[23] He argues that the degree people trust each other around the world is decreasing rapidly. Covey argues that when "trust goes down, speed of business will also go down and costs will go up." In organizations, the data show a great absence of trust:

- Only 51 percent of employees have trust and confidence in senior management.

- Only 36 percent of employees believe their leaders act with honesty and integrity.

- Over a 12-month period, 76 percent of employees observed illegal or unethical conduct on the job.

This is critical because we have entered a global, knowledge-worker economy that revolves around partnering and relationships. The ERO Spiral is plain to see—*simply telling someone what you think they want to hear to save time and effort with no follow through on your part, self-deception that it does not matter much, a break in employee trust, disengaged employees thinking it is okay—even fun—to sabotage your strategies and plans.*

Here is what you should do:[24]

- Be honest by saying what will be done and do what you say you will do.
- Give credit for good work that is being done.
- Be willing to acknowledge, accept responsibility for, and repair perceived breaches or betrayals of trust with employees. Take responsibility rather than making excuses.
- Ensure that organizational policies, procedures, and rules are applied consistently and equitably. There will be no vengeful actions.
- Send the message that employees will be trusted. Speak in terms of "we" rather than creating "us and them."
- Unclog organizational communication channels by implementing open-door and open-book policies and establishing user-friendly networks.
- Value each other's background and experience and do not discredit each other's competence.
- When problems are investigated, attempt to determine what went wrong and why rather than who was responsible.

Admit

Galford and Seibold Drapeau in *The Trusted Leader,*[25] list several factors that hinder organizational cultures of trust. These factors are as follows:

- Personal agendas that do not align with the organization's strategies
- Volatile personalities that reflect a need for vengeance or abrasive and abusive conduct
- Perceiving coworkers or management to be incompetent
- An organizational environment with a history of numerous reorganizations or management changes
- Ambiguous behaviors by leaders and supervisors
- Perceptions about the culture of the organization—"how we do things here"

Trust also breaks down in organizations because of a "good guys and bad guys" mentality between management and labor. Each group believes that the other wants radically different things and will be willing to hurt the other side to get them. Yet, in conflict management and team-building work, the answer routinely comes back that people generally want the same things—respect, participation, clarity, fairness, understanding, and the opportunity to achieve something worthwhile. Understanding and cutting through these assumptions and differences is a key to creating trust and a good communication culture.

The ways trust is broken are numerous.[26] It can come from mismanaged change efforts, mergers, acquisitions, and layoffs. Interpersonally, it may occur through a single act, such as violating a confidence or telling a lie, or a continuous stream of minor acts, such as gossiping and talking about others behind their backs or consistently arriving late for meetings. Regardless, if unintentional error or fraudulent, vengeful act, employees interpret them as acts of betrayal. Strong leadership can help organizations overcome these barriers to organizational trust. Trust is a reciprocal process and leadership is often the key for creating a trust-based organization. Leaders do this by getting out, being vulnerable, and listening.

And remember that there are cross-cultural differences in organizational trust and similarities cannot be assumed.[27] Individualist cultures, like that of the United States, focus on the self, while collectivist cultures, like that of Japan, focus on the group. It could be assumed that organizational trust should be higher in collectivist cultures. However, this is not the case. Organizational trust and the propensity to trust are higher in the United States than in Japan, Korea, Hong Kong, Taiwan, China, and Malaysia. This might be due to the differences in openness among these cultures. Americans are three times as likely to express discontent within the workplace as the Japanese are to express such feelings.

Ask yourself these questions:[28]

- Is my behavior predictable or erratic?
- Do I communicate clearly or carelessly?
- Do I treat promises seriously or lightly?
- Am I forthright or dishonest?

Adjust

Rebuilding trust has much in common with experiencing a death.[29] There is a sense of loss and healing after a betrayal which requires us to move through a series of emotions:

- Become aware of what happened and acknowledge the impact on you and others.
- Feel the upset and find ways to voice to your feelings.

- Frame the experience: consider the bigger picture and take responsibility for what part you may have played in what happened.
- Forgive and forget—let go and move on.

When trust is broken, most people experience the impact as a loss—tune into how employees are responding to that loss. Acknowledge their experience and listen to what's important to them. Provide people with nonthreatening environments to express their feelings and begin to work through them. Share key information and insights to help employees feel involved in the solution. Make up for failing to do what you said you would do. Remember that rebuilding trust takes time and patience. It is *rebuilding your credibility.*

Key Behaviors
The key behaviors for rebuilding trust are as follows:

1. Remind yourself that not all is lost. Don't do anything rash without thinking about it first.
2. Acknowledge what happened and apologize. Also apologize for lying by omission. Take full responsibility for your actions and choices.
3. Allow feelings to surface through team meetings or one-on-one conversations. Give the others a chance to speak and be clear about your feelings.
4. Reframe the experience into a larger context. Help people to see the bigger picture, such as the business reasons behind a set of decisions.
5. Help people recognize where they are stuck and how they can shift from blaming to problem solving.
6. Make constructive changes based on employee input.
7. Be extra dependable, consistent, and responsive. Be sure that all promises you make *are* promises you keep.
8. Accept that sometimes it is going to feel like you are moving two steps forward and three steps back but continue to hold employees accountable.

Blame

Recognize
How many times have you heard someone who said or did something that is mean and hurtful and they justified it by saying you made them do it?[30] That's an example of using blame to excuse their own bad behavior—

severe self-deception. Blame can also allow a person's emotions to override self-control in order to achieve an often selfish end. People who blame others tend to *overemphasize themselves while at the same time underemphasizing the negative effects of their actions.* Blame closes you up and everyone around you. Blame is an obstacle on the end of a long ERO Spiral.

Admit

Many people's actions are based on either gaining something pleasurable and avoiding something unpleasant. We all make selfish, self-serving, and lazy decisions now and then. It's called being human. However, using too much blame to bolster ourselves or our self-esteem is self-defeating. Blame is often used to cover fears, so examine your motivations carefully in this section.

Adjust

If you can own up a mistake as soon as you make it and do your best to correct it, you can prevent it from turning into a huge problem that is then difficult to solve.[31] We often justify failures by saying we could turn things around if only X, Y, or Z would happen. This kind of "faceless" blame simply keeps you from acting and solving problems. Get over the idea that making mistakes is being stupid. Try not to judge others. Lastly, stop blaming yourself—this kind of blame keeps others away and does nothing to foster a learning environment in your work area.

Key Behaviors

The key behaviors for avoiding the blame game are as follows:[32]

1. Step up and confess as soon as you realize what went wrong.
2. Don't skate around the issue. Don't try to shift even a part of the blame to someone else.
3. If you do or want to blame others, ask yourself "Why?"
4. Define the box that blame has built for you and find ways to get out of that box.
5. Shift to "What" and "How" questions. Do not say "If only."
6. Accept the consequences. Realize that the truth will be discovered eventually.
7. Recover gracefully. Hold your head up and move on.

Vulnerability: Shame and Pessimism

Recognize

There's a saying—"Don't believe everything you think."[33] It applies to a lot of our negative thinking—shame, pessimism, and defensiveness.

Shame-based thinking has several characteristics—dire predictions, doubt in your coping skills, selective focus on negative aspects of events, negative explanations of others' or one's own behavior, and rigid rules about how people should behave. We all have had some of these thoughts when we feel like we can't do something well or we have done something we are not proud of. This leads to feelings of not liking yourself. We usually keep those hidden, but sometimes, *it keeps us from being open—and vulnerable—to others. And these apprehensions lead to huge obstacles for a leader.*

Admit

Some leaders don't really believe they are capable of their positions; yet, they are probably very capable. This is just a self-sabotaging brain exercise. Lots of professionals in hard science areas haven't been prepared well for the messy world of managing people. They were taught to manage things— things are predictable and much more manageable than people. If you feel unworthy or incapable of doing something well—like connecting to people, being vulnerable with other people, dealing with people without being defensive, or you don't deserve your job—you have short circuited the entire communication process before it even starts. Inner thoughts that make us closed and not transparent create the wrong kind of communication culture. But that self-sabotaging thinking can be stopped and turned around.

"Confirmation bias" describes our brain's tendency to latch onto information that matches our pre-existing beliefs, and to shun information that contradicts it. Knowing this, we need to consciously tamp down our knee-jerk reaction to feel shame, be pessimistic or defensive. You can work on becoming more optimistic.[34] Pessimistic thoughts—"I can't do this" or "I'll look like an idiot"—close you up and only make matters worse in communication culture. Catch yourself when the self-talk turns negative and consciously make it positive—"I can deal with this" or "I can take care of myself." Positive thoughts really do lead to positive actions. We invite you to read Martin Seligman's book, *Learned Optimism: How to Change Your Mind and Your Life.*[35]

When good things happen, pessimists dismiss it as a fluke; optimists take the credit. When bad things happen, pessimists blame themselves and expect to suffer a long time, while optimists see bad events as having little to do with them, and as one-time problems that will pass quickly. During difficult times when solutions seem to be beyond your reach, *remember it is not personal, not pervasive, and not permanent.* Seligman's entire book shows that optimism and pessimism both boil down to little more than our "explanatory" style—a person's distinct way of interpreting life's ups and downs. An optimist doesn't go looking for a scapegoat and will acknowledge his contribution to a problem so he can make it better. Great leaders lead through optimism because pessimism can often be a self-handicap.

Adjust

The really good news is that we can all develop skills to improve optimism. *Learned optimism* includes a test to determine your own style and strategies for growing a more optimistic and hopeful attitude. You can take the test online at http://web.stanford.edu/class/msande271/onlinetools/LearnedOpt.html.

The best thing to do with negative thinking is to work in baby steps and use your ability to think to turn things to the positive. Choose a specific thought that you'd like to work with, then challenge this thought by asking the questions mentioned below.

Key Behaviors

The key behaviors for overcoming shame are as follows:

1. Pick a thought that is shame-based or pessimistic.

2. Work through the following list to challenge the thought.
   a. Is this thought really true?
   b. How do I know it's true?
   c. What is the evidence for or against this thought?
   d. Is this thought helping me or hurting me?
   e. Who would I be or what could I do if I let go of this thought?
   f. Am I willing to release this thought?
   g. What's the worst that could happen if I let go of this thought? Can I live with that?

3. Find a more appropriate thought and say it over and over until you believe it.

For more help on this, read Nigel Paul Miller's, *How to Remove Negative Beliefs and Free Your Mind,* CreateSpace Independent Publishing, 2013.

Defensiveness

Recognize

Defensive communication is a form of fighting—a defense mechanism. When we sense a threat to our self-esteem, we automatically protect ourselves by defensive verbal or nonverbal responses. It is often the visual clue to shame or other feelings of unworthiness. It is excessive sensitivity to criticism and the things you do to deal with criticism.

Admit

When you or an employee is automatically defensive, ask "why?" Is it as simple as a word being used that triggers long suppressed emotion, or is it a defense against any and all criticism—constructive or not? It is a reaction to a trigger, so find and moderate the trigger.

Adjust

When defensiveness occurs, it is best to slow down.[36] Deliberate action when in conversation with an employee allows time to ask why the defensiveness is occurring and what to do next. Also, detach. You know what pushes your hot buttons, so cut off your usual response at the pass. Finally, start over. Step away and come back when you are cooled down and not emotionally wrapped up in the issue. Reschedule with an employee and start again after analysis to determine what you said or did to cause or set off the defensiveness. The fastest way to change other people's perception of you as a poor leader is to work on being less defensive.

Additionally, there are several ways to avoid sending defensive messages. One is to focus on the problem, not on the person. The speaker should focus on situations and solutions, and not on personal traits. The communication should validate; invalidation arouses negative feelings and defensiveness. It should be specific and useful, not global. The more specific a statement is, the more useful it is and the more likely you are to avoid defensiveness. In addition, appealing to a common goal is preferable to exercising control over the other person. Finally, avoiding judgments of the person's behavior is helpful.

Key Behaviors

The key behaviors for handling defensiveness are as follows:

1. Listen carefully and paraphrase by reflecting both the person's content and feeling messages. (Repeat if necessary).
2. Verify your perceptions by asking for clarifications.
3. Do not allow yourself to get defensive too.
4. Continue to treat the person with respect in spite of his words.
5. Appeal to the common goal of mission or a shared task.
6. Make "I" statements when expressing thoughts and feelings.
7. Focus on behaviors and actions, not on personality traits.

Hindering Expression of Doubt

Recognize

Not allowing expression of doubt in meetings or any similar lack of two-way communication is self-limiting. A common example in business is continually using presentations rather than allowing discussions in small group or team meetings. The wisdom of the crowd (see the Chapter 7, Decision Analysis) cannot be heard and many ideas and issues will be passed over. These can come back to haunt team or departmental efforts to excel or change. It can also cause the development of "undisscussables"—things people won't bring up in a meeting but talk about it extensively at work among themselves. The leader is then often oblivious to major issues in the workforce that can hobble him, or his area.

Admit

Employees withholding information that could benefit the organization can be caused by fear of retribution, but that seems to be the exception. Most of their silence is from employees feeling they have little to gain by venturing forward with their doubts or ideas for solving problems. The prevailing belief among mangers that having an open door policy will encourage employees' input isn't enough. It isn't enough because it is passive. It requires employees to initiate the conversation. A major key to allowing expression of employee fears and doubts is to hold open-ended small group or one-on-one meetings that give each team member the opportunity to share concerns and ideas. The ERO Spiral starts with the excuse, "It is not my job to force employees to tell me their apprehensions," causing time to be saved and problems hidden as undiscussables, employees not sharing critical information, and failed initiatives.

Adjust

Employees are much more likely to be forthcoming when *their input is solicited*. You must find ways to draw them out. Taking inventory of the diversity of employees in workplace and accommodating their various styles of interacting upward is also important. If you have not done these things, is it due to lack of time for multiple meetings, avoiding the complications of dealing with the employee concerns, lack of respect for the employees' opinions, or fear of being transparent or of possibly failing in responding to the employee concerns?

Key Behaviors

The key behaviors for encouraging expression of doubts and concerns are as follows:[37]

1. Develop an efficient and effective method for collaboration and the sharing of ideas that *you are comfortable using.*

2. Whatever it is, stick to it. It could be a software tool, small group meetings, or a regular protocol for interactive electronic communication.

3. Let it be known that participation is welcome and expected.

4. Specifically ask for concerns, doubts, and fears. Do this repeatedly as the employees will not trust the process yet.

5. Meet any sharing of ideas, insights, and concerns with positive reinforcement. Never reproach or interrupt.

Assertiveness

Recognize

Managers who are assertive express themselves honestly, openly, and responsibly and are therefore more effective in creating an open communication culture. Aggressive, passive, or passive-aggressive communication does not. The first step in becoming more assertive is to understand the differences between assertive, passive, and aggressive behaviors. A comparison among these three ways of communicating appears in Table 8.2.

Admit

All communication has a payoff for the communicator and consequences for the recipient. For example, when you communicate aggressively, you may vent your anger and feel superior (payoff), but the recipient may feel humiliated, hurt, and angry (consequence). The recipient may be complying with your wishes out of fear of aggression, but later, he may seek revenge and hold a grudge against you. When you are passive, you *don't* get what you want. If you feel anxious or resentful, that usually means you have communicated passively. How you feel about yourself as you communicate can be a clue to how you are presenting yourself. The ERO Spiral starts here when the leader acts aggressively, gets his way, keeps doing it, employees become passive-aggressive and disengaged, and they sabotage initiatives.

Adjust

Very few people are assertive all the time. Those who live in a hierarchical world can be very passive-aggressive—passive up and aggressive

---

Table 8.2 Passive, Assertive, and Aggressive Communication

	Passive	Assertive	Aggressive
Intent	To please others	To communicate to others	To dominate or humiliate others
Verbal behaviors	Does not express true wants/feelings or expresses them in a self-depreciative way	Expresses wants/feelings in a direct way	Expresses wants/feelings at the expense of others
Nonverbal behaviors	Looking away or down, smiling, clearing throat, soft voice, mumbling, or whining	Direct eye contact, open and relaxed expression, firm and clear voice	Looking down your nose, staring into the distance, overly loud or sarcastic speech
Communicator's feelings	Anxious, disappointed with yourself. Angry and resentful later	Confident, feel good about self throughout	Self-righteous, superior
Other person's feelings	Shamed, disgusted	Respect and appreciation	Angry, vengeful, feel used
Outcome	Don't get what you want	Get what you want or compromise	Get what you want, anger others
Payoff	Avoid conflict, tension, confrontation	Feel respected and self-confidence, better relationships	Vent anger, feel superior and in control

Source: Adapted from M Chenevert, *Special Techniques in Assertiveness Training for Women in the Health Professions.* St. Louis, MO: Mosby, 1978.

down. Many of us who are aggressive think we are being assertive, but we aren't. Simply ask the recipient how they felt and you may get an indication of where you stand. No response probably means aggressive on your part. Great leaders communicate in a way that takes away from neither themselves nor their employees. Note the following main points about assertive communication:[38]

- Avoid over-apologizing. When saying no or making a request, you do not have to apologize for it.

- Avoid adverse reactions such as defensiveness, tantrums, backbiting, slander, sarcasm, and threats.

- Use body language that is appropriate to and matches the verbal message (e.g., eye contact, open body posture, gestures, and facial expressions).

- Accept manipulative criticism while maintaining responsibility for your decision. For example, if you are asked for a favor and you say, "No." The requester says, "What's wrong with you, you lent it to me the last time." You say, "You are right, I did, but I don't want to this time."

- Calmly repeat a request or reply without justifying it. Be persistent.

- Be honest about feelings, needs, and ideas. Use "I" statements.

Key Behaviors

The key behaviors for assertive communication are as follows:

1. Express wants, ideas, and feelings in a direct and appropriate way. Use "I" statements.

2. Maintain direct eye contact and maintain an open and relaxed stance.

3. Use an appropriately firm, warm, and clear voice.

4. Avoid over-apologizing, defensiveness, or other adverse reactions when challenged, and always remain respectful. When criticized, accept and/or acknowledge your faults calmly without apology.

5. Look for a win-win situation to resolve the conversation. Calmly repeat what you are saying without justifying it.

6. Quit the conversation and come back at a later time if you find yourself being passive or aggressively defensive.

7. Do not think about retaliation or how bad you are for performing poorly, look at the key behaviors and come back to the conversation and do better.

Handling Complaints

Recognize

You will receive complaints from a variety of sources—customers, employees, peers, bosses, and vendors. Knowing how to deal with these effectively is important. While some larger employers have developed dispute resolution and arbitration procedures, informal procedures are often the best methods for leaders. If employees feel that they are being treated with respect and fairness, they are more likely to accept the resolution you suggest, even if it is not exactly what they wanted or expected.

Admit

Start by getting out of the formal talk. Refer to your "chat" with a customer rather than your "correspondence" with them. Speak to your employees like you care. A little familiarity can go a long way toward getting folks who complain on your side. Really listen to them.

Great entrepreneurs know every complaint gives them an opportunity to differentiate their company from others. Only 4 percent of dissatisfied customers complain; the remainder quietly go away, without a word. Even worse, they tell at least 274 people of their experience through stories being passed down across four layers of friends and relatives—social networking just speeds up the process. Smart leaders make it easy to complain, and then use the complaints to address the causes behind customers' or employee's dissatisfaction. Too many companies ignore their customers because it is too difficult to change service delivery to match customer's desires—some manager's do the same.

Adjust

It is best to actively solicit complaints from employees and customers. Persuading people to complain could be the best leadership tactic you can make. When people complain and their problems are resolved quickly, a majority are happy and they engage again. If you think you're doing a good job because your employees or customers aren't complaining, think again. Customers and employees think complaining won't do any good; complaining is usually difficult and time-consuming and they feel awkward or pushy. *Most people don't like to complain so you must go to them, ask, and listen.*

Key Behaviors

The key behaviors for handling complaints are as follows:

1. Listen openly to the person's complaint. Do not speak until the person has completed what he has to say. Make sure that you understand the problem.

2. Avoid reacting emotionally and don't get defensive.

3. Ask for his expectations about a solution to the problem. Ask the employee what he would like to see in the way of a resolution.

4. Don't make a decision until you have obtained all the facts. If you must talk to others, explain that to the employee.

5. Discuss and agree on steps to be taken to solve the problem— solve it for them or reward them for the time it cost them.

6. If the employee's complaint is without merit, explain it to the employee in a pleasant, low-key manner. If the complaint is sound, thank the employee for calling it to your attention.

7. Set specific deadlines for the actions to be taken. Follow through with corrective action as soon as possible.

8. Check back after taking action to determine if the issue has been resolved.

Final Personal Takeaways

Action Plan—Communication Culture

Take a few minutes and complete this action plan about communication culture.

Communication Culture Self-Handicaps	What Is the Situation?	Trigger	Impact on Others	What to Do/When?
Basic communication issues		__Expedient __Avoiding __Apprehension __Self-deception		__Deliberate action____ __Self-efficacy_____ __Face it_____ __Look and listen_____
Barriers to communication		__Expedient __Avoiding __Apprehension __Self-deception		__Deliberate action____ __Self-efficacy_____ __Face it_____ __Look and listen_____
Transparency		__Expedient __Avoiding __Apprehension __Self-deception		__Deliberate action____ __Self-efficacy_____ __Face it_____ __Look and listen_____
Saying "I'm sorry"		__Expedient __Avoiding __Apprehension __Self-deception		__Deliberate action____ __Self-efficacy_____ __Face it_____ __Look and listen_____
Listening		__Expedient __Avoiding __Apprehension __Self-deception		__Deliberate action____ __Self-efficacy_____ __Face it_____ __Look and listen_____

continued

Communication Culture Self-Handicaps	What Is the Situation?	Trigger	Impact on Others	What to Do/When?
Developing and maintaining trust		__Expedient __Avoiding __Apprehension __Self-deception		__Deliberate action____ __Self-efficacy_____ __Face it_____ __Look and listen_____
Blame		__Expedient __Avoiding __Apprehension __Self-deception		__Deliberate action____ __Self-efficacy_____ __Face it_____ __Look and listen_____
Vulnerability		__Expedient __Avoiding __Apprehension __Self-deception		__Deliberate action____ __Self-efficacy_____ __Face it_____ __Look and listen_____
Optimism		__Expedient __Avoiding __Apprehension __Self-deception		__Deliberate action____ __Self-efficacy_____ __Face it_____ __Look and listen_____
Defensiveness		__Expedient __Avoiding __Apprehension __Self-deception		__Deliberate action____ __Self-efficacy_____ __Face it_____ __Look and listen_____
Expression of doubt		__Expedient __Avoiding __Apprehension __Self-deception		__Deliberate action____ __Self-efficacy_____ __Face it_____ __Look and listen_____
Assertiveness		__Expedient __Avoiding __Apprehension __Self-deception		__Deliberate action____ __Self-efficacy_____ __Face it_____ __Look and listen_____
Handling complaints		__Expedient __Avoiding __Apprehension __Self-deception		__Deliberate action____ __Self-efficacy_____ __Face it_____ __Look and listen_____

Baby Steps

This chapter has examined many actionable items—some may be overwhelming. Some baby steps are provided that you are start practicing tomorrow in relation to your communication culture.

The baby steps for this chapter are as follows:

- Write down all of the commitments made for one day—track whether done or not—follow up with person tomorrow explaining why not done.
- Choose a coworker to have a conversation with and practice paying attention and listening.
- Get rid of one thought you keep thinking that is not helpful.
- Say "I'm sorry" one time sincerely in front of two or more people when you foul up and it is all your fault.

The key behaviors for maintaining attention are as follows:

1. Stop talking—listen to what the person is really saying.
2. Look at the speaker directly and maintain eye contact throughout the conversation.
3. Do not rush to add to the conversation—process the information before you take your turn to speak.
4. Use your own body language and gestures to convey your attention.
5. Help the speaker to feel free to speak. Encourage the speaker with small verbal comments like yes, and uh huh.

(*See the Key Behaviors for Listening mentioned previously*)

Here are the key behaviors for getting rid of a "bad" thought.

1. Work through the list mentioned here to challenge the thought.
    a. Is this thought really true?
    b. How do I know it's true?
    c. What is the evidence for or against this thought?
    d. Is this thought helping me or hurting me?
    e. Who would I be or what could I do if I let go of this thought?
    f. Am I willing to release this thought?
    g. What's the worst that could happen if I let go of this thought? Can I live with that?

2. Find a more appropriate thought and say it over and over until you believe it.

Here are the key behaviors for saying "I'm sorry":

1. Apologize as soon as you realize that you've wronged someone.
2. Say "I'm sorry," or "I apologize" sincerely to express remorse. With full eye contact.
3. Admit responsibility for your actions.
4. Make amends if possible. Don't give empty promises.
5. Say you will not do it again.

Follow-Up Questions

1. What are some situations where you should use verbal and written communications?
2. What are some situations where you tend to use blame when you shouldn't?
3. How can you create a more trusting culture?
4. How can you open up communication at your organization?

Endnotes

1. Summarized from Phil Decker, Blackboard website for HADM 5033 Leadership, University of Houston Clear Lake, 2014 (accessed February 10, 2015).
2. From Boris Groysberg and Michael Slind, "The Silent Killer of Big Companies." https://hbr.org/2012/10/the-silent-killer-of-big-companies and Leslie Allan, "Costs of Poor Workplace Communication." http://www.businessperform.com/workplace-communication/poor-communication-costs.html (accessed February 10, 2015).
3. Adapted from Boris Groysberg and Michael Slind, "The Silent Killer of Big Companies." https://hbr.org/2012/10/the-silent-killer-of-big-companies (accessed February 10, 2015).
4. Summarized from Towers Watson, "Capitalizing on Effective Communication—How Courage, Innovation and Discipline Drive Business Results in Challenging Times" originally published by Watson Wyatt Worldwide, 2010, http://www.towerswatson.com/assets/pdf/670/NA-2009-14890.pdf (accessed February 10, 2015), and Survey: Poor Communication Causes Most IT Project Failures, Computerworld Inc., 2010, http://www.computerworld.com/s/article/9012758/Survey_Poor_communication_causes_most_IT_project_failures, and M Leonard, S Graham, and D Bonacum, "The Human Factor: The Critical Importance of Effective Teamwork and Communication in Providing Safe Care," *Quality and Safety in Health Care*, 2004, 13, 85-90, http://www.ncbi.nlm.nih.gov/pmc/articles/PMC1765783/pdf/v013p00i85.pdf, and Warren Shepel, *Health & Wellness Research Database*, 2005, http://www.shepellfgiservices.com/research/stats.asp (accessed March 10, 2015).

5. Summarized from University of Northen Iowa, "Differences in Communication Culture." http://business.uni.edu/buscomm/buscomcourse/ReadingsSummer07/Differences%20in%20Communication%20Culture.pdf (accessed November 2, 2014).

6. Summarized from Mike Myatt, "5 Keys of Dealing with Workplace Conflict." http://www.forbes.com/sites/mikemyatt/2012/02/22/5-keys-to-dealing-with-workplace-conflict/ and Edmonds Community College, "Conflict Resolution Skills." http://www.edcc.edu/counseling/documents/Conflict.pdf (accessed November 2, 2014).

7. See Gayle Cotton, *Say Anything to Anyone, Anywhere: 5 Keys To Successful Cross-Cultural Communication* Circles of Excellence, Hoboken, New Jersey, 2013, or Sana Reynolds, Deborah Valentine, and Mary Munter, *Guide to Cross-Cultural Communications*, Prentice Hall, Upper Saddle River, NJ, 2011.

8. Summarized from UK Essays, "The Importance of Effective Written Communication English Language Essay." http://www.ukessays.com/essays/english-language/the-importance-of-effective-written-communication-english-language-essay.php (accessed November 2, 2014).

9. Adapted from Skills You Need, "Non-Verbal Communication." http://www.skillsyouneed.com/ips/nonverbal-communication.html (accessed November 2, 2014).

10. A good reference is Barbara and Allan Pease, *The Definitive Book of Body Language*, Bantam, New York, NY, 2004.

11. From Maynard Brusman, "Transparent Leadership – Fostering a Culture of Trust and Transparency." http://ezinearticles.com/?Transparent-Leadership-Fostering-a-Culture-of-Trust-and-Transparency&id=2929559 (accessed November 2, 2014).

12. From Glenn Llopis, "5 Powerful Things Happen When a Leader is Transparent." http://www.forbes.com/sites/glennllopis/2012/09/10/5-powerful-things-happen-when-a-leader-is-transparent/ (accessed November 2, 2014).

13. Summarized from JRS Consulting, "How to Encourage an Open and Honest Communications Environment." http://www.jrsconsulting.net/freearticles_20.html (accessed November 2, 2014).

14. Summarized from Reliable Plant, "Seven Steps to Creating a More Transparent Organization." http://www.reliableplant.com/Read/23472/Seven-steps-transparent-organization, Leading with Trust, "Four Strategies to Increase Organizational Trust and Transparency." http://leadingwithtrust.com/2012/09/23/four-strategies-to-increase-organizational-trust-and-transparency/ and Jacquelyn Smith, "How to Create an Authentic and Transparent Work Environment." http://www.forbes.com/sites/jacquelynsmith/2013/10/04/how-to-create-an-authentic-and-transparent-work-environment/ (accessed November 2, 2014).

15. Manuel J. Smith, *When I Say No, I Feel Guilty*, Bantam, New York, NY, 1985 and Martin Antony and Richard Swinson, *Shyness and Social Anxiety Workbook: Proven, Step-by-Step Techniques for Overcoming Your Fear*, New Harbinger, Oakland, CA 2008.

16. Summarized from Succeed Socially. http://www.succeedsocially.com/ (accessed November 2, 2014).

17. Ibid.

18. Adapted from Betty Kupperschmidt, Emma Kientz, et al. "A Healthy Work Environment: It Begins with You." http://www.nursingworld.org/MainMenuCategories/ANA Marketplace/ANAPeriodicals/OJIN/TableofContents/Vol152010/No1Jan2010/A -Healthy-Work-Environment-and-You.html (accessed March 24, 2015).

19. From Keith Jackson, "How to Apologize: Asking for Forgiveness Gracefully." http:// www.mindtools.com/pages/article/how-to-apologize.htm (accessed November 2, 2014).

20. Summarized from Aanya Rose, "How to Improve Listening Skills to Be a Better Manager." http://everydaylife.globalpost.com/improve-listening-skills-better -manager-8835.html and Tom Lewis and Gerald Graham, "Seven Ways to Improve Your Listening Skills." http://gvillage.org/gv/index.php/management-tips-21/21 -management/50-seven-ways-to-improve-your-listening-skills (accessed November 2, 2014).

21. Ibid.

22. J Becky Starnes, A Truhon Stephen, and Vikkie McCarthy, Organizational Trust: Employee-Employer Relationships ASQ, Human Development and Leadership Division, Milwaukee, WI.

23. MR Covey Stephen, *The Speed of Trust: The One Thing that Changes Everything.* Free Press, New York, 2006.

24. See The Trusted Leader. http://www.thetrustedleader.com/ (accessed November 2, 2014).

25. Ibid.

26. From Dennis Reina and Michelle Reina, *Rebuilding Trust in the Workplace: Seven Steps to Renew Confidence, Commitment, and Energy,* Berrett-Koehler Publishers, San Francisco, California, 2010.

27. Ibid. Also see Note 7.

28. JS Kouzes and BZ Posner, *Credibility: Why Leaders Gain and Lose It, Why People Demand It*, Jossey-Bass, Inc. San Francisco, California, 1993.

29. Ibid. Also see Note 25.

30. Abstracted from Marc Macyoung and Dianna MacYoung, "Blaming Justifies Your Own Bad Behavior." http://www.nononsenseselfdefense.com/blameBadBehavior .htm (accessed November 2, 2014).

31. Summarized from Brett and Kate McKay, "Personal Responsibility 102: The Importance of Owning Up to Your Mistakes and How to Do It?" http://www.artofmanliness .com/2013/02/19/how-to-own-up-to-mistakes/ (accessed November 2, 2014).

32. Taken from WikiHow, "How to Accept Blame When You Deserve It?" http:// www.wikihow.com/Accept-Blame-when-You-Deserve-It (accessed November 2, 2014).

33. Summarized from Behavioral Health Evolution, "Overcoming Shame-based Thinking." http://www.bhevolution.org/public/overcoming_shame_based_thinking.page (accessed November 2, 2014).

34. From Mosaic Online, "During Challenging Times you can Learning to be an Optimist." http://www.mosaiconline.ca/during-challenging-times-you-can-learn -to-be-an-optimist/?gclid=CKbr_4r8vb8CFXNo7AodgygA2Q and Jane Adams,

"The Pessimist's Guide to Being Optimistic." http://www.prevention.com/mind-body/emotional-health/pessimists-guide-being-optimistic (accessed November 2, 2014).

35. Adapted from Martin Seligman, "Learned Optimism: How to Change Your Mind and Life." Vintage Books, New York, 2006.

36. Summarized from Jim Tamm, "Buzz Off!" http://www.businessknowhow.com/growth/defensive.htm and Ridge Training, "Overcoming the Destructive Dynamics of Defensiveness." http://www.ridge.com/downloads/DestructDynamicsDefensive.pdf (accessed November 2, 2014).

37. Summarized from Brene Brown, "How to Practice Vulnerability." http://inpursuitofhappiness.net/blog/2013/03/28/how-to-practice-vulnerability and Henna Inam, "Why Vulnerability Can Be Your Biggest Strength." http://www.transformleaders.tv/why-vulnerability-can-be-your-biggest-strength/ (accessed November 2, 2014).

38. Adapted from RE Alberti and ML Emmons, *Your Perfect Right: A Guide to Assertive Behavior.* San Luis Obispo: Impact, Atascadero, California, 1990.

9

Talent Development

- ▶ Be on the lookout for promotable employees in your workforce

- ▶ Overcome you bias in employee selection

- ▶ Learn why using an interview guide is important

- ▶ Learn how easy and effective on-the-job training can be

- ▶ Hone your coaching skills

Leaders find good workers and keep them proficient in their work. Talent development refers to the process of selecting, training, promoting, mentoring, and sponsoring employees. For us it means finding and keeping energetic, self-developing employees throughout the organization. Talent and leadership development practices are positively related to employees' intention to stay and their commitment to the organization.

Leaders often get in their own way in this process. They can hire people who are too much like themselves, thereby not adding to the needed diversity in the organization; or they hire people who will not threaten the status quo—"yes people." Leaders can also have a tendency to rely on selection tools that look good but don't work well. Some go outside the organization to hire good people while others focus on only developing talent in-house to lower selection costs; employee selection is a balancing game between these two focuses. Leaders can also get too busy or focused and ignore the people around them who are striving to better themselves and get ahead.

Employee selection is the process of matching people and jobs, which usually involves multiple steps to evaluate candidates for a specific job—interviewing and testing are common. Employee selection can

---

range from a very simple to a very complicated process, depending on the position and employment laws. Employee selection processes are preceded by *recruiting* that brings candidates to the firm to be evaluated. Leaders are always part of each process because they know what is needed of candidates on the job and have to work with the individuals in the end. *Flaws in employee selection will always fall on the leader, no matter how involved or uninvolved.*

Beyond selection, many leaders have a tendency to avoid coaching and mentoring because of the time commitment or being uncomfortable with that level of interpersonal interaction. *Coaching* is helping individuals on new tasks or to find better ways to do the work; *mentoring* is a relationship in which a more experienced person helps guide a less experienced individual; and *sponsoring* is introducing a colleague to someone, matching a protégé to projects where they will learn, and otherwise opening up opportunities. While talent development has been proven to foster high-performance, less than 10–20 percent of managers are usually held accountable for developing talent.

Impact

As much as 80 percent of employee turnover is due to bad hiring decisions. The total cost of recruiting the wrong employee is very high; it includes hiring, total compensation, coaching, poor performance, eventual severance pay, and other factors like legal fees. It can be in the hundreds of thousands of dollars for a mid-level manager. Overall, the United States is devoting $105 billion a year (1 percent of the total US GDP) to correcting problems associated with poor hiring and people management practices.[1] According to a The Future Foundation study, management hires do not work out because of performance issues, a poor skills match, unclear performance objectives, and cultural mismatch—the perfect candidate who clashes with the organization's culture. Furthermore, 23 percent of the United States workers surveyed believe their colleagues are incompetent and the United States managers waste an average of 34 days per year dealing with underperformance. Senior executives claim they spend over an hour per day managing poor-performing employees. Even worse, employees admit that 68 percent of the mistakes they make never come to their managers' attention. This time and effort could be used on value-adding tasks—it is a huge handicap.

The talent development self-handicaps are one of the easiest areas to avoid—just a little extra attention is needed. To save enormous time correcting the results of poor hires and promotions, great leaders spend the time to clarify what "talent" means in the organization, make talent development an integrated process, and organize it as a coherent effort. The time spent upfront on these functions will save time and energy later on performance management, disciplining or firing employees, dealing with significant turnover, or trying to improve productivity of a disengaged workforce. Accept the premise of "pay me now or pay me later" and attend to the tools readily available.

The Real Issues

At issue here are the following:

- The process of always being on the lookout for eager, smart talent in your workforce and those you see in other worlds
- Analyzing candidates against a competency standard defined by outstanding performance and outcomes and making good decisions
- Mentoring/sponsoring/training talent to even greater heights

Little of this is the kind of self-handicapping that falls into the fear or self-deception categories—while some leaders may hire "yes-men," most leaders usually don't fear finding great talent, they just don't know how or it isn't the highest priority. They may have delegated this function inappropriately. Most leaders *know* that lack of time is no longer an excuse in this day and age; none of us have enough time in the day. But poor talent development due to lack of time or avoidance means the leader will spend more time down the road fixing the problems. Exercising good talent management will preload skill and ability into a workforce and help lead the team to excellence.

Leaders can have a tendency to commit errors of judgment or errors of bias in the talent development process. Leaders join groups that represent their shared interests and they carry this tendency into work—they go to lunch with friends, talk around the coffee maker about football, and other activities. If they aren't careful, they can carry this behavior into the search for job candidates—they can excuse a lack of work competency for a shared love of golf or a deficit in education/certification for graduating from the same college. Bias in employee selection is easy to miss, but once recognized and acknowledged, it is easy to eliminate.

Most new careerists view having a mentor as a ticket to greater visibility and better assignments and promotions.[2] Mentors can enjoy influence when their protégés rise to stardom. There are benefits for both, except mentoring can go bad. Some mentors end up neglecting their protégés because they are preoccupied with challenges in their own careers. Mentors can manipulate, especially when the mentor is the protégé's manager in the same department. Protégés can also manipulate and harm a mentor's reputation and career. Sometimes protégés rely on their mentor too much—they become codependent. A protégé can find a poor mentor and has no way of knowing this mentor is out of favor or out-of-date and providing poor advice. These situations are all clearly self-handicapping for both individuals.

A fundamental premise of this book is that self-handicapping behavior often doesn't look like failure to the manager who is self-handicapping. Remember the guy on the roof tearing up newspaper; he thought he was being successful keeping the wolves away. On the best day, a 30–50 percent hit rate is the definition of success in employee selection, so someone doing a bad job in employee selection doesn't necessarily look too bad. Furthermore, the manager may be hiring exactly the kind of people he really wants to hire—they're just not good for the customer or the organization. Controlling managers usually expect superior performance without superior selection, delegation, or training.[3]

Do You Practice Poor Talent Development?

Survey: Do I Practice Poor Talent Development or Not? (Y = Yes, N = No, DK = Don't Know)

____ I am not always on the lookout for developing talent in my area.

____ Leaders here have a tendency to hire the wrong people.

____ I don't seem to very good hiring people who can work independently and grow.

____ I don't always walk around my organization in different ways so that I can talk to different people.

____ I don't feel comfortable confronting employees when there are performance problems.

____ I am not always good at paying attention to the fit of new hires to the team/organization.

____ I tend to hire people from my alma mater.

____ I am not mentoring anyone.

____ I am guilty of allowing coaching and mentoring from bad leaders in my area.

_____ I think of my staff as a means to an end—that is, meeting departmental goals rather than a group of people trying to live their lives well.

_____ I am not a good interviewer.

_____ We do not have a clear competence model for each position.

_____ We made up our competencies; there is no data or proof they cause good customer outcomes.

Scores

10–13 Y's—You are greatly self-handicapping your talent management.
5–9—You are inconsistent on your approach to talent management.
1–4—You are good at talent management.

Beware of fudging on this evaluation. It is easy to be self-deceived in talent development activity.

What to Do?

Organizations thrive on talented employees. What to do to foster effective talent development is as follows:

1. *Align talent selection criteria to mission.* Pick talent with the mission/vision in mind. These items will dictate your competencies and needs—which should then guide the selection process. This is rare in organizations even though most leaders won't admit to it.

2. *Define and use competencies for your selection process.* Competencies guide the process and help avoid biases.

3. *Use an interview guide.* Using a guide will increase the validity of interviewing for many reasons and can serve as a record of the interview. It makes the process easier for the manager.

4. *Evaluate the interviewers.* Good hires depend on good interviewers. The outcomes of the process should be evaluated—tenure and productivity of the hires.

5. *Be on the lookout for internal talent that can be promoted.* Doing this can help in multiple ways (increase morale) and it can be financially better to groom an internal employee rather than training a new one.

6. *Coach your employees.* Teach your employees how to improve. In a few months you will know who is promotable and who isn't

and your employees will feel appreciated because you took time to speak with them.

7. ***Sponsor employees.*** Introduce and match your employees with a colleague. Arrange a special project for your employee to help your colleague on. Focus on growth.

8. ***Mentor employees.*** Mentoring can either be formal or informal, usually outside the junior employee's chain of supervision.

9. ***Provide training.*** As things change, make it easy for employees to keep up-to-date.

10. ***Ensure mentors and coaches are good.*** Allowing poor coaching or mentoring can derail and even ruin the career of a junior employee.

11. ***Pay attention to fit of people in teams and the organization.*** The culture of an organization will always win. Fit the hires to it.

Why Don't You?

Expediency

Often, poor recruiting and hiring are simply lack of skill or of understanding the process. Leaving this important function totally in the human resource (HR) office—or even undone—is self-handicapping. Lack of understanding how to find and keep talent in an organization is a behavioral handicap caused by reduced effort—the effort to educate oneself about the process and practice doing talent development activities. HR starts the process, the leader owns it and ends it with the final decision. *The leader always lives with the outcomes of the process.*

Most selection is done to match a person to a job, so the first thing that must be done is to understand the job—what does it take of an individual to do it. That will result in a list of competencies. *Competencies are characteristics of a person that cause superior performance.* These resources may be:

1. ***Motives***—The things a person consistently thinks about or wants that cause action

2. ***Traits***—Physical characteristics and consistent responses to situations or information

3. ***Self-concept***—A person's attitudes, values, or self-image

4. ***Knowledge***—Information a person has in specific content areas

5. ***Skill***—The ability to perform a certain physical or mental task

Some characteristics (self-concept, traits, and motives) may be difficult to measure and can be skipped by leaders, while others (skill and knowledge) are somewhat easier. Managers have traditionally used selection tools measuring mostly skill and knowledge competencies—with a little motivation thrown in. They either assume that applicants have the underlying attitude and trait competencies or that these can be instilled by good management. However, in most jobs, the opposite is true. Today, with the independence of workers, what distinguishes superior performers are motivation, attitude, interpersonal skills, self-concept issues, and political competencies. Furthermore, some managers actually think they can judge these through a quick interview. This attitude on the part of the leader is a self-handicap. Leaders who avoid handicapping know how to develop competency models and to develop reliable and valid selection tools. They also understand that knowing the customers' desired outcomes is critical to competency development and assessment—*competencies cause good customer outcomes.* Leaders accomplish things through their workers; poor workers produce poor results. It all starts with talent development.

Furthermore, most organizations miss the opportunity to evaluate the effectiveness of managers as interviewers, mentors, or trainers. This is difficult to do in most cases because the manager doing the poor hiring or training is also the manager who is completing the performance appraisal of those employees, which is the outcome measure in any such evaluation system. Regardless, a formal or informal method of evaluating interviewers shouldn't be overlooked. What is measured is what gets done. Sometimes in-depth reference checks can be used for this.

What talent development handicaps are you creating because of expediency issues?

Avoidance

One issue never to avoid is when selection systems do not support the leader's or organization's strategy and vision. The authors can't count the number of organizations we have walked into where the executives have told us they were trying to change some aspect of the culture of their organization; and when we walk into the HR office, we don't find a single selection or performance management system measuring those aspects. Simply put, organizations talk about strategic HR, but they rarely practice it.

Leadership creates strategy and HR develops selection systems. Guess who's in the middle when they don't match—the manager. Almost all organizations use interviews by managers as part of their selection system. So, managers are involved. *The mission, vision, and values of the organization and the competencies required in the job must be translated into interview questions asked of candidates.* It is time consuming to work through this process, but avoiding it is a severe self-handicap.

There's no reason why any manager can't draw a list of the departmental strategies and develop a competency list for each. The trick here is to keep it simple *and do it.* Take a look at Table 9.1 as an example of how to do this.

The next step in this process is to translate these competencies into a valid selection system. Since managers are usually involved in the interview, they can develop specific questions mentioned in Table 9.1 and put those questions into an "interview guide." An *interview guide* is a prewritten list of questions, probes, and interviewing hints that guide the interview. Developing such a guide is one of our "behaviors to change." What is important is that this guide will help ensure that the mission/vision guide selection, help a manager remember the questions developed prior to the interview, increase validity of the process, protect him from legal issues, and provide a format to take notes so that candidates are compared on the same information. To the extent that a leader takes the extra time to develop a guide and use it, he will enhance both the

Table 9.1 Developing Competencies to Meet Departmental Strategies

Strategy	Competency	Behaviors	Selection Methodology	Training Strategy	Performance Management Strategy
Lower costs	Be cost conscious	**1.** Know item costs **2.** Waste less of the expensive items	Interview question— "How do you lower costs through employee interventions in your current position?" or "How would you lower costs here?"	**1.** Training on item costs **2.** Identify expensive items and develop strategies to lower waste	Reminders of cost strategy Coaching on same Incentives

candidate/job fit and candidate/strategy fit and will be seen as one of the better leaders in the organization. Leaders who hire self-starters spend less time coaching employees and finding new employees.

What talent development issues are you avoiding?

Apprehension

Consider the following situation in interviewing two applicants—Sam and Dave. Both possess the minimum requirements for the position; however, you notice some differences during the interview process. Sam's previous work experience shows a man with independent thought, and he tends to excel in IT—one of the requirements. While you admit that Sam is a wonderful candidate, but he wasn't overly friendly to and you gathered that he isn't afraid to speak his mind on professional items. While Dave's resume and interview show him meeting the minimum requirements of the job, he is probably not independent at solving problems. He seems agreeable and nonthreatening. You hit it off immediately with him because he was in the same fraternity as you, has a background in finance—just like you—and he just seems like a likable guy.

So who do you hire? We know the socially acceptable answer—Sam. But, the reality in many cases is that Dave is less threatening and it seems that he would fit in with little disruption. The question that every leader has to ask in this situation is can he choose the candidate that's best for the department and organization or best for himself? You recognize Sam's talents and know he would be a valued member of the company, but he could be a problem for you down the road. Dave, on the other hand, does possess the minimum requirements for the position and you know that is no threat to you now or later. This type of hiring may not be handicapping for you, but it is self-defeating for your organization.

Most leaders know that they should be continually searching for young talent to cultivate and move higher in the organization, but why don't they do it? Often it is time—too many conflicting problems. But some leaders feel they shouldn't hire independent thinkers or look for junior employees to mentor, because, "What if they become more successful than me?" They then take the safe route; hire the 4 instead of the 7 (and down the rabbit hole they go). The team is stuck with a 4, and it plods along; this is an organization that spends a lot of energy to just stay steady. And it builds because the 4's probably hire 2's. When a manager has this mindset, he is essentially keeping the team from growing, and that is handicapping

---

everyone. *Inhibiting the better players from entering the game and playing just sends them to your competition which makes them better.*

The authors have seen many leaders consistently make their hiring decisions based on perceived or actual loyalty. While some degree of organizational loyalty is a required competency, asking for too much loyalty and conformance is not. Furthermore, hiring loyal and nonthreatening candidates can foster a codependent relationship in a department, which continues to build with more hires. The longer Dave continues as a mediocre employee, the less able he will be to find another job—thereby increasing the manager's and organization's hold over him—the longer he stays and the more loyal he becomes. While we all appreciate loyalty, the organization is less innovative, Dave is a less productive employee, the workforce becomes less customer-friendly and the manager is seen as less than effective.

One of the things that is critical in mentoring is the degree one trusts that the protégé will not embarrass him in some way. We coach those who we may not trust, we may mentor those who we don't completely know, but sponsoring and long-term mentoring relationships must involve knowledge of the individual and a relatively high degree of trust.

The key decision points in deciding to sponsor or mentor depend on getting to authentic trust; a leader must understand the level of goodwill an employee has for him as well as have belief in that person's competence. The leader will not reach a state of authentic trust until he believes that the protégé has both. Most of us know trust when we feel it, but sometimes it can be useful to ask—"Does the employee care about me?" and "Is the employee competent?" You can use the following chart to help sort this out for different employees and understand underlying feelings about mentoring and sponsoring them.[4]

Does the employee care about me?

	No	Yes
Yes	Affection	Trust
No	Distrust	Respect

Is the employee competent?

Do any fears play in into your talent development?

_____

_____

Self-Deception

Many leaders are unaware of the biases they bring to employee selection and development. An *implicit bias* is a positive or negative mental attitude toward a person that a person holds at an unconscious level. It is difficult to get people to acknowledge that it actually exists and should be changed. If a leader is hiring people he is comfortable with, he is probably very happy with the situation. The problem is that the workforce hired is not doing a great job. Furthermore, given that the easiest way to stop poor hiring is to remove the manager doing the poor hiring, that leader may not want to find himself in this predicament.

And, don't forget the old "in" group. Managers tend to give their "in" group more leeway, trust them more, assume they have an internal locus of control, forgive their errors more readily, etc. *They will also give them the most coaching and training attention.* But guess who is in more desperate need of that attention—the "out" group. This is a huge bias that should not be ignored. We have some hints on how to approach effective training. None of it is difficult; you just have to do it. Great leaders know how to effectively coach, mentor, and train their employees.

Finally, Manfred Kets de Vries suggests some of us are motivated less by a desire to help others than by a deeper emotional need within ourselves.[5] If you fall into this category, you may be a "rescuer," who builds inappropriate dependency relationships with the people you want to help. People become rescuers because they have a need to be liked or just a basic personality as a "helper." In this kind of relationship, both parties inevitably suffer. The person being helped may receive no real beneficial help, while the rescuer may become overburdened with the dependency of the other—they become a time leech. So if you find yourself being emotionally and physically drained by a professional colleague you feel responsible for, perhaps you should take a serious look at why you feel compelled to help that person.

What talent development may you be missing because of self-deception?

Behaviors to Change

Knowing the Competencies Needed in the Job

Recognize

The first step to talent management is to know what is needed. Ask yourself this question—"In my workforce, where do most of the problems occur?" Is it lack of skill and knowledge to do the job or is it that the employee does not have the "right" attitude, motivation, or self-concept to be effective? We have asked this question of thousands of managers and always get the same answer—attitude, motivation, and self-concept. We believe, as do those in companies such as Apple and Google, that selection should increasingly be based on the personality that it takes to be innovative and effective in today's high paced, complex world—in other words, not self-handicapping. We suggest a complete review of any organization's selection processes and a possible rebuild of competencies assessed. More focus on personality and motivational/self-concept competencies can force us all away from self-handicapping the selection process. Granted, this makes for a more expensive selection process, but finding effective employees—and especially leaders—can quickly pay for it.

Admit

Keep in mind that the manager practicing poor talent management is still hiring on attitude and self-concept; it's just on the dysfunctional side of the coin—unquestioning loyalty, codependence, willingness to take abuse, etc. If this is you, it can be difficult to admit that you need to refocus on the functional and effective side of attitude, motivation, and self-concept. If you are comfortable with all of your direct reports, you should examine what you have been doing. Innovative, independent people are irritating. No irritation may mean poor hiring.

Just to be clear—civil rights laws or the affirmative action guidelines do not prohibit measuring attitude, motivation, or self-concept. What federal and state civil rights law says is that *you may not discriminate against a person in any employment decision (e.g., selection and assessment) because of the race, sex, religion, color, national origin, age, mental or physical impairment, veteran status (and other state classes such as marital status, sexual orientation, etc.).* What this really means is that you can assess anything as long as it is not race, color, sex, etc., does not adversely affect a protected class, you do not treat individuals differently, and you can prove what you did use to decide is job-related. Traits and self-concept are fair game in most cases if required by the job.

Adjust

Step one is to list your biases. Take out a sheet of paper and draw a line down the middle vertically. On the left, list any and all biases you have—don't worry, you can burn it in a few minutes. Whatever they are—"I hire only from my alma mater," "Overweight people are lazy," "People who know Cisco are wonderful," "Red heads are never introverted"—get it all out and look at it. Say, "Yes, this is me." Then, on the right side of the sheet write down the impact for you, your department, and organization each of those biases can create. Hiring only from one school perpetuates one kind of thinking or knowledge base, I am missing out on all the non-skinny people who are super productive, and so on. Now ponder this and see how important those biases are to you. While some biases are suppressed and they may not be conscious, 80 percent are conscious and you can admit to them. You choose to have and use them. Some may be based on good data; just remember it is not really valid data, it is only your limited experience. So, choose to counteract your biases. Take deliberate action and change your thinking.

Now that we have that out of the way, let's get serious about how you really determine what is required of a person for great performance. A selection system should be based on a job analysis to ensure that the selection criteria are job-related. This analysis will determine the knowledge, skills, ability, and other characteristics (traits, attitudes, self-concept, motivation, etc.) required to perform the job successfully—*competencies*. In employee selection, tests and interviews are used to determine if a candidate possesses these competencies.

Key Behaviors

One easy way to determine competencies is to use Table 9.2. Write down the core tasks/responsibilities of a job, what the customer wants from that task and then what it takes of the person to provide it.

For more information on developing a competence model, see Marrelli, et al. "Strategies for Developing Competency Models."[6]

Interviewing

Recognize

There are countless tools, methods, and approaches to making good selection decisions. Most are marginal at best. The most valid methods are

Table 9.2 Developing a Competence Model

Competency or Job Task	Customer Need	Subcompetency	Behavior
Provide nursing care	Get well	Perform nursing task Document care	
	Not hurt	Be quick	
		Distract patient	
	Be respected	Don't talk down to patient	

expensive and time consuming (e.g., assessment centers and work sample tests). Most companies fall back on the tried and true interview because managers know the job, need to see and talk to the candidate, and interviews are quick and cheap. So, let's discuss how to approach the interview to avoid self-sabotaging talent development. We refer you to your HR department or Farr & Tippins for more information on other employee selection methods.[7]

Admit

The interview remains the single most common technique used in the hiring process, yet research suggests that it is not highly valid. Not only are interviewers likely to inject their personal prejudices or first impressions into the selection decision, but they also may not be using effective or relevant questions to gain information from the candidate especially about competencies. Interview guides help structure the interview and this increases validity. Managers often use the resume or application for this, but that does not usually help get at any real competencies and it is essentially spending time asking about information one already has on the application. Furthermore, the most accurate selection decisions are those made by choosing the best of several applicants rather than a yes or no decision made after each applicant is interviewed—all should be interviewed with the same questions and then one chosen. Lack of advance preparation in preparing an interview guide may lead to poor outcomes.

Adjust

One of the best ways to become a productive, efficient interviewer is to prepare and use an interview guide. An interview guide is a written document containing questions, interviewer directions, and other pertinent information so that the same process is followed and the same basic information is gathered from each applicant. Structuring the interview with an interview guide:

- increases its effectiveness by helping reduce the interviewer's bias
- makes for easy note taking so the interviewer recall of information about each applicant and can be stored to later justify the selection decision
- reduces the tendency of managers to make snap judgments based on superficial criteria
- allows for required note taking per question on the actual interview guide
- reduces the tendency of managers to use the interview to simply confirm first impressions

- gives the interviewer the same basic information on all candidates allowing for a more thorough comparison of candidates on the same criteria

Here is a sample interview guide.[8]

INTERVIEW GUIDE

The interviewer should record responses to each question during the interview.

Candidate: _____

Interviewer: _____

Date: _____ Position sought: _____

REVIEW OF APPLICATION FORM

Notes:

OPEN THE INTERVIEW AND ESTABLISH RAPPORT

Warm, friendly greeting.

Names are important—your's and the applicant's. (Use first and last name correctly.)

Break the ice—talk about the trip in, hobbies, weather, etc., and talk briefly about your position, hobbies, etc.

Notes:

OUTLINE TOPICS TO BE COVERED IN THE INTERVIEW

Education

Work history

Miscellaneous

Job preview

Notes:

QUESTIONS ABOUT EDUCATION

Notes:

QUESTIONS ABOUT WORK HISTORY

Notes:

QUESTIONS ABOUT COMPETENCIES

Notes:

OTHER TOPICS

Self-evaluation

Relocation

Technical licenses/certificates

Availability

REALISTIC JOB PREVIEW INFORMATION

Thank the applicant.

Questions?

The most useful questions are *open ended* ("How do you feel about . . . ?" or "Give me your opinion on . . . " or "Tell me about . . . ") or *work sample or behavioral* ("Given situation X, how would you handle that?" or "How do you create _____ function in MS Excel?"). Avoid *leading questions* where the answer is implied in the question ("We have a lot of overtime the last week of the month. How do you feel about working overtime?" or in behavioral interviewing, "Tell me about a time you have a difficult situation and what you did" which only asks for triumphs not failures. Avoid questions every applicant has prepared for in advance ("Tell me about yourself." "What are your strengths for this job?"). Use *closed-ended* questions only as probing questions to follow up an open ended or work sample question (e.g., where, what, when, why, how many, etc.). If you are typically more intuitive or emotional, include more technical skill questions; if you value specific technical competence, ask more about character traits like motivation and interpersonal skills. If you find yourself liking the candidate, probe for negative information, and vice versa. Remember, some degreed interviewees may have more interview training than you have. And, the more you speak the less you learn.

Finally, as you ponder questions for your interview guide, go back to the first two chapters of this book and think about how to look for individuals who do not self-handicap. We know that self-handicapping is done by those who are uncertain, so self-esteem and self-efficacy come to mind. They are difficult to measure in an interview, but you can assess true confidence at some level. Also, goal orientation is important. Those with a drive to mastery—not being best or avoiding error—but continually growing and learning would be preferable. We think humility and theory of intelligence are predictors of a mastery goal orientation. An openness to recognizing, admitting, and adjusting self-sabotage could be assessed. Finally, any knowledge of the ERO Spiral would indicate a candidate who is likely to do less self-damage on the job. If eliminating self-handicapping becomes your quest, make sure your selection instruments reflect that strategy.

Interviewing and Hiring

Key Behaviors

First, some hints:

1. Do you have a written list of required competencies for your department and most jobs? An interview guide?

2. When interviewing, if the candidate is starting to look perfect, step back and reexamine the situation. Why are you so comfortable with the candidate?

3. Develop a quality control function for interviewing and employee selection. Keep a list of your assessments of candidates and track performance—are you selecting people who stay and are successful?

4. Admit you and no one else are very good at employee selection. Keep trying to do it better.

5. Look for those who self-handicap.

The key behaviors for interviewing are as follows:[9]

1. Opening the interview
   a. Give a warm, friendly welcome—relax and smile.

    b. Talk about yourself or some other neutral subject to put the person at ease.

    c. Tell the person what you will cover during the interview.

2. Probing for information

    a. Probe for unfavorable information.

    b. Seek information to refute your first impression.

    c. Don't ask leading questions.

    d. Ask only one question at a time.

    e. Use such words as *How, What, Why,* and *Tell me.*

    f. Use the interview guide!!

3. Giving a realistic job preview

    a. Take a genuine interest in the person—discuss hobbies or interests.

    b. Make a point to discuss those aspects about the job and the institution that lie within the applicant's interests.

    c. Describe the job and the institution realistically, using a job preview checklist for the particular job. Discuss both good points and problems.

4. Closing the interview

    a. Summarize applicant's strengths and weaknesses.

    b. Ask if he or she has anything to add.

    c. Tell him or her the next steps in the employment process.

    d. Thank the applicant.

    e. Complete interview notes after the interview.

Being on the Lookout for Talent to Grow Inside an Organization

Recognize

Companies sometimes have trouble retaining their talent. There are many reasons for this. Eric Jackson suggests the following:[10]

1. ***Big Company Bureaucracy***—No one likes rules that make no sense.

2. ***Failing to Find a Project for the Talent That Ignites Their Passion***—Top talent is driven by something that will change the world.

3. ***Poor Annual Performance Reviews***—Ineffective performance reviews leave the employee with the impression that the boss isn't really interested.

4. *No Discussion of Career Development*—Everyone wants to have a discussion about their future.

5. *Shifting Strategic Priorities*—Top talent hates to be "jerked around."

6. *Lack of Accountability*—Top talent demands accountability from others and doesn't mind being held accountable themselves.

7. *Top Talent Likes Other Top Talent*—If you want to keep your best people, make sure they're surrounded by other great people.

8. *Missing Vision*—If the future of your organization is not exciting, good people will find where it is.

9. *Lack of Open-Mindedness*—The best people want to share their ideas and have them listened to.

10. *The Boss*—If a few people have recently quit your company who report to the same boss, it's likely not a coincidence.

Jackson suggests that smart organizations are the ones who get out in front of these 10 things and that organizations attending to them will keep more superior employees. However, in our consulting, we continually see one very simple-to-fix "up-front" problem that is not on this list: interacting with people on a daily basis and identifying those who are potential top talent—those who want to get ahead, make changes, innovate, grow, or act entrepreneurially.

Admit

Large companies often have a complex succession planning program where managers identify their potential successor. A good resource for examples is http://www.workforce.com/topics/115-talent-management-systems. Smaller companies identify a key person and then prepare that person for the job in various ways. The first problem is that neither of these techniques really work. Organizations are not stable and succession charts are quickly out of date. Second, competence at one level of an organization does not guarantee competence at the next level. Functional managers do not always make the transition to broader leadership roles. The key is to develop "bench strength" of several individuals at each level who might fulfill roles at the next level. Bench strength creates greater flexibility for both the individuals and the organization. This can only be done by interacting with your people, analyzing who wants and can get ahead, and then moving them into coaching and mentoring opportunities.

This is done in conversations between a leader and his employees. Beverly Kaye in *Help Them Grow or Watch Them Go*, talks about these conversations.[11] In these talks, it should be a priority to understand what is important to each employee. When employees are recognized for making gains toward career advancement, they feel valued and appreciated. Never take high-performing employees for granted; their success is probably due to seeking challenge and doing the right things toward advancement. Admire their accomplishments and help them move up.

Adjust

We have a very successful system CEO friend who consciously walks to regular scheduled meetings through different routes in the buildings, simply so that he can stop and interact with different employees. He does this not only to see and be seen, but also to find out what people are doing and thinking about their futures. Most of us are where we are professionally because of help from someone who recognized our talents—maybe on one of those walks or in a meeting. Pass that favor forward by adding the following technique to your talent development efforts. This is one of the easiest ways for you to be a great leader.

Key Behaviors

Here's how. Whenever you interact with an employee either you or your assistant can add to the following table (Table 9.3). After some time, you will know who deserves mentoring and further development. Don't try to sit down and do this all at once. Talk to them!

Table 9.3   Who deserves mentoring and development?

Rate each employee on each trait—low 1 to 10 high. Add the scores for each. Higher scores indicate talent to develop, mentor, sponsor.												
Employees												
Talent Trait												
Avoids office gossip and instead builds positive/constructive relationships within the department and organization												
Volunteers for projects and helps coworkers												
Deflects attention from themselves and credits others where appropriate												
Successfully completes difficult or ambiguous projects without close supervision												
Mentors new employees without having to be asked												

Table 9.3 *continued*

Criterion											
Looks at failures as opportunities and is always looking for growth opportunities											
Arrives on time, goes to work immediately, and wastes little time											
Joins professional associations or seeks development outside the office											
Demonstrates leadership in the community											
Helps other employees stay on track and manages projects without a formal title											
Despite adversity or difficulty, persistent effort is made to solve problems											
Accepts feedback and criticism well											
Avoids gossip and negative "gripe" groups											
Takes ownership of tasks or problems. Gets them done right the first time											
Is always looking for better ways to do things											
Demonstrates a passion for the job											
Treats customers and coworkers with respect and always tries to add value											
Always presents self and acts professionally											
Understands customer desires and always adds value to customer relationships											
Exemplifies the image you wish your company to project											
Total score											

Adapted from Elaine Stattler, "Is Your Employee Promotable?" http://www.managingpeopleatwork.com (accessed January, 2013).

Avoidance of Coaching and Discipline (Performance Management)

Recognize

Once promotable individuals have been identified, this talent pool will need development.[12] Leadership development requires three ingredients: (1) Formal training, (2) Performance management, and (3) Mentoring/

sponsoring. Formal training is necessary, but not sufficient. Developing leaders also need coaches or mentors; mentors and protégés should select each other voluntarily. For coaching to be effective it is has to be relevant, job-related, specific, and frequent. Sponsoring people at the level for which they are being developed allows those individuals to receive development and the organization has an opportunity to assess their work.

Admit

Most likely, it didn't require you reading the preceding paragraph to know that you should be mentoring, coaching, and sponsoring your employees. But why don't we do it? What is holding you back from realizing your potential for influencing ownership in employees? Is it an issue of lack of interest in people, being introverted, fear of competition, avoidance of getting too psychologically close, or perhaps just needing reminding from time to time? Maybe you are thinking that if you don't talk about it they may not think about it and the status quo will be safe. Maybe you think employees need to own their careers, and their development is not your job. Or maybe you just think everyone wants more, so why bother. Those attitudes are self-handicapping and can be costly in the long term.

In our experiences, one of the most costly, but preventable times, in an organization's life is that of leader transitions, namely, a situation of a manager/director/executive leaving the company—with no one to fill that position internally. Potential costs may include loss of productivity, training of external hires, marketing the position externally, and the costs of making a hiring mistake—time to hire, realize the mistake, fire, and second transition. It adds up and can literally cost years.

We believe the most common reasons for avoiding coaching and mentoring are lack of time and skill, so we offer quick tools to help in both areas.

Adjust

On a daily basis, managers coach employees on performance problems—it is part of standard performance management. Before meeting with a subordinate, the manager should prepare for the coaching session. Part of this preparation includes a quick diagnosis of the performance problem. A strategy for diagnosis is as follows:[13]

1. Is the performance discrepancy caused by a basic skills/knowledge problem or lack of motivation?
2. If the performance discrepancy is caused by lack of a skills or knowledge, how can that be solved?

a. Can the job be changed so that the employee's present knowledge and skill levels are satisfactory?
b. Can the employee learn the knowledge or skills required for effective performance?
c. Should the employee be reassigned to another job and a new employee hired?

3. If the performance discrepancy is not caused by a problem in skills or knowledge, why is the employee not performing up to standards?

   a. Is it caused by a performance obstacle such as incorrect tools, equipment, or materials?
   b. Are good employees *punished* by being given more work or harder work?
   c. What is the reward for good work?
   d. Are poor performances rewarded in some way?
   e. Are performance expectations clear?

4. What is the most effective course of action to correct the performance?

   a. Is it coaching, training, of changing the rewards?

Key Behaviors

The key behaviors for coaching are as follows:[14]

1. Always prepare before the meeting with the questions mentioned previously.
2. State the problem in behavioral terms. Focus on the problem, not the person.
3. Tie the problem to a customer outcome, the organization, or to the person's self-interest.
4. Try to bring the reasons for the problem into the open.
5. Ask the employee for suggestions and discuss his ideas on how to solve the problem.
6. Listen openly.
7. Agree on steps each of you will take to solve the problem. Write them down.
8. Plan and record specific follow-up dates and times.

The coaching session should last only a few minutes and should address small problems before they become bigger. It is important to state the problem in behavioral terms; this helps reduce defensiveness and keeps the focus on the performance problem. Encourage the employee to state the reasons for the problem; don't assume that you know the reasons. Asking for the employee's suggestions on how to solve the problem cannot be overemphasized as that is a key to ownership of it. Be sure that there is agreement about the solution and always document the steps that will be taken. Remember that 80 percent of the development of your employees will take place in day-to-day coaching.

Key Behaviors

Finally, coaching is different from correcting a rule violation. The following are the key behaviors for dealing with rule violations:[15]

1. Prepare before the meeting (e.g., is the employee aware of the rule, how employee will react, has the rule been consistently enforced.)

2. Without hostility, describe the behavior that violated the rule.

3. State the rule that has been violated.

4. Ask for and listen openly to the employee's reasons for the behavior.

5. Explain why the behavior cannot continue (and offer your help in solving the problem, if you think it would be useful).

6. Set and record a specific follow-up date.

Avoidance of Mentoring and Sponsoring

Recognize

While coaching is often a managerial job requirement, mentoring is something that is usually done outside the scope of one's duties, and sponsoring falls in the middle. A leader or manager can often arrange special projects and assignments as temporary duties performed by the employee on a full-time or part-time basis. These can be used to:[16]

- Enhance an employee's knowledge or skills in a particular area
- Work with a mix of people with expertise in different areas
- Prepare an employee for career advancement
- Broaden an employee's knowledge of other functions and departments
- Motivate and challenge an employee

Mentoring is a formal or informal relationship between two people—a senior mentor (usually outside the protégé's chain of supervision) and a junior protégé. Mentoring has been shown to be an important influence in professional development. More and more organizations are creating formal mentoring programs, but successful mentoring programs do not just happen. Organizations must devote the time, attention, and resources to make a formal mentoring process work. The US Office of Personnel Management has developed a good 20 page guide for creating mentoring programs. See http://www.opm.gov/policy-data -oversight/training-and-development/career-development/bestpractices -mentoring.pdf.

Admit

As discussed earlier, *authentic trust* is being fully self-aware and cognizant of all the conditions and limitations involved in trusting someone. An authentic trusting relationship doesn't simply happen, nor can it be mandated; it is built over time.[17] ASQ, an organization that shares information about quality improvement, has developed a useful white paper on trust. Visit http://asq.org/hdl/2010/06/a-primer-on-organizational -trust.pdf. Trust leads to productive mentoring relationships.

Ask yourself the following questions:

- How was I sponsored and how were doors opened for me to get where I am?
- Do I really think I did all this on my own?
- Do my employees deserve the same breaks I got?
- Why am I afraid to pay those favors forward?
- Do I have a network where I can sponsor my employees?
- Is there some reason employees should not be developed to their full potential in my unit?
- Am I trying to keep my employees where they are rather than help them develop? Why is that so?

As you answer these questions, you may find that you are the barrier to this kind of employee development in your unit—self-handicapping. Lack of development and engagement of employees has no good outcome.

Adjust

Many of us have LinkedIn accounts originally created to do our own networking. Over time these networks grow but should not be forgotten. Just as you use that LinkedIn account to network with potential mentors and sponsors, you can use the same account to help sponsor

---

your employees. If you're not familiar with LinkedIn and do not have an account, go to https://www.linkedin.com/reg/join.

When you identify a potential employee for talent development, you should do the following:

- Define the relationship making clear meeting times, roles, and expectations
- Request or recommend topics to cover at mentor/protégé meetings
- Present other ideas to enhance the mentoring relationship
- Ensure an agreement of confidentiality
- Establish termination of agreement rules—the "exit strategy"

Key Behaviors

Mentoring can be a challenge that is well worth the time and effort. Use these key behaviors to get the most out of mentoring sessions:[18]

1. Set aside time so that you can devote your full attention to your mentee.
2. Be fully present and keep eye contact. Mentoring requires your full attention.
3. Make a personal connection. This may be hard for some of us, but get to know the person.
4. Ask open-ended questions to understand the mentee's situation and concerns. Pay attention to the emotion and energy of the mentee.
5. Listen with curiosity, not judgment. Strive for understanding rather than problem solving.
6. Tell your story. People often learn best through storytelling.
7. Follow through on your commitments. If volunteering a book, a referral to one of your contacts, to review a resume, or some other service, make note of your promise and follow through.
8. Schedule your next meeting then and there.

Allowing Mentoring of Employees by Poor Manager Mentors

Remember that employees learn what they are given regardless of source. Allowing poor coaching and mentoring in your area is almost always self-handicapping. Many of us have had the opportunity to be mentored by a great leader. You likely adopted many of their lessons or styles. Maybe you learned to avoid some practices from poor leaders. But imagine being mentored by a poor leader. Think about the poor guy in a unit where there are only 1–2 managers and no formal training or mentoring programs. Does that stop the up and coming employee from watching their leadership? Typically not. If all the managers are not good models, some of those junior employees are mature enough to learn what *not* to do. Many will not be.

When an organization allows junior employees to be mentored by poor mentors/trainers, the future will consist of more soon-to-be poor managers and leaders. If your position allows you the discretion of choosing mentors for your junior staff—it is then your responsibility to ensure that only the mentors who possess the leadership competencies you wish for the future of your company to be mentors to junior employees.

Avoiding Training Opportunities

Recognize

There are several principles that guide training activities. These are as follows:

- *Motivation to Learn*—Trainees must be motivated to attend to the training content—give them a reason better than "because you said so!"

- *Practice*—What is practiced is learned and complex tasks should be broken down into smaller parts.

- *Over-learning*—Practicing beyond the point of getting it right is critical for retention and transfer—using it on the job.

- *Transfer of Training*—Learning will be transferred to the job when the training looks like the job and is reinforced on the job.

- *Self-Efficacy Is Motivational*—If an employee thinks they cannot do something, learning one small step at a time (baby steps) builds confidence and the feeling that it can be done.

- *Increasing Self-Efficacy, Confidence, and Mastery Goals*—These are key to eliminating self-handicapping and can be incorporated into training.

Admit

Do you do all of these things when someone is taught how to do a task? Training isn't really difficult, but the trainee has to see the training content, practice it in steps, be given feedback to get it right, and be rewarded for doing it. Often, the trainee is only told to watch and never gets to try it out or practice. Or, the trainee is put on the task with no demonstration or explanation; training requires lots of practice with demonstration and feedback.

Adjust

Self-sabotage in training usually means not doing one or more necessary parts of it. But if an employee needs training to perform successfully, and the manager is not supplying it because of time commitments, lack of training skills, or procrastination, it is self-handicapping. Go back to "Pay me now or pay me later." A little work up front in selection and training will save enormous heartache down the road with most employees.

Key Behaviors

The key behaviors for training someone in most tasks are as follows:[19]

1. Tell the trainee the objective of the task and ask him to watch you demonstrate it.

2. Show the trainee how to do it without saying anything.

3. Explain the key points or behaviors (give the trainee the key behaviors written out, if possible).

4. Show the trainee how to do it again.

5. Have the trainee do one or more simple parts of the task. If mistakes are made, have the trainee practice until accurate reproduction is achieved.

6. Have the trainee do the entire task and praise him for correct reproduction.

7. Praise the trainee for his success in learning the task.

Almost all training is based on these principles; they should be incorporated in all on-the-job training. If they are not used in the expensive training program offered to you—don't buy it. The only difference between you and one employee/trainee and the expensive program should be the fancy handouts or videos.

One important thing to remember: *You can't train someone to do something that you can't write down (or film it) and describe the steps.* Table 9.4 is an example. This form simply helps you write down the steps in an operation with the key learning points that may be needed to accomplish each step. *Some tasks are cognitive*, that is they are only in our head. Decision-making, analysis, and auditing are examples. You may think that you can't use this form and these methods to teach cognitive skills, but you can. You need only two things besides the key behaviors of training and these are: (1) A list of questions or decision tree showing the thought process and (2) A number of cases for demonstration and practice purposes.

Table 9.4 How to Make a Paper Cup?

Steps in the Operation		Key Points
A logical segment of the operation in which something is done to advance the work		Any directions or bits of information that help perform the step correctly, safely, and easily
	Place 8½" × 11" sheet of paper in front of you on flat surface	Be sure surface is flat, free of interfering objects
	Fold lower left hand corner up	Line up the right hand edges Make a sharp crease
	Turn paper over	Pick up lower right hand corner with right hand and place it at the top Folded flap should not be underneath
	Fold excess lower edge up	Line up right hand edges Fold should line up with bottom edge Make sharp crease
	Fold lower left hand corner flush with edge A	Keep edges B and C parallel Hold bottom edge in the center with finger while making fold
	Fold upper corner to point D	Hold cup firmly with left hand Bring upper corner down with right hand

continued

Table 9.4 *continued*

Steps in the Operation		Key Points
	Separate lower right hand corner and fold back	Hold cup with left hand Fold back with right hand Make sharp creases
	Turn cup over and fold remaining flap back	Make sharp creases
	Check cup to be sure it will hold water	Open cup and look inside

Source: PJ Decker and B Nathan, *Behavior Modeling Training: Theory Applications.* New York, NY: Praeger, 1985.

Not Paying Attention to Fit of People in the Team/Organization

Fit is a very important element of the selection process, and often over-looked. The culture of an organization will always win. When the new employee comes on board, he is immersed in the organization's culture. If his values differ from the organization's, he will be presented with two options—(1) To leave (and retain his values), or (2) Stay (and accept or buck the system).

Determining whether a specific candidate is the right fit for your organization's culture is critical and it can be very challenging to do. To do it, you need to understand your department or organization's culture, define what it takes in a candidate to fit into that culture, and of course, determine the candidate's values and personality. There are a number of instruments available to assess the culture in your organization. The Organizational Culture Assessment Instrument (OCAI) is a validated instrument used by many companies worldwide. It takes only a few minutes to measure the current as well as the preferred culture. Visit http://www.ocai-online.com/ and you can complete this survey for free. It is a good start, but remember that if completed only by you it is only your opinion of your organization's culture.

The next step is to assess your candidate. You need to separate skill and knowledge items that are found on a resume from the attitude and motivation and self-concept items since you will find fit answers on the attitude side. None of these steps are easy and they all take time. The Bridgespan Group has a useful white paper on this topic. Visit http://www.bridgespan.org/Publications-and-Tools/Hiring-Nonprofit-Leaders/HiringTools/Making-Right-Hire-Assessing-Candidate-Fit.aspx#.UrB_3U2A3y8.

Final Personal Takeaways

Action Plan—Talent management

What will you do about your talent management?

Tunnel Vision Self-Handicap	What Is the Situation?	Trigger	Impact on Others	What to Do/When?
Hire the "wrong people"		__Expedient __Avoiding __Apprehension __Self-deception		__Deliberate action____ __Self-efficacy_____ __Face it_____ __Look and listen_____
Don't use competencies in the selection process		__Expedient __Avoiding __Apprehension __Self-deception		__Deliberate action____ __Self-efficacy_____ __Face it_____ __Look and listen_____
Poor interviewing skills		__Expedient __Avoiding __Apprehension __Self-deception		__Deliberate action____ __Self-efficacy_____ __Face it_____ __Look and listen_____
Not using an interview guide		__Expedient __Avoiding __Apprehension __Self-deception		__Deliberate action____ __Self-efficacy_____ __Face it_____ __Look and listen_____
Not being on the lookout for promotable employees		__Expedient __Avoiding __Apprehension __Self-deception		__Deliberate action____ __Self-efficacy_____ __Face it_____ __Look and listen_____
Avoid coaching/ discipline		__Expedient __Avoiding __Apprehension __Self-deception		__Deliberate action____ __Self-efficacy_____ __Face it_____ __Look and listen_____

continued

continued

Tunnel Vision Self-Handicap	What Is the Situation?	Trigger	Impact on Others	What to Do/When?
Avoiding mentoring and sponsoring		__Expedient __Avoiding __Apprehension __Self-deception		__Deliberate action____ __Self-efficacy_____ __Face it_____ __Look and listen_____
Permit poor leaders/managers to serve as mentors		__Expedient __Avoiding __Apprehension __Self-deception		__Deliberate action____ __Self-efficacy_____ __Face it_____ __Look and listen_____
Don't pay attention to fit of people within teams/organization		__Expedient __Avoiding __Apprehension __Self-deception		__Deliberate action____ __Self-efficacy_____ __Face it_____ __Look and listen_____
Poor training skills		__Expedient __Avoiding __Apprehension __Self-deception		__Deliberate action____ __Self-efficacy_____ __Face it_____ __Look and listen_____

Baby Steps

The baby steps for this chapter are as follows:

- Take one job and ask yourself what is the most important competency that leads to satisfied customers. Ask a customer.
- Spend 2 minutes the next day with a random employee—get to know their aspirations.
- Decide who you may consider mentoring. You don't need to act on it, just think it through and choose a name.

The key behaviors for competency determination are as follows:

1. Choose a job at random.
2. List the internal and external customers for that job.
3. Choose one or two important customers.
4. Ask what those customers want from that job. Be open; frame this well.

5. Step back and ask yourself what motivation, trait, or self-concept traits lead to that outcome.

6. Complete the competency chart (Table 9.1) down to the behavior level.

The key behaviors for time with employees are as follows:

1. Ask what is happening in their lives.

2. Ask about their professional or job concerns. Address them, if possible.

3. Recognize good performance.

4. Ask one or more questions to begin completing the talent chart (tables).

The key behaviors to mentoring are as follows:

1. List current people you know to determine best fit for your mentoring.

2. Rank them on trust.

3. Ask for each—Are they motivated to succeed and excited to do what it takes to get there? Are they open to learning? Are they confident—it can be very challenging to build confidence in someone who doesn't have it? Rank again.

4. Determine what you would need to discuss in your first meeting— items such as the frequency of meetings, level of confidentiality, exit plan, etc. Rank one last time.

5. Choose a mentee.

Follow-Up Questions

1. Did you have any mentors? What did you get out of them? Can you pay it forward?

2. Can you identify someone in your organization who would benefit from mentorship/training/sponsorship? Where would you start?

3. How can you improve your personal process of finding promotable employees in your organization?

4. How would an interview guide help you?

Endnotes

1. Summarized from Laurence Karsh, "The Hidden Costs of Poor People Management." http://www.inc.com/articles/2004/12/karsh.html (accessed April 10, 2015).

2. Summarized from Dawn Chandler, Lillian Eby, and Stacy McManus, "When Mentoring Goes Bad." http://online.wsj.com/articles/SB1000142405274870369920 4575016920463719744 (accessed April 10, 2015).

3. Adapted from John Sullivan, "20 Reasons Why Weak Managers Never Hire A-Level Talent." http://www.ere.net/2011/03/25/20-reasons-why-weak-managers-never -hire-a-level-talent/ (accessed April 10, 2015).

4. Adapted from Peter R. Scholtes, *The Leader's Handbook: A Guide to Inspiring Your People and Managing the Daily Workflow*, McGraw-Hill, New York, NY, 1988.

5. Manfred F. R. Kets de Vries, *The Dangers of Codependent Mentoring*, HBR Blog Network. https://hbr.org/2013/12/the-dangers-of-codependent-mentoring/ (accessed December 3, 2013).

6. AF Marrelli, J Tondora, MA Hoge, "Strategies for Developing Competency Models," *Adm Policy Ment Health,* May-July 2005, 32(5-6): 533–561.

7. L James Farr and Nancy Thomas Tippins. *Handbook of Employee Selection.* Routledge Chapman & Hall, New York, NY, 2010. http://books.google.com/ books?vid=9780805864373 (accessed April 10, 2015).

8. Adapted from PJ Decker, *Management Micro Training*, 1982.

9. Ibid.

10. E Jackson, "Top Ten Reasons Why Large Companies Fail To Keep Their Best Talent Investing." http://www.forbes.com/sites/ericjackson/2011/12/14/top-ten-reasons -why-large-companies-fail-to-keep-their-best-talent (accessed December 14, 2011).

11. Kaye Beverly, *Help Them Grow or Watch Them Go—Career Conversations Employees Want*, Berrett-Koehler Publishers, San Francisco, CA, 2012. http://site.ebrary.com/ id/10597156?ppg=1 (accessed April 10, 2015).

12. Adapted from Harold Resnick, "Cultivate Leaders From Your Existing Talent Crop," *Jacksonville Business Journal,* March 2005. http://www.bizjournals.com/ jacksonville/stories/2005/02/28/smallb2.html

13. Adapted from IL Burr Ridge and D Richard Irwin, *Human Resource Management: Gaining the Competitive Edge*, McGraw-Hill, New York, NY, 1994.

14. Ibid.

15. Ibid.

16. Adapted from U.S. Office of Personnel Management, "Learning Strategies for Creating a Continuous Learning Environment." https://www.opm.gov/policy -data-oversight/human-capital-management/reference-materials/leadership -knowledge-management/continuouslearning.pdf (accessed April 10, 2015).

17. Adapted from Becky J. Starnes, Stephen A. Truhon, and Vikkie McCarthy. *Organizational Trust: Employee–Employer Relationships.* ASQ—Human Development and Leadership Division. http://asq.org/hdl/2010/06/a-primer-on-organizational-trust .pdf

18. Ibid. Also see Note 12.

19. Adapted from PJ Decker, *Management MicroTraining*, and PJ Decker and B Nathan, *Behavior Modeling Training: Theory and Applications*, New York, NY: Praeger, 1985.

10

Micromanaging

Chapter Takeaways

► Identify triggers that urge you to want to micromanage

► Learn the relationship between needing predictability and micromanagement

► Set and enforce boundaries

► Learn how to appropriately delegate

Theodore Roosevelt said, "The best executive is the one who has sense enough to pick good men to do what he wants done, and the self-restraint to keep from meddling with them while they do it."[1] Scott Berkun said, "Good leaders are brave and generous with trust in their people. They want them to mature in their judgment and grow in their skills, preferring to err on the side of trusting too much than trusting too little. They take pleasure in letting go and giving power away to their staff, accepting that when someone who works for them shines, they shine too."[2] Finally, Glen Blencoe says good leaders:[3]

- Surround themselves with high quality employees

- Invest in training and praise good work

- Communicate their vision and empower employees to achieve it

- Lead by example and listen

- Manage each employee differently

The golden rule of great leadership is that when employees succeed, leaders succeed. So, great leaders foster an open and engaging environment that allows employees to succeed and thrive. A major obstacle to that in business is the need to micromanage. *Micromanagement* means the

---

leader in question acts as if the subordinate is incapable of doing the job, giving close instruction, offering many "helpful" suggestions, dumping all responsibility on the subordinate without any authority or accountability, and checking everything the person does.[4] Micromanagers seldom praise and often criticize. Whatever their subordinates do, nothing seems good enough. Good delegation is the antithesis of micromanagement.

Much has been written about micromanagement—it is frequently the correct diagnosis for management ills. Many managers know no other way and simply don't believe that outstanding work can be done without their constant intervention. They are like the guy on the roof tearing paper; micromanagement has always worked in the past and there is no understanding that it is harmful or that people suffer from it. The result is diminished team performance and lack of accountability on the part of employees. Why should they try to own their jobs or competence? The boss owns it all and will fight to let it go. Micromanagement is likely one of the most difficult areas of self-handicapping to deal with. It comes from some deep-seated feelings about life and how to operate.

This chapter is about letting go, giving power away, and managing each employee differently. By another name—we are talking about *great delegation*. Micromanaging can be difficult for many of us and it is not something you can change with a training program. But remember this, "the difference between how a person treats the powerless versus the powerful is as good a measure of human character as we know."[5] There is no faster way to hurt yourself with self-handicapping than to abuse those who get the work done for you. The problem of self-handicapping arises when the leader does not realize that what he does can be abusive.

Micromanagement comes in different *flavors*. It can be dominating or passive, overt or subtle—one thing for sure, it is always persistent. We all know controlling bosses, *but control is much more pervasive in organizations than just the autocratic bullies who stand out*. The *dominant methods of micromanagement* can include taking over, anger, verbal assault, rewriting history, intimidation, ever-changing standards, and constant close instruction. Each of these categories can be broken down further. For example, temper tantrums, tirades, character assassination, ridicule, caustic jokes, and verbal put-downs are all assaults. Once a leader has a reputation for assault and a willingness to actually attack once in a while, he is in a perfect position to manage through intimidation alone. All he has to do is *look* as though he is about to explode and he will get his way.

Those of you with dogs can think about how dominance is established in the pack—the alpha male corrects the beta dogs as needed—no more or less, then they live in harmony with the authority structure established. This is what all dogs do naturally. It was how businesses were ran for a millemium, but the information age has disrupted that style of leadership. We can no longer afford that level of codependency, the hierarchy, or the wariness from the beta employees—always watching the boss. Workers today must *own* their own work competence, and add value for the customer—without direction from management. Micromanaging is a severe handicap in today's business world.

Passive micromanagement can be just as powerful and much more hidden. *Passive micromanagement* techniques include using existing vulnerabilities (poor me), deception, withdrawal, caretaking, crisis orientation, and entrapment. Other tactics include false flattery, carrot-dangling (holding out rewards which won't really get realized), playing dumb, helplessness, and denial. Another is "band wagon"—telling someone that everyone else has already agreed to the plan to get you to go along. All can be broken down further; for instance, withdrawal is used in eye contact, conversation, touch, proximity, supplying information/ data, and cooperation. A classic passive control maneuver is triangular communication. Here, a person will communicate to everyone else but you. The intent is to get a third person to relay the message to you so the originator avoids confrontation with you. All of these are passive or passive-aggressive and are designed to control another person— micromanagement. *It is important to understand that one can be controlled passively just as abusively as by the dominant micromanager.*

You may also see a relationship build between a micromanaging leader and his employees. Micromanagers tend to collect employees that are caretakers—passive micromanagers. These employees may have a higher need for security and are more willing to work for a leader that seems to have a tight handle on everything and is willing to tell them what and how to do it. This symbiotic relationship is in itself self-handicapping. These teams are not as innovative, productive, or customer friendly as empowered teams. It takes two—the micromanager and the codependent—to equal one independent person seeking mastery. The codependents are spending their time looking up at the boss to assess his moods and the micromanager is supervising everything below; neither is looking down to help solve customer problems.

If the following rules govern your organization, micromanagement is present in abundance:[6]

1. The leader must be in control of every aspect of the organization at all times.

2. When problems arise, find a guilty party to blame, immediately.

3. Don't make mistakes; if you do, cover them up and never let it get reported.

4. Never point out the reality of a situation; never express your feelings unless they are positive.

5. Don't ask questions, especially if they are tough ones, because they will rock the boat.

6. Don't do anything outside of your role.

7. Don't trust anyone.

8. Nothing is more important than giving to the organization and keeping up the *image* of the organization.

One of the things that usually goes hand in hand with micromanagement is a *need for predictability*. We all want some stability and consistency. It is a core function of organization. But predictability is different. It is the need to predict a future state, regardless whether it is calm or chaotic. When there is a constant striving for predictability, we can handicap ourselves. Picture yourself wanting to play tennis. You can call Fred because you are usually better than him or John who often wins. The micromanager will call Fred for predictability; the non-self-handicapper, seeking mastery, will call John. He can learn from John. Need for predictability behaviors include getting uneasy when things go too smoothly, avoidance of uncertain situations or being helpless in such situations, worrying constantly, checking up on employees or coworkers repeatedly, finding out what the "boss" wants before you decide how to act, trying to keep emotions out of what you do, and avoiding intimacy. Some people are often driven to micromanagement to insure a stable environment. This set of behaviors can prevent us from taking risks or opening up to employees. It can prevent learning because we avoid situations that are not thoroughly planned or controlled before we enter.

Impact

At the management level, micromanaging causes many problems with employees such as:[7]

- *Feelings of Incompetence*—No one wants to be made to feel like they aren't intelligent, incapable, or lack necessary skills when it comes to completing a task.

- *Reduced Accountability*—Groups sometimes become "leader dependent" or fear unreasonable punishment so they refuse to voluntarily take responsibility and ownership of tasks and their own competence.

- **Added Extra Pressure**—A boss watching over employees can cause them to make more mistakes because the workers may feel extra pressure to perform and perform well.

- **Limited Independence**—Micromanagers limit a worker's sense of independence, and thereby lower job satisfaction and morale.

- **Unwillingness to Add Value for Customers**—Employees are too busy watching the boss to attend to customers.

- **Decreased Confidence**—Micromanagement decreases and often eliminates employee confidence, which inevitably decreases the quality of their work and causes them to self-handicap.

- **Stifled Creativity**—Constantly checking on someone's work (and telling how to do it) puts a damper on creativity.

Micromanaging doesn't work except in task-oriented, time sensitive situations, with low power employees—and not always then. Reinforcing employees to rely so heavily on the leader is self-handicapping for customers. The employees will hunker down, not drive for anything unless told, and the micromanagers' reaction to problems is to do it alone, work harder, do more, with no collaboration and sharing of the leadership burden. Their heroism is often their undoing.[8] Martin, in his book, *The Responsibility Virus*, says that when heroic leaders take on too much responsibility and approach the point of failure, they often do an abrupt turnaround, flipping to an under-responsible stance in order to avoid the accountability of a failure.[9] Then, as failure looms, followers begin to be angry with the leader for not leading and the leader becomes angry with followers for not helping to solve the problem—the Box of Blame. We have all seen it—if the micromanager is supreme, then failure would be on his shoulders; so his only out is to throw a fit blaming the staff to duck the accountability for the failure. We have already said that blame causes more blame (and retaliation). Martin also suggests that team-based organizational structure and empowerment have not solved this problem.

Here are a few more tidbits about micromanagers. They are often "organizational gatekeepers" and try to isolate their subordinates from all outside information.[10] They keep their employees out of vital meetings and ensure information they do get is distorted to match their goals. *Any attempt to change the behavior of the micromanager will be perceived as a personal threat and he will retaliate. He will be motivated to eliminate the source of resistance.* Micromanagers can read people and identify those who will accept control. It is like there is a special radar between those with a need for control—dominant controllers will quickly find those willing to follow. Micromanagers only *share responsibility with others, not authority.* They use a lot of corporate buzzwords, and communication is cluttered with complexity as just one more way to never be personally accountable. *Finally, they focus on activity rather than outcome.* Their techniques of control are so deft that they stay out of accountability's reach in many ways.

All poorly run systems, whether it is an addictive family or an organization riddled with micromanagement, are often in a state of confusion and crisis.[11] Since organizational management is about creating a steady state, many executives make the assumption that this crisis can be reduced if confusion is reduced. They see the two as separate, but they're not. A micromanager creates crises to avoid accountability. Throw in some intimidation and their staff fall all over themselves to try to predict what will happen next, what the boss wants, and how to deal with it. This is their attempt to create order. But it prevents anyone from taking responsibility and accountability. When the staff is busy trying to figure out what's happening with the boss, they are not taking responsibility for the customer and being accountable for customer outcomes. This confusion is a self-imposed handicap by itself, which leads to an even larger handicap—lack of accountability throughout the team.

"Living the promise" is a situation where the organization or the leader directs the staff eagerly to the future and some hoped for future reward in the middle of the confusion of micromanagement. It can be a way of distracting attention away from the ineffectiveness of the present situation. The focus is on expectations rather than the current state. Unfortunately, this constant focus on the future is the very thing that keeps everyone from focusing on the present and is therefore self-handicapping. The real knot here is that there may be very little real productive activity going on in the organization, or if it does take place, it is taking an inordinate amount of effort. That often is what the crisis orientation is hiding.

Most leaders who find themselves with an organization in a state of confusion, crisis management, and living for the "future promise" believe that it is possible to "figure out" what is happening in the organization and solve it. But they often cannot. This is called "stinkin thinkin" in AA meetings—to believe that this kind of crazy (addictive) system is understandable *is not* a rational, logical way of thinking. Doing this means constantly going back to understand how you got to a certain state and few dysfunctional people will agree on the history. When management consultants say, "you have to understand the history of this," they are not being helpful because you can't negotiate the past in micromanagement. It is best to move forward, illuminate the self-handicapping, be outcome-focused, and negotiate future action and agreements.

But in this kind of system, the future is often another crises. Crisis creates a great deal of directed effort and intense feelings. It brings people to work together and allows them to feel responsible for an important goal. Guess what you need in a crisis—a task-oriented, micromanaging, "strong" leader. That is a cycle leading right down the rabbit hole. Around and around we go until the organization is bypassed by another organization that can get the work done more productively or effectively. The key to breaking the cycle is getting rid of micromanagement, everyone accepting accountability to the customer, and allowing the workers to do their work.

Real Issues

Working for a micromanager makes most subordinates become timid and tentative—even paralyzed. This *paralysis* a form of learned helplessness (a mental state caused by abuse) where the person becomes unable or unwilling to have future encounters with the same abusive behavior because he has learned that he cannot control the situation. Beat a dog enough and it will not move. Pessimists are more prone to learned helplessness; and interestingly, people can learn to be helpless through observing another person encountering uncontrollable events. Many people who work for micromanagers are prone to say "No matter what I do, it won't be good enough." This, of course, strengthens the perception by the leader that the employees need closer supervision.

Micromanagement often is rooted in one's personality and prescriptive lists of what to do differently are not a solution. Maybe it is all a manager learned along his management career ladder. More likely it was learned it at an early age. A micromanager tries to control every little detail, but they are not super human and their attention span is limited. They usually bog themselves down to the extent they lose the bigger or more important picture. We see this a lot in business—benchmarking in one area excessively and losing the big picture in another much more important outcome measure or building the best "tool" available to accomplish something and losing sight of the fact the customer no longer wants that "something." Micromanagement causes tunnel vision. Employees will often use this weakness and keep the boss focused on detailed procedures or documentation rather than their lack of outcomes.

Of course, a leader may reasonably not trust his employees either because there is evidence to support this, the newness of the relationship, or a high-risk situation that merits extra management attention. Lack of trust is a rationale reason for close management. But in situations where the leader overly fears failure, feels (or want to feel) superior to the employees, or knows no other way of interacting, it is self-handicapping. Let's go back to the guy on the roof tearing up paper and throwing it off. He fears quitting the one thing he "knows" works and is unwilling to risk losing it for a risky new behavior that may not work. This is why changing micromanagement is so difficult.

As organizational consultants, one of the ways that we determine the degree of micromanagement in an organization is to look at the administrative/staff ratio. Nearly 90 percent of companies staff assistants to vice presidents at a 1:1 ratio and most staff assistants to directors at a 4:1 ratio. There are many places to find appropriate staffing levels by industry and position; and it should be done.[12] When you see too many assistants (avoiding accountability) or not enough (doing it all yourself) you may have a case of micromanagement. Leaders who are micromanaging avoid accountability through too many assistants. There is a tendency to dump everything on the assistants and when it goes right, claim credit; and when it goes sour, blame the assistants. Micromanagers like to fire orders out and never follow up. The opposite is also true: Not enough support or the support is unused indicates the leader is trying to do everything himself. Recently, assistants have taken on more management and supervisory roles—even more long-term project management. The trend is toward more responsibility of assistants, not larger staffs. Large staffs are suspect. If you are looking to reduce your leader to assistant ratio, reducing micromanagement and working on helping leaders accept accountability may help.

Do You Micromanage?

There are many ways to run down the rabbit hole to micromanaging.

Survey: Do I Micromanage or Not?
(Y = Yes, N= No, DK = Don't Know)

Do I:[6]

    ___find myself looking over employee's shoulders to offer "advice."

    ___get called a "control freak."

_____ often listen to my employees discuss a problem and feel compelled to voice an opinion.

_____ sometimes don't cope with uncertainty or the unexpected well.

_____ suggest a solution, rather than ask others to propose solutions.

_____ have a high need to help people with their work or problems.

_____ often succumb to the urge to finish a task that was started by an employee.

_____ often delegate *some* tasks within the project but never the *whole* project.

_____ have employees relate that they feel unfulfilled in their job.

_____ "lose it" because things are unpredictable.

_____ think my workplace suffers from a high employee turnover rate.

_____ usually solve one problem before I move on to the next one.

_____ often wonder why my employees are so lazy.

_____ sometimes avoid the tough conversations until it is too late.

_____ like my employees to uphold the image of my unit no matter what.

Scores
11–15 Y's—You are micromanaging.
6–10—You are somewhere between a poor delegator and a micromanager.
1–5—You are empowering.

What to Do?

Let's start by reviewing delegation (see Chapter 3, Accountability). When you delegate tasks, you must delegate responsibility, authority, and accountability:

- **Responsibility**—An obligation to perform assigned duties to the best of one's ability

- **Authority**—The power assigned to a leader in order to achieve certain organizational objectives

- **Accountability**—The answerability for performance of the assigned duties and living with the outcomes

Many leaders delegate responsibility but forget authority or accountability which is the focus in the Accountability chapter. Micromanagers almost never let the delegated individual have any authority or get to the point where they alone must live with the outcome of their actions. They dump a lot of responsibility and it looks good, but in truth it is self-handicapping for all.

Delegation also includes developing skill in juggling and multitasking—micromanagers are very linear and have trouble keeping several employees' issues and projects in the air at once and all moving forward. A flexible leader can do these things and avoid the attitude that an issue must be completely solved before he can move to another issue. Delegation can be the most important management tool that you use. It can save you time, motivate employees, and help them develop. Poor delegation can cause frustration, act as a demotivator, and disengage people.

Here is *what to do* about micromanagement; we will talk about *what it takes to do it* later.[13] For now, on each item, plan further education or an action step to develop the skill or deal with the issue (Table 10.1).

Table 10.1   Micromanagement Behaviors to Work On

Behaviors to Work On	Where It Occurs/ With Whom	What Will I Do?
Ask yourself why. If you're micromanaging, there's probably an underlying reason		
You are not the only one who can accomplish an end result. *Trust* others to be capable of achieving it		
Assign one task to two team members. Give them the responsibility for dividing the work and finding a solution. They should come to you only if they cannot find an answer together		
Encourage employees to ask about your way of doing things. You can then explain the thought process behind your approach (or maybe even that it is just your control issue). **Then, leave it up to them to decide to adopt it or not.** Employees maybe more likely to adopt it this way or at least respect the thought-process		

Table 10.1 *continued*

Behaviors to Work On	Where It Occurs/ With Whom	What Will I Do?
Delegate whole pieces of the job rather than just tasks and activities		
Delegate challenges and define success. Delegate the problem and let them determine the intermediate steps or detailed output		
Don't ask for a list of options and recommendations. We all know the employees will search for what the micromanager "really" wants and provide that		
Agree on the frequency of feedback meetings or reports between yourself and the person to whom you are delegating. **Then stick to it**		
Encourage your employees to speak up if they have a better idea—with enough time for discussion and decision. **Listen and adopt**		
Resist the urge to solve someone else's problem. They need to learn for themselves. Give them suggestions and perhaps limits but let them take their own action		
Never take back a delegated item because you can do it better or faster. Help the other person learn to do it better after they ask		
Share experiences, don't instruct. Allow the learning to take place by allegory and not turn the learning into "just do these steps"		

continued

Table 10.1 *continued*

Behaviors to Work On	Where It Occurs/ With Whom	What Will I Do?
Listen to progress, don't review it. Let folks report on the progress		
Provide feedback, don't course correct. This type of course correction can disempower and demotivate		
Don't correct everything you receive. When an update comes in, the sender was probably hoping for a job well done reply. Don't criticize the work in minute detail with every incoming email		
Communicate serendipitously, don't impede progress. All projects have more work and less time than they need. Reduce the call for reviews or updates in a formal manner (meetings, written reports). This type of communication can slow things down		
Practice being absent. Parents do it if they want their children to be more independent. Spend more time away from the office or simply keep your door closed		
Rein in workplace bullying. Those with a tendency to bully others at work may create resentment and diminish feelings of self-esteem and autonomy		

A leader can use a decision analysis meeting to reinforce the message that the leader did not intend to make all the decisions himself but rather to make choices as a group (Vroom and Yetton, Chapter 7). This is a conscious choice by the manager to bring the employees or team together to make decisions and assign responsibilities and accountabilities as a team rather than one micromanager being in charge. It is an attempt by the manager to let go and give power to subordinates. This process includes framing the choice, brainstorming options, specifying conditions and barriers, analyzing alternatives, and making a choice of approach as a group (this is also front-loading the delegation).

When it is too late to use that process, the leader can reframe the issue without a meeting of subordinates. The micromanager sees his existing frame as "the leader knows the right answer." The reframing process is to develop a new frame that suggests the leader may not know all the answers. The task in the meeting is helping him redraw different frames using the perspective of employees and customers.

Micromanaging by Email

Very few leaders enjoy confrontation, and many micromanagers do whatever they can to avoid it—including hiding behind email.[14] Unfortunately, this often aggravates the problem. No matter how much you dislike confrontation, you have to be very careful about using email. It is easy for those typed words to get interpreted a hundred different ways. Refrain from shooting off the quick email; rather use face-to-face conversation when needed. Email doesn't convey emotion well. It is not empathetic or open. Email and texting are a "read-and-reply" culture. If you are really angry, it's all too easy to "vent and send" before investigating the facts. Also, online conflict spreads like wildfire. It's too easy to forward email to lots of people, many of whom may not need to get involved.

There is a fine line between micromanaging by email and not. You need to practice email skills so your unanswered email does not bury you. Do not delay email to show how important you are.[15] Get your message across quickly and effectively. If a message is too long, it risks getting pushed aside to be revisited. At the same time, you want to be thorough in your email so there is no room for misinterpretation or need for your recipient to request more information. Do not send multiple messages in one email. Anticipate the questions you might receive ahead of time, and answer them. Write detailed subject lines so that the recipient has a clear understanding of the issue. Do not ask executives multiple questions—they will answer the first or last one. Do you know how frustrating is it when you've presented a number of options in the email only to receive a response that says, "Sounds good!"? To avoid this, make sure your objectives are clear from the get-go. Never be afraid to pick up the phone or walk down the hall. Your willingness to come out from behind the email veil shows assertiveness and initiative. It is engaging.

Working for a Micromanager

So what should you do when your boss is a micromanager?[16] Sure, you may be tempted to bolt, but at a time of high unemployment, you might not have that option. So, better to master the art of managing the micromanager:

- Recognize that it is their issue, not yours. This probably means they lack certain abilities and you are going to have to handle it. Don't be defensive. It is a waste of your time and plays into their game (that you are the problem).

- Avoid any power struggles or too much feedback about micromanaging. This will likely result in the micromanager using all his formal power to beat you into submission or get rid of you.

- Listen patiently and attentively when they tell you what to do (they hate being ignored or disrespected).

- Try to ensure you cannot be blamed for the micromanager's decisions (keep notes, emails) but don't expect this to always protect you. They rewrite history easily.

- Help your boss delegate to you more effectively by prompting him to give you all the information you will need up front, and to set interim review points along the way. Volunteer for projects that you are good at as this will increase his confidence in you.

- Look for patterns. As annoying as micromanagers are, they're incredibly predictable. Knowing their pressure points can help you ease them.

- Show empathy. Remember, the micromanager is under pressure to produce (much of it in his own mind). Show that you understand his plight and are willing to share the load.

- Be super reliable. This goes back to the fact that a micromanager hates feeling out of control and needs predictability.

Piaget devotes much of his book, *Control Freaks*, to discussing techniques for coping with micromanagers.[17] He outlines five approaches—four don't work. His fifth category, *the Aikido alternative*, parallels the philosophy of the martial art—that is, don't react to a controller by trying to stop him but move with his energy for a while; then as you move with him, attempt to influence, redirect, or neutralize him in some way. He sees this technique as neutralizing the micromanager's great energy and drive to control while doing as little harm as possible to everyone involved. The four basic Aikido skills and the tools suggested by Piaget include:

1. *Centering*—relax and stay balanced no matter what. Manage the adrenaline-induced need for "fight or flight," blushing and anger, and your emotions. Know your limits.

2. *Observing and paying attention*—observe what goes—understand the emotional hooks used and the patterns. Listen for feelings as well as facts; don't jump to conclusions.

3. *Aligning*—move with, rather than fight against, his energy. Mirror their position, accepting the rightness of it.

4. *Redirecting*—deflect or change the attacking force. Respond selectively to mixed messages, negotiate and compromise, and nudge the situation to be less micromanaged (use baby steps).

Assertiveness is critical with micromanagers because you should never judge them, try to control them, pity them, or fight back. In other words, do not be aggressive or passive with them. You must try to subtly teach your micromanaging boss how to behave. This can be done through behavior modification—*subtly* rewarding appropriate behavior and not rewarding or *subtly* punishing inappropriate behavior. The reward should be affirmation and attention. Go slow and be careful. Remember that you probably can't overhaul the boss's basic personality by setting limits, but you can teach him how to act in acceptable ways by clearly defining what he can and cannot do in the relationship—micromanagers are bullies and can be made to back off. You just have to do it slowly and gradually. Also, you must be willing to leave or quit to pull this off. You must be willing to accept the consequences of your actions. Remember, most micromanaging bosses have a significant resistance to growth. They view the employees as the ones with the problem, not themselves.

Probably the biggest key to working with most micromanaging bosses is to understand their need for affirmation. Many dominating controlling people find a passive controlling mate who continually provides this. Your boss may be expecting the same with his workforce. Loyalty is his big issue. His symbiosis is with the employees and if you try to take that away, he will react violently. So affirm while practicing Aikido. Watch carefully for the subtle, insidious pressure to affirm. This can be hypnotizing for some and drives independent people away.

Why Don't You

Expediency

To figure out how to delegate properly, it's important to understand why leaders avoid it.[18] There are several reasons people do a poor job delegating—it takes a lot of up-front effort, they don't like the confrontations needed to correct or guide those who are avoiding accountability, they fear losing control of the outcomes (the root of most micromanagement), or they want to use the word "accountability" with employees to actually hide from it. Avoiding the up-front effort can stem from two reasons: (1) It's easier to do it yourself than explain the process to someone else, or (2) It is too time-consuming to include all the elements for front-loading accountability. Delegation is most appropriate when:[19]

- It is not critical that you do it yourself (micromanagers don't see this)
- The task provides an opportunity to grow and develop another person's skills
- The task will recur, in a similar form, in the future
- There is enough time to delegate the job effectively
- Your skills are better used elsewhere—on strategy
- There is a need to spread the work load evenly across your span of control
- There is someone else who has (or can be given) the necessary information or expertise to complete the task

How to "front-load" the accountability (proactive accountability) and the skills/motivation to reward and correct avoidance of delegated accountability are discussed in the Chapter 3—Accountability. This chapter is about one reason we don't do those things. You can take a quiz on how well you delegate at MindTools Team Management (https://www.mindtools.com/pages/article/newTMM_60.htm).

What micromanaging do you do because of expediency?

_____

_____

Avoidance

Delegation is an area where many mangers struggle.[20] The difficulty stems from their need to control outcomes and the belief that they know the best way of doing things. These are the traits that brought them to management in the first place that were often rewarded. Companies often promote workers who produce good work, not necessarily workers who are excellent leaders. Rather than working on improving delegation skills, sometimes leaders simply keep hold of more tasks and become overworked. Or they learn how to "manage up" very well. True delegation means managing down in order to manage up. It means giving up some measure of control and not holding on to the accountability. But the micromanager is thinking, "What if the employees don't do it correctly? What if they do it better than me? What if I become less essential to the business?" It is easy to want to hang on to control, but don't protect your job by hiding it, protect it by teaching others how to do it. This builds depth within the organization and promotes individual trust. Find something for everyone to take ownership in—give them a reason to be engaged at work. This is the path away from micromanaging. Delegation means taking true leadership responsibility and giving up control. It is the opposite of micromanaging, which we know is the greatest self-handicap of all.

What micromanaging do you do because of avoidance?

Apprehension

At this point, you may have begun to accept that you do a little micromanaging. What is left are the big challenges:[21]

- Identify your insecurities behind the micromanaging
- Understand and respect personal boundaries

Looking in the mirror and "accepting" what we see can be one of the hardest things we ever do. People may not recognize bad outcomes, or they may woefully misperceive the impact they have on the people around them. Typically, the more severe the problem, the stronger the denial. "Identifying your insecurities" isn't easy. You may be insecure about your ability to manage or your team members' ability to get the job done. One possible insecurity is perfection. The desire to be perfect hits a lot of us and causes much unhappiness. The need for perfection can be a statement that "I'm not good enough just as I am." We are judging ourselves; but we need to decide what's more important—having the work completed to "perfection" (the way we would do it), or having it completed successfully in a different way by someone else in a timely manner. *At work and in sports, being consistent is better than perfect most of the time.*

The ability to judge ourselves makes us uniquely human, but can also be our downfall. If we have an exaggerated sense of our own shortcomings—maybe because we received messages as children that we weren't good enough—we are in immediate trouble with perfection. This self-judgment is so ingrained, so normal, we don't even recognize it. But remember two things: (1) No one is ever really "perfect"—even Olympic gold medalists want to be better and better. That is mastery goal orientation. (2) To eliminate self-handicapping means to dump performance goals and strive for mastery. In order to let go of a need for perfection, we need to decide to stop judging ourselves so harshly and then to stop using our judgment of ourselves as a guide.

Many organizations operate with an undercurrent of fear; people fear change; they fear failure at work, their boss, speaking up and taking risks. Fear is easy to see in an organization, especially in a highly competitive work environment. Fear is at the heart of command and control, bureaucratic organizations; employees are expected to submit to authority, deny self-expression, sacrifice for future rewards, and believe that all the rules and regulations imposed are just. This is self-handicapping. The best advice we can give is to select competent employees, front-load delegation, help employees own customer outcomes, and then get out of the way. Go interact with a peer, do some planning, or go to a professional association meeting. Do anything to leave your subordinates alone so that you discover: (1) They can handle their own work, and (2) Them handling their own work does not threaten you but strengthens your position. That is the only reinforcement over time that will defeat your fears and help you move beyond micromanaging.

What micromanaging do you do because of apprehension?

Self-deception

Managers and professionals can treat others as objects to help accomplish goals (being *in the box*) as opposed to viewing others with their own hopes and dreams. When this continues to spiral downward, they blame those folks for all of the problems (the Box of Blame).[22] This self-deception blinds leaders to the true causes of problems and creates the inability to see themselves as the probable cause of these problems.[23] The trigger for this self-deception is the act of self-betrayal—when we act contrary to our sense of what is appropriate and betray our own sense of how we should behave.

Being in the Box, a leader begins to feel justified in blaming others—forcing his employees into their own boxes. He then feels their blame is unjust and blames them more. Once this cycle begins, it grows, creating obstacles such as lack of commitment, conflict, stress, poor teamwork, lack of trust, lack of accountability, and communication issues. It is easy to see how leaders and employees in this mode interact in addictive and destructive ways thus justifying the manager's choice to micromanage the employee, and so on. The problem is that there are no easy ways to jump out of the Box of Blame. It is understanding, baby steps to change, and possibly a final realization of how the ERO Spiral takes you into the Box of Blame and micromanagement. If a leader can climb out of his box, the employees will follow. We recommend reading *Leadership and Self-Deception: Getting Out of the Box*[24] as a start. After that, it is a long hard climb and staying out of the ERO Spiral every day.

How is your micromanaging associated with self-deception?

Behaviors to Change

Not Letting Go

Recognize

If leadership is committed to fully engaged employees and acts that way, then fear tends to slowly disappear and trust develops. If leadership is okay with a culture of fear, on the other hand, then all the great empowerment programs in the world *are going to fail.* You have the choice of adding to a dysfunctional culture or taking on one of the major jobs of a manager—that is, standing as the bulwark between the leaders and the workers, taking heat from both sides. Just because the leadership above you is dysfunctional does not mean that you need to pass that dysfunction down to your employees. And just because your employees are fearful and lack trust in their leadership, does not mean that you need to project those attitudes upward from your department or let them be okay in it. It is helpful to know how much of your situation is affected by your need to control.[25] Keep track of difficulties in trusting others, perfectionism, having unrealistic expectations, or taking command too much—these are all characteristics of being a "control freak."

Admit

The overall problem is circular. How do you change micromanaging without changing your sense of self and how do you change your sense of self without reducing micromanaging? You can't control without others being willing to be controlled. So, you may have selected a group like this and you may use that as an excuse to control them. Regardless, they can't grow with over control. It causes a disengaged workforce, makes everyone look to you rather than their customers, and stops development of employees. Everyone is "in the box." Only you can stop the merry-go-round here.

If you are a control freak, you are undoubtedly using a lot of brain power to manage things. Your mind is constantly whirring to keep the parts of your area moving *and monitored*. You are a vision of efficiency, though probably very tired of managing it all and you will burn out. *You need to come to the realization that your real problem is that you are always expecting something to be a certain way. Great leaders are calm, delegate, and put their expectations into visions, not controlling behavior.*

Adjust

Burns, a well-known authority on the effects of self-talk, suggests the following triple column technique.[26] Simply draw two lines down the center of a piece of paper, dividing it into thirds. Label the left-hand column, *fear or insecurity*; the middle column, *my distortions*, and then the right-hand column is *my self-defense* (Table 10.2).

Key Behaviors

In the left-hand column, write down all the things you think might drive your micromanaging. In the second column, you need to diagnose the distortions that you're making in your thinking. Burns (p. 303) suggests that these distortions can include the following:

Table 10.2 Overcoming Distorted Thinking

Fear/Insecurity Causing Control	My Distortions	My Self-Defense

1. *All or Nothing Thinking*—Seeing things in black or white—either perfect or a failure.

2. *Overgeneralization*—You see a single negative event as a never ending pattern.

3. *Poor Frame*—You pick out a single negative detail and focus on it exclusively.

4. *Magnification or Minimization*—You exaggerate the importance of things.

5. *Emotional Reasoning*—You think that since you feel it, therefore, it must be true.

6. *Should Statements*—You try to motivate yourself with "should" and "ought."

7. *Labeling*—Instead of describing an error or mistake you or an employee make, you attach a negative label to yourself, such as you are a loser.

We would add *over-excitement*. In stressful times, folks with a tendency for micromanaging can build themselves up to a fever pitch—and their employees, too. Dogs do this when playing in a pack—they wind themselves up and up to the point you have to sit one down, holding its collar, and say forcefully, "settle." Sometimes you just have to back off and tell yourself to settle; the world will not come apart in the next few minutes.

After writing down your micromanaging drivers and figuring out what mental distortions you are using, the third step is to substitute a more rational, less upsetting thought in the right hand column like "settle." *And then think it—over and over* (in third person). In this column you must recognize the truth of the situation and be kinder to yourself or your employee. By facing these distortions, you will begin to cope rather than feel like a victim—at least give yourself time to find a better coping response that does not create obstacles to effective leadership. Don't forget that self-deception is a defense mechanism used to help avoid unpleasant thoughts, feelings, beliefs, or fears. That is why Burn's technique is so powerful. Table 10.2 will help break through any possible self-deception and self-betrayal.

Boundaries

Recognize

Most people have personal boundaries which are the limits set on things like self-disclosure, touching, asking and giving help, sharing confidences, demonstrating feelings, and exposing vulnerabilities. These

---

boundaries exist in all areas—intimacy, professional life (work space and responsibilities), territorial (home and property), etc. Yet, folks who micromanage often don't see and respect these boundaries.

Boundaries are like layers—you have an internal boundary, an external personal boundary, and a territorial boundary. Your internal boundary protects your thinking and feelings. You don't blame others for your own actions or feelings when you adequately use your internal boundary. Your external boundary allows you to keep a distance between yourself and others. It also enables you to control who (and when) someone touches you through verbal and nonverbal signals. Territories are the areas of land, personal belongings, and job responsibilities that you consider yours. Boundaries are about permission.

People feel tension when their boundaries are violated. They move away or attempt to block the intrusion to protect their space. *No one can control someone with intact boundaries without that person's permission. In business, all employees agree to give up some personal boundaries in trade for a job and income. Those who want to be controlled give up control to the controller—the key is how much is given up.*

Admit

We all learn about boundaries as children. We are taught to have boundaries by parents who do not over or under-control, who respect us, or do not make us play inappropriate family roles or make us do things we did not actively choose to do. We are also taught to respect others' boundaries in school—when not allowed to interrupt, take others' toys, or physically abuse others. Without this education, we can become adults with no boundaries or weak and incomplete boundaries. Some people go through life being victimized and violated because of their lack of boundaries. Some go through life violating others.

Having boundaries creates a whole new set of rules about how people interact:

- People need to ask permission before they cross over one's boundaries
- People must accept ownership and accountability for their boundary violations
- One person does not belong to or allow oneself to be over-controlled by anyone else

Adjust

You can see where we are going—micromanagers often have a tendency to see a subordinate as an extension of themselves and freely violate their boundaries. And employees with poor boundaries have little sense of being abused or being used may search for bosses who are controlling. But trust is destroyed. People with poor boundaries can, at certain times say no and set some limits, but in most situations, find it difficult to set boundaries. You may know people who are perfectly capable of setting boundaries at work, but when it comes to their personal lives, they leave themselves open to whatever use and abuse any other person who comes along wants to heap on them or vice versa.

Key Behaviors

Take a blank piece of paper and put your employee's names at the top. Add your name too. Then divide the paper so that it accurately represents the proportion of your energies devoted in the previous week to managing them—delegating, instructing, and handling problems. You may find that you have but a small corner of the paper left for your job requirements and needs.

You can also keep track of the questions to answers ratio in conversations with your team. The goal of this is to raise your awareness of when you provide an answer or tweak a finished product and to build your alternative skill of asking open-ended questions like, "What are your options?" "What do you think you should do?" "How can you get that done?"

Ultimately, the task is to separate yourself from others and create intact boundaries which help you identify *you* and *yours* from *others* and *theirs*. The simplest way to deal with this is to look at the ownership of problems and accept that others' problems are not yours. The next step is to tell your employees to continually instruct you on boundary intrusions, which isn't easy! Don't retaliate. You have to learn to respect your own boundaries and accept accountability for your intrusion into other's boundaries. It is a complicated process that calls for responsibility and accountability at several levels.

Setting a boundary is not an attempt to control the other person. It is a part of the process of defining what is acceptable at work. It is a vital step in taking responsibility for oneself and one's leadership position. The difference between setting a boundary in a healthy way and manipulating is—*when we set a boundary we let go of the outcome.* You don't micromanage the entire process; you just set the boundary and let the employees go. Which defined another way is good delegation. More information can be found at http://www.pennbehavioralhealth .com/documents/setting_boundaries_at_work.pdf.

Table 10.3 is an action plan for you to think about your boundary violations (Table 10.3):

Table 10.3   What to Do for Boundary Violations?

Boundary Violation	To Me or Mine to Others	What to Do?

Managing Without Intimidation

Recognize

Effective communication includes asking questions, being a great listener, helping people self-discover, being sincere, and empowering. If you find yourself doing all of the talking and maybe "talking down" to employees, you may be intimidating with or without micromanaging. With any power comes the power to hurt—there are many ways to hurt others deliberately. But sometimes, powerful people hurt others inadvertently because they say or do careless things. It is easy for leaders to unthinkingly hurt employees because they are less likely to strike back or complain.

Remember that assertiveness helps, but the key is self-esteem. Those with lower self-esteem are not sure of their capabilities and can compensate by taking it out on subordinates. So the solutions are: (1) Increase self-esteem and self-efficacy, or (2) Try to be more humble despite your inner feelings. Humility has nothing to do with self-deprecation or not being strong. Humility actually comes from a sense of power—but not the sense of power that comes out of ego, pushiness, or indigestion. It comes from knowing who you are, what you can do, and what you can't—self-efficacy. *Great leaders are humble.* A humble person isn't concerned with who he is or who he should be. He isn't concerned with himself at all; but instead he's concerned with other people—employees and customers.[27]

Admit

Imagine you are a leader/owner of a hair salon. One of your employees is working on someone's hair and is about finished. You notice that (what soon will be the end product) isn't what you would have given the client. It is not a "bad" haircut, but rather something that you would have done differently. You then take this opportunity to speak to your employee about what you would have done, if you were the stylist—in front of the client. Why not—no time like the present for a "teachable moment" right? What implications will result in this action? Your employee's (and customer's) boundaries just got violated, you got to show off, the haircut did not change, you might have lowered the satisfaction of the client, and the client now thinks that there is a negative environment in the salon (and might not return because of it). The stylist is embarrassed and resentful. The owner thought this was education; everyone else thought it was intimidation.

Adjust

One should never be intimidating to hurt someone's feelings, to show off, educate, or just to make oneself feel better. If this is what you want, you are self-sabotaging yourself severely. Don't get in the habit of being intimidating or your new personality might become permanent; humility disappears. Make sure to watch yourself when you feel uneasy. If it feels a little too good to be intimidating, or you intimidate when uneasy, then it's time to back off. Bragging, being a "know it all" and other forms of intimidation simply make coworkers lose respect for you and that is a quick slide down the ERO Spiral.

And watch your nonverbal actions. A good deal of your communication is nonverbal and can be intimidating even when the verbal message is humble. One way to understand nonverbal cues is to classify them into two categories. These are: (1) Paralanguage, and (2) Visual cues. Paralanguage consists of voice tone, pitch, intensity, and fluency. For example, a low monotone voice may indicate a depressed mood; a tense, loud voice suggests anger. Visual cues include facial expressions, eye contact, body posture, and actions. Gestures, posture, and eye contact may indicate the masked or denied emotions of the speaker. For example, a tapping finger may indicate impatience, or a slumped body posture may indicate negative feelings about the self. Physical appearance is a major determiner of intimidation. Obviously, nonverbal cues are complex and numerous. Yet, it is important for leaders to gain a good understanding of nonverbal cues in order to increase interpersonal communication skills. Do not try to sound sweet when all your nonverbals are showing superiority and intimidation. It will not work.

Here are some final hints. You have heard them before but imprint them in your brain; they are the keys to staying humble.

- Know what you can do and what you can't
- Stop comparing yourself to others
- Remain teachable but also willing to help others
- Go last

- Listen more than you talk
- Don't take all the credit; avoid bragging

Key Behaviors

What is provided here are more baby steps than sequential key behaviors. We want you to practice each of these, once a day, and maybe even keep a log of your efforts (Remember—what gets measured gets done).[28] Feel free to investigate this endnote further as it has 50 such items to follow in a quest to be more humble. Keep adding new ones each week or month as you master the current ones. You will be more humble and less intimidating in the end.

1. Use the response "It's my pleasure." when someone thanks you for something.

2. Use the response "I'd be honored." when someone asks you to help them do something.

3. Count to three before adding to a conversation to ensure the other person is done.

4. Be willing to follow another person in conversation even if you don't get to talk about your idea.

5. Give someone credit for what was done on your watch publically before employees or bosses.

Flexibility

Recognize

Our ability to deal with change is becoming a major factor at work. Flexibility is very important for a business because changes must be made constantly. Flexibility means "having the power, authority, and skill to change accordingly, with ease."[29] The practices that leaders are adopting to make their organizations more competitive often ignore the human need for predictability. Reengineering throws out all the old procedures; continuous-improvement programs promise only that an organization's rules will continue to change. The need for predictability is part of micromanagement.

Admit

When change is thrust upon us, we often resist and try to prevent it from happening. Sometimes we try to stick with the original plan. When we try to resist change, we often end up sabotaging our own success because we're using our energy in wasteful, unproductive, even destructive ways, which causes more frustration and fatigue.[30]

When you are resisting change, your focus is trying to make life into the way you think it *should* be. When you adapt and respond creatively to change, your focus is to acknowledge that things will be different and you have power to adapt. Many times it takes less energy to adapt and respond creatively to change than it does to resist change.

Adjust

Flexibility is a trait and some can be more flexible than others. If you find yourself blowing up when things get unpredictable, work on this—it is self-handicapping. Try to calm yourself when you feel the panic.[31] Planning ahead, having alternative options in case things go wrong, is very useful. This takes time, so if you have the tendency to blow up in these situations, budget the time and plan ahead. Practice thinking quickly to respond to sudden changes in circumstances. Learn to take on new challenges at short notice. Just remember, that throwing a fit does not create solutions or reduce the time needed for changing gears to another direction.

Here are six ways to find your balance and keep moving when change is thrust upon you. These are as follows:

1. Acknowledge the part of you that's been resisting the changes. It is trying to keep you safe.
2. Let go of the present. Express your disappointment, sadness, fear and anger—grieve.
3. Don't focus on what you can't control, or put energy and attention into things that you can't change. Focus on and do what you can change.
4. Cut out victim language and complaining. Remember—"What?" and "How?"
5. Decide what's important to you. Change usually means you lose something. Find the new that you want.
6. Find the hidden opportunities.

Key Behaviors

Here are the key behaviors for handling change:[32]

1. Write down what is changing, how you feel about it, what status you are losing in the change, and how you might transition to the new (Table 10.4).
2. In determining what status you are losing, you will have to face fears about the change. Get past "Why me?" and "It isn't fair!" Negative thoughts block your creativity and problem-solving abilities. Positive thoughts build bridges to possibilities and opportunities.

Table 10.4 Handling Change

What Is Changing?	How Do I Feel?	What Status Am I Losing?	What Can I Do to Let Go and Transition?

3. Determine where the opportunity is in the change. Find the benefit somewhere in the change. Let go of the old way and move toward that opportunity.

4. Set SMART goals so you can consciously guide how you respond to the change. Write out your goals and plans to meet them.

Juggling Projects

Recognize

Micromanagers tend to be linear and have problems managing too many projects. Managing multiple projects is a juggling act; managing multiple projects with intertwined dependencies can be a nightmare. Letting go of the problems of one project and finding your way back into another one generally isn't easy. When you are only juggling one project, you can get away with bad habits like procrastination, disorganization, and lack of planning. But when your projects begin to expand, these bad habits catch up with you.

Admit

The problem here is not particularly about over-commitment.[33] That is somewhat easy to handle—keep in mind that if it's not your ball; don't keep it—delegate. Then, think through your priorities and do the most important task first. Sequence whenever possible. Some of us work best by focusing on one thing at a time (linear or tunnel vision) and rather than having all the projects going at once, we would be less overloaded by doing them sequentially. But we can't, the projects may need to be completed around the same time. Set time boundaries for each project. You need time chunks long enough that you believe you'll make real progress. Time boundaries have a hidden benefit. They help you make choices about how you'll proceed. Here are some more hints:[34]

- Make a list in a spreadsheet or whiteboard with columns for "projects," "time," and "due date." Keep track of sub-deliverables and what has been done. Use the freed space in your head for the going back and forth.

- When you calculate how long it will take you to finish a project or any part of one, be generous. Add a 20–30 percent contingency cushion.

- Write down all of your time commitments on calendar and then block out periods of time on calendar to work on the projects you listed earlier.

- Schedule only one or two truly creative project activity per day. Creativity wears you out. Any time constraints put stress on your creative capacity and you will not get it all done.

- Even if the best project in the world lands in your lap, learn to say "No." Honor your previous commitments (or delegate them). If the customer *really* wants you, they'll wait until you have an availability.

- Try speed dating your tasks. Putting focus in 5–10-minute chunks helps you get into a groove and build momentum, knowing there's a preset time when each project will make progress.

- Set boundaries and let them guide your actions. They help you make choices about how you'll proceed. Do this for the project and each subdeliverable.

There is a fine line between successfully juggling several needed projects and using juggling to self-handicap. You *may* juggle multiple projects to insulate yourself from failure. To commit to one thing requires courage and persistence. It means you will do what is required to make it work. Also, when you're flipping your focus between different projects, it's very easy to hit resistance in one and then switch to another—one with a win. But all projects have resistance, which must be overcome. Playing this game is very handicapping in the larger scheme of things. "Energy flows where attention goes." remains true. You may be losing time and energy with every switch you make.

Adjust

Project 2010 provides tools to help you manage cross-project dependencies, even tasks in one project that are dependent on the completion of another project. When things get even more complicated, you can use Project Professional 2010 and tap into Project Server, SharePoint, and Outlook. Always look at MindTools.

Final Personal Takeaways

Action Plan—Micromanaging

What will you do about your micromanagement?

Micromanagement Self-Handicap	What Is the Situation?	Trigger	Impact on Others	What to Do/When?
Fully delegate responsibility, authority, and accountability		__Expedient __Avoiding __Apprehension __Self-deception		__Deliberate action____ __Self-efficacy_____ __Face it_____ __Look and listen_____
Delegate whole pieces of the job		__Expedient __Avoiding __Apprehension __Self-deception		__Deliberate action____ __Self-efficacy_____ __Face it_____ __Look and listen_____
Delegate challenges and define success		__Expedient __Avoiding __Apprehension __Self-deception		__Deliberate action____ __Self-efficacy_____ __Face it_____ __Look and listen_____
Share experiences, don't instruct		__Expedient __Avoiding __Apprehension __Self-deception		__Deliberate action____ __Self-efficacy_____ __Face it_____ __Look and listen_____
Resist the urge to solve someone else's problem		__Expedient __Avoiding __Apprehension __Self-deception		__Deliberate action____ __Self-efficacy_____ __Face it_____ __Look and listen_____
Never take back a delegated item		__Expedient __Avoiding __Apprehension __Self-deception		__Deliberate action____ __Self-efficacy_____ __Face it_____ __Look and listen_____
Provide feedback, don't course correct		__Expedient __Avoiding __Apprehension __Self-deception		__Deliberate action____ __Self-efficacy_____ __Face it_____ __Look and listen_____
Don't correct everything you receive		__Expedient __Avoiding __Apprehension __Self-deception		__Deliberate action____ __Self-efficacy_____ __Face it_____ __Look and listen_____

continued

Micro-management Self-Handicap	What Is the Situation?	Trigger	Impact on Others	What to Do/When?
Respecting boundaries		__Expedient __Avoiding __Apprehension __Self-deception		__Deliberate action____ __Self-efficacy_____ __Face it_____ __Look and listen_____
Having boundaries		__Expedient __Avoiding __Apprehension __Self-deception		__Deliberate action____ __Self-efficacy_____ __Face it_____ __Look and listen_____
Managing without intimidation		__Expedient __Avoiding __Apprehension __Self-deception		__Deliberate action____ __Self-efficacy_____ __Face it_____ __Look and listen_____
Being flexible		__Expedient __Avoiding __Apprehension __Self-deception		__Deliberate action____ __Self-efficacy_____ __Face it_____ __Look and listen_____
Juggling projects well/ not being linear		__Expedient __Avoiding __Apprehension __Self-deception		__Deliberate action____ __Self-efficacy_____ __Face it_____ __Look and listen_____

Baby Steps

The baby steps for this chapter are as follows:

- Delegate the whole piece of one job/project rather than simply tasks and activities to one employee/team. Delegate the challenges and define success. Let the employee/team determine the intermediate steps and detailed output. Watch what happens without speaking.

- Don't ask for a list of options and recommendations the next time you feel like doing so. We all know the employees will search for what you "really" want and provide that. Instead tell the employee/team to solve the problem and report back when it is solved. Watch what happens without speaking.

- The next time you need to train someone; share experiences, don't instruct. Allow the learning to take place by allegory and not turn the learning into "do these steps."

The key behaviors for sharing experiences are as follows:

1. Identify the lesson or "main point" of the experience before you start speaking.

2. Keep story short—make sure the details add to it rather than drag out the story.

3. Make sure to say how you personally benefitted from the experience.

4. Call to action—tell the person how you believe that he/she can benefit from a similar experience.

Follow-Up Questions

1. What task can you delegate to someone today?

2. If micromanaging comes from our upbringing, how can we get out of it?

3. How can you practice having flexibility to change?

4. Where do you have problems with boundaries or violating boundaries?

5. How could you learn to be more flexible?

Endnotes

1. Summarized from Scott Berkun, "Blog." http://scottberkun.com/blog (accessed June 19, 2015).

2. Ibid.

3. From Leadership Thoughts, "The Superleader, Greg Blencoe." http://www.leadershipthoughts.com/superleader-greg-blencoe/ (accessed June 19, 2015).

4. From Changing Minds, "Micromanagement." http://changingminds.org/disciplines/leadership/articles/micromanagement.htm (accessed June 19, 2015).

5. RI Sutton, *The No Asshole Rule*, Business Plus, New York, NY: Grand Central Publishing, 2007, 25.

6. Adapted from Shala Marks, "Micromanagers: 6 Reasons yor Employes Don't Like You," https://www.recruiter.com/i/micromanagers-6-reasons-your-employees-dont-like-you/ (accessed June 19, 2015).

7. S Arterburn and J Felton, *Toxic Faith: Experiencing Healing from Painful Spiritual Abuse*, Colorado Springs, CO: Shaw Books, 1991.

8. R Martin, *The Responsibility Virus*, New York, NY: Basic Books, 2002.

9. Ibid.

10. Adapted from Softpanorama, "Understanding Micromanagers and Control Freaks." http://www.softpanorama.org/Social/Toxic_managers/Micromanagers/understanding_micromanagers.shtml (accessed June 19, 2015).

11. Much of this section is discussed in AW Schaef and D Fassel, *The Addictive Organization*, New York, NY: Harper & Row, 1988.

12. From Best Practices, http://www.best-in-class.com/ (accessed June 19, 2015).

13. Adapted from David Wolinsky, "How to Stop Being a Micromanager." http://www.nbcchicago.com/blogs/inc-well/How-to-Stop-Being-a-Micromanager-176461561.html, Elizabeth Eyre, "Preventing Manager Dependency: Teaching Your Team to be More Independent." https://www.mindtools.com/pages/article/preventing-manager-dependency.htm, Tom Searcy, "4 Ways to Avoid Becoming a Micromanager." http://www.inc.com/tom-searcy/4-ways-to-stop-being-a-micromanager.html#/tom-searcy/4-ways-to-stop-being-a-microleader.html, Forensic Magazine, "What's the Opposite of Micromanagement?" http://www.forensicmag.com/articles/2014/01/whats-opposite-micromanagement, Steven Sinofsky, "5+1 Ways to Delegate Effecicely Without Micromanaging." http://www.linkedin.com/today/post/article/20130618165146-2293107-5-1-ways-to-delegate-effectively-without-micromanaging, Jan Fletcher, "5 Ways to Give Workers More Autonomy (and Why It's Important)." http://blog.intuit.com/employees/5-ways-to-give-workers-more-autonomy-and-why-its-important/, and Steven Sinofsky, "3 Patterns to Avoid Micromanaging and Lead Instead." http://www.linkedin.com/today/post/article/20130321171818-2293107-3-patterns-to-avoid-micromanaging-and-lead-instead (accessed April 19, 2015).

14. Adapted from Angie Ward, "3 Reasons Not to Confront by Email." http://www.christianitytoday.com/le/2012/october-online-only/3-reasons-not-to-confront.html (accessed June 19, 2015).

15. Adapted from Megan Broussard, "6 Ways to Get Your Emails Read." http://www.themuse.com/advice/6-ways-to-get-your-emails-read (accessed June 19, 2015).

16. Adapted from Changing Minds, "Micromanagement." http://changingminds.org/disciplines/leadership/articles/micromanagement.htm and Deborah Jacobs, "How to Manage a Micromanager." http://www.forbes.com/sites/deborahljacobs/2012/05/07/how-to-manage-a-micromanager/ (accessed June 19, 2015).

17. GW Piaget, *Control Freaks–Who They Are and How to Stop Them From Ruining Your Life*, New York, NY: Doubleday, 1991.

18. Adapted from Elizabeth Eyre, "Successful Delegation: Using the Power of Other People's Help." http://www.mindtools.com/pages/article/newLDR_98.htm (accessed June 19, 2015).

19. Ibid.

20. Adapted from Elizabeth Eyre, "The Delegation Dilemma." http://www.mindtools.com/pages/article/newTMM_96.htm (accessed June 19, 2015).

21. Visit Alyssa Gregory, "How to Stop Micromanaging Right Now." http://sbinformation.about.com/od/businessmanagemen1/a/stop-micromanagement.htm (accessed June 19, 2015).

22. See The Arbinger Institute, *Leadership and Self-Deception: Getting out of the Box*, San Francisco, CA: Berrett-Koehler Publishers, 2010.

23. Adapted from JFD Performance Solutions, "Leadership and Self-Deception. Getting out of the Box : Book Summary." http://www.jfdperfsolutions.com/modules/news/article.php?storyid=26 and The Intentional Workplace, "Is Self-Deception Keeping You in the Box?" http://intentionalworkplace.com/2010/06/24/is-self-deception-keeping-you-in-the-box/ (accessed June 19, 2015).

24. Ibid. Also see Note 22.

25. Summarized from Susan Steinbrecher, "Taming Your Inner Control Freak: Why Letting Go Can Help You Stay in Control." http://www.huffingtonpost.com/susan-steinbrecher/taming-your-inner-control_b_5531069.html (accessed June 19, 2015).

26. DD Burns, *Feeling Good: The New Mood Therapy* (Preface by Aaron T. Beck). New York, NY: Wm. Morrow and Co (hardbound), 1980; New American Library, 1981 (paperback). Revised and updated, 1999.

27. Taken from Unban Dictionary, "Humble." http://www.urbandictionary.com/define.php?term=humble (accessed June 19, 2015).

28. Adapted from Learn This, "50 Ways to Be More Humble and to Act Humbly." http://learnthis.ca/2011/01/50-ways-to-be-more-humble-and-to-act-humbly/ (accessed June 19, 2015).

29. Taken from Marketing Deviant, "Flexibility in Business." http://marketingdeviant.com/flexibility-in-business/ and Howard Stevenson and Mihnea Moldoveanu, "The Power of Predictability." https://hbr.org/1995/07/the-power-of-predictability (accessed June 19, 2015).

30. Taken from Make it Happen Now, "Top Tips for Dealing with Unexpected and Unwanted Change at Work." http://www.makeithappennow.org/advice/top-tips-for-dealing-with-unexpected-and-unwanted-change-at-work/ (accessed June 19, 2015).

31. Adapted from University of Kent, "Adaptability and Flexibility." http://www.kent.ac.uk/careers/sk/adaptability.htm (accessed June 19, 2015).

32. Adapted from Terri Babers, "How to Deal with Change." http://www.positive-changes-coach.com/how-to-deal-with-change.html (accessed June 19, 2015).

33. Adapted from Steven Robbins, "How to Juggle Multiple Projects." http://www.quickanddirtytips.com/productivity/time-management/how-to-juggle-multiple-projects and Thomas McKee, "The Smooth and Elegant Art of Juggling." http://www.advantagepoint.com/articles/staffdev/art3.html (accessed June 19, 2015).

34. Adapted from Steven Robbins, "How to Juggle Multiple Projects." http://www.quickanddirtytips.com/productivity/time-management/how-to-juggle-multiple-projects#sthash.IO6nsv3i.dpuf and Courtney Johnston, "10 Tips for Juggling Multiple Projects + Priorities." http://www.rulebreakersclub.com/home/10-tips-for-juggling-multiple-projects-priorities.html#sthash.skOhJrQA.dpuf (accessed June 19, 2015).

11

Driving for Results

Chapter Takeaways

▶ Start your day with a simple task—build self-efficacy daily

▶ Learn why a personal vision and action plan are important

▶ Learn goal-subdivision

▶ Understand about master-orientation goals

▶ Align daily processes with consumer-directed goals

Effectively driving for results is a benefit and result of eliminating self-handicapping behavior. Driving for results is constant attention to how daily actions align with a larger goal and *having a mindset to master that goal.* One of the enemies of driving for results is being in our "comfort-zone." When everything is going "fine," and we are maintaining the "status-quo," there is little incentive to perform better or reach a goal. This is the mindset of staying out of trouble and just getting the task done. Many people and organizations have the potential of being "great," but they are comfortable being "good" because of lack of clear goals, a mastery mindset, or well-defined action plans to get there. Compounding these issues is the tendency to not take risks—we have a tendency to "not fix what's not broken." While no one endorses taking unnecessary risks, without some risk an organization can remain stagnant while the competition is innovating.

How often do you surf the web, go on social-media, read blogs, shop online, talk about sports with coworkers, gossip, allow "short" distractions, gripe about the company or boss, or open your email whenever you get an alert? The authors are not advocating for a complete abolishment of the aforementioned distractions—we just want to get you thinking about how all of that takes away from being "results and mastery-oriented." When we drive for results, we ensure daily processes align to larger outcomes, identify and control distractions, develop game plans to reach the goals, quickly find the root cause for problems, and are directed by our action plans. We do not work for the sake of being "busy," focus on ourselves or monetary reward, try to be better than everyone else, or focus on staying out of trouble. We all have that coworker who likes to announce how much he has worked that day—for some reason, they "are just *so* busy." But the curious thing is—they produce very little, and it takes them longer than others to complete a task. While the obvious short-term issue may be excuses leading to poor "time management," the longer-term obstacles are lack of mastery goals and clear plans driving for results.

Athletes, especially those competing alone, always have a goal in mind and they use that vision to guide what they have to do to achieve it—to master it. The vision (a certain speed or score) sustains their energy and is the motivation to align their daily processes. They understand that they must stay away from distractions, work everyday, and continually strive to be better. There is a thin difference in goals. Their goal is usually not to win but to reach their personal goal to improve—their reason for being. This is a mastery mindset. Due to the abundance of opportunity in the business world, leaders can fall prey to being "good enough" or just to win and not continually strive to be great. Some business guru's suggest business is all about winning. We think business is an open game where the aim is to keep everyone playing. That means to keep getting better and better at it. Often, when leaders stop at "good enough or focus on winning," workers are too removed from the customer or organization strategy to have that central sense of being mastery-oriented. Neither ruins careers nor businesses, but it does self-handicap them—dooming them to mediocrity.

Recall from Chapter 1 and 2 that: (1) Individuals have different theories of intelligence, and (2) This explains why they strive to achieve for different purposes—mastery, performance-approach, and performance-avoidance goals. Mastery goals represent a desire to *continually develop* competence, performance-approach goals reflect a concern to *demonstrate* competence by outperforming others, and performance-avoidance goals represent the desire to avoid appearing incompetent or less competent than others—fear of failure and making mistakes. Leaders are more likely to self-handicap when they have performance goals—particularly performance-avoidance goals. *Simply put—those with mastery goals do not self-handicap. They drive for results—particularly results good for customers.* The adoption of these goals is influenced in part by cues, or goal-related messages, from the work, the boss's approach, and from within. It is a mindset—one that should become part of any organization's talent development efforts. It is a mindset that management can influence with effort and focus.

Driving for results means continually asking yourself if your day-to-day efforts support and are directed toward a predetermined goal and vision (hopefully, the customer's or the organization's) and whether mastery of it is important to you. Do you want to master the process? Is the goal of adding value for customers important to you? A lot of people self-handicap in these areas by not connecting their work activities with outcomes they really need to achieve; this may be due to lack of engagement, lack of accountability, or other obstructions. We suggest asking yourself on a daily basis the following questions:

- Does everything I do further an organizational goal?
- How did I help customers today?
- Do I have a passion for this; do I want to master it?
- Does my to-do list today align with larger outcomes?
- Before I go home for the day, do I have a game plan for tomorrow?
- How will I handle distractions throughout my day?
- What am I doing to detract from this organizational goal?

A leader that drives for results:[1]

- Sets personal goals based on personal vision that aligns with customer needs
- Develops action plans to meet those goals
- Consistently meets or exceeds his goals and deadlines
- Attends to all projects until completion
- Challenges himself and meets his own high expectations
- Meets all commitments
- Prepares for barriers to success by planning for them before they happen

From our experience, the actions that go along with driving for results are the best predictors of future success in leadership—wanting to master the competency, going above and beyond on assignments, looking for learning opportunities, exceeding standards, looking for internships and volunteer opportunities to enhance competencies, etc. This is not to say that the great student/early careerist won't cut corners and find better ways to master the goal—they will. After all, they are "managing" their education or career. But, *when a person sets mastery goals, develops action plans, and doesn't let barriers or obstacles get in their way, they practice what is required for exceptional leadership and they become leaders.*

Impact

We all know the drill. Performance management is created to ensure that goals are met in an effective and efficient manner. It is supposed to help employees reconcile personal goals with organizational goals and increase productivity and profitability—aligning their objectives to strategic and operational goals. Dashboards tell us where we are. We are told that using integrated software for this may deliver a significant return on investment by unlocking the time every employee spends not actually doing their job. Benefits far and wide are proposed—grow sales, reduce costs, decrease the time it takes to create strategic or operational changes, improve employee engagement, and improve management control. But do all of these management tools really drive performance? Not very well.

Regardless of how sophisticated our organizational tools are, we are all guilty at some point of not driving for results. Have you ever been in a situation where a series of good events has happened to your organization or you personally—so you "downshift" the next couple of weeks/months/year to enjoy your success? An issue stopping or delaying driving for results is believing things are going "just fine"—being good at what you do. Jim Collins wrote a book on this topic entitled, *Good to Great: Why Some Companies Make the Leap... And Others Don't.*[2] Collins states that "good" is the natural enemy of "great." He said we have lots of "good" organizations that survive in America, but very few "great" ones—those that generated stock returns higher than the average stock market 7 out of 15 years. So what did Collins recommend to achieve this level of success? He suggested seven principles. These are as follows:[3]

1. Leaders who are humble, but driven to do what's best for the company.
2. Get the right people on the bus, then figure out where to go. Finding the right people and getting them in the right positions is important.
3. Confront the stockholder paradox and deal with its short-term mentality but keep a vision and drive.

4. Determine the space in the middle of three overlapping circles—"What makes you money?" "What could you be best in the world at?" and "What lights your fire?"

5. Develop a culture of discipline—get rid of the fat.

6. Use technology to accelerate growth, within the three overlapping circles mentioned earlier.

7. Create an additive effect of many small initiatives; they act on each other like compound interest.

What do all of these principles have in common? They all focus on a vision and a drive to get there. No fat and no messing about is allowed; everyone is working toward the goal—driven to meet the goal. That is what many organizations think driving for results is all about. But of course, many years after the book was published, at least half of the great companies he identified are no longer doing so great. "Circuit City is bankrupt, Fannie Mae went bankrupt/nationalized, Wells Fargo needed a bailout, Nucor's stock and revenue crashed, Pitney Bowes went down significantly, and Gillette is no longer independent."[4] One issue is his methodology—he measured a company's "greatness" by its sustained stock market value being a certain percentage (150 percent) above the general market. There are too many factors involved here to say that vision and driving for results will overcome the effect of the economy. *Yet, it does seem strange that "greatness" was so easily lost and so quickly.*

We think that many companies do a great job visioning, aligning, and developing dashboards and other tools to keep that alignment. Many do better than the market average for these reasons. They stay focused and driven. They also are driven by their customers. Yet, most are not. What fails is the drive—there is no mastery mindset and the drive diminishes over time. At this point, you begin to see the self-handicapping ERO Spiral. Employees and leaders alike can only keep up with the superhuman level of work so long without some motivation. Without the spark that comes from something that "lights your personal fire," all of us will eventually let up—"go back to normal" and "regress toward the mean." Organizational goals will only carry us so far and after that you have to be doing something you truly love doing for this type of sustained effort. Otherwise, excuses set in for the very purpose of allowing reduced effort. Sometimes a leader is trying to soften the blow of the inevitable let down of pressure, sometimes he is looking for enhancement so he does not look bad. But we all know we can only do so much without rest, without burnout. Excuses can take us off the hook and lead into reduced effort we need to "go the long haul." The vision and dashboards stay but the effort must meet reality. Saying "we are doing just fine" starts it.

So, what is the answer? Are we almost always doomed to fall back to a more normal performance after superhuman effort (market value 150 percent above the general market)? We think moving from good to great and staying there is more than vision, goals, dashboards, and especially, a driven culture. In fact, we think much of that will inevitably lead to "failure"—a "regression toward the mean." Any superhuman drive to greatness is not sustainable unless you are willing to burn out your employees and throw them out when used up, or replace good workers with overseas workers because they are cheaper. Operations can be made less costly (we can cut the fat) but not forever. Take the analogy of dieting. Any physician or dietician will tell you that "binge dieting" does not work. Yes, you lose weight quickly, but after the sustained effort meets its inevitable leveling off point, you will go back to the way you were (overweight) because you resumed the old habits. The way to lose weight is to change your lifestyle—eat healthy and exercise. Moving to healthy organizational living is to eliminate self-handicapping and the ERO Spiral and replace it with a mastery goal orientation focused on adding value for all customers—that builds an open-ended game that is sustainable.

We think that any executive who has tried binge dieting in his organization for any long-term strategy change (not just a quarterly stock return), and sees it peter out over time, will begin to appreciate that healthy living in an organization is to reduce self-handicapping. That is the only way you can cut out the wasted effort and sustain a palatable pace forever in an organization. When leaders, managers, and workers start to understand self-handicapping—that the excuses they are using (which are very successful in the short-term) lead to obstacles that hurt them, their customers, and the organization's goals—healthy organizational living can start. And, it does not take superhuman ability to change the lifestyle to overcoming self-handicapping. In fact, the employees will find it a refreshing and exciting new leadership style (remember that they take the brunt of most of the leadership self-handicapping as it falls down the ERO Spiral).

Healthy living in an organization means accountability, open awareness and vision, proper decision analysis, talent development, real efforts at engagement and competence mastery, and eliminating micromanaging. These can be achieved through the reduction of self-handicapping. This healthy living can be sustained with effort truly focused on being better at achieving customer outcomes. The bus can be loaded with employees that have mastery goals for what they are doing. We all know that any dashboard in any organization and any organizational mission/vision can be ignored by employees. Any failure to meet a goal can be excused. Because of this, we think dealing with self-handicapping is the recipe for greatness. A drive for results must be based on removing self-handicapping.

The justification of "doing just fine" is what often starts the ERO Spiral. "It won't matter if I take a little time to order something from Amazon." "The customer won't know if I cut this corner on their order." "The boss is being a jerk; I am not going to do this task very well just to show him who really is boss." "These customers are really a pain, I am not going to hurry up just for them." "I don't like this job, I am going to go slower." These excuses get us through the hard times and it is easier to do the same the next time. Slacking off can become habit. Blaming everyone except yourself (boss and customers) becomes habit. This blame and excuses then produce self-defeating behavior. This creates major obstacles—dissatisfied customers (who go away rather than complain), an annoyed boss (who does complain and causes more employee disengagement), and goals not met, behind schedule, or over budget. Self-handicapping slowly bogs down the organization.

The Real Issues

Accountability is fundamental when driving for results. Have you ever been in a meeting where the leader/executive spends more time making excuses for why there are shortcomings in the organization than making a plan of action? Suppose Company "A" had a history of tremendous market share in their industry, but because of changing demographics, more competition, and static management, the company is losing the majority market share. The leader comes in to a meeting of directors and explains the reasons why (mostly excuses) they lost share—more competition, competition is innovating more, etc. Basically, the leader starts most of his sentences with, "the competition." This creates a lack of focus on the true customer (stockholder, product consumers) and shifts it to competition—a non-customer/stakeholder. This type of ERO Spiral at the Board level can be deadly for organizations. It all starts with excuses, which lead to reduced effort to retool the strategy.

Remember from Chapter 1 and 2, incremental theorists believe that working hard toward a goal is a way to get better—to master the goal. On the other hand, entity theorists think that if they have to work hard, they must not be very good. So, they choose easier targets, which when achieved, do little to expand their skills or provide learning opportunities.[8] Entity theorists want to look good but not put in the work to do so; and because of that, don't drive for results as hard. Incremental theorists will do whatever it takes to master the job. Furthermore, incremental theorists persist longer under adversity. They believe effort toward a goal gives meaning to life. They also know that mastery can be stressful and painful—they know "learning hurts." Finally, they know that mastery is something you never ever reach. There is no quitting point. So, goal orientation is critical in thinking about driving for results. In the short-term, you may not even notice, but when everyone is working to avoid errors or stay out of trouble, it could mean organizational death. Mastery goals are the key to sustaining driving for results. And, this should be your new focus in talent development efforts.

Those with mastery goals have a personal vision and an action plan for at least the next steps of getting there. They are accountable for their own learning. They have alignment between everyday processes and desired customer outcomes at work. Once there is a vision, a way of dealing with this is, "microplanning," or making sure that what you do every year, month, and day aligns with your multi-year goals and vision. Everyone has experienced arriving at work and not knowing exactly what to do or how to fit tasks into specific time periods—time optimization. Imagine arriving at work at 7:30 and you have a manager's meeting at 8:00. What do you do during that 30-minute window? If you are like many—you might use that 30 minutes to wake up, get coffee, or even find out what's new on social media. Now imagine using that time to practice before the meeting, get a task on your "to-do" list checked off, or review information from other industries. Think of the confidence boost you would have walking into the meeting after already crossing off one line-item on your list or being ahead of the game in other ways. When we complete tasks—even the small ones, we experience a boost to our confidence and self-efficacy—we approach the next tasks with more "grunt" and vigor. This confidence is the key to eliminating your self-handicapping.

As an example, do you know why people in and retired from the military always make their bed when they get out of it? In the 2014 University of Texas—Austin commencement address, Admiral Bill McRaven, head of the US Special Operations Command and a Navy Seal, urged graduates to make their beds every morning. Admiral McRaven said, "If you make your bed every morning, you will have accomplished the first task of the day. It will give you a small sense of pride and it will encourage you to do another task and another."[5]

Sometimes, behavioral change doesn't make much logical sense. Why would you make your bed *every* morning? It has no intrinsic value except to keep the dog/cat off the sheets and it takes time—time that would be better spent drinking that first cup of coffee. But we humans need to be reminded everyday to be proactive. Imagine if the first item of the day was an enormous task that would take at least 3-4 hours to complete. If you get your engine warmed up with a small, completed task, it will give you confidence and pride to complete that larger 3-hour task. By now, you have noticed all of those "baby-steps" at the end of each chapter. Upon first glance at them, you may have said to yourself, "that is such a small and mundane task, I don't need to practice that." We have given you those baby steps to build self-efficacy in each area—these, like bed making, will give you the confidence to keep going. You must first learn to walk, and then you can run. And if you have a bad day—at least you will come home to a made bed—that you made!

At the organizational level, you are probably thinking, "Why not just hire only incremental theorists with mastery goals?" Well, like all good things, they are rare and picky about where they work. No one knows the proportion of incremental versus entity theorists out there, but we all know not many people around us are truly mastery driven. In our classes it remains about 10 percent each year. And, even those who know to look for these individuals do not have the employee selection systems to find them or the organizational culture to support and keep them. If you are reading this book as a leader trying to change an organization, you must find ways to attract those with mastery goals. You are probably trying now, but haven't defined it or really know what to look for. Understanding of the ERO Spiral and "The Box of Blame" will help you develop tools to find those with mastery goals. But more importantly, it makes the search behavioral—things you can see and measure much more easily than mental mindsets.

And keep in mind that you can create an organizational culture that will kill mastery. People with mastery goals need autonomy and purpose. Long ago, Hackman and Oldham said that there were several core dimensions to any work that increased satisfaction and motivation.[9] They showed that workers experience three psychological states in work:

1. *Meaningfulness of Work*—It has meaning; it is something to which one can relate. This causes intrinsic motivation—the work is motivating in and of itself.
   a. Meaningfulness of work comes from having *skill variety*— An opportunity to use variety of skills and talents; *task*

identity—being able to identify how something is done and why; and *task significance*—being able to identify the task as contributing to something wider, to society or a group.

2. *Autonomy*—One is given the opportunity to be a success or failure and have the ability to make changes and incorporate the learning gained in doing the job.

3. *Knowledge of Outcomes*—Providing feedback on how successful the work has been, which in turn enables one to learn from mistakes. Also to connect emotionally to the customer of the output which gives purpose to the work.

Knowing these critical characteristics, it is then possible to derive the key components for designing jobs, teams, and work culture. It is possible to create a culture that provides purpose and autonomy where those with mastery goals will thrive. A poor culture will drive those seeking mastery out. In order to do this, you must first address the preceding chapters of self-handicapping issues. In other words, you must have personal accountability and an accountable staff, a proactive communication culture, an engaged management workforce, little micromanagement, an aware workforce, etc. When those items are aligned, and you begin to attract those with mastery goals, driving for results will happen naturally.

Do You Not Drive for Results?

Survey: Do I Drive for Results or Not?
(Y = Yes, N = No, DK = Don't Know)

___I avoid challenge.

___I typically set easily attainable goals for myself and like to stay in my comfort zone.

___I find myself daydreaming about how things should be, instead of taking action.

___I ask "Who?" "When?" and "Why?" much more than "What?" and "How?"

___I do not really have a personal vision or mission.

___I don't have an action plan that is written behaviorally and results-oriented.

___I pride myself on my ability to stay busy.

___My processes are not linked to outcomes for the organization.

___Distractions often get the better of me.

___I don't write a list of tasks to complete the next workday.

___This company has no dashboards to show us where we are.

___I blame management a lot for our problems.

___I am not sure what "adding value" means.

Scores
9–13 Y's—You are greatly self-handicapping your drive for results.
5–8—You are inconsistent on your approach to driving for results.
1–4—You are pretty good with driving for results.

What to Do?

Creating a culture of driving for results occurs at both the personal and organizational levels and is is the constant force of forward and directed motion. There are several reasons why this is avoided—lack of company vision (where are we going?), lack of personal vision which puts you in the right spot for continued mastery (what do I need for the next step of my career/life?), lack of action plans (how do we get there?), lack of company or personal values (why?), lack of personal action plan (how do I get there?), or just a simple disinterest in customer outcomes (what do *they* need?). So what to do?

Many leaders think motivation and payment are the same things—but *they are not to workers*.[6] The reality is that people come to work for money—most are paid to be there during work hours and to stay out of trouble, but not for exceptional work (mastery goals). They work hard and excel because of all kinds of other things— creation of something, challenges, ownership, identity, mastery, and pride. Seeing the fruits of our labor makes us more productive; and the less appreciated we feel our work is, the more money we want to do it. Often, the harder a project is, the prouder we feel when it is accomplished. Knowing that our work helps others usually increases motivation and makes us more likely to work harder. Positive reinforcement about our abilities may increase performance. Finally, images that trigger positive emotions may actually help us focus—pictures of happy customers enjoying something you designed or built may help you design the next product. *These are all things that come from leaders and the nature of the work, not money.* Simply put, we show up and stay the work hours for the money, but we seek mastery for other things. Furthermore, do not confuse driving for results with control. They are two separate ideas. Controlling people can be quite Machiavellian—a controlling boss doesn't rely on a solid infrastructure of employees and ideas to achieve results but on his micromanagement and the willingness of his employees to be driven to their tasks. Conversely, a workgroup without self-handicapping allows a leader to guide a group of accountable, engaged, visionary, and courageous staff to achieve results more effectively—they will not tolerate a control freak. You can be the captain of your own nuclear submarine—give your workforce a vision and actionable steps to achieve it, and get out of their way.

There are five things to do to drive for results:

1. *Get Yourself Straight*—Why are you there?
2. *Adjust to the Work*—Understand *your* "why do it?"
3. *Organize*—Create "mastery goals" and figure out the "what" and "how."
4. *Work Better*—Keep improving the "how."
5. *Recharge*—Find ways to keep motivated.

Get Yourself Straight

The first step is to literally decide between leadership and followership—right now. Leaders know where they are going and why. They know their accountabilities. And they understand the customer is the end-all, be-all in outcomes—it is all about adding value for the customer. You must embrace these concepts to be a leader—it isn't about you anymore. In fact, very little will be about you in true leadership. Most leaders can tell you the exact time that they knew they were different. They were smarter than those around them, they wanted to change things, they were willing to put in the time to figure out how, and they had a need to produce something of value for another person. Once they figured out this about themselves, they started to develop the path to get there. They stopped working on an "hourly" basis and started to work to produce "outcomes." Those who wanted to create wealth became entrepreneurs. If you have not had this moment yet, you must reach down and find it. Without it, you may find leadership a weary climb.

Most leaders are *servant leaders* in whole or part. They have or are trying to make servant leadership a part of how they run their businesses.[7] When the organization chart looks like a steep pyramid with the leader at the top, people in those organizations focus on pleasing the bosses to the exclusion of doing as much as they can for the customer. One of the most central tenets of servant leadership is listening to the customer and finding ways to add value to their experience. This requires a flatter organization. Servant leadership also influences how one treats suppliers—it is important to care about everyone that the organization touches. The values of servant leadership include empathy, awareness of the customer, foresight—understanding lessons from the past and realities of the present, stewardship—leaders are holding their institutions in trust for the greater good of society, and building community.

While most employees are paid to be there, leaders are paid for results. Leaders must look at stock returns, budgets, and customer satisfaction. All leaders must accept that adding value for customers—*all customers (internal employees or customers outside the organization)*, is a key to their position. Adding value is to increase the functionality or the use of a product or service while holding costs constant, reducing the cost while not reducing functionality, or to increase functionality more than cost. One of the best ways to identify value-added activities is to assess if a particular product or process does *nothing* for a customer. Another is to ask if there is a better solution for the customer—even if you can't provide it. The best is to anticipate their needs and wishes and provide a product that satisfies needs the customer did not know they had. This has been Apple's secret. If you can't supply what a customer needs, then by definition, adding value means to find an alternative source for the customer and direct them there. Satisfied customers return even when directed to an alternate source and appreciate the relationship where they are taken care of regardless of company products or policies (or lack of). Adding value to customers is an attitude or value needed in leadership. Lacking this value is very self-handicapping.

Adjust to the Work

Even if you were destined for leadership, believe the community and customer come first, and have fully equipped yourself mentally for the job of leadership, your organization may not put you where you belong. You still have to find something to lead that suits you. Some of us are entrepreneurs who want to build and sell; some are helpers who want to make other peoples' lives better; some of us want to build things, be first, make a splash; some want to be part of a larger organization and make a contribution wherever it is required. It really doesn't matter who you are, what matters is that you know it and find a place where your personal "why do it?" is always satisfied so you can stay focused and driven without burning out. We all burn out when we are in the wrong place.

A personal vision is extremely helpful here. It will guide you to accept positions better suited to you. It may guide you to seek out different circumstances. Many entrepreneurs start in organizations and slowly discover they are not destined for corporate life—they need to strike out and create wealth. Determine your vision and goals and find the spot that satisfies those goals. To do otherwise is self-handicapping. And this is often where the excuses start the ERO Spiral—"I can't quit this job because of my family responsibilities." "I can't start my own business because I have to guard our nest egg for retirement." This leads to reduced effort—not doing what it takes to move on to what is your real vision or suppressing vision for reality. Then the unhappiness and burnout set in—obstacles. And so on, down the Spiral.

Organize

Organizing consists of two main activities: (1) Setting goals, and (2) Planning. Setting goals includes determining customer needs and wants. It is asking nothing but "what" and "how." Asking "*Who* will 'rescue' me," "*Why* can't I do what so-and-so is doing," and "*When* can I get out of this mess of a job?" will really get you nowhere and are part of the excuses starting the self-handicapping cycle. We all know people who spent their careers on these questions and they are now stuck in their positions without the credentials to move, blaming everyone but themselves, and in denial about the whole situation. So plan out your vision in your current organization or outside of it—it may be both with a progression up from this organization and into another or one of your own. Remember two things: (1) This will require a plan—a detailed, actionable plan and a commitment right now to take charge of mastery and execute it. (2) This is where you break the Spiral. Action plans, focus on mastery rather than performance, and courage will get you beyond excuses and reduced effort to the places you want to be. Break the cycle before it breaks you.

Employees who are mastery-oriented focus on effort, use appropriate learning strategies, are persistent, make choices that are challenging and engaging, and develop a positive orientation toward learning. Leaders should emphasize goals of understanding and improvement (rather than being best or avoiding error). They should convey an activity's meaning and real-world significance. Employees should be involved in decision-making to develop responsibility, independence, and self-directed learning strategies. They should feel they can take risks, make mistakes, and reveal their lack of understanding or apprehensions. Thus, employees will develop a high sense of self-efficacy and attribute poor performance to controllable areas like insufficient practice. Success should be defined by improvement, with value placed on the process of learning.

Obviously, making these leaps is easier when you know your customer and help employees want to please them. No matter if you ever see a customer, customers still pay the bills. Keeping busy, pleasing the boss, and drifting in the wind are viable ways to operate in many corporations. Employees do these things, but in the end, the corporation loses. You are different—you are a leader. Leaders find ways to motivate their employees to a commitment to customers—stockholder, consumer, employee, and corporation—and determine what they need and want. Leaders reinforce this constantly. Find better ways to do this and you will always be a successful leader.

Work Better

Leaders are usually smarter—they keep improving the "hows" of what they do. They plan ahead, organize, are efficient, and bundle. In sports, the guy who gets the penalty is usually behind—not in the right spot at the right time—and he strikes out and is caught. Leaders do not get penalties because they plan and organize to be in the right spot. Sure, there are mistakes, but they use those to learn and get better. That is why a progression of jobs is good—make your mistakes in the small places and learn. Leaders seek out internships and places to volunteer when they are starting out. Mistakes are forgiven there and used as learning opportunities by preceptors. We quickly found out that the best students—*the* ones who moved quickly into the C-suite—practiced efficiency, avoided meetings, organized teams and delegated, skipped the "make work," and found all the loop holes. Well, guess what? They were just managing a tough situation. And, they were teaching others their methods. Leaders organize to solve problems and produce desired outcomes. Great leaders know their customers well and do as needed to satisfy their customer outcomes.

In our classes, we make students draw out a "goal subdivision chart." It can be easy to become distracted what your big goal should be and lose the linkage between that big goal and what you should be doing in the short-term. Similarly, when your organization is going through change, it can sometimes be hard to maintain focus due to worries about how it will affect you. In either situation—goal setting or change management, consider examining goals and subdividing time periods. Put those goals on paper so you really look at them.

Let's look at a simple example using easy numbers. Picture this situation. You acknowledge that your finances are out of order, you have too much charge card debt, and want to save (not accounting for time-value of money) $6,000 in the next 5 years to get out of debt. You need to attain a yearly goal of $1,200; a monthly goal of $100; and a weekly goal of $25. You know the big goal and made a plan—subdivide the savings needed by week. You now know the "what." Next continue to take on the mindset of mastery—"how" do I do it? How do I personally cut out $25 of spending not really needed week to week without suffering? Suffering will take you back to the old ways. You will continually have to look at what you do and adjust every week—learning and getting better at saving (without suffering too badly). Reaching a large goal over a long time-frame may be difficult and can even seem daunting. It is easy to slip into excuses and reduced effort so you do not save the $25 needed each week. Then, the lack of saving adds up to the major obstacle of not being able to pay the bills. And, you start to blame everything and everybody—car repairs, increase in cable bill, inflation, and spouse. The point is that having the sub-goals and approaching each week with a mastery goal mindset will keep you focused on the goal and plan. The first step, of course, is subdividing the outcome goal and time-period so you can impose baby-step goals that give your encouragement along the way when you reach them—increasing motivation and learning. The second is to think mastery—only "what" and "how." If not trained as a child to prefer mastery, this is one way you can work into that mindset.

Recharge

Finally, we all wear out; we need to find ways to keep motivated. Leaders know this and keep their resume current and in their back pocket at all times. Why? Because, (1) They realize that they learn and recharge by moving, and (2) They will never settle for the organization "owning them" when they are prepared to move on. Leadership is a transportable skill; it is needed everywhere. In fact, great leadership is always in great demand in organizations. We think this is because so many let the ERO Spiral drive them out of greatness. But that is the story of this book. It is self-handicapping to not keep a current resume and LinkedIn account, to not keep up with your network, to avoid learning opportunities due to expediency, to be unwilling to move to new leadership positions, and to find other ways to recharge. Find a place to go and relax—a cruise, lake place, or library. It does not matter how or what, just a place to recharge. Extroverts will recharge in their LinkedIn; introverts will recharge in the library or their Kindle. Recharging is another way to stop the excuses leading into the ERO Spiral—recharge and then go out again for the fight; don't hide down the rabbit hole.

Here is a worksheet to think about these things (Table 11.1):

Table 11.1 What Will I Do to Drive for Results?

Behaviors to Work On	Where/When It Occurs	What Will I Do?
Avoiding challenge—Challenges help us grow as people and professionals.		
Who are our customers?—Do you know?		
Is your mind straight?—Who do you own accountability? Are *you* in there too much?		
Can/will you add value?—How will you add value to every interaction you make at work—list all your customers here.		
No personal vision/action plan—Without a vision and action-items, you may be going 80 mph down the wrong highway.		
Confusing "time-based" productivity with outcomes-based processes—Align what you do everyday to an outcomes-based goal.		
Allowing distractions to derail purposeful pursuits—Don't make distractions more important than achieving goals.		
Symptom-based fixes vs. finding and addressing the root cause of an issue—When you get to the root, the symptoms will disappear.		
Daydreaming—Allowing dreams to interfere with your day-to-day tasks.		
Focus—How can you focus to make it count? Fewer projects, more focused outcomes, dashboards?		
Adjust to the job—How will you find your place at work or beyond?		

continued

Table 11.1 *continued*

Behaviors to Work On	Where/When It Occurs	What Will I Do?
Do you need to find a new place?—What do you need to do to make that happen? Resume?		
How will you recharge?—How do you recharge? Where do you recharge?		

Why Don't You

Expediency

Driving for results is something that you never really achieve. You have to constantly remind yourself to be on guard against distractions in the workplace, to have servant goals, to make sure your tasks are aligned with outcomes, and have the courage to take on challenges that will help you grow as a person and professional. It is too easy to let distractions creep up and take time away from important tasks. These distractions aren't just external—a lot are internal. Your daydreams consume time that should be devoted to getting work done and they are really excuses for reduced effort. While you dream nothing gets done.

Don't forget that being good enough is a comfortable place to be. Being good enough produces satisfactory results with a satisfactory amount of effort, but with time marching on, it allows for others inside and out of the organization to grow and learn. And you become obsolete. Much like a lobster being in a pot of lukewarm water that slowly rises to a boil, we often don't realize that our lack of action in the short-term is detrimental to our long-term success. We like to say, "I am playing the long game" and put off what we can do today because we "have plenty of time" to achieve those goals. As time goes by, this thinking persists, and we fail to realize goals. The reasons could be that we simply don't know how to connect the long-term with short-term actions (expediency), we fail to accept challenge (avoidance), we may treat the symptoms of a problem because we fear what may be the root cause (apprehension), or we may simply believe what we are currently doing is great, but everyone else needs to step up (self-deception).

What handicaps do you use to not drive for results because of expediency?

_____

_____

Avoidance

Not driving for results can be the result of a more nuanced cause—focusing on internal outcomes rather than outcomes that affect the external consumer. This is related to tunnel vision. Ideally, all operations of an organization should focus on consumer outcomes—will this project generate a net positive for the external consumer that pays the bills, buys the stock? Of course, some industries like healthcare have multiple customers with conflicting demands which causes problems. Sometimes, too much effort can be wasted on activities that do not have any effect on consumer benefit and this is avoidance of the real issues. Distractions and daydreaming are avoidance. So is lack of developing personal visions, action plans, and keeping up a resume and network. So is not sorting out conflicting customer demands so employees know where to focus.

What handicaps are you creating because of avoidance?

Apprehension

If the planning and preparation are not done (avoidance), driving for results requires mental toughness, discipline, and grit. That can be scary. Does change cause anxiety for you—to the point where you do your best to avoid it? Are you easily distracted from your goals—letting small interruptions derail purposeful pursuits? Do you avoid learning because it is hard? Do you justify this by saying it will not hurt the organization or the customer won't know? If so, you are not being accountable to the customers and organization probably due to apprehension.

The key here is to translate the vision into action. Plans are one step but baby steps are needed next. Successive small and successful steps toward a goal will help one keep on track, overcome hurdles, and build confidence. Taking one big leap is always hard and often leads to failure that saps one's motivation to continue.

What handicaps to driving for results do you create because of apprehension?

Self-Deception

To some extent, this entire book comes down to this one paragraph. Leaders have vision and work to accomplish that vision. Without that, there is no leadership. Great leaders have no self-deception as to where the drive should be directed and how. Can you sum up your career in one sentence? We can—*we educate*. It is all we do—in writing, class, conversations, everywhere and always. And we are driven to continually develop ourselves and help others grow. Our wives are often a victim of that. You are a victim of this sentence right now in reading this book! When you can sum up your life in one sentence, it becomes very hard to deceive yourself. You just keep repeating the sentence over and over and it gets more difficult to blame others or hide from a vision. Without that simple sentence to sum up your personal vision and the mantra of repetition, you could become the victim of your self-handicapping. That one sentence can keep you from spiraling into the Box of Blame. Remember, when others are at fault, you have to work extra hard, everything is unfair, and you are the "hero," you are in self-deception. This typically means you are driving very hard but in the wrong direction and probably for too long—time to stop, reflect, and maybe recharge. At minimum, reassess the underlying reason for the blame. If you step back and look, we will find *you* have put yourself into a Box of Blame. When employees are ducking their heads and provide no feedback of any kind, look and listen very, very carefully. *It is easy to confuse the "Box of Blame" for driving for results.*

How does self-deception affect your communication efforts?

Behaviors to Change

As you read this section, be very honest with yourself—remember, you must be the example to your staff—when you demonstrate behaviors that drive for results and make those results meaningful, your staff will want to jump on the bandwagon—success is attractive.

Developing a Personal Vision

Recognize

Visions direct action. Without a vision, how do you know where you want to go? You are at risk of a derailment and "blowing in the wind." But having just a vision won't result in much without an action plan. Many people go through life without either of these items—floating from one job to another without any logical progression. In order to find where your passion fits you must first create a personal vision and action plan in order to give you direction.

Admit

Admitting that you don't have a personal vision is a difficult thing to do. However, it is helpful to realize how different your life can be when you do. This vision statement will provide a compass for you to gauge career decisions, personal decisions, and financial decisions.[10] Once the vision statement is in place, developing an action plan logically follows (there are action plans throughout this book as an example). Not only does the action plan contain specific actions, but also should contain potential barriers to achievement. The better you can plan for barriers (relapses) —the more likely you will be able to overcome them.

Adjust

If you currently don't have a personal vision statement—make one. Before you put pen to paper, ask yourself what you truly want out of your professional career.[11] Your goals need to be specific to you—no one else. Just because you overheard someone sharing their vision doesn't mean you should automatically adopt it—be true to yourself. This is going to take time! Your vision statement will come from your desires, values, and dreams.

Key Behaviors

Here are the key behaviors for developing a personal vision:[12]

1. Keep it simple, clear, and brief.
2. Focus on "wants" and not "shoulds." Keep it positive.
3. Then ask "what"—what do you want to become as a person? Why is that important to you?
4. Include positive behaviors, traits, and values that you consider important.
5. Balance your dreams with logic.
6. Create a clear statement that will guide you in day-to-day actions—remember the one sentence mantra to sum up your life.
7. Think about how this vision affects other parts of your life. Is it consistent? Where will it conflict?
8. Make it emotional. Including an emotional payoff infuses your vision with passion and makes even more compelling.

Just remember that a mission statement is for now while a vision statement is for the future. Here is a good website that helps you build a mission statement from scratch http://www.franklincovey.com/msb/.

Confusing "Staying Busy" with Mastery Goals

Recognize

It can be very easy to confuse "staying busy" with processes that align with a mastery goal. Managers often use time as a unit of measurement of achievement. You know that hardworking coworker who stays busy and is overwhelmed, but achieves little, and worst of all, does not grow and get better. That coworker is not working toward a mastery goal. It is likely he is working toward performance goals that represent the desire to avoid appearing less competent than others. This is very self-handicapping.

Admit

Not aligning your day-to-day activities with mastery goals can have multiple implications. Personally, you may have a difficult time meeting task goals and becoming responsible for more tasks (promotions). Most importantly, you do not grow, and in the world we have today, that will lead to problems as you quickly become obsolete. There are fewer and fewer places to hide with obsolete skills. The issue of goals is as important as any concept in self-handicapping. Self-handicapping is caused by uncertainty. Performance goals will always cause some level of uncertainty—one is trying to be better than others (performance-approach goals) or not make mistakes (performance-avoidance goals). Ask yourself how much of your time is spent asking, "Who?" "Why?" or "When?" Only a mastery goal and a clear plan to reach it will eliminate the uncertainty and therefore self-handicapping. When one falls short on a mastery goal, he will learn and go right back at it—no real uncertainty there. They spend their time on "What" and "How" questions.

Adjust

Remember, when managers emphasize performance goals, employees have a tendency to evaluate their lack of ability as a cause for failure. The best solution here is to not fail—to avoid error at all cost. The best way to do that is to duck down and do as little as possible. Managers should emphasize goals of understanding and improvement (rather than being best or avoiding error). They should convey an activity's meaning by involving workers in decision-making to develop responsibility, independence, and self-directed mastery learning strategies.

Great professors help students understand mastery by defining it in a mastery grid—showing what is needed to progress from beginner, novice, practitioner, to mastery. They also ask students to think in terms of their "portfolio" or collection of their work and competencies. You may have seen neither—if not, develop a mastery grid and start to collect evidence of your competencies in a "portfolio." Ask your employees to do the same. Celebrate and model learning, improvement, and the success of keeping external customers happy.

Here are some basic rules:

- Provide tasks that are meaningful to employees—given their interests, *or* explain why it must be done and for whom.
- Place the emphasis on mastery of a skill, rather than performance.
- Focus on the value of learning (and what can be gained) in all interactions and in formal and informal evaluation.

Key Behaviors

Here are the key behaviors for *modeling* a commitment to mastery goals and creating an environment of mastery.[13]

1. Model a positive attitude, a willingness to take risks, and continual learning whenever you personally encounter challenging tasks.

2. Approach all employee tasks as learning tasks—not something for punishment or reward.

3. Focus attention on persistent effort and strategy use, not on employee intelligence.

4. When an employee fails, give constructive feedback about work behaviors and strategy use. Emphasize that success is related to one's preparation and effort and continual learning.

5. Teach adaptive strategies. Model how employees should plan, monitor, and evaluate their own work, and especially, their learning.

6. Encourage involvement and a sense of personal accountability. Let employees own their work and their competence.

7. De-emphasize the negative consequence of making errors. It is a part of the learning process; making mistakes help employees improve their skills.

8. Decrease any emphasis on social comparison at work—the "have to win" mentality. Recognize them as individuals taking responsibility for their work and competence, not being better than someone else.

Avoiding Challenge

Recognize

Avoiding challenge is a good way to disengage yourself from work. When you aren't challenged—there is no celebration of conquering the unknown. This isn't to say that those who avoid challenge are bad at what they do. But remember this chapter is all about transforming from good to great—breaking out of that comfort zone at work to achieve at a higher level. Contrary to popular belief, most challenges are not self-initiated. They come in the form of day-to-day tasks that we shy away from because of expediency, avoidance, fear, or self-deception.

Admit

We all avoid challenge at some point, but this can be self-handicapping. Avoiding challenge will stifle your professional growth and seriously limit future promotions. When you accept a challenge a few things happen. These are:

- You learn something you didn't know before.
- You demonstrate ability to take on more responsibility—you are more promotable.
- There is potential to meet new people within the organization—networking.

When people fear the repercussions of challenge—they are focused on not making mistakes and maintaining the status quo. These are performance goals, not mastery goals. This ultimately stifles growth and limits the forward motion of you and your organization. It requires courage to take on the new "uncharted" challenge. If you think you are fearful of taking on new challenges, try to think about remaining static and not growing with the organization. Don't get left behind!

Adjust

All challenges that present themselves should not be accepted. The crux of this section is to learn to be able and willing to accept challenges that will help you grow and learn—not challenges that have no "upside" and will spread your efforts too thin. Mastery is the key. There is a saying that if you want to know what you will be like in 5 years—look at the people you surround yourself with. Surround yourself with people that challenge you to grow and learn.

It is also important to challenge your employees. It can re-engage your employees to the organization. As a leader, you are responsible for the forward momentum of your employees. Help them grow, give them special challenges, motivate them to have the courage to go where they haven't gone before.

Here are a few ways to challenge employees:[14]

- Make sure employees know their purpose in the organization
- Allow them to create their own challenges to support their career advancement
- Clearly communicate their compensation—why they make what they make, and how to get a promotion
- Seek their input and ideas—engage them in decision-making
- Trust them and give positive feedback
- Let them think! Challenge them to critically think about how to complete a task
- Learn from each other's mistakes—they are good things!
- Develop a culture where employees can encourage one another
- Recognize good performance

Key Behaviors

Lana Kravtsova gives an exercise to help with the avoidance of challenge.[15] She says to take a clean sheet of paper and draw a vertical line to create two columns. In the first column, list some of your life's challenges that you have had or are going through currently; in the second column, list the corresponding positive lessons that you learned from going through the challenge. Here are a few examples—first day at a new company | overcoming fear; not being a micromanager | learning to trust; fear of increased work responsibilities | increased self-efficacy. Here are the key behaviors for accepting challenge.

1. When a challenge is presented to you (from yourself or others) acknowledge the challenge.
2. Evaluate potential "upside"—promotions, capable with more responsibility, etc.
3. Evaluate potential resources needed to accomplish the challenge.
4. Read the Chapter 7, Decision Analysis and analyze the risks, ambiguities, and uncertainties associated with the challenge.
5. Make a decision to accept or reject challenge.

Daydreaming and Other Distractions

Recognize

Does your brain wander at work? Do you find yourself thinking about how things should be, how things would be different if you were boss?

While there is nothing wrong with visualizing a better work environment or mentally preparing for your next promotion (it is actually good for your brain)—dreaming about those things can detract time and mental effort away from your day-to-day responsibilities and developing an action plan for those dreams. Furthermore, other distractions can creep up—they promise only a 5-minute break from what we are doing which turns into half an hour on the computer or counseling an employee.

Admit

All of our brains wander into creativity; the issue is whether or not it fits the mission. You can press pause on the wandering and start developing the idea on paper—give it legs. This should be a quick process (dream, refine vision, plan, and action) and not a half-day affair to avoid something.

Douglas Cootey has described the four stages of daydreaming:[16]

1. Normal—When attention drifts away. You lose focus temporarily. This stage is when you come up with new ideas—mostly everyone does this.

2. Dangerous—This is when time runs away from you. You are so entertained in your daydream that you are not conscious of time. This stage can be problematic for your day-to-day tasks and deadlines.

3. Serious—This stage is when you experience physiological changes. Your heart rate increases and you feel emotions. This stage will cause you to make mistakes at your job—it will detach you from reality.

4. Mentally Unstable—This is when you are unable to come back to reality. You live in a constant state of confusing fantasy with reality. Most of us never get here.

The next time you are reading a work-related email or document investigate how many times you stop when you hear an email "ding," another person interrupts you, you mentally shift to another issue, or something else takes your attention away from the work email/document. Research has shown that office workers experience an interruption every 3 minutes.[17] Moreover, it can take up to 23 minutes for a worker to resume their task after the disruption initiated. Distractions are often boundary violations. These violations can range from the obvious (someone interrupting your work), to the ones that "sneak in"—checking email constantly, responding to social application "dings," or thinking about that summer vacation coming up soon.

Adjust

The best way to limit your time daydreaming is to identify what triggers your daydreams and avoid or limit doing them.[18] It is also important to get enough sleep. Research suggests that men need 7-8 hours of sleep per night, while women need 8-9. Not achieving these numbers can result in lack of concentration, daydreaming, and being out of touch with reality.[19] Finally, you can retrain your brain with a timer. Use a timer on your phone or a timer on the Internet to retrain your brain to daydream for a certain amount of time. Set the timer for 5 minutes. Allow yourself that time to go into the creativity dream—when the buzzer goes off—it's time to refocus.[20]

Distractions are like eating—you need to eat every now and again, but eating constantly will lower your effectiveness. In the same way, distractions can allow your brain to unwind and relax in between mental strain. The issue that many people have is becoming distracted constantly because they do not like their work or they let technology run their life.

Key Behaviors

Here are the key behaviors for daydreaming and other distractions:[21]

1. Identify and list possible triggers for your daydreaming.
2. When you feel yourself slipping into a dream—set the timer for 5 minutes. When the time goes off—refocus on your task.
3. Get enough sleep *every* night.
4. Schedule and enforce a set amount of time in your day for email—preferably in a "low productive" time of the day for you. Once you are finished—close the email application.
5. If you work at a computer—close all Internet and social messaging applications during productivity hours.
6. If you work in a cubicle, you may want to invest in some noise-cancelling headphones.
7. Allow 5 minutes on the hour to get up, stretch, move, and be distracted.
8. When you must head to meetings, allow time for distraction. This is how you engage your employees and practice good talent management.
9. Set times and durations for distractions. Try not to think about work during these times.
10. Establish boundaries for others. Tell them about your "peak productivity hours" and ask them not to interrupt. If they continue to interrupt—ask them gently to respect your set boundary.

Not Giving Employees Meaningful Work

Recognize

People have strong motivation to seek meaning in their work. Employees want to feel worthwhile and make a difference; so, there must be a balance between work requirements and an employee's own personal purpose and interests. Disengagement occurs when the employee does not have a personal connection to their work role so learn about employees' goals and determine which roles would enable them to express themselves best.

Admit

There are many things that managers can do to make work meaningful to employees. Questions to ask are—Do you personally learn about employees' goals and determine which roles could be best for them? Do you find ways to give employees autonomy and allow them to make decisions pertaining to these issues? Do your employees have opportunities to learn new skills? Do you keep meaningful work from some employees—your "out" group? Do you give employees information about the organization, so they can find a more rewarding position in it? Are you on the lookout for talent (see Chapter 9: Talent Management)? Do you let employees "see the books" and explain how their roles are vitally important to the organization as a whole? Do you give honest performance feedback? All of these things are part of making work more meaningful for employees. Great leaders learn to make these part of their job because they want engaged employees.

Adjust

Unfortunately, too many managers don't even try to make work meaningful for the people doing it; they don't see it as their job. Managers in such companies seem to think that paying people is reason enough for them to perform at their best. But extrinsic motivation only goes so far. Even the "self-starters" need feedback and encouragement. And, the company may not help you—their mission statements fall flat, their selection systems are all about technical skill, and they may not care if a person's values match the job or not. So your job is to kick in and do it for the company. These employees work for you and your team will stand out with true engagement. So match people to tasks and jobs that will engage them.

Key Behaviors

Here are the key behaviors for match people to jobs to increase engagement:

1. In your interview guide (Chapter 9, Talent Management) add questions that get at personal needs for engagement and even advancement. Learn about employees' goals and determine which roles be best for them.

2. In your interviewing process, add a realistic job preview so employee expectations are realistic.

3. Let employees arrange task or jobs to suit their needs.

4. Ask your employees if they want opportunities to learn new skills and what.

5. Ask yourself if an employee is in your "in" or "out" group when assigning tasks or projects. Be fair to the "out" group (who you may not trust, give less feedback, and give less discretion) in assigning work.

6. Make sure you give employees information about the organization—job openings, other areas—and even other companies.

7. Give honest performance feedback.

Not Adding Value for Customers

Recognize

Adding value to customers requires long-term customer relationships, diagnosis of their needs and wants, a personal strength and foundation to move away from one's own needs to those of the customer, knowledge of what the employee and company can offer as well as what the competition can offer, networking to find this out, and honesty with the customer. There is a complete shift to the customers' point of view—from short-term indices or sales quotas to long-term customer relationships, from capturing or manipulating the customer to servicing the customer, and assessing success not by sales or number of interactions but by customer satisfaction.

Admit

Consumers' habits have begun to change dramatically. They now trust online information such as the opinions of strangers shared in public forums. Consumers have become savvy researchers and are considering reviews in context and examining advice to suit their particular needs. You may try hiding the fact that you can't do the best job for a customer, but it won't work. Sometimes adding value requires losing to win. If you can't add value, someone else can; and your customer will find them. You should tell the customer who that is. You may lose a sale but you will gain a committed, loyal customer. If your department or company cannot supply what the customer wants or needs, you and your employees should have the integrity to say so, and the authority to tell the customer where to find what is needed.

Adjust

Start by letting employees know that the customer is your prime focus *and practice it*. Ask yourself, "What will my customer think about this?" each and every time you make a decision. Life no longer revolves around just what matters most to you. We know that whenever our customers (or students) are becoming a nuisance is when we have stopped trying to add value. Encourage employees to develop creative ways to serve customers. Engaged employees add value for their customers.

Key Behaviors

The key behaviors to try out in adding value are as follows:

1. Develop a plan to build long-term customer relationships.

2. Diagnose customers' needs and wants.

3. Develop the personal strength to move away from your needs to customer needs.

4. Develop a full knowledge of what you can offer as well as what the competition can offer.

5. Network to find this out.

6. Offer value in every transaction even if it is from another company or department.

7. Do not forget to attend to your communication style and interaction with a customer. It is not all transaction.

8. Acknowledge your appreciation for and by the customer.

Final Personal Takeaways

Action Plan—Driving for Results

Take a few minutes and complete this action plan about driving for results.

Driving for Results Self-Handicaps	What Is the Situation?	Trigger	Impact on Others	What to Do/When?
Having no personal vision/action plan		__Expedient __Avoiding __Apprehension __Self-deception		__Deliberate action____ __Self-efficacy_____ __Face it_____ __Look and listen_____

continued

Driving for Results Self-Handicaps	What Is the Situation?	Trigger	Impact on Others	What to Do/When?
Developing mastery goals for yourself (getting yourself straight)		__Expedient __Avoiding __Apprehension __Self-deception		__Deliberate action____ __Self-efficacy_____ __Face it_____ __Look and listen_____
Modeling mastery and creating an environment of mastery for employees		__Expedient __Avoiding __Apprehension __Self-deception		__Deliberate action____ __Self-efficacy_____ __Face it_____ __Look and listen_____
Avoiding challenge		__Expedient __Avoiding __Apprehension __Self-deception		__Deliberate action____ __Self-efficacy_____ __Face it_____ __Look and listen_____
Staying "busy" without aligning processes with outcomes		__Expedient __Avoiding __Apprehension __Self-deception		__Deliberate action____ __Self-efficacy_____ __Face it_____ __Look and listen_____
Daydreaming without results		__Expedient __Avoiding __Apprehension __Self-deception		__Deliberate action____ __Self-efficacy_____ __Face it_____ __Look and listen_____
Allowing distractions		__Expedient __Avoiding __Apprehension __Self-deception		__Deliberate action____ __Self-efficacy_____ __Face it_____ __Look and listen_____
Making work meaningful for employees		__Expedient __Avoiding __Apprehension __Self-deception		__Deliberate action____ __Self-efficacy_____ __Face it_____ __Look and listen_____

continued

continued

Driving for Results Self-Handicaps	What Is the Situation?	Trigger	Impact on Others	What to Do/When?
Adding value for customers		__Expedient __Avoiding __Apprehension __Self-deception		__Deliberate action____ __Self-efficacy_____ __Face it_____ __Look and listen_____
Learning to recharge		__Expedient __Avoiding __Apprehension __Self-deception		__Deliberate action____ __Self-efficacy_____ __Face it_____ __Look and listen_____

Baby Steps

This chapter is the final step in eliminating self-handicapping. Lots of issues were discussed, but here are a few baby steps for you to implement now.

The baby steps for this chapter are as follows:

- Every day, start with a small and easy task that you can complete quickly. Don't forget to make your bed every morning! Be proud of it.
- Write out a personal vision of building competence and develop an action plan that aligns with that vision.
- From the plan, identify a longer-term goal and break it down into yearly, monthly, and weekly target checkpoints.
- Take a piece of paper and write down all of the things you did last week that were not mastery-oriented. What did you do to be better or to stay out of trouble? Think about the proportion of time spent in performance goals and how that is affecting your career.

Follow-Up Questions

1. Does your personal vision conflict with your organization? Job?
2. Why do you get consumed by distractions? Because you are extroverted? Hate your job? Are just bored? Or, are performance-oriented?
3. How can I be more mastery-oriented? Or is it something innate that I can't change?
4. What more do I need to know about adding value for customers? Where will I find it?

Endnotes

1. Adapted from Zenger Folkman, "The 16 Days of Competencies: #6 Drives for Results." http://zengerfolkman.com/the-16-days-of-competencies-6-drives-for -results/ and Justine Beem, "Competency Spotlight: Driving for Results." http:// www.assess-systems.com/thought-leadership/articles/competency-spotlight -driving-for-results-and-delivering-results/ (accessed June 5, 2015).

2. See Jim Collins, "Good to Great: Why Some Companies Make the Leap...and Others Don't." HarperCollins, New York, NY, 2001. http://www.amazon.com/ Good-Great-Some-Companies-Others/dp/0066620996/ref=sr_1_1?s=books&ie=U TF8&qid=1416599068&sr=1-1&keywords=good+to+great (accessed June 5, 2015).

3. Chad Kettner, "A Review: Good to Great, Why Some Companies Make the Leap... and Others Don't." http://www.goodreads.com/book/show/76865.Good_to_Great (accessed June 5, 2015).

4. Ibid.

5. See David Larter, "Top Navy SEAL's Life Advice: 'Make Your Bed.'" http:// scoopdeck.navytimes.com/2014/05/19/top-seals-life-advice-make-your-bed/ (accessed June 5, 2015).

6. Adapted from Jessica Gross, "What Motivates Us At Work More Than Monday." http://blog.ted.com/2013/04/10/what-motivates-us-at-work-7-fascinating-studies -that-give-insights/ (accessed June 5, 2015).

7. Adapted from Josh Spiro, "How to Become a Servant Leader." http://www.inc.com/ guides/2010/08/how-to-become-a-servant-leader.html, and Larry Spears, "Ten Principles of Servant Leadership." http://legacy.butler.edu/volunteer/resources/ principles-of-servant-leadership/ (accessed June 5, 2015).

8. Summarized from DH Pink, *Drive: The Surprising Truth About What Motivates Us*, New York, NY: Riverhead Books/Penguin Group, 2009.

9. See JR Hackman and GR Oldham, *How Job Characteristics Theory Happened*. The Oxford Handbook of Management Theory: The Process of Theory Development, 2005, 151–170.

10. See Susan Heathfield, "Create Your Personal Vision Statement." http:// humanresources.about.com/od/success/a/personalvision.htm (accessed June 8, 2015).

11. See PR in your Pajamas, "How to Create Your Personal Vision." http:// prinyourpajamas.com/how-to-create-your-vision/ or Randall Hansen, "The Five-Step Plan for Creating Personal Mission Statements." http://www.quintcareers. com/creating_personal_mission_statements.html (accessed June 8, 2015).

12. Summarized from Jesse Stoner, "Personal Vision: 6 Guidelines to Create a Vision for the Life You Really Want." http://seapointcenter.com/personal-vision/ and Carroll County Public Schools, "Writing a Personal Mission Statement." http:// www.carrollk12.org/Assets/file/MVH/Resources/Portfolio%20-%20Mission% 20Statement.pdf (accessed June 8, 2015).

13. Summarized from Northern Illinois University, "Guide for Creating Mastery Oriented Classrooms." http://www.niu.edu/eteams/pdf_s/GO_GuideCreating MasteryOrientedClassrooms.pdf (accessed June 8, 2015).

14. Summarized from Roy Saunderson, "Top 10 Ways to Challenge Employees to Perform." http://www.incentivemag.com//Strategy/Ask-the-Experts/Roy-Saunderson/Top-10-Ways-to-Challenge-Employees-to-Perform/ (accessed June 5, 2015).

15. See Lana Kravtsova, "Life Purpose: Do you Avoid Challenges." http://daringclarity.com/life-purpose-do-you-avoid-challenges (accessed June 5, 2015).

16. See Douglas Cootey, "The Shocking Truth about Daydreaming." http://douglascootey.com/2012/10/the-shocking-truth-about-daydreaming.html (accessed June 5, 2015).

17. Summarized from Rachel Silverman, "Workplace Distractions: Here's Why You Won't Finish This Article." http://online.wsj.com/articles/SB10001424127887324339204578173252223022388 (accessed January 5, 2015).

18. Summarized from Daydreaming Disorder, "Possible Treatments." http://daydreamingdisorder.webs.com/possibletreatments.htm (accessed June 5, 2015).

19. See Holly Carling, "Daydreaming or Inability to Maintain Concentration?" http://www.cdapress.com/news/healthycommunity/article3bf3df0a-a162-579b-b09d-a922e23f5394.html (accessed June 8, 2015).

20. Adapted from Douglas Cootey, "Hack Your Mind: 4 Steps to Take Charge of Your Daydreaming." http://douglascootey.com/2012/10/hack-your-mind-4-steps-to-take-charge.html (accessed June 8 2015).

21. Summarized from Sarah Pavey, "Minimizing Distractions: Managing Your Work Environment." http://www.mindtools.com/pages/article/distractions.htm and University of Reading, "Study Advice: Avoiding Distractions and Staying Motivated." http://www.reading.ac.uk/internal/studyadvice/Studyresources/Time/sta-distractions.aspx (accessed January 5, 2015).

12

What Happens Next

So there you have it. We have emptied our brains to help you begin the conversation about self-handicapping in business and start your journey to overcome the habits of self-handicapping. It may be a bit overwhelming at this point, but think of the positive: you made it all the way through this book. Many didn't. We don't profess to have all the answers, but we know you are on the road to overcoming whatever major constraints you have placed on yourself in leadership. And you have your reference manual in hand (Don't lose this book; review it each quarter to see what needs work). At this point, you can help the business world begin to focus less on impression management and more on adding value to customers because that is what you will model for others to do. You will move further and further into this adventure because you will continue to grow. Many of our readers will have suggestions and critiques. Researchers will gear up to answer many of the unanswered questions about self-handicapping in business. Some will question our model and the ERO Spiral. And, we will be happy—the conversation has begun, in earnest.

A Quick Summary

When we were kids, we all said, at one time or another, "It wasn't me!" That could have been the very start of our self-handicapping. As we got older, the excuses become obstacles for life. As leaders they bog down our ability to be effective. These excuses and self-defeating behaviors have negative impacts on organizational and customer outcomes. When we use excuses, we typically point fingers at an inanimate object—"my allergies," "the company," "my computer crashed." Yet, when those become habit and turn into self-defeating behavior, we cannot hide behind the excuses anymore and we need heavier ammunition. When our negative behaviors create obstacles our employees feel it. This is often the point where we start blaming other people for our problems—the biggest obstacle of them all. The impact of that is hurt feelings and retaliation. You have heard about this spiral into poor leadership enough. You have pored over ways to overcome self-handicapping—whether excuses, self-defeating behavior, or actual obstacles. You have tried some of the baby steps to move away from the self-defeating behavior. Now, it is time to really commit for the long haul. No more excuses, no tolerance of obstacles, and nothing but "What" and "How" questions and a mastery orientation.

You can't achieve a mastery orientation overnight or legislate it on your employees with a memo. First, it takes getting out of a performance goal atmosphere—aiming to win or not making mistakes. That won't be easy in business, but self-handicapping is the greatest drag on being exceptional. *Learning, competence, and adding value should be the rewarded goals.* Second, it takes every group member working to overcome the habits leading them down the EPO Spiral—eliminating excuses and self-defeating behavior. Group members need to agree to call each other out on the slipups. New behaviors must be learned. Like all things, this takes attention and practice—"recognize, acknowledge, admit, and adjust." But, we can all do it once it is out and discussed. Like most things, it will be easier being allowed to laugh at the mistakes and regressions, but that is part of a mastery climate. And remember, it is ok to "fall off the wagon"—just be sure to recognize when you do and apply what you have learned.

What will work look like when there is no self-handicapping? We know that great managers motivate every single employee to take action and engage them with a compelling mission and vision, have the assertiveness to drive outcomes and the ability to overcome adversity and resistance, create a culture of clear accountability, build relationships that create trust, open dialogue, and full transparency, and make decisions that are based on productivity, not politics. The exceptional leader is always thinking three steps ahead and working to master his environment with the goal of furthering the aims of his organization and its customers and vendors. Exceptional leaders do not let self-handicapping overwhelm them or their employees. They will help their workforce attend to the excuses, point out where excuses are leading to reduced effort, and identify self-defeating behaviors. They will help those in the box. They know—much like competence or adding value for customers—there will never be an end to overcoming self-handicapping. It is habitual, we often learned as children, and it may be a generation or two before it is truly managed. Exceptional leaders know it is up to them to start and perpetuate the self-handicapping conversation at work and support research in business to learn more. They know it is a team effort.

The difficult group is all of us normal people who will have a tendency to say, "Yes, I see that. I know my employees do this and I need to put a stop to it. Sure am glad I don't do that stuff!" That denial will be your downfall with your own behavior as well as your employees'. Unless you can begin to change your self-handicapping, your employees will not believe they have to do so. Soon, all of you will be back in the same way of operating you have always had. This takes a group commitment, an open discussion, and a true turn towards mastery goals.

When tasks are simple, both performance and mastery goals will increase effort and performance. However, when tasks are complex— such as in team projects—different goals trigger different reactions.[1] Employees with performance goals become worried about failure and lack of competence. They offer excuses and reduce effort. Those with mastery goals do not self-handicap and persist in the face of difficulty. While most employees are oriented one way or the other, research suggests that an individual may adopt both performance and mastery goals at the same time. In teams, it gets more complex because of workers' misperception of the situation.

Team members who perceive the team having mastery goals or believe teammates hold mastery goals have more satisfaction and better performance. However, research also shows that individuals hold less accurate perceptions of their teams' mastery goals than they do of their performance goals. Team members often believe that other members are less motivated by skill development than those members report themselves to be. Exceptional leaders work to change this in teams. This issue of misperceived goals in teams and dealing with those in the box are the most difficult areas of self-handicapping to change. Exceptional leaders work to know individual worker's perceptions of team goals and work with them because these perceptions are more likely caused by their own individual goal preference than actual team goals. Sometimes team culture does not overcome individual preference and self-handicapping in teams goes on. We know that instruction or training programs can shift an employee's attention toward the goal type to which he or she is not predisposed. Leaders can develop these skills in a world where there is a discussion about self-handicapping.

Without self-handicapping and leaders/employees sliding down the ERO Spiral, we expect to see much less blame at work and fewer people in the box. Yet, there are many in the box now. We have offered suggestions to help these folks, but readily admit that "in the box" people don't want help, have cut themselves off from constructive feedback, and may simply take too much counseling time to turn around unless they see the light, work to eliminate blame, and ask the *What* and *How* questions. We do know that with a conversation and team effort to overcome self-handicapping, many that might go into the box will avoid it. That alone makes working with self-handicapping a worthwhile pursuit.

Leaders Have Impact on Those Around Them

After a leader understands self-handicapping and moves toward overcoming his own self-sabotage, he will want to change the world (as discussed earlier). You, as a leader, can work with employees to change some behaviors; but, remember that trying to change mindset is considerably more difficult. An analogy is dealing with sexual harassment under labor law. It would be nice if all men respected women and vice versa, but you can't *make* that mindset happen. What you can make happen, and you do—as it is company policy—is eliminate certain well-defined behaviors. All companies keep employees from making sexual issues a condition of employment, the basis for an employment decision, or creating an intimidating, hostile, or offensive working environment (this is the US law). These behaviors are spelled out in legislative law, court cases, and innumerable training programs. There is clarity about the behavior and the sanctions are clear. So, the bad behavior is not done—very often.

You can make this approach work in eliminating self-handicapping behavior. Once the conversation around self-handicapping is well-established, teams can define what they want to work on and how to start. They need the vocabulary, clarity of behavioral definition, and a lot of practicing better ways of handling situations—just like dealing with sexual harassment (it takes role-play practice for most men to even realize the different ways they sexually harass women). As an example, let's say an issue is that employees don't engage employees or customers well. Behaviors defining engagement include making eye contact throughout a conversation or within a certain time frame after the customer enters an office, greeting or shaking hands with every employee, team member, or customer you see in a meeting or conversation, and asking employees or customers what they need to make things easier. There are more complex things to do, but take these as your first "baby steps." They are fairly clear and not terribly hard to do. Picture everyone practicing and doing two or three of these simple behaviors consistently for the next month. Sometimes it may be awkward, sometimes you may not be able to do it. Sometimes, hopefully, you will laugh at each other. But over time, you will become more comfortable and your employees/customers will respond. You may see reciprocation, trust, openness, and who knows what more. This is the path of baby steps. We believe that the team's attitude toward engaging fellow employees and customers will change and they will keep growing in this regard. We think their attention will shift to customers and mastery of their ability to solve customer problems. Of course, you can't micromanage this process. After these baby steps, you will choose the next two behaviors to work on. Keep doing this and you will fairly quickly have an engaged workforce and possibly be the envy of most leaders in the organization.

Working With Others' on Self-Handicapping

We hope all managers and leaders do speak up and try to get the problem of self-handicapping on the table. There are several levels at which self-handicapping can be confronted other than within yourself:

- Boss to employee
- Peer to peer
- Executive coach or trainer to leader
- Employee to boss

Talking to anyone about self-handicapping is difficult because it typically has been an undiscussable topic at work. Team members often misinterpret peer's goals driving the discussion. Furthermore, there would need to be a solid connection and a fair amount of trust between the individuals discussing self-handicapping. Peer to Peer and Employee to Boss will only happen where the leaders are open, connected, and trusted and usually only when the boss initiates it. An organization-wide discussion of self-handicapping can start this process but not finish it. A boss can confront an employee as they do with all work-related problems. This would be a crucial conversation and be dependent on the connection and trust between the individuals. Many leaders may self-handicap because of general unease with talking about "personal or psychological issues." Their coaches will point it out.

Helping Employees

Most of this book is dedicated to helping a leader manage employees without excuses, self-defeating behavior, and the creation of major obstacles. We don't need to reiterate *how* to coach employees about self-handicapping. Let us talk here about two issues: (1) Creating a climate for mastery of competence (and overcoming self-handicapping), and (2) How self-handicapping training should be organized and delivered.

A Climate for Mastery of Competence

Climate is a set of properties of the work environment, perceived by the employees, that influences employee behavior.[2] As organizations become more complex, the need to establish a positive climate is increasingly critical to employee satisfaction and productivity. Employees in large organizations today often work on multiple teams and report to a variety of managers, so their work life can be complex and frustrating. They often do not understand mastery goals at the individual or group level. Good organizational climate is based on clarity, accountability, flexibility, and team commitment. Employees should know that mastery goals are expected—individually and for team tasks—and what is precisely required to get there. In other words, they should be given authority to accomplish tasks, be able to get rid of unnecessary rules, policies and procedures, to make mistakes, learn, and continually develop competence in what they do, and they should be proud to belong to the team and add their competence to it.

There are two more things to expand on in that list: (1) Mastery orientation and (2) Vulnerability. Employees should be recognized and rewarded for a mastery orientation. The goal should be for the employee to become as competent as possible in adding value for customers. Furthermore, employees must be allowed to feel free to express their worries and vulnerabilities. Without this they will close up or go back to the uncertainty and insecurity. This leads to self-handicapping in the face of performance goals—to win or not make mistakes. Here are some examples of what this climate should look like.

Experienced employees know when they've made a mistake.[3] Instead of lecturing them or telling them how to fix it, take yourself out of the situation and let them work it out. Once *they* realize they made a mistake and take ownership of it, they're less likely to repeat it. To help you back off, put things in perspective like you would with your children. Telling oneself, "She is just a five-year old," does seem to help get one in the habit of avoiding criticism and harsh punishment. It also helps you wait to catch the five-year old in the act of doing something good, and then praising her. "Children" rules work on employees too.

Remember that employees inherently attend to bosses. By telling them exactly what it is that they did right or that you want, you empower them with the knowledge of exactly what to *repeat* to get your attention again.

Instead, focus on the effort to be competent—then they will take pride in their own effort and what they have accomplished. This helps employees develop a sense of internal evaluation, allowing them to take responsibility for their action and pride in their achievements. They must feel free to make some mistakes, ask questions, and express when they feel vulnerable or apprehensive. This is not the war mentality of many business gurus, but exceptional leaders build this type of climate. Interestingly, most dog trainers will tell you the same things.

Last, how you say "thank you" is important. Many of the situations where we use "good job!" are situations that make *customers' lives* easier. Why not come out and state that connection directly? Saying, "Thank you for doing that. Now, these customers don't have to worry about when it might get done!" will convey much more than "good job!" Much of this sounds like you are raising children, and it may be because developing a mastery climate at work looks a lot like helping our children become independent adults sure of their own abilities and independence. But for employees or children to get there, they must be allowed to express their fears, uncertainties, and when they feel vulnerable, to ask questions, and learn from their mistakes. Environments where workers are over managed and feel powerless over their jobs and competence, do not support them being in charge of what they do or working toward mastery goals.

Expressing Vulnerability

One way to help employees express their worries is to express yours.[4] But, many leaders think showing weakness will relegate them to the back of the pack, that admitting mistakes means they cannot handle being the leader. Vulnerability does not mean being weak or submissive; it really implies the courage to laugh at yourself. Opportunities for vulnerability come up every day—calling an employee whose child is sick, reaching out to someone who has just had a loss in their family, taking responsibility for something that went wrong, or asking someone for help. When a leader tries to appear perfect or strong, it often has the opposite effect. Employees are particularly sensitive to signs of trustworthiness in their leaders and trust in a leader improves employee performance.

When employee vulnerability is not welcome in the workplace, employee ideas are being stifled. If an employee doesn't feel comfortable offering worries or new ideas, they will keep it to themselves. A working environment in which people don't feel free to be open or make mistakes can also be corrosive. This is where self-handicapping takes hold—people avoid blame and accountability goes out of the window. Engagement dies. And the leader slides down the ERO Spiral into the box.

Allowing the expression of vulnerability also may increase the resilience of employees.[5] Resilience is the capacity to absorb recurrent disturbances while moving forward. Not all employees have high levels of resilience. Resilience is important for the discussion of vulnerability for several reasons—it helps employees evaluate hazards and make plans, it puts the emphasis on the ability of a person to deal with a hazard—absorbing or adapting to the disturbance, and it is forward-looking and helps one explore options. Furthermore, leaders accepting expressions of vulnerability can give an employee a positive view of themselves, confidence in their strengths and abilities, increase employee skill in communication and problem solving, and moves them very firmly away from performance goals. Finally, it increases their capacity to manage strong feelings and impulses. Building vulnerability and resilience into work is an effective way to cope with change and build a mastery climate.

Training Employees

We have used two types of training in exposing people to self-handicapping—(1) Reflective workshops and (2) Behavior modeling. We think both are needed. It takes time for leaders to recognize, acknowledge, and admit to self-handicapping. Recognition of excuses comes first, and then self-defeating behaviors and obstacles are recognized. Only then are participants ready and motivated to find new ways to operate—alternative key behaviors. This can be done in groups but most require their own thoughts in individual reflection to work through it at first. We have used the worksheets provided here as action plans to help trainees see their behavior in context and plan strategies. It takes time to absorb the model of self-handicapping and the ERO Spiral. The reflective activities must come first or the behavioral work has no context. It becomes just another management training program.

We have provided key behaviors for many new non-self-defeating behaviors as a way to overcome obstacles to effective leadership. Those come from training using behavior modeling techniques. Taylor, et. al.[6] in a meta-analysis, shows that behavior modeling training is one of the most widely used, well-researched, and highly regarded training interventions. The approach, based on Bandura's Social Learning Theory, differs from other training methods because of its emphasis on the following: (1) Describing to trainees a set of well-defined behaviors (skills) to be learned, (2) Providing a model or models displaying the effective use of those behaviors, (3) Providing opportunities for trainees to practice using those behaviors, (4) Providing feedback and social reinforcement to trainees following practice, and (5) Taking steps to maximize the transfer of those behaviors to the job.[7] Although other training approaches often include one or more of these components, behavior modeling emphasizes the importance of including them all. We strongly encourage this type of behavioral training be used in dealing with self-handicapping at the behavioral level—it works.

Furthermore, we provide relapse training: (1) To anticipate high-risk situations, (2) Develop coping strategies for avoiding high-risk situations, and (3) Make slight slips or relapses predictable outcomes that need not become full-blown relapses. These techniques increase trainees' self-efficacy (feelings of control over the situation). Mental rehearsal can also be used as a self-control device. If a person pictures him or herself doing the correct behaviors before actually going out and attempting that new behavior, they are more successful. Finally, our final training bit of wisdom is to *not* just terminate those in the box or excessively self-handicapping and pass the problem on to the next department or organization. *There are few non-self-handicappers out there to be hired and if placed in a poor climate would just leave anyway.* It is best to build a team culture around overcoming self-handicapping in your organization and watch everyone master it together. Some "Box" people will leave willingly.

Hiring Employees

Throughout reading this book, you probably had thoughts on how to hire employees and leaders who do not self-handicap or have mastery-goal orientation and you must have an idea of what to look for in a candidate by this point. They are as follows:

- Humility (not to certain and not too uncertain)
- High self-efficacy and resilience
- Understanding of self-handicapping
- Having mastery goals versus performance goals

We have provided an entire chapter on poor talent development which is one of the major obstacles to exceptional leadership. Whether you employ interviewing or more sophisticated techniques, your dilemma is the same—"How do I find candidates that do not self-handicap and particularly do not let self-handicapping lead to self-defeating behavior and major obstacles to leadership?" "How do I find leaders who build mastery-oriented work climate and teams?" We believe the first step is to measure or look for humility. Those individuals have self-efficacy and will likely be resilient in finding solutions. They will also likely be ethical and place the customer and organization before themselves. Of course, it may be best to not assume humility automatically leads to these. Separate them out and measure them apart. We suggest this because most employee selection methods are flawed and not very valid. It is best to measure in different ways and multiple times.

Second, self-efficacy and resilience can be measured with established tests.[8,9] Those interested could explore these tests or develop questions for their interview guide. If you have made it this far, you should be able to assess what one knows about self-handicapping.

And finally, we have no magic bullet for measuring goal orientation concepts with leaders. There are existing survey-based measures of goal orientation used with students. One of the most commonly used measures is the Patterns of Adaptive Learning Survey (PALS).[10] The PALS contains measures of students' personal goals, as well as their perceptions of classroom goal structures and has been used with a wide range of age groups, including young children, adolescents, and college-aged students. Other student measures are also available.[11] Most survey measures of achievement goals assess students' reasons for engaging in academic tasks; however, Nichols and his colleagues conceptualized their measures of goal orientations in terms of how students feel about learning.[12] Those interested should explore these tests or develop questions for their interview guide.

Helping Bosses

Two in five people work for someone they consider a "bad" leader.[13] Generation Xers seem to be the most disgruntled—45 percent of them say they work for a bad boss, 39 percent of millennials, and 35 percent of boomers are unhappy with their bosses. Over a third of employees say that the poor leadership at work is the most stressful part of the job and that their boss makes them feel controlled, manipulative or defensive. Additionally, 25 percent feel their career progress is limited because of their boss's poor leadership. Employees who classify their supervisor as bad are more than twice as likely to say they plan to look for a new job within the next year. This adds up to a lot of obstacles to overcome. Yet, for the "good" bosses, 91 percent of employees feel positively about their work, enjoy going to work each day, 80 percent say their work makes a positive difference in the world, and 74 percent feel empowered to be a leader at work. *"Good" leaders seem to be developing mastery climates and more leaders.*

Good and bad leader behavior impacts employees and it filters right down to customers, vendors, and organizational outcomes; so this research stresses the importance of self-awareness and feedback systems that allow leaders to face the truth about their leadership. Up to 40 percent of the people on your team will thank you for overcoming your self-handicapping and possibly not leave your team. Where are you with your boss? How can you develop this feedback mechanism?

Bosses self-handicap for the same reasons we all do—uncertainty. When he talks too much, makes a decision only to start second-guessing himself, changes his mind constantly, asks for your opinion more than once, or is micromanaging, he is self-handicapping. Of course, you have just read about all of the obstacles. One thing has always been clear in working with this type of boss—anticipate your boss' needs and always stay one step ahead. Take the initiative to look ahead and be ready to react. We all know that past behavior is the best predictor of future behavior; most of us are predictable, if studied. So take a positive approach to this; study your boss and find ways to help him overcome self-handicapping. Mention what you are doing with yourself. Start the conversation in your work group; it will filter back up one way or the other—just make sure it is positive.

You have a source of power in the employee-boss relationship because bosses may be dependent on you and may even do anything to keep you. But push too hard with a controlling boss and you are history. By setting limits and initiating new, non-self-handicapping behaviors, you are upsetting the balance of power in the relationship. He is not going to give up what he is doing—easily. And, you understand self-handicapping. So, you are really the stronger of the two, but also the more vulnerable of the two.

You have to subtly teach your bosses how to behave. This can be done through modeling and behavior modification; show your boss your lack of excuses, recognition of self-defeating behavior, and asking the What and How questions. Say, "Let's concentrate on what we can control," a lot. Then, reward appropriate behavior in positive ways and not rewarding or subtly punishing inappropriate behavior. And remember, the reward is often affirmation and attention.

The most controlling/blaming bosses have a significant resistance to growth. Furthermore, it is important to understand that controlling behavior works—most people either give in to control attempts, get out of the way, or actively enable them—the guy on the roof again. In any job, there are disagreements over any number of issues and while these issues may cause conflict, the conflict is short and the resolution is usually negotiated. However, with controlling bosses, negotiation and compromise don't appear. The relationship is played out in a situation where the boss is driven to win—performance goals. Controlling bosses have a large repertoire of scare tactics, insults, comments and other intimidating behaviors. So, be very careful; be willing to move on and don't *live for the promise*. Never attack or label the boss; align and redirect.

Helping Peers

Bringing up self-handicapping to peers is one of the most difficult but important things you will do. Almost everyone has a colleague who comes to every meeting unprepared and uses the excuse, "I didn't get that email." You know he got it because he was on the same distribution list as you, but for every meeting he does this, he ends up not being assigned any tasks. Is this a confrontation issue, something for the boss to bring up, or a time to bring up self-handicapping as poor impression management? Since this peer is clearly rewarded for his behavior—at first it probably changed attributions of the team, but now he is still getting out of work and accountability—it is affecting the team. They are getting tired of it; so it is becoming self-defeating behavior. But, no one says much except talk about him behind his back. If confronted directly, he would deny seeing the emails and deny that he is using the excuse as a self-handicap. That kind of confrontation probably won't work and no one wants to take the accountability to do it. Who wants to be the bad guy?

You have been told all the "right" things to do for these "crucial confrontations"[14]—wait until a private, opportune moment to talk over a particular incident, focus the conversation on a particular action or behavioral pattern, rather than the person's character or personality, focus on observation rather than inference, be respectful and keep it within the person's power to address, give feedback with future improvement as a goal, and be aware of feedback overload. We think self-handicapping is different than other work behaviors. It just slips out fast and easily and passes by so quickly that a big crucial conversation/confrontation will miss the opportunity and just lead to denial and more self-handicapping. We would like a team commitment to call each other on self-handicapping excuses. We believe the only way to handle it is to provide feedback proactively, not just when peers request it. Because peers only have influence, not formal authority over each other, the method of delivering peer feedback is important.[15] Consider joking about the person self-handicapping themselves without even knowing it (the rabbit) or saying "be careful where those excuses take you." Regardless, to get your peers to listen and to motivate them to stop self-handicapping, use a nonconfrontational approach. *Do Not*:

- Present several issues at once
- Use generalized language or characterizations
- Use value judgments or insert your opinion or feelings
- State your interpretations of your observations
- Focus only on negative feedback
- Provide feedback on nonwork contexts
- Talk down to the feedback recipient
- Become defensive or argumentative when receiving feedback back from a peer

Remember, the way people give feedback, especially negative feedback, can actually cause the conflict they want to avoid. When the focus is on an attitude, such as "You are blaming everyone," "You don't respect the customers," "You are so self-righteous," you will *not* get the person to focus on their own self-handicapping behavior. When the behavior cannot be easily observed, you are bound to cause a defensive reaction. You must stick to the ERO Spiral—mention only excuses, self-defeating behavior, and outcomes for employees, peers, and customers. Do it with the intent to help, be light—not serious, and expect some very hard hitting advice back on your self-handicapping. *But if everyone talks about it, self-handicapping moves out of the undiscussable realm into the open and something we are all helping each other avoid and overcome. That is mastery.* Make it fun.

Of course, all of this is easier if there is trust in the team. But this is a vicious circle that is hard to break into—you need some trust to talk about self-handicapping and there is no trust if everyone is self-handicapping. We have discussed how to build trust—be honest, open, transparent, do what you say you are going to do—really walk the walk, meet in small groups, care about your employees, expose yourself and show your vulnerability, open yourself to others, let your team know that you are just like them, be willing to admit your own failures and take the hit when undesirable outcomes happen—no blame, only humility and a desire to master the situation. Do these things and you will earn the team's trust and respect. Then you can move into the self-handicapping conversation.

One thing to think about is Richard Lewis' model of how different cultures view trust.[16] He said there were three types of cultures and trust was built in different ways:

1. *Linear-Active cultures* (Northern Europe) help people trust institutions. People will trust you if you do what you say you will do and if you are consistent. Eye contact shows you are honest, open, and have nothing to hide.

2. *Multi-Active cultures* (Southern Europe) help people show their weaknesses to convey trust. Compassion is key and the truth is flexible. Eye contact is used to build relationships because trust is found in intimates.

3. *Reactive cultures* (Asia) are those where reciprocity is the way to build trust. Truth is very flexible and saving face is of paramount importance. Reactives avoid conflict (someone will lose face) and eye contact is avoided.

This is a very simplified way of describing Lewis' Model, but it gives you an idea that trust is cultural and very fluid. Therefore, being open about self-handicapping must be flexible depending on the team nationalities and backgrounds. Furthermore, many of us are hybrid because Asians come to the US, and vice versa. We learn new behaviors in our new contexts. Understand that different ways of building and experiencing trust exist in your team. For us in the US, we make an effort to maintain more eye contact and accept any discomfort because this is how business generally operates.

Prescription for Teams

Our prescription for teams is to:

- Agree to make self-handicapping a joke—use the self-handicapping rabbit going down the hole to start the conversations (confrontations). Make it all about getting to mastery goals—adding value for customers.

- Agree to call each other and everyone on the team out every single time self-handicapping occurs—at every level. Let nothing slip by or become undisscussable.

- *This one is really important.* Agree to own the success of one team member—not as a coach, but rather like a Secret Santa at Christmas—just watch over someone and specialize in calling them out. Everyone has a "Secret Santa." After some time, the whole team switches Secret Santas and everyone avoids becoming stale by focusing on only one person and being the bad guy too much.

- Get over whatever issues you have and listen openly to the feedback coming your way without retaliation.

When to Be Careful

We have said you must first overcome your own self-handicapping to start to change the world around you. When you can say to others, "This is what I did and these good/bad things happened" others may listen; they will tune you out if you start with a criticism. We also suspect that, as you progress, the urge to help others will grow, but you must be careful. There are several types of individuals and situations you may be approaching about self-handicapping. What you reveal can be used against you and others will resist any discussions of their issues. So, start slow—interact with your family, then employees, your team, and finally your peers or bosses, in that order. You should approach each differently as you can see in the figure below. Be careful, self-handicapping is not currently discussed in business settings for a reason—everyone is uncomfortable with the topic. Don't be the reformed smoker coming around gripping about your peers smoking.

Should I say anything about self-handicapping?

		Strong relationship	Deep denial	Risk of retaliation
Low	Subordinate			
	Team	Why not	Proceed but slowly	
	Peer	Test the waters	Be very, very careful	
High	Boss			

Open → Communication culture → Closed

Risk: Low → High

Risk increases as you go from subordinate to boss. The subordinates may think you are a little weird and even make fun of you as you reveal yourself. You may find self-deception, defensiveness, resistance, and even some forms of retaliation. But overall, your management skills will prevail in most of these situations. Just make perfectly sure your house is in order first.

When you reveal to peers or confront them on their behavior, you must tie it to organizational outcomes and tread very carefully. Make it somewhat of an emergency to solve customer problems and to be exceptional at it. Make it okay to keep learning and growing to get the mission done. Talk about how much effort goes into excuses and impression management and not into the mission. Obviously, the depth of your relationship and trust level with others, the extent of their self-deception, and risk of backlash determine the openness of the communication culture you have with any group. The less open the culture, the scarier it is to discuss self-handicapping or any other "touchy-feely" subject. But stopping the self-handicapping will allow you to focus on the true mission of excellence and customer service.

Even so, you can't control them nor should you try. You are responsible for you first. Clean up your act and be a role model. Start to use yourself as an example and use your self-handicapping vocabulary.

Final Notes

Goulston and Goldberg, in discussing self-defeating behavior, suggest a number of things we can learn from watching others[17]—such as public figures. One is to work on it now—don't wait. Procrastination gets you no further ahead than you are today. Furthermore, avoidance is no solution. Denying the problem or pretending it will go away if left alone usually solves nothing and causes a bigger mess. Make sure that you do not jump from the frying pan into the fire. In the haste to change a self-handicapping behavior, it is easy to just substitute another self-handicapping behavior that may be even worse. If you are avoiding confronting a coworker because of fear of conflict, don't substitute keeping your feelings to yourself. This may build up to anger and an explosion of emotion down the road. Understand that you can't fix something until you admit it is broken. Awareness and recognition of self-handicapping are tough issues. Admitting to the impact is an even bigger deal. Changing it takes work.

Some Special Values for Book Readers

We invite you to go to our website *www.shleadership.com*. For professors who might use this text in management or leadership courses, we will have BlackBoard content, self-assessments, and PowerPoints for you; for trainers and professors, we will have available a trainer's manual with all handouts and program instructions; for researchers, we have a complete bibliography of self-handicapping articles in several formats (alphabetical, by content area) and needed testable hypotheses; and for everyone, we have a blog at *www.shleadership.com/blog*, a self-survey of self-handicapping, and an available survey that can be given to employees as part of a self-handicapping behavior assessment using the wisdom of the crowd. Don't forget to follow us on Twitter—*@Leadership_SH* and Facebook at *www.facebook.com/selfhandicappingleadership* and let us know what works and what doesn't work. As part of our ongoing quest to learn more about self-handicapping, we would appreciate hearing about your experiences and successes. Your ideas and suggestions will help others on the same quest. Feel free to contact the authors with questions, suggestions, or complaints at *shleadership@gmail.com*.

Endnotes

1. AAL Kristof-Brown and CK Stevens, "Goal Congruence in Project Teams: Does the Fit Between Members' Personal Mastery and Performance Goals Matter?" *Journal of Applied Psychology*, 2001, 86(6), 1083–1095.

2. From WikiPedia, "Organisation Climate." https://en.wikipedia.org/wiki/Organisation_climate (accessed July 1, 2015).

3. Summarized from Sumitha Bhandarkar, "How I Learned to Stop Nagging my Kids and Start Motivating Them." http://lifehacker.com/how-i-learned-to-stop-nagging -my-kids-and-start-motivat-1464670051 (accessed July 2, 2015).

4. Summarized from Emma Seppala, "What Bosses Gain by Being Vulnerable." https://hbr.org/2014/12/what-bosses-gain-by-being-vulnerable and Monica Parker, "Embracing Vulnerability at Work is the Key to Employee Engagement." http:// www.theguardian.com/sustainable-business/embrace-vulnerabilty-workplace -employee-engagement (accessed July 2, 2015)

5. Summarized from Fikret Berkes, "Understanding Uncertainty and Reducing Vulnerability: Lessons from Resilience Thinking." http://research.arch.tamu.edu/ media/cms_page_media/3494/Berkes_understandinguncertainty_nathaz.pdf (accessed July 2, 2015).

6. Taylor, et. al. "A Meta-Analytic Review of Behavior Modeling Training," *J Appl Psychol*, 2006, 90(4), 692–709.

7. PJ Decker and BR Nathan, *Behavior Modeling Training: Principles and Applications.* New York, NY: Praeger, 1985.

8. See Charles A Scherbaum, Yochi Cohen-Charash, and Michael J. Kern, "Measuring General Self-Efficacy a Comparison of Three Measures Using Item Response Theory," *Educ Psychol Meas*, December 2006, 66(6), 1047–1063.

9. Windle, G, Bennett, K, et al. "A Methodological Review of Resilience Measurement Scales," 2011, Health and Quality of Life Outcomes, 9:8. See http://www.hqlo.com/content/9/1/8 and http://www.hqlo.com/content/pdf/1477-7525-9-8.pdf (accessed July 2, 2015).

10. C Midgley, A Kaplan, and MJ Middleton, (2001). "Performance-Approach Goals: Good for What, for Whom, Under what Circumstances, and at What Cost?" *J Educ Psychol,* 93(1), 77–86; C Midgley, A Kaplan, MJ Middleton, et al. "The Development and Validation of Scales Assessing Students' Achievement Goal Orientations," *Contemp Educ Psychol,* 1998, 23, 113–131; and C Midgley and T Urdan, "Academic Self-Handicapping and Achievement Goals: A Further Examination," *Contemp Educ Psychol,* 2001, 26(1), 61–75.

11. See DE Conroy, AJ Elliot, and SM Hofer, "A 2×2 Achievement Goals Questionnaire for Sport: Evidence for Factorial Invariance," Temporal Stability, and External Validity, *J Sport Exerc Psychol,* 2003, 25(4), 456–476 and CS Dweck, *Self-Theories: Their Role in Motivation, Personality, and Development.* Philadelphia, PA: Taylor & Francis, 1999.

12. See JG Nicholls, *The Competitive Ethos and Democratic Education.* Cambridge, MA: Harvard University Press, 1989.

13. See Barna Group, "The Different Impact of Good and Bad Leadership." https://www.barna.org/barna-update/leadership/707-the-different-impact-of-good-and-bad-leadership#.VZViBk0o7RY (accessed July 1, 2015).

14. See Richard L, Daft and Marcic Dorothy, *Building Management Skills: An Action-First Approach,* Mason, OH: South-Western, Cengage Learning, 2014.

15. See Corporate Executive Board, "Informal Peer-to-Peer Feedback Guide." http://www.ucalgary.ca/hr/files/hr/providing-informal-peer-feedback.pdf (accessed July 3, 2015).

16. See Marianne Mol, "Team Management: How to Build Trust." http://www.whiteboardmag.com/team-management-how-to-build-trust/ (accessed July 3, 2015).

17. M Goulston and P Goldberg, *Get Out of Your Own Way,* New York, NY: Perigee/Penguin, 1996.

Index

Page numbers followed by "*f*" and "*t*" indicate figures and tables, respectively.

risk, 368
  economic wisdom and, 26
risk averse, 201–203
role modeling, 130
rule violations, dealing with, 274
Russo, J. E., 186, 188, 201

S

Schmidt, Eric, 142
Schoemaker, P. L. H., 186, 188, 201
Scientific American Mind, 136
score, 56–57
The Self-Assessment Library, 96–97
self-assessments, 94–97
  asking others for help, 94
  book reading for, 97
  flawed, 96
  Gallup's analysis, 97
  Meyers Briggs, 96
  strengths-based approach to, 97
  tools for, 96–97
self-awareness, 5, 85–118
  acknowledging behavior, 90–91
  action plan, 116t–117t
  apprehension, 101–102
  assessment, 94–97
  avoidance, 101
  behaviors to change, 102–116
  boundary violation, 92–93
  burning bridges, 107–109
  concept, 85–86
  emotional intelligence, 102–104

environment/surroundings, 111–113
executive coaching, 97–98
expediency, 100
impact, 87–89
issues, 89–91
lack of, 88–89
leadership, 93–94
learning, 86–87
managing up, 109–111
networking, 113–114
overview, 85–87
reading the room, 104–106
self-deception, 102
spotting threats and opportunities, 111, 112
steps to follow for, 94
survey on, 91–92
things to be done, 92–100
wisdom of the crowd, 98–99
work-life balance, 114–116
self-confidence, 40
self-deception
  accountability, 62–63
  analyzing decision alternatives, 198–200
  communication, 227–228
  driving for results, 337–338
  engagement, 163–164
  framing decisions, 194–195
  handling, 38–39
  micromanaging, 302–303
  overview, 20
  reversing/eliminating, 43–45
  self-awareness, 102
  talent development, 261
  tunnel vision, 134–135
  types of, 38

Sutton, Robert, 20

T

taking deliberate action.
See deliberate action
talent development, 6,
251–283
   action plan, 281t–282t
   apprehension and,
    259–260
   avoidance and, 257–259
   behaviors to change,
    261–281
   competencies and, 261–263
   effective ways of, 255–256
   errors of judgment/bias
    in, 253
   expediency and, 256–257
   fit and, 280–281
   impact, 252–253
   interviewing and, 263–268
   issues, 253–254
   mentoring and, 276–277
   overview, 251–252
   self-deception and, 261
   succession planning
    program, 269
   survey on, 254–255
   training and, 277–280
   troubles in, 268–269
talent management, 25
talking about other people,
172–173
task identity, 327–328
task significance, 328
TCSH. See Total Cost of
Self-Handicapping (TCSH)

teams
   dysfunctions of, 56, 106
   prescription for, 366–367
theory of intelligence, 28–29.
  See also intelligence
Total Cost of Self-Handicapping
  (TCSH), 20–22, 21t
training
   behavior modeling, 360–361
   key behaviors for, 278–279
   principles guiding, 277
   reflective workshops, 360
   relapse, 361
   self-sabotage in, 278
   for talent development,
    277–280
transaction, engagement and,
171–172
transparency, communication,
224–225
triangular communication,
  boundary violations
  and, 93
triggers, self-handicapping.
  See alsospecific trigger
   apprehension, 20, 36,
    37–38
   avoidance, 19, 36
   deliberate action, 36
   expediency, 19, 36
   habitual behavior, 34–35
   handling, 34–39
   self-deception, 20, 36,
    38–39
   self-efficacy, 36–37
trust
   authentic, 275
   breaking, 232–233